THE MATTER OF EVIL

THE MATTER OF EVIL

From Speculative Realism to Ethical Pessimism

Drew M. Dalton

Northwestern University Press
Evanston, Illinois

Northwestern University Press
www.nupress.northwestern.edu

Copyright © 2024 by Northwestern University. Published 2024 by Northwestern University Press. All rights reserved.

Printed in the United States of America

10 9 8 7 6 5 4 3 2 1

Library of Congress Cataloging-in-Publication Data

Names: Dalton, Drew M., 1978– author.
Title: The matter of evil : from speculative realism to ethical pessimism / Drew M Dalton.
Description: Evanston, Illinois : Northwestern University Press, 2024. | Includes bibliographical references and index.
Identifiers: LCCN 2023028393 | ISBN 9780810146402 (paperback) | ISBN 9780810146419 (cloth) | ISBN 9780810146426 (ebook)
Subjects: LCSH: Good and evil. | Ethics. | Pessimism.
Classification: LCC BJ1408.5 .D35 2024 | DDC 170—dc23/eng/20230620
LC record available at https://lccn.loc.gov/2023028393

For my father . . .

Contents

	Acknowledgments	ix
	Introduction. The Matter of Evil	1
1	After Kant: The End of Western Metaphysics and Ethics?	13
2	Absolutes within the Bounds of Reason: Speculative Realism and the Return of the Absolute	41
3	Toward a Post-Critical Ethics: Meillassoux and Badiou on the Mathematization of Nature and the Possibility of Absolute Metaphysical and Moral Claims	63
4	The Science of Entropic Absolutes: The (Dis)Order of Nature	85
5	The Value of Science and the Science of Value: Reevaluating the Moral Neutrality of Material Reality	114
6	Moral Value and Absolute Necessity: Baruch Spinoza's Metaphysical Monism	137
7	The Monstrous Will of Nature: Arthur Schopenhauer's Ethical Monism	164
8	The Specter of Nihilism: Friedrich Nietzsche's Moral Naturalism	186
9	The Ethical Potency of Pessimism: Schopenhauerian Negation, Buddhist Renunciation, and the Political Activism of Philipp Mainländer	210
10	New Directions in Pessimism: Cosmic Pessimism, Afropessimism, and Extinctual Nihilism	244
	Conclusion. Speculative Absolutes and Pessimistic Activism: The Evangel of Entropy and the Ethics of Resistance	275
	Notes	287
	Bibliography	319
	Index	331

Acknowledgments

This volume would not have been possible without the generous institutional support of Dominican University. I'd like to especially thank the members of the Philosophy Department, Tama Weisman, Kelly Burns, and Nkuzi Nnam. Without their understanding and solidarity, I would not have been able to balance my research interests and teaching responsibilities. In that same spirit, I'm also grateful to Chad Rohman, the Dean of the Rosary College of Arts and Sciences, for supporting faculty development wherever and however he can and ensuring that I had all the funds possible to present this material in its seedling form at various conferences and invited lectures. I'm especially grateful to Dominican's Post-Tenure and Sabbatical Review Committee for granting me sabbatical leave for the Fall semester of 2020 in order to complete the first draft of this project.

I'm equally grateful for the support of my colleagues in the Philosophy Department at Brock University who have continued to provide a platform for me to test my ideas on them and their students for years through an annual invited lecture. I'm especially thankful for the support, feedback, and pushback of Michael Berman, Athena Coleman, and my dearest friend and closest confidant Rajiv Kaushik.

I'm also lucky to have found understanding and support in my editor, the canny and clever Faith Wilson Stein, whose insight, advice, and suggestions were essential in bringing this manuscript to publication. For her hard work and all of the hard work of her colleagues at Northwestern University Press I am truly grateful.

To my friends and family, who have supported me in more ways than I can enumerate and are always quick to offer a word of succor, support, and the occasionally sarcastic jab: I am humbly thankful most of all, for your patience and love. Robin and Thea—you are my first and last line of defense against melancholy. Without you I would have given up long ago. Thank you. Thanks are also due to Robert Walsh and Liz Barnett for always being advocates, friends, and constant allies—quick with a beer or an "old man" walk to sort through my "melancholic fancies" with grace, good will, and the music of Protomartyr and visions of a "Life without Buildings."

I'm equally grateful for all of my students. I'm especially thankful to those whose hard work remind me to never give up on the value of thought. Luke Jenner, Katrina Cano, Jack Maddock, and so many others; your friendships and successes mean more to me than you could ever imagine. Keep fighting the good fight. To my friends Tyler and Danny, you are the "platonic ideal" of loving friendship and philosophical agony. Thank you for constantly reminding me that my life, and perhaps life as such, is bigger than the immediate travails of the present. I'm also grateful to Chris Yates, David Hoffner, and David Banach for always being interested in ideas, ready for a chat, and quick to offer a laugh, if only at my own expense.

Finally, my deepest thanks are due, as always, to Rudi Visker and to my father, Donald Dalton, without whom I would not be what I am, or know what I do about what I am.

THE MATTER OF EVIL

Introduction

The Matter of Evil

The Inhumanity of Absolute Truth
and the Question of Moral Value

The differences which separate opinion from truth are similar to the differences which separate our individual experiences from the nature of reality. Each is a matter of perspective and scale. Our experience of reality and the opinions we develop from it conform to the scale of the limits which circumscribe the boundaries of our singularity. For this reason, our opinions are irrevocably extensions and representations of our bodily experiences, time in history, and place in the world. They are the product, in other words, of our embodied finitude—the fact that, as individuals, our engagement with reality is structurally restricted to a particular viewpoint and singular perspective. For this reason, our experiences and the opinions which follow from them are destined always to be relative to us alone, or perhaps, at best, our culture or generation.

The absolute truth of reality is only achievable, then, if and when we transcend these limitations and perceive things not as they merely *appear* from any one, individual, cultural, or generational perspective, but rather as they actually *are* within the nature of the universe itself. Absolute truth is accomplished, in other words, only when we scale out, as it were, and move above and beyond the singularity of our human engagement with the world to conceive reality from the perspective of the cosmos as a whole. Only inasmuch we are successful in achieving this cosmic overview can we hope to escape the particularity of our human limitations, conventions, and convictions and aspire to understand the truth of matters as they actually are, universally and absolutely.

It is the aim of mathematics, science, and philosophy to help us to ascend to this cosmic scale and to see reality from the overview which is achieved from a universal, inhuman, and truly absolute perspective. It is only through them, therefore, that we can ever know the truth of what actually is, over and at times against the way things appear to us from any given human perspective. This unique power of mathematics, science, and philosophy to show us the truth comes from their capacity to enable us, as individually embodied and limited human beings, to conceive of reality in a universal, abstract, and inhuman way. In this regard, their power grows from their ability to liberate us from the confines of our unique time in history and place in the world in order to see ourselves and our world from the perspective of time and the cosmos itself.

A perfect example of their power to this end can be found in the Copernican Revolution of the sixteenth century which, through the application of mathematical abstraction to the testimony of empirical observation, proved definitively that our human perspective on the position and motion of the objects in our solar system (i.e., the fact that from the limited perspective of the earth, the sun seems to revolve around us) was only relative to our terrestriality and, as such, incorrect—a merely human or earthborn opinion and not actually representative of the truth of the matter. The essence of the Copernican Revolution was to use math and science to enable us to see ourselves and our position in the universe, both locationally and existentially, from the perspective of the universe itself—to free us, in other words, from the confines and limitations of our all too human and terrestrial perspectives and opinions, and to elevate us into the absolute and inhuman truth of reality as it actually is. The achievement of such an overview effect has always been the unique function and aim of mathematics, the sciences, and any philosophy worthy of its name.

Of course, as a natural consequence of this scaling out of perspective which is granted by mathematics, science, and philosophy, some of our previously held "truths" concerning the nature of "reality" are revealed to be nothing more than "opinions"—nothing more than a product of human "experience" alone. At the same time, other accounts of these "experiences," which may have been judged to be nothing more than controversial "opinions," will be confirmed as facts and become recognized as universal truths. As a result of this process, in other words, some of our deepest held beliefs will be exposed as false and, as such, hopefully and eventually, eliminated from discourse. Others still will be relativized and, as such, must be reconsidered, recontextualized, and reevaluated—no longer considered as subjects of scientific investigation, but of the humanities instead, though of no less critical importance to our well-being or way of life. Meanwhile, others still will become elevated from the status of experience and opinion alone to be recognized, finally, as absolute and universal truths.

One of the most important tasks of contemporary philosophy is to distinguish between these three categories: to unmask, debunk, and strive to uproot what is merely *opinion*, while simultaneously working tirelessly to rethink the foundations, functions, and methods for determining the validity and scope of questions of *human* import, by surveying, recounting, and applying the absolute, inhuman, and universal *truths* which are discovered in mathematics and the material sciences. And, no question is more important within this epistemological sorting or, as a result, more controversial, than the question of moral value and ethical responsibility.

Since the advent of modern mathematics and science, it has been the general consensus of philosophers that normative questions of this sort, questions concerning the moral or ethical evaluation of reality, are a merely human affair and not, as such, the proper subject matter of mathematics or the material sciences; but, rather, perhaps only of the humanities. Outside of this relative consensus, debate has raged. For some, the cosmic perspective granted by mathematics and the sciences fundamentally discredits the concept of normative value, relativizing it not merely to the human scale but, even more damnably still, to the perspective of particular groups of people (i.e., cultures and times); or, worse still, single individuals. For these thinkers, what the overview granted by the modern mathematical sciences demands is the realization that concepts of moral value and ethical normativity are ultimately meaningless from the cosmic perspective. For these reasons, they argue, these questions are best abandoned entirely as relics of our dogmatic and superstitious past in favor of a kind of moral nihilism which they think is more reflective of the truth of reality itself. For other thinkers, of course, this relativization of concepts of moral value and ethical normativity is not cause for their condemnation, dismissal, or nihilation, but rather for their reestablishment within the compass of human existence itself—as a product, for example, of human reasoning, or of human evolution. Whatever the position, the vast majority of modern and contemporary philosophers agree that ultimately, from the absolute and cosmic perspective which is granted by the material and mathematical sciences, questions of moral value and ethical normativity are, at the end of the day, strictly human affairs, and, as such, relative to our way of being alone, or perhaps, at its most expansive, biological organisms in general. The general consensus of modern and contemporary philosophy is, in other words, that these questions are not grounded in or supported by the inhuman truths of the raw matter of the cosmos itself as it is explored by and exposed in the modern mathematical sciences; and, as such, they cannot be illuminated through the exposition of those absolute and universal truths which pertain to it.

But is this necessarily the case? Or is it possible that moral value and ethical normativity might be derived from these inhuman scientific truths; and, as such, become reconsidered and reevaluated as more than merely relative, human concerns, but rather as integral and essential to the underlying structure of material reality itself? The central tenet of this book is that a universal and radically inhuman account of ethical and moral value can be established in and extracted from the cosmic perspective of reality which is granted by the contemporary mathematical sciences; and that, moreover, a practical ethics and politics can be developed from this account of absolute moral value. To show how all this might be possible, however, requires unsettling a number of long-accepted philosophical assumptions concerning the possibility of absolute knowledge, the nature of good and evil, the moral significance of matters of fact, the kind of normative claims that can be derived from those facts, not to mention the nature of ethical reasoning itself. Nevertheless, it is the contention of this book that when these tasks are accomplished properly, a new and universally *absolute* normative system can be established on and extracted from the account of reality which is provided by the modern sciences. The first step in this process is to reconsider the primal origin of our moral concerns themselves.

The Moral Trauma of Reality

Ethical concern is born of suffering. It germinates from those first moments when we begin to realize that existence does not conform to our hopes, expectations, and desires; but is in fact cruelly indifferent to them, and at times even structurally bent against them. This nascent ethical concern grows and expands as we realize through experience that a tragic divorce separates what we instinctively feel, however vaguely, *should* or *ought* to be the case from what actually *is* the case. So, we increasingly find ourselves with maturity questioning how or why the world is the way it *is* and wondering if it might be made *otherwise than*, or somehow *better than* we actually find it to be. In this way, our early experiences of the primal division between our values and the facts of the matter eventually buds into our first concepts of *good* and *evil*. And it is from the cultivation of these initially naïve concepts that philosophical ethics blooms.

Our philosophical concern with the moral value of reality does not proceed, then, as is generally agreed upon by the history of Western thought, from some primal affirmation of or delight in our experience of that which is. How could it? The principal quality of such gratifications is that they leave us feeling satiated, sedate, and "without a care in the world"—untroubled, unquestioning, unconcerned, and entirely content with our lot in life. It is only when such satisfactions are interrupted that we grow discontented and begin to worry about the potential value of our existence. Ethical inquiry thus begins precisely when and where our felicity ends. Our philosophical concern with the moral value of reality only arises, in other words, because we have cause to question what we naively expect to enjoy—because we are rudely awakened from our passive delights and are forced to actively reckon with the fact that existence consistently fails to conform to our needs and desires and appears to contain within it a recalcitrance which refuses to be integrated to our ends. Our concern with the moral value of the universe does not grow, then, from some primal recognition of what we come to think of as "goodness." On the contrary, this sense of goodness develops from our rejection of what we experience to actually be the case. It develops instead from our refusal to accept reality as it is. Our primary experience of reality is of its independence from us, its indifference to us, and, moreover, its tendency to harm us. Our primary ethical experience of reality is much more closely linked, then, to what we come to think of as "evil"—that apparently malevolent force which opposes and inhibits our flourishing—than it is with what we tend to think of as the "good"—that which contributes to our salubrity and well-being.

This primal origin of our ethical categories is exemplified in our instinctive tendency to respond to bad news by crying out, "No, it can't be!" It is from this spontaneous rejection of the malevolency of what actually *is* that our hope for the possibility of some eventual goodness, which we think *should be*, is born. From this it is clear that our concept of goodness emerges *negatively*, as the theoretical extension of our instinctive recoil against, rejection of, and attempt to escape from our primal encounter with existence. Hence our identification of the good with what we think *should* or *ought to be*, and not what actually *is*. Conversely, our concept of evil appears to arise *positively* as a theoretical reflection, extension, and expansion of our primal experience of the independence, indifference, and irreducible otherness of existence. Thus, whereas our nascent concept of goodness seems to appear as an ontological potential or logical possibility alone, our instinctive concept of evil appears as a direct representation of the ontological actuality of reality itself. In this sense, our concept of goodness must necessarily be less real than or logically privative to our concept of evil. And yet, the general consensus of Western philosophy is precisely the opposite

There, as is evident from even the most cursory survey of Western philosophical ethics, the concept of goodness is generally accounted for as a direct expression of the true nature of existence. Evil, by contrast, has generally been accounted for as a privative concept, one which is emergent from some misguided negation of, derivation from, inversion within, or failure to comprehend reality as it actually is. While this was especially true in the medieval period of philosophy, this apparent reversal of our ethical instincts has been upheld throughout the history of the Western

INTRODUCTION

intellectual canon. Indeed, from the ancient period onwards, evil has almost exclusively been defined in Western thought as an *accidental* phenomenon, one which bears no existential weight in its own right. Following this, the vast majority of Western philosophers since have accounted for evil, against what we have just seen, as a concept which is ontologically hollow, representative ultimately of nothing at all—little more, at most, than a consequent of some fissure within the otherwise perfect nature of that which is; something which results, in other words, solely when we fail to understand rightly or to act faithfully in response to the true nature of existence, as a result, perhaps, of some misjudgment or misbehavior on our part. In this way, the bulk of Western thinkers deny that evil exists in any real way and further reject the possibility that it is representative of some fundamental, structural, or intractable problem within existence itself. Instead, they tend to treat it as the result of a lack, gap, or interruption in the wholeness of existence—a fold in the totality of being, one which does not testify to the ultimate truth of reality, but, at best, merely to how we misperceive, misunderstand, mistreat, or misuse reality. And so, the argument goes, for someone who has a proper understanding of the totality of reality and the fullness of time, the "problem of evil" disappears, if not practically, then at least logically. Indeed, one of the classical apologias for the goodness of reality is the argument that for the truly enlightened, evil is nothing more than a function of or means to some final and greater good. So it is that the problem of evil, that seemingly natural problem from which our moral concerns first arise, has been "solved" time and time again by the canonical thinkers of Western philosophy, and our primal repulsion at the cruel indifference of reality has been repeatedly dismissed as logical nonsense.

It is only relatively recently, in the modern era, that this alleged "solution" to the problem of evil has been challenged or questioned at all. Oddly, however, this disputation does not come by reversing or re-evaluating the primal identification of reality as a moral good, nor does it proceed by reassessing the ontological status of evil. Instead, the modern critique of these ethical categories comes through a contestation of the ontological status of moral values in their entirety, good and evil alike. Indeed, the motivating principle of modern moral philosophy is the suggestion that neither the concept of good nor the concept of evil has any objective ontological weight. Instead, it contends that both are ultimately epistemological categories alone—nothing more than products of human understanding and judgment. Good and evil, most modern philosophers thus argue, are not substantive concepts for understanding reality in its own right, but are exclusively productive to understanding how humans operate within and navigate through that reality by way of reason, or perhaps at times their cultural or individual understanding of reality. For this reason, most modern philosophers have concluded that existence itself bears no inherent moral value; but that it is our thinking alone which would make it seem so. As such, they argue, if moral philosophy is going to have any real propaedeutic power, it must acknowledge the fact that existence is objectively morally neutral. Only by acknowledging this fact, they contend, can we finally rid ourselves of the metaphysical baggage which comes from our traditional (i.e., ancient and medieval) notions of moral value and begin to speak meaningfully of and understand properly the nature of reality and our ethical experiences and normative commitments alike. From this it becomes clear that despite their apparently revolutionary rejection of the claims which preceded them, modern philosophers, like their ancient and medieval predecessors, are just as guilty of failing to take seriously the kind of primal moral experience that gives rise to our ethical concerns in the first place: the cruel indifference of reality to itself.

This reluctance to take seriously the insight which grows spontaneously from this fact—namely, the possibility that evil is an ontologically real phenomenon in its own right, one which is inherent to and inseparable from the fundamental structure of material reality itself—is so complete in the canon of Western philosophy, in fact, that anyone who has dared to challenge it and consider evil as a product of existence itself has been laughed out of the history books, labeled a morose crank, a gloomy mystic, or a melodramatic misanthrope—in a word, a pessimist. It is time that this tendency within Western philosophy is overturned. It is time that we follow the trajectory of our first moral experiences of reality and take seriously the possibility that existence may not be good, or even value-neutral, but may in fact be inexorably and irrevocably evil. It is time, in other words, that pessimism is redeemed from the margins of the history of Western philosophy, rescued from the periphery of our moral discourse, and placed squarely at the center of our ethical considerations as a reflection of a primal ethical truth that is immanent in material existence itself. Only by taking this possibility seriously can we hope to craft a theory of moral value which affirms our primordial ethical instincts and develop from it a more realistic and more effective model of moral normativity, and perhaps even social and political responsibility. To this end, it is essential that philosophers turn to the contemporary mathematics and sciences as a thoroughfare to the absolute and horrifying truths of reality.

In Pursuit of an Absolutely Grounded Ethical Pessimism

The aim of this book is to accomplish a pessimistic reappraisal of the moral significance of the absolute truths of nature and to craft from it a practical ethics and effective politics. To do this first requires articulating an epistemology which would allow us to speak of the absolute metaphysical and ethical truths of reality, as achieved in the sciences. This requires challenging the prevailing modern assumption that reality is value-neutral—that, in other words, it is not only impossible to ascribe any proper moral value to existence itself, but that it is also impossible to talk meaningfully about existence as it is in its own right, rather only how it appears to and is evaluated by us—existence, in other words, as it merely seems from the human perspective. Only by showing how we might talk meaningfully of existence in itself, on a cosmic, universal, and inhuman scale, can we then show how it might possess a moral power on its own and develop from this fact a new model for moral normativity and political activism. The first aim of this work, then, is to establish a new kind of postmodern epistemology by reassessing the philosophical applications of modern mathematics and science. To this end, the first half of this volume brings the claims of speculative materialism to bear on the conclusions of the contemporary sciences concerning the primacy of the principle of entropic decay. Through this dialogue I will show how the limitations which have hampered philosophical epistemology since the advent of modernity can be overcome, and a new account of the absolute structure of existence can be established in such a way that a new metaphysics of the absolute nature of being itself can be developed. Specifically, I will show how existence might be reconceived in light of a new speculative epistemology of the contemporary sciences as irrevocably finite and actively "unbecoming," rather than eternally static or infinitely transformative, as has been traditionally claimed.

Having developed this metaphysics of "unbecoming" from a new speculative approach to the products of the contemporary sciences in the first half of the book, I will dedicate the second half to showing how a new account of moral value and ethical responsibility might be deduced from it. To this end, I will question the legitimacy of the so-called "is/ought" distinction in Western philosophy, reassess the classical definitions of good and evil maintained therein, and demonstrate how a moral evaluation of the principle of entropy is both logically sound and rationally justified. In this way, I will argue that not only can we legitimately defend the claim that existence possesses an inherent and absolute moral value; we can also assert that its moral value is demonstratively evil, as our ethical instincts testify. By overturning our assumptions about the nature and value of reality in this way, I will show how ethical normativity can be developed from moral pessimism, as well as how this pessimism might ground a new justification for absolute ethical duty and sociopolitical activism.

To lay the foundation for this task, chapter 1 begins by exploring the nature of Kant's critique of dogmatism as the apotheosis of the modern rejection of the concept of absolute being (metaphysics) and value (ethics), paying particular attention to the effects of his critique on contemporary philosophy and social and political discourse.

Chapter 2 then shows how the limits established by Kant's critique can be overcome through speculative realism in order to develop a new absolute metaphysics and ethics. To this end, this chapter explores the work of Quentin Meillassoux. Through an analysis of Meillassoux's work we will see how it might be possible to speak meaningfully of absolute reality without betraying the limits of Kant's critique of reason. As we will see there, such a possibility is operational if and only if philosophical reasoning is constrained by what Meillassoux calls a "special" set of parameters. These parameters, he argues, are that reason be guided by the methods and conclusions of the contemporary sciences wherein, he argues, a complete "mathematization of nature" is accomplished. When philosophers are constrained by and work within the limits of what has been discovered by the contemporary sciences, Meillassoux concludes, they can begin to rationally speculate on the nature of absolute reality without risking any form of dogmatism and develop in this way a new metaphysics of absolute reality upon which moral evaluation, ethical normativity, and sociopolitical action might be reestablished.

To develop this claim further and see how an ethical and political system might be extracted from a new materialist metaphysics of absolute nature, chapter 3 explores what Meillassoux and his closest philosophical ally, Alain Badiou, mean by the "mathematization of nature" which they think is accomplished in the sciences, as well as how both suggest such a "mathematization" might be used to develop a new and practical sense of ethical normativity and political activism.

Chapter 4 proceeds from this account of the power of the mathematical sciences by attending to the actual conclusions of those sciences to see if and how some account of the absolute structure of existence might be identified from which a new speculative metaphysics and ethics can be developed. To this end, this chapter surveys the conclusions of leading figures in contemporary biology, chemistry, and physics in pursuit of some absolute law immanent within material nature which might carry some inherent or latent moral value. As we will discover, there is at

INTRODUCTION

least one principle which nearly every material scientist is convinced structures, defines, and determines the origin, operation, and eventual end of reality at every level: the principle of entropy as outlined in the laws of thermodynamics. If there is any one metaphysical absolute from which we might deduce a moral value, I conclude, it is this: that all material things move, by virtue of their very existence, toward their own destruction and the eventual abolition of reality itself. This inherent teleological aim that is immanent to and inseparable from material reality itself, I conclude, is sufficient to establish a new, natural, and absolute metaphysics and account of moral value.

In defense of this conclusion, chapter 5 addresses the kinds of objections which contemporary philosophers are likely to make to this attempt to extract a moral value from the material fact of entropy. To this end, this chapter addresses two major challenges to this project: first, the potential charge of Alan Sokal and Jean Bricmont that by drawing from the natural sciences, speculative thinkers may indulge in what they famously call "fashionable nonsense"; and second, the concern that by attempting to derive some moral *value* from a purely scientific *fact*, I am potentially committing the so-called "naturalistic fallacy," which distinguishes matters of fact from matters of value. To respond to the first of these potential critiques, I lay out Sokal and Bricmont's account of "fashionable nonsense" and address each point in turn to show how and why my conclusions are justifiable and, if anything, are operating in obedience to the modern challenge to philosophy to follow the testimony of the natural sciences in the service of truth. Having settled this potential objection, I then turn to the potential criticism that by attempting to extract some moral *ought* from that which *is*, I must commit the commonly held "naturalistic fallacy." To respond to this possible criticism, I examine David Hume's and G. E. Moore's respective accounts of the naturalistic fallacy and show how, when read through the historically established definition of evil as the absence of any apparent good, their work actually supports the evaluation of existence as a moral evil. I conclude this chapter by showing how an evaluation of the structures of material reality as a moral evil is not only possible, but is in fact logically necessary.

Having settled these possible objections, chapters 6 through 10 take up the second goal of this work: to show how a new normative moral system might be developed from this account of nature as a pernicious force. To this end, chapter 6 begins by asking how it is possible to conceive of moral responsibility within an ethically monistic system by interrogating the concept of free will as the necessary condition for the possibility of moral responsibility. To aid in this examination I take up the materialistic and monistic ethics of Baruch Spinoza, who argues that normativity is not incompatible with an account of nature as a singular moral power. On the contrary: in Spinoza's system a true and effective ethics is in fact empowered by such an account of nature. By engaging with the respective strengths and weaknesses of Spinoza's ethics, chapter 6 shows how it might be possible to develop a normative system of ethical responsibility from an entirely materialistic and morally monistic account of nature in which free will is denied.

From this demonstration, chapter 7 proceeds by exploring how the strengths of Spinoza's moral metaphysics are ameliorated and its weaknesses overcome by the metaphysical and ethical pessimism of Arthur Schopenhauer, who famously sought to revise Spinoza's monism through a revaluation of nature as primarily evil. In Schopenhauer's ethics, we begin to see how we might develop a normative system from a speculative evaluation of existence as a moral evil which is more suited to the facts of science. Chapter 7 concludes by exploring the relative weaknesses of Schopenhauer's ethics, weaknesses which, I argue, must themselves be overcome if we are to develop an effective ethical system.

To examine how these weaknesses might be surmounted, chapter 8 investigates the work of Friedrich Nietzsche, who drew from both Spinoza and Schopenhauer in his pursuit of a new scientific account of moral value and ethical duty. Through a critical examination of Nietzsche's attempt to reanimate ethical responsibility within his own version of materialistic monism, we will see even further what must be accomplished if we are to successfully derive an effective account of moral normativity from the evaluation of nature as an absolute evil. Ultimately, as I show, this requires rereading the positive power of Nietzsche's ethics back into Schopenhauer's pessimistic metaphysics and ethics.

This conclusion drives the aim of chapter 9: to probe the possibility of developing a less quietistic, fatalistic, or nihilistic ethics within the basic parameters of Schopenhauer's metaphysics. To this end, I examine the roots of Schopenhauer's pessimism, exploring his account of Buddhist metaphysics and ethics, and conclude by showing how both of these sources inspired the work of Philipp Mainländer, who drew from them equally to develop a robust account of pessimistic responsibility *and* political activism. To aid this examination, I provide an entirely new and original translation of key sections of Mainländer's principal work. Through an analysis of this work, I show how Mainländer's pessimism effectively overcomes the risk of quietism immanent in Schopenhauer's ethics and exemplifies how a robust account of ethical responsibility and political activism can be developed from a purely scientific account of material reality. By extending Mainländer's work, I conclude, we discover how the conclusions of the natural sciences might be used to develop a new, absolutely justifiable pessimistic account of ethical duty and political activism.

This conclusion leads us, in chapter 10, to see how Mainländer's work might be updated and expanded by drawing from three different contemporary pessimisms: the "cosmic pessimism" of Eugene Thacker, Georges Bataille, and Emil Cioran; the Afropessimism of Frank B. Wilderson, Saidiya Hartman, and Calvin Warren; and what I call the "extinctual nihilism" of Jean-François Lyotard and Ray Brassier. This chapter argues that by bringing Mainländer's work into dialogue with these contemporary pessimisms it might be logically strengthened, historically informed, and more pointedly directed in order to become a practical and effective model of ethical, social, and political normativity.

I conclude all of this by exploring in greater detail what can be practically gained from the kind of speculatively driven ethical pessimism I have argued for. Despite the apparently dreary outlook it seems to promote, I argue that some good news and cause for hope exist beneath its *prima facie* gloominess. Specifically, this speculatively empowered ethical pessimism engenders a novel response to the age-old existential problem of meaning. By embracing a speculatively emergent ethical pessimism grounded on the claims of the contemporary sciences, I suggest that we can finally identify the absolute meaning, moral value, and ultimate purpose of human existence, and indeed even existence itself, although admittedly not in a way which is easy to accept. Nevertheless, as I show, this new account of the absolute and inhuman meaning and purpose of existence has some strategic advantages; namely, it grants our moral efforts a clear aim and direction. This, I conclude, is unquestionably good news as it provides a new foundation upon which philosophy might rediscover an objective sense of moral normativity and thereby reclaim its relevance to the world.

1

After Kant:

The End of Western Metaphysics and Ethics?

After Kant

The history of philosophy in the West is in many ways a history of reckoning with the concept of the absolute. The ancients sought to establish its existence outside of and beyond the sublunary realm of human perception, generation, increase, and dissolution. In the Middle Ages, philosophers hoped to forge a direct connection (re-*ligio*) to the absolute and deduce from it rules (*regula*) by which they believed they might acquire some surety for the human condition, its permanence and significance in the universe. The moderns, for their part, aimed to immanentize the absolute: to pluck it from the supernatural heights of medieval religion and Scholastic faith and establish it anew upon the material world of empirical experience and/or within the rational domain of human cognition. Upon such natural absolutes modern philosophers endeavored to erect an encyclopedic understanding of the cosmos and achieve through it complete mastery over existence.

If such is the history of philosophy in the West, then Immanuel Kant represents the apogee and end of that history; for in his work we find the most exhaustive and systematic examination of the frontiers of thought and experience in relation to the possibility of the absolute, as well as the most systematic reasoning for excluding it from the realm of human actuality. In this regard, Kant's critique represents simultaneously the fulfillment of the ambitions of Western philosophy as well as its abolition. For Kant's critique is nothing less than the systematic demonstration of the insurmountable abyss which seems to exist between human thought and experience, on the one hand, and any potentially absolute reality which might exist "out there," on the other. Thus, inasmuch as Kant's work can be seen as the culmination of Western metaphysics, it must also be seen as its conclusion. Hence Nietzsche's infamous assessment that with Kant the "god" of philosophy is well and truly "dead"; and with its death, as Heidegger sees it, the history of Western metaphysics as a whole.[1] Indeed, one of Nietzsche's greatest insights was to realize the irrevocable devastation that Kant's critique had brought to the general aims of Western thought. After Kant, according to Nietzsche, the concept of the absolute is no longer available to those who endeavor to labor within the constraints of rational argumentation and empirical evidence alone.

Since Kant, then, Western philosophers have been forced to reconsider the validity of their hope in some final surety, much less the certainty of their claim: they have had to design some new way of achieving it without reference to any absolute. As a result, the Western philosophical project changed after Kant, fracturing and separating into distinct camps and spheres, each with its own response to the dilemma created by the Kantian project. A synthetic accounting of the history of Western philosophy thereafter finds one of three ways philosophers have attempted to justify their account of the good, the right, and the true afterwards. Many, for example, (1) explored the possibilities, limits, and uses of philosophical reasoning without recourse to any absolute position upon which to ground their claims—thus giving up, in effect, the promise of certainty that the concept of the absolute had secured for them in the past. Think, for example, of Albert Camus as the quintessential representative of this branch of post-Kantian philosophy. For Camus, famously, the task of philosophy in the wake of the "death of God" effected by Kant's critique is to explore the possibility and potential meaning of a life lived without reference to any absolute—an absurd life; or, as Jean-Paul Sartre put it, a life condemned to be free of any and every absolute.[2]

Of course, this approach to post-Kantian philosophy was not without its detractors and critics, those who feared that attempts to philosophize without reference to any fixed or universal points would necessarily result in nihilism or relativism. To guard against this possibility, the majority of post-Kantian philosophers sought instead (2) to discover within the realm of human reasoning alone some relative "absolute" upon which they might reestablish the Archimedean hopes of their predecessors. Think of Kant himself as the first representative of this project. What Kant hoped to achieve in his work, as is clear in his second *Critique*, and we will see in greater detail later in this chapter, was to discover within the structures of reason and logic alone the same kind of universal and fixed point that philosophers had once hoped to achieve in the absolute itself, whether some principle in nature or some transcendent or divine being. In this way, Kant sought to reestablish the traditional pursuits of philosophical reasoning—a universal and rationally justifiable sense of the good, the right, and the true—upon the structures of human reason itself, operating, in this sense, as a kind of new non-absolute ground for philosophical claims. Kant argued thusly that the philosophical pursuits of the past could and indeed must continue after his critique, only now in a new way: not through the certainty of any actual absolute, but by reference to the universal structures of human existence.

Another example of this kind of post-Kantian redemption of the traditional aims of Western philosophy can be found in the work of the Vienna Circle, and later of Bertrand Russell and the subsequent tradition of Anglo-American analytic philosophy. What these thinkers all have in common is the hope that by purifying language from the vagaries of everyday use, they might extract from it a logical lever by which some facsimile of universal certainty might be achieved anew. In this way they sought to rescue the traditional project of philosophical reasoning by establishing it upon an allegedly better account of meaning and sense. Meanwhile on the Continent, a similar project was pursued within the structures of subjective experience alone. Think, for example, of Johann Gottfried Fichte's analysis of the foundations of "I-hood," G. W. F. Hegel's expansion of that project into a survey of a universal world-spirit, and Edmund Husserl's endeavors to identify and describe the underlying elements of a universal "transcendental subjectivity." What these seemingly disparate systems share in common is their recognition that if any sense of certainty is to be achieved through the use of reason, it must be accomplished within the limits of human experience, meaning-making, or logic alone. In this way, what all these Continental and analytic traditions have in common is the hope that some simulacrum of the kind of certainty once promised in the concept of the absolute might be achievable within the realm of the non-absolute: that is, in human experience, structured reasoning, or logical discourse. While each of these traditions acknowledges that after Kant no rationally accessible absolute can ultimately be determined to exist, they nevertheless argue, each in its own way, that a secure enough foundation for the classical project of philosophical inquiry can be achieved to justify its continued pursuit and relevance.

Of course, there were still other thinkers who rejected both of these approaches and proposed another, more radical path for the course of philosophy after Kant; namely, (3) to reject the limits his critique placed on the philosophical enterprise by asserting, against those limits, the possibility of discovering and connecting to some actual transcendental absolute. To accomplish this task, they argued, one need only transgress the limits of reason established by Kant by giving oneself over, for example, to the singular experience of faith, to the particularity of sensuous delight, or to the sublimity of individual ecstasy. Think of the neo-fideism of someone like Søren Kierkegaard as a good example of this route—someone who saw in the "madness" of personal religious faith a way to escape the strictures of post-Kantian philosophy and directly encounter some sense of the absolute anew. Another example of such a rejection of the Kantian critique of the absolute can be found in the work of Georges Bataille or Gilles Deleuze, both of whom sought in the transcendental experiences of enchantment, rapture, or psychosis some way outside of and beyond the limits of human rationality; a path by which they argued one might discover anew the power of the absolute. As disparate as these two approaches might appear at first glance, what they have in common is the claim that through some "line of flight," as Deleuze characterizes it, we might recover the concept of the absolute in philosophy and secure through immediate and individual contact with it a sense of some kind of certainty, significance, and even potentially beatitude which philosophers of the past sought to achieve through it.

Until very recently nearly every iteration of Western philosophy after Kant could be situated within one of these three responses to his critique of the concept of the absolute.[3] So it would seem that after Kant, as the saying goes, *le deluge*: the dissolution of the traditional methods, ends, and aims of philosophy, and its subsequent dispersion into warring camps—camps which are not only dialectically opposed to one another, but are often even unwilling to acknowledge one another as inheritors of the same history. And yet each is, in its own way, a child of the same rift that Kant's critique effected between human reasoning and the idea of the absolute. In this regard, each of the above approaches, as disparate as they may at first seem, ultimately bears a sibling relation, affinity, and resemblance to its others.

The problem, of course, is that while each of the above approaches maintains some internal logical consistency and offers some value to the contemporary thinker, it does so only by sacrificing the original power and promise of philosophical reasoning: the hope that some absolute position might be achieved which could ground, validate, and stabilize human existence, understanding, meaning-making, and moral evaluation. Perhaps this explains the enduring temptation of dogmatic metaphysics in the contemporary world—the promise that some sense of a universal absolute might still be achievable if we just believe hard enough. It also explains, I think, the ongoing erosion of the perceived value of philosophical argumentation to the general public, not to mention its slow transformation into an object of mockery and derision within political discourse, something better abandoned for a career in welding.[4] Indeed, there is too little scope and dimension to what philosophy can accomplish within the compass of Kant's critique to excite much interest beyond the rarified sphere of academic circles and readers of professional journals. No wonder, then, that the role of philosophy in popular discourse has shrunk to the point it has today, and our ranks grow fewer every day.

Post-Kantian Politics

But the effects of Kant's critique have been even more devastating outside the cloistered world of scholarly philosophy. The most horrifying repercussions of his critique can be found in the realm of contemporary social and political activity. Denied access to the power of a rationally justifiable concept of absolute goodness upon which to ground some hope for universal peace and justice, political aspirations after Kant have wavered between self-righteous quietism on the one hand, and bigoted sectarian barbarism on the other.

Following the various approaches to the question of human meaning-making sketched above, political reasoning in the West after Kant has likewise adopted one of three routes. Perhaps the most common of these has been (1) to abandon all hope for the possibility of achieving a universally agreed-upon vision of goodness, peace, and justice, and as such to renounce the efficacy of political projects entirely, opting instead to sneer cynically at those who strive to maintain some belief in "the system," whether as naive "bleeding-heart" liberals or as conservative "true believers." Against what proponents of this approach characterize as the childish pretenses of such political "dupes" on "both sides" of the political spectrum, they argue that the only authentic option for those who, like themselves, have taken the "red pill," "woken up," and now "know better" is to abandon hope in the value of political activity and to give up on thinking that any lasting change, peace, or justice might be possible. Instead, they suggest, the only meaningful goal to life is to accumulate as much private wealth, power, and pleasure as can be achieved, and to die "with the most toys."

The variety of such political nihilisms is easy to find in any number of post-Kantian cultural trends. They have ranged from the *bon vivants* of the late nineteenth century, who happily fiddled away at their private romances while the world burned around them, to the hippies and eventual hyper-consumers of the middle and late twentieth century, whose demands for "peace, love, and understanding" were ultimately nothing more than a passionate plea to be left alone to relish their private luxuries, personal reveries, and individual well-being—never mind its cost to anyone else, its effects on the possible survival of future generations, how it might unbalance global equality and security, or the devastation it might wreak upon the environment. Examples of such idiotic renunciations of political hope in favor of some version of "tuning in, turning on, and dropping out" are abundant after Kant. Indeed, more often than not, they are the real face of even those who seem to encourage political conviction, so long as that conviction doesn't upset the apple cart too much or disturb the status quo from which they personally benefit.

Against such hedonistic nihilisms there are many who still (2) hold out hope for the possibility of achieving some universally accepted route to "perpetual peace." The problem, of course, is that those who would pursue such a global project of universal diplomacy are denied access to any actual or rationally available absolute ground upon which to establish a shared vision of the good life, much less ground a practical foundation for the accomplishment of these aspirations. As a result, proponents of such doe-eyed hopefulness are forced to discover some new ground for their project, one which is localizable within what they see as the universal parameters of human nature; for example, within the "indominable human spirit," or the idea of "liberty" itself. Upon such virtual ideals, devotees to these political projects strive to promote universally agreed-upon goods which they think should serve as a "common ground" upon which everyone of good faith might work together "for the good of all." This, of course, was the approach pursued by Kant himself, not to mention Hegel, the inheritors of Adam Smith's account of capitalism, and, though many may think it somewhat ironic, Karl Marx's vision of an eventual communist utopia as well.

The problem with each of these attempts, however, as evidenced by the radical differences between them, is that it's not as easy as it might seem to agree upon what such a shared universal human conception of the good might be. Nowhere is this problem clearer than in the critical voices of the various post-colonial movements which have emerged since Kant, voices which have demonstrated clearly and concretely, as we will in greater detail soon, that every operative definition of an allegedly universal good has been, in the end, nothing more than a projection of a definitely local, and more often than not exclusively Western, white, and male ideal. As such, they convincingly argue, such projects, despite protestations to the contrary, are not ultimately universal. On the contrary, they are merely the fantasies of a European utopianism that ultimately proves itself to be little more than the groundwork for a new colonialism. It would seem from this fact that the post-Kantian liberal's hope that he or she might appeal to some universal account of human nature, reasoning, and the good life without reference to any absolute existential reality is not only doomed to fail; it is destined, tragically, to wreak actual harm upon others when it is practically pursued. Thus, while such projects may claim to operate from some set of universally acceptable and rational ideals, these ideals are, in the end, ultimately wholly contingent, local, and culturally unique, and are useful, perhaps only and at best, within the boundaries of their specific culture of origin. For, as the history of the last three centuries can testify, when these ideals are applied beyond those boundaries, they inevitably cause catastrophic harm. This explains in large part, I think, the tragic history of international politics since Kant, the heartbreaking fact that nearly every time a political action has been justified in the name of some allegedly universal good, the civil liberties of others have inevitably been trampled.

To make this terrible irony clearer, note the number of times in the late twentieth century alone that war has been declared in the developing world in the name of protecting and securing "human rights" precisely, it would seem, at the cost of those rights. What this tragic history reveals is the fact that the kinds of principles outlined in the Universal Declaration of Human Rights, though perfectly rational and universally appealing in theory, are, in actual practice, nothing more than the groundwork for an effective political colonialism. Indeed, nearly every attempt to apply such principles across national borders and cultural differences has resulted in what has ultimately amounted to some form of cultural imperialism whereby the West imposes its vision of the good, the right, and the true through the erasure of any already existent local conceptions of these ideals. So it is that after Kant, civic-minded Western liberals must inevitably face a choice: either (a) cling to the illusion of the universal rationality and impartial goodness of their values by sacrificing the capacity to act effectively in their name in order to keep from trampling the actual freedoms and values of other peoples and nations—and thus, in effect, resign themselves to a life of narcissistic quietism; or, alternatively, (b) act upon those values, but, in doing so, establish some form of colonial imperialism. Every political system after Kant which aspires to some vision of a universal concept of justice without reference to any absolutely guaranteed idea of the good, the right, or the true is assured one of these two fates.

In recognition of the inevitable failure of these two approaches, many post-Kantian political thinkers have taken a third route, by striving (3) to maintain some sense of the absolute, only now restricted exclusively to the domain of the individual, local, or indigenous. By rejecting the liberals' pretense to universality, eschewing all such trans-national ideals, and renouncing every assertion of a potential global sense of the good, advocates of this approach have promoted instead a variety of nationalisms, each promising to infuse the life of local communities with a renewed sense of well-being, meaning, and purpose. Such is the internal logic of every form of post-Kantian political fascism, whether those which rose to power in the middle of the twentieth century or those growing in popularity again at the start of the twenty-first.

While such political ambitions have the benefit of drawing from the real experience, actual history, and authentic forms of life of the communities for which they speak, their value as a basis for policy and political action are exclusive to an ever-diminishing definition of the local, native, domestic, regional, and eventually, if not immediately, even the human itself. The problem with such nationalistic and ethnic parochialisms is, in other words, that they demand the exclusion, excision, and ultimately, the elimination of any competing claimant to the good, the right, or the true. As such, these nationalisms are inherently at war, not only with liberalism, but with every other form of nationalism, and eventually with every other dissenting or differing position within their own political history. Hence the inevitable obsession with the idea of "purity," whether ethnic or ideological, in such political projects, not to mention their eventual collapse into internal backbiting and, eventually, civil war.

But the root of these problems lies in the fact that such nationalisms, like their globalizing liberal counterparts, have no access to an actual absolute power by which to justify their account of the good, the right, and the true. As such, they cannot accomplish even what they promise in the lives of the local communities to which they appeal. And so, in their pursuit of some singular sense of absolute reality, whether defined nationally, locally, or regionally, these political projects inevitably devolve into obsessional madness and chaotic violence, all to maintain a relevance and power which they can never hope to achieve without the support of some actual absolute. Hence, against their allegedly local interests, they must inevitably proselytize the value of their "way of life" to and for all. So it is that the post-Kantian nationalists, like their liberal counterparts, must eventually face a choice: either (a) resign themselves to a life lived exclusively within the confines of an ever-shrinking definition of the local, hoping to interact and engage only with those who share a similar set of values and vision of the good life, a choice which ultimately appears to be nothing more than another form of nihilistic quietism; or, alternatively, (b) abandon the façade of political provincialism and defend the relevance, power, and value of their traditions in the "marketplace of ideas" against other competing claims, a decision which, of course, ultimately betrays their founding aims and effectively erects a trans-national form of political imperialism. In this way the fate of post-Kantian nationalism is no different from that of post-Kantian global liberalism. Both eventually collapse into a dialectical antimony that forces them to choose between a shrinking quietistic regionalism or an expansionist fanatical dogmatism.

From this brief survey of the kinds of political projects which have dominated Western history since Kant, the inherent danger of political activity without access to any truly universal absolute should be clear. Without some real sense of an actually existent universal absolute upon which to ground and defend a universal concept of meaning, value, and truth, every political project must inevitably collapse into some form of ethical nihilism and quietism or give way to some form of moral dogmatism or cultural imperialism. After Kant, truly, *le deluge*.

What then is to be done? How is philosophy and politics to move forward after Kant? Where are we to turn to envision meaning, value, and truth anew, much less act upon them, without risking one of the sociopolitical horrors evidenced in the history of thought after Kant? It is far too late, of course, to return to any pre-Kantian conception of the absolute. Nor should we hope to! After all, as Alfred North Whitehead notes, the kinds of dogmatism that such absolutes provided were a "refuge of human savagery," and the history of the political reasoning which they supported justified a "melancholy record of horrors."[5] Indeed, the elimination of such savageries was in large part the explicit target of Kant's critique. The problem is, however, as we have just seen, that although Kant's critique was intended to liberate us from such a "melancholy record of horrors," it has only contributed to it.

We cannot hope to escape our own period of savagery and horror by looking backwards to the political systems of the past. If we are to overcome the terrible history of political mishaps since Kant without resurrecting those which preceded him, then we must find a new way of conceiving of the absolute for the future; one which is not dogmatic but is nevertheless actual and universal. This requires, as Kant argued, working within the constraints of reason alone, without, however, equating the absolute with the operation of reason itself. To see how this might be accomplished, we must first understand Kant's claims concerning the power and limitations of reason with respect to absolute knowledge, as well as the potential pitfalls of his claims. Only in this way can we see how we might overcome the limitations of the philosophies and politics which have followed from Kant's claims without reverting to the kinds of philosophies and politics which preceded them, and in this way potentially discover a different route to an absolutely grounded sense of meaning, value, and truth for the future.

The Aim of Kant's Critique

Kant's critique of the limits of reason is, of course, a double-edged sword. On the one hand, it aims to curtail the claims of religious dogmatism as well as the influence of church doctrine over social and political life. In this regard, Kant's critique is intended to restrict religious faith to the bounds of "reason alone," as the title of his 1793 treatise put it, and thereby further empower what he took to be the spirit and destiny of the Enlightenment: *sapare aude*—to "dare to know" freely, to let reason guide thinking and the pursuit of truth.[6] At the same time, and on the other hand, Kant's critique also aims to curtail what he saw as the exaggerated counter-claims of empirical skepticism and scientific materialism in the modern world, claims which he thought might destroy entirely the concept of the social good and the possibility of political hope.[7]

"Dogmas and formulas," Kant famously argued, whether religious and spiritual in nature or empirical and scientific in origin, are both "instruments" for the "misuse" of reason.[8] Because of this, he continues, they function as fetters upon the actualization of human freedom and should be seen as "the ball and chain of [human] immaturity" and enslavement.[9] In order to free humanity intellectually and politically from the encumbrance of such "dogmas and formulas," Kant concludes, we must endeavor to liberate ourselves from every form of thinking which promises "to extend human cognition beyond all bounds of possible experience," whether through faith or through science, and come to understand instead what can be accomplished "merely with reason itself and its pure thinking"—what, in other words, he thinks can be assured and guaranteed by and within human thought and experience alone.[10] The problem with those dogmatic programs, as Kant demonstrates throughout his work, is that they all too "confidently take on the execution of [the] task [of defining metaphysical absolutes like 'God, freedom, and immortality'] without an antecedent examination of the capacity or incapacity of reason for such a great undertaking."[11] The first task of his critique of every dogma and formula, whatever its nature and origin, is therefore to initiate "a science of the mere estimation of pure reason, of its sources and boundaries."[12] This, he suggests, is the precondition for the dissolution of the pretensions of every form of dogmatism, whether religious or scientific, and thereby the realization of the full expression of human freedom and flourishing. By establishing the proper limits of reason and assessing the effective range of its claims, Kant suggests, not only can we curtail the exaggerated pretensions of religion and science alike, but we can solidly ground philosophy's pursuit of truth, meaning, and the good. Hence, Kant's assessment that the "utility of [his critique of pure reason] [is really] only negative, serving not for the amplification but only for the purification of our reason, and for keeping it free of errors," as well as his suggestion that it is only by way of such a negative approach that the future of philosophical reasoning and human well-being in general can be secured.[13]

This purification is essential, Kant asserts, because "if the understanding cannot distinguish whether certain questions lie within its horizon or not, then it is never sure of its claims and its possession, but must always reckon on many embarrassing corrections when it continually oversteps the boundaries of its territory (as is unavoidable) and loses itself in delusion and deceptions."[14] Hence Kant's claim that while primarily negative in its rejection of dogmatism, "a great deal is already won" by way of a critique of the effective power of reason.[15] Indeed, Kant argues, "critique, and that alone, contains within itself the whole well-tested and verified plan by which metaphysics as a science can be achieved."[16] Only by passing philosophical reason through the purifying fire of such a critique, he concludes, can a truly scientific approach to our questions concerning the nature of the existence, the good, the right, and the true finally be secured.

On the basis of this conviction, Kant contrasts those inquiries which emerge from a proper critique of the power of reason with "the ordinary school of metaphysics precisely as chemistry stands to alchemy, or astronomy to the fortune-tellers' astrology."[17] Against such "sophistical pseudosciences" and "empty wisdoms," Kant endeavors to clear the way for a truly scientific account of the good, the right, and the true that is rigorously grounded, entirely rational, and empirically justifiable.[18] But herein lies the double edge of Kant's critique. Inasmuch as he hopes to limit the excesses of dogmatic metaphysical claims concerning the nature of the absolute, Kant equally expects his critical evaluation of the effective power of reason "to negate the impudent assertions of materialism, naturalism, and fatalism" as well, all positions which he argues equally "constrict the field of reason."[19] We should be careful then not to take Kant's critique of dogmatism in favor of a properly scientific and wholly rational metaphysics to be a full-throated endorsement of what has since been called "scientism." On the contrary: according to Kant, such a reductionistic understanding of the empirical and materialistic sciences is just as dangerous to human flourishing and the pursuit of truth as classical dogmatism. Indeed, Kant devotes just as much, if not more, of his first *Critique* to dressing down what he sees as the miscarriages of scientific reasoning as he does to dismantling the claims and excesses of classical religious dogmatism. But, and this is essential to understanding Kant properly, despite their apparently contrasting claims, their problems are essentially the same; namely: both err in their assessment of the effective range of human rationality. Thus, where dogmatism promises too much to human understanding, for example, a knowledge of absolute reality in itself, outside of and beyond the realm of human experience and, in this way, oversteps the proper limits of rationality, Kant argues that the tendency toward skepticism and fatalism in materialistic empiricism and scientism expects too little of human rationality. Indeed, he argues, at their most extreme they expect nothing at all, and in this way they obliviate what he suggests is the effective power of rational intellection. In this regard, inasmuch as Kant's critique aims to curtail the extravagances of spiritualism and religious dogmatism, it likewise endeavors to enliven the diminutive reductionism of materialistic empiricism. By surveying the frontiers of reason and establishing its proper perimeters, Kant thus aims to defend philosophy from two forms of epistemological extremism; and by doing so, he aims to reestablish the proper ground, aim, and end of philosophical reckoning anew. After all, while "materialism will not work as a way of explaining my existence," Kant reasons that "spiritualism is just as unsatisfactory."[20]

Against "materialism," Kant thinks that critical philosophy must work positively to make room for a full expression of the human powers of reason and show "that [in fact] there is an absolutely necessary practical use of pure reason (the moral use), in which reason unavoidably extends itself beyond the boundaries of sensibility."[21] Against "spiritualism," Kant argues that critical philosophy must operate negatively to limit the "dogmatic procedure of pure reason," to "teach . . . us never to venture with speculative reason beyond the boundaries of experience."[22] Through these twin rebuffs, Kant concludes, "we sever the very root of materialism, fatalism, atheism, [and] of freethinking unbelief . . . and finally also of idealism and skepticism," while weeding out simultaneously the "enthusiasm and superstition" demanded by dogmatic fideism.[23] But for such a critically productive limitation to occur, Kant insists, we must begin with an "inventory of all we possess through pure reason, ordered systematically."[24] Only in this way, he argues, can philosophy reestablish itself through a proper understanding of the nature and limits of reason.

It is important to note that for Kant this bi-directional critique of the powers of reason is not merely "theoretical." Its aims are not, in other words, solely epistemological. To the contrary, its aims are first and foremost ethical and political. Indeed, Kant begins the *Critique of Pure Reason* by analogizing the domain of philosophical discourse with the polis, seeing in dogmatism an avatar for political despotism and in skepticism a representation of political anarchy, both of which he critiques as respective expressions of tyranny. Against both, Kant likens his critical philosophy to the rule of law—the only means, he suggests, which exists to mitigate the threat of tyranny and promote the possibility of true peace. The aim of Kant's critique is from the outset, then, a fundamentally ethical and political project, even when it is at its most epistemological and metaphysical. Hence Kant's claim that the ultimate aim of his critique is "to institute a court of justice, by which reason may secure its rightful claims," so that lasting intellectual, social, and political peace might be secured.[25] For Kant, then, critical philosophy is more than merely a means of safeguarding the sovereign epistemological territory of philosophical inquiry. It is the only route by which social and political well-being can be pursued. It is therefore ultimately against every form of sociopolitical "fanaticism" that Kant's critical philosophy takes its aim.

By Kant's account, this "fanaticism cannot make headway in an enlightened age except by hiding behind a school of metaphysics, under the protection of which it can venture, as it were, to rave rationally, [and so] will be driven by critical philosophy from this, its final hiding place."[26] Through an analysis of the appropriate dominion of rational philosophy, then, Kant intends not only to eradicate the decadence of dogmatic metaphysics and materialistic scientism, but to abolish the kinds of political fanaticism which spring from such excesses and to end, thereby, the ethical toll they inevitably levy upon the lives of their human subjects. In this regard, Kant's aims are no different than our own: to establish a justifiable philosophy capable of grounding the pursuit of a truly good and just world.

The problem, however, as we have already seen, is that insofar as Kant's critique successfully accomplishes its aim to limit the power of dogmatic fideism and materialistic scientism, and thereby curtail their accompanying social and political expressions, it gives rise to a new set of epistemological and ethical problems which have resulted in entirely new versions of dogmatic fanaticism and nihilistically quietistic fatalism. Indeed, as we have just shown, the horrors of the history of politics since Kant are a direct result of the effectiveness of his critique. To understand how we might escape these horrors without giving rise to those which preceded Kant's critique, it is therefore incumbent that we understand the nuances of that critique. Only thus might we discover a route beyond both.

The Content of the Critique

Kant's review of the compass of reason's scope famously begins with a systematic accounting of the various kinds of judgments it can produce. It begins, in other words, by identifying and defining the various ways in which reason makes sense of the world. Such judgments, Kant outlines, are made according to one of four possible modes. A judgment can be either *analytic* in nature (i.e., explicative or formed by definition and containing no information outside of itself) or *synthetic* (i.e., ampliative or extended by attribute or further information); and either *apriori* in nature (i.e., emergent from understanding and reason itself) or *aposterori* (i.e., informed by the empirical or sensible experience of something seemingly outside of reason).²⁷ According to Kant all knowledge, which is to say every possible form of rational judgment, must, by definition, appear in some combination of these four possible modes of understanding. From this it follows that there are really only four kinds of knowledge which are even theoretically possible for Kant—four possible combinations of these forms of judgment. Plotted along the classic Aristotelian square of opposition, Kant's analysis of the kinds of knowledge claims which are *possible* for reason is illustrated in figure 1 below. Of course, the first of these four possible quadrants, those judgments which would apparently be simultaneously *analytic* and *aposterori* (the top-left quadrant), are fundamentally impossible, as they express a possibility which is internally contradictory—an idea which is both simple and complex at the same time.²⁸ Since such forms of knowledge are impossible, Kant maintains that in effect there are only three kinds of *actual* knowledge claims: (1) *analytic apriori* judgments—that is, concepts which are emergent from the operation and structure of reason alone and are formed by definition; (2) *synthetic aposterori* judgments—concepts which emerge from the combination of *analytic apriori* structures and some empirical content which is received from sensory experience; and (3) *synthetic apriori* judgments—concepts which are formed through the extension of *analytic apriori* structures by logical analysis.

In order to complete his survey of the nature and operation of rea-

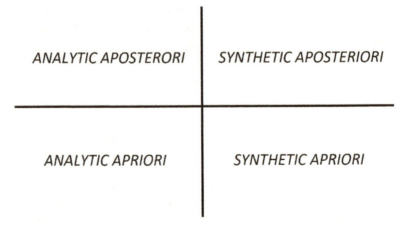

Figure 1. Kant on the possible forms of knowledge

son, Kant must identify what he claims are the four different ways in which reason can organize the content of its judgment into knowledge claims. This he does by maintaining the classical definitions of logical thought established by Aristotle. Hence Kant's claim that the concepts of reason can be connected either (1) *quantitatively*, whether universally, particularly, or singularly; (2) *qualitatively*, whether affirmatively, negatively, or singularly; (3) *relationally*, whether categorically, hypothetically, or disjunctively; or (4) *modally*, whether problematically, assertorically, or apodictically.[29] According to Kant, through the operation of these four logical "concepts of understanding" upon the three kinds of rational judgment which are possible, reason constructs the entirety of its understanding of reality. Everything that we can think, claim to know, or hope to experience, Kant concludes, is the product of one of the three forms of judgment extended through one of the four possible modes of logical combination, either with itself or with its other.

The Absolute Limits of Knowledge

This survey of the nature, content, and operation of reason, while perhaps overwhelming and difficult to comprehend at first glance, is relatively intuitive once it is properly understood, and a number of excellent commentaries exist which can aid in this endeavor.[30] But an exhaustive understanding of Kant's account of the operation of reason for the production of its understanding of the world isn't strictly necessary for the task at hand. It is sufficient for now to understand the conclusions which Kant draws from his survey of the nature, content, and function of reason; namely, that everything which can be known by it, which exists for it, or which can be hoped for from it must be understood as fundamentally conditioned by and circumscribed within its nature, function, and operation alone. In other words, what Kant thinks his survey of the structure of human rationality proves is that everything that we can possibly know is ultimately the product of our own cognition and, therefore, is ultimately *human* in origin and nature. All knowledge for Kant, in other words, is irrevocably shaped by and inextricably confined within the limit and structure of our own cognitive faculties.

What this means is that it is impossible, according to Kant, to know or say anything meaningful about the nature of reality as it *actually* exists in-itself, outside the structures of reason. All such claims, he thinks, fail to acknowledge the proper scope and effective limits of reason; the fact, in other words, that everything which appears to us and can be thought by us is necessarily constituted within us and is limited by and structured according to the nature of our perceptual and cognitive apparatuses. To claim to have knowledge of some *absolute* truth or reality, some "thing-in-itself," as Kant calls it, as it might exist outside these apparatuses, is therefore, according to him, inherently mistaken. Indeed, such claims, he suggests, are in fact demonstratively self-contradictory; for they pretend to have *knowledge* which exceeds the very nature of *knowing* itself. Yet it is precisely claims of this sort which Kant thinks populate every form of dogmatism, whether spiritual or scientific. If philosophy is going to free itself from the claims of such fundamentally irrational and demonstratively false and self-contradictory systems, he concludes, it must start by accepting the irrefutable fact that every knowledge claim is inseparable from the nature of its claimant. In this way, Kant renders meaningless what had been the prospect and project of Western philosophy up until then: to achieve some absolute knowledge through which all that we know, experience, and hope might be assured.

"Everything in our cognition that belongs to intuition," Kant writes, "contains nothing but mere relations," and "through mere relations no thing in itself is cognized."[31] All that we know and everything that could ever exist for us, according to Kant, is necessarily ordered by and inextricably bound to the architecture of human cognition and rationality. In other words, reality as we know it is fundamentally structured and organized by the nature of our mind. Thus, Kant claims, even when we think that we perceive objects which seem to exist outside of ourselves, somewhere "out there," as it were, beyond us, in the world itself, "it is [nevertheless] just this subjective constitution that determine[s] its form as appearance."[32] Kant concludes that "through sensibility we do not cognize the constitution of things in themselves merely indistinctly, but rather not at all."[33] Indeed, he writes, "appearances are not things in themselves, but rather the mere play of our representations, which in the end come down to determinations of our inner sense."[34]

It follows from this that for Kant no perception, whether material or metaphysical, is ever of some "thing" that actually exists outside of ourselves and consists of its own true nature. On the contrary, he reasons, all such perceptions are irrevocably structured and conditioned by the nature of human reason and cognition alone. Thus, Kant concludes, while some absolute "out-there" may exist independently from us, it can never be known as such. Instead, he argues, all that we can ever hope to know is the rational representation of that thing, one which is organized and filtered by the constraints of our own understanding and nature. With this, Kant's critique renders the concept of the absolute meaningless for philosophy thereafter.

It is important to note, however, that it is not Kant's claim, as is commonly misunderstood, that there is *nothing* at all outside of ourselves; that in other words, everything that we experience originates with us and is exclusively the product of the structures of our thought; or, in other words still, that we are not in contact with anything outside of and beyond ourselves. On the contrary, Kant's critique is in large part directed precisely against such solipsistic idealisms.[35] Hence his insistence that "all our representations are in fact related to some object through the understanding, and, since appearances are nothing but representations, the understanding thus relates them to a something, as the object of sensible intuition."[36]

It is clear from this that Kant expressly denies the conclusions of any transcendental idealism which rejects the independent and absolute existence of external reality. Against such idealisms, Kant insists throughout his work that human reasoning is fundamentally in contact with some absolute order. But, and this is the crux of his claim, human understanding can never be brought into *immediate* relation with or connection to that absolute order. Instead, he argues, all contact with such an absolute reality will be fundamentally and inescapably mediated by the structures and nature of human understanding. And so, he concludes, any claim concerning the nature of this presumed absolute reality is not rationally justifiable, even if it happens to be correct. As such, he thinks, claims of this nature must be tempered and limited through an informed understanding of their inescapable relativity to the structure of human reasoning from which they spring and by which they are formed.

The aim of Kant's critique, then, is not to deny the possible existence of some absolute reality in and of itself. Its aim is instead to show the impossibility of sensing, knowing, understanding, or making any rationally justifiable judgments about the nature of that absolute as a thing-in-itself. For Kant, all such judgments must necessarily be limited to the nature and structure of human reason. Hence, Kant's conclusion that while we most certainly *do* encounter some absolute reality which exists entirely outside of our being, whatever actual existential qualities we may want to attribute to that reality (e.g., its size, shape, density, color, etc.) must be recognized as originating in "my kind of intuition and not [from] these objects in themselves."[37] Our apparent experiences of the absolute, Kant concludes, are never representative of the actual nature of being, but only of our own capacity to cognize it. Hence Kant's claim that while some absolute reality may indeed be "given to us by means of sensibility," this reality must always be "thought through the understanding, and from it arise [our] concepts" of it.[38] Thus, while Kant acknowledges that all knowledge must ultimately be related, "whether straightaway (*directe*) or through a detour (*indirecte*)," to some absolute existence, he insists that our understanding of that presumed existence must be acknowledged as irrevocably molded and crafted by the structures of our own rationality and perception and never taken to be a pure representation of the thing-in-itself.[39] The heart of Kant's argument is not that there is *no* absolute reality in and of itself then, nor is it that we are entirely divorced from such an absolute. His claim is rather that "all empirical cognition of objects is necessarily in accord with [rational] concepts, since without their presuppositions nothing is possible as objects of experience."[40] Hence Kant's conclusion that "sensibility and its field are themselves limited by the understanding, in that they do not pertain to things in themselves, but only to the way in which, on account of our subject constitution, things appear to us."[41]

What all of this means, and this is the truly revolutionary heart of Kant's critique, is that while some absolute reality *must* exist outside of and beyond the limits of our understanding—and, indeed, such an absolute must serve as the actual ground for and condition of our perception, knowledge claims, and understanding of reality—nevertheless, the absolute nature of that reality, existent as it is in and for itself, can never be known purely, nor accessed directly by us. For Kant, reality in its absolute form is categorically impossible and fundamentally inaccessible. Thus, he reasons, while we may make assumptions, and even achieve rational conclusions concerning what such an absolute *might* be like on the basis of our perceptions and conclusions, we can never *actually* know its nature as it is in and for itself. Such "hyperbolic" claims concerning what Kant calls *noumenal* reality must be understood as "always be[ing] encountered [exclusively] in relation to the subject" and filtered through the structures of our own being and consciousness.[42] At best, he thinks, we might use reason to extrapolate from our *phenomenal* experiences the *possible* nature of the absolute. But, Kant assures us, such *possible* projections of absolute reality can never be verified by us against the absolute itself; for we can never know the true nature of *noumenal* reality as it *actually* exists, in and for itself.

Because Kant insists that whatever absolute reality must exist out there, as a "thing-in-itself" (*Ding an sich*), can never be known or accessed by us, he argues that claims concerning its nature cannot and should not serve any practical philosophical or political purpose. They should not be used, in other words, to certify our judgments or support our sense of the meaning and value of the world.[43] At best, Kant suggests, the concept of the absolute might be treated as "a something = x, of which we know nothing at all nor can know anything in general (in accordance with the current constitution of our understanding)"—nothing more, in other words, than the limit or boundary which defines the proper domain of philosophical reasoning.[44] As such, instead of hoping to secure human knowledge or to ground our hope in the meaning and value of human existence upon such absolute, Kant suggests that philosophy is better served establishing itself upon an understanding of the "constitution of our understanding." This, he thinks, is the best and only way in which we might hope to confirm our judgments, test and secure the nature of knowledge, and ground our ethical and political hopes anew. Indeed, according to Kant, if anything is to be treated as the ultimate ground and condition for our philosophical hopes, and in this capacity replace the position traditionally occupied by the absolute, it should be the organizing structure of rationality itself, which Kant calls "transcendental" in nature, indeed a "transcendental subjectivity."[45] Hence our identification at the start of this chapter of the Archimedean nature of Kant's project and all those who have followed the route he charted—all those, in other words, who have strived to define some new universal ground for philosophical thought within the "transcendental" nature of human cognition and its products.[46]

Kant's Critique and the Birth of Modern Ethics

This is precisely the aim, of course, of Kant's ethical works. There he endeavors to show how a new foundation for moral judgments might be established upon, secured by, and deduced from the "transcendental" structures of reason alone, rather than intuited from or dictated by the nature of some independently existing absolute being or value (i.e., noumenal reality or a dogmatically asserted God). For Kant, following the logic of his *Critique of Pure Reason*, the proper foundation for morality cannot be anything which might exist "out there," in some presumably "real" noumenal world, since such a world is by his definition inaccessible. Instead, he reasons, the proper foundation for moral claims must be located "within me"; it must be emergent, in other words, from "my invisible self, my personality," and "discoverable only by the understanding."[47] In other words, the proper foundation for morality, according to Kant, is not the transcendence of some presumed absolute reality, but a "transcendental power" that exists within the structures of reason itself. So, Kant concludes, if any ethical principle, law, or edict is to be properly grounded, it must be discoverable within or deducible from "the concepts of pure reason" alone.[48] Following this line of reasoning, Kant endeavors to extract not only a new foundation for morality from the "universal and necessary" operations of logic itself, but even practical moral edicts and commandments instructive for everyday conduct.[49] In this way, Kant hoped to sever the last ties which he felt bound us to the dogmatisms of the past and forge a new, modern, and enlightened guide for life that would "hold not merely for human beings but for all rational beings as such, not merely under contingent conditions and with no exceptions, but with absolute necessity."[50]

This is, in many ways, the ultimate end of Kant's critique of *pure reason*: to develop from it a foundation for *practical life*—a foundation for the kind of reasoning which we need to make effective ethical judgments and regulate our moral actions. As Kant notes, "the moral law in its purity and genuineness (which in practical matters is of the greatest significance) is to be sought nowhere else than in a pure philosophy; it (metaphysics) must thus come first, and without it there can be no moral philosophy at all."[51] Having secured a foundation for this new metaphysics in and through his survey of the categories of understanding inherent to the structure of pure reason, Kant suggests that it is incumbent on us to deduce a new set of ethical *imperatives* which can be used to structure and guide human behavior and direct our political projects.[52] Only if this task is accomplished, Kant suggests, can the work of his first *Critique* be fulfilled and the legacy of dogmatism finally concluded.

The most famous of the imperatives Kant thinks can be deduced from the transcendental structure of reason in the formation of a new practical morality is, of course, the "categorical imperative," which, he argues, enjoins us "[to] act only according to that maxim through which you can at the same time will that it become a universal law."[53] Despite common misperceptions, this rationally grounded moral imperative does not contain any practical instruction or actual content. On the contrary, it is merely an expression for Kant of the formal conditions or logical requirements to which any actual practical moral edict must conform if it is to be valid. In this regard, it is for Kant merely the measure of whatever "practical law" or moral edict one might want to establish—a safeguard, in a sense, against the return of dogmatism within morality.[54] In other words, what this iteration of the categorical imperative defines is the limits or bounds within which the actual content of any practical moral claim must conform in order to retain any logical or rational validity. Nevertheless, Kant thinks that from this imperative alone, a number of other moral imperatives and ethical edicts can be deduced; for example, "I ought not to lie," and "I ought to try to advance the happiness of others," and so on.[55] Perhaps the most famous example of the kind of practical moral content Kant thinks can be deduced from this imperative is his assertion that "a human being is not a thing, hence not something that can be used merely as a means, but must in all [one's] actions always be considered as an end in itself."[56] Whatever its actual content, however, the emphasis of Kant's extension of his critique of pure reason into the realm of the practical is to show how a new, universally valid conception of moral regulation can be deduced from the transcendental structures of reason alone, and not from any absolute reality which exists outside of or beyond those structures. In this way, Kant sought to replace the old dogmatic assertion of a supreme absolute good as the foundation of moral normativity with a new "supreme" good, one from which he thinks a new set of modern ethical imperatives can be derived. The superiority of this good over its predecessors, Kant thinks, is that it need not be merely supposed in faith or accepted in obedience, but can instead be deduced by any rational agent from a proper understanding of the operation of reason alone.[57] So it is, Kant thinks, that the new foundation for the good lies immanently within the rational agent itself, and not in the absolute structures of any independent existence.

Kant names his account of this new "supreme good" the "good will" of the rational moral agent, which is for him nothing more than the practical expression of the operation of pure reason itself.[58] Hence Kant's definition of this new supreme good: "A good will is good," he writes, "just by its willing, i.e., in itself."[59] Indeed, according to Kant, the "practical" function of reason is precisely "to produce" this "good in itself," an in-itself which is not cordoned off and inaccessible as some noumenal hyperbolic object "out there," but which is instead immediately available and directly accessible "in a rational being."[60] This reference to "good will" as a good "in itself" is clearly an allusion by Kant to the function it serves in his new morality. For Kant, "good will" is in effect a new absolute—a new moral thing-in-itself, only one which is not actually absolute, derived as it is from the structures of reason immanent within us. By establishing a new "groundwork" for morals in the operation of the will of the rational subject in this way, Kant cuts the final tie binding us to the dogmatisms of the past. No longer are we forced to search for some absolute moral object out there which we must assert in faith in order to secure a practical ethics. Instead, we can now deduce a concept of a universal good, and indeed a "supreme good" "in itself," from within the nature and operation of our own being.

The Death of God, Nature, and the Absolute Good

Through such a critique of every conceptual form of the absolute (whether metaphysical or ethical) by means of a comprehensive mapping of the function of reason, a mapping which, he asserts, establishes a radical break between the merely theoretical possibility of *noumenal/absolute existence* and the actual lived reality of *phenomenal/practical* existence, Kant effectively ends the philosophical project of the West up to that point. By abolishing the pretensions of dogmatism and materialism alike, he fundamentally demolishes philosophy's hope that it might define itself in relation to some absolute reality which might secure its conception of the good, the right, and the true. In its place, Kant shows how we might hope to rediscover the power and potential traditionally ascribed to such an absolute within the decidedly non-absolute structures of reason itself. In this way, what Kant takes away with one hand, he alleges to grant anew with another. Nevertheless, the final consequence of his critique is to abolish the concept of *absolute* existence (the ultimate "hyperbolic" object of dogmatic thought), *absolute* moral values (the supreme "good" of traditional premodern ethics), and even the *absolute* laws of an independent material world (the "final truths" of scientific empiricism). After Kant, it seems, all such conceptions of the absolute must be reassessed as ultimately resting upon, emergent from, and organized by the schemata of human reasoning alone. As such, he argues, rather than continuing to aspire to some allegedly absolute conception of existence, goodness, or reality, philosophers should endeavor to recover the security once hoped for in the absolute through reference to the nature, structure, and operation of reason alone. Hence Kant's insistence that the only valid path for establishing any claim anew is through the crucible of logical reasoning.

It is important to emphasize at this point that while such logical and rational analyses are for Kant the only legitimate ground for a practical reasoning, and in this regard provide a new good "in-itself," they do not amount to a new absolute in themselves. Indeed, as Kant notes, the best we can hope for is that the products of our rational scrutiny might be representative of whatever absolute reality exists out there, beyond the scope of reason. And so he enjoins his readers to act "as if" the products of rational analysis accurately correspond to whatever absolute reality might exist outside of and beyond us, while insisting that we nevertheless not forget that an insurmountable boundary separates those products from this reality and prevents them from ever being treated or understood as actual absolutes themselves.[61] Thus, while Kant thinks such a practical "as if" is sufficient to found and justify a new hope for the pursuit of a universal conception of the good, the right, and the true, he insists that we acknowledge that such universal conceptions never bear the status or structure of the kind of absolutes traditionally esteemed by philosophy. To the contrary, Kant concludes that every knowledge claim, whether of the "starry heavens above" (nature/God) or of "the moral law within" (morality/God), be understood as inexorably circumscribed, conditioned, and shaped by the structures of reason itself.[62] Thus, Kant argues, if any conception of the absolute is to be retained within this new understanding of the nature and limits of reason, it must be divorced from its traditional connotations.[63] If we want to maintain some conception of the absolute, Kant insists, it cannot be taken to indicate some "thing-in-itself" which exists independently from us. For, as we have seen, the idea of such noumenal "hyperbolic objects" is entirely speculative for Kant and only useful *negatively* as a "boundary concept, in order to limit the pretension of sensibility," signifying exclusively that which can never be thought or known rationally.[64] Kant concludes, then, that the only sense of the absolute which could still possibly be achieved in the wake of his critique is of a product of the will alone, a product he figures as the ultimate accomplishment of the perfect "unity of reason."[65]

In service to this possible unity, Kant dedicates a good portion of the first *Critique* to exploring the nature, value, and uses of what he calls the unifying *ideas* of reason; that is, the metaphysical concept of the *I* or soul (which he sees as the foundation of a new moral law), the understanding of the *world* or cosmos (which he posits as the foundation for a new concept of nature), and the idea of *God* or the divine (which he views as the foundation for a new hope in some ultimate truth or meaning of existence).[66] In references to these new potential "absolutes," Kant makes clear that such "ideas" are not really absolute in the traditional sense. They do not signify any potential independently existing objects or *things* which might derive their meaning and existence from themselves alone. On the contrary, Kant claims, each of these "absolutes" are nothing more than a product or extension of the *analytic apriori* structures of reason alone, each is achieved, in other words, in accordance with the categories of human understanding alone. Such transcendental or metaphysical ideas are for Kant then always only *synthetically* derived from the structures of human understanding and are not then ultimately separate from us as absolute *things* and noumenal objects in their own right. Instead, each of these synthetic "absolutes" is a product of reason alone which grows from and appears exclusively within us alone. Hence Kant's insistence that while we may, and indeed *should* act "as if" these ideas have some absolute existential import, they must be recognized ultimately as nothing more than an extension of the logical operation of reason itself.[67] As such, rather than assume that such objects may have some absolute correlate in the noumenal realm itself, Kant suggests that we doubt the independent existence of any such metaphysical objects and accept them instead as a product of and project for human existence alone. After all, he reasons (as Ludwig Feuerbach famously noted), it is much more likely that such ideas are an outward projection of our innermost nature than they are an inner reflection of an outer/absolute reality which exists independently from us.[68]

It is essential, then, to a proper understanding of Kant's argument and the legacy of his critique that we not take his claims about the nature of the self, the world, and God to contain any positive assertion of the independent or absolute existence of such epistemological objects.[69] Hence Kant's insistence that his exploration of such ideas is not "constitutive" of any formal proof for the existence of the soul, the independent existence of the world, or God.[70] Instead, he insists time and time again, the proper function of such transcendental ideas is "merely regulative."[71] Their use, he argues, is solely to guide *reason* in the development of a rationally justified sense of moral norms, scientific laws, and ultimate hope. Thus, while these ideas may be treated as theoretically "absolute," Kant states clearly that they are not ultimately absolute. Nevertheless, he concludes, such ideas should supplant and take the place of the classical absolutes of Western thought in order to found and empower a new, modern metaphysics and ethics.

This is the final aim of Kant's critique of the concept of the absolute then: to undermine the pretenses of any claim to the absolute existence of moral, scientific, and theological objects. For as Kant makes clear, the foundation for such claims about the Soul, the World, and God are demonstrable products of human reasoning. As such, he concludes, these ideas cannot be used to determine anything meaningful about the *actual* nature of *noumenal* reality as it exists in and for itself. Instead, he claims, they might only be used to help us to relate *practically* to *phenomenal* reality as we experience it either ethically, naturally, or metaphysically, respectively.[72] The function of these ideas for Kant then is exclusively to guide and govern human reason as it constructs a coherent and practical understanding of itself, its world, and its projects and aims. Constrained as they are within and occasioned by the architecture of human reasoning, Kant insists that the value of such ideas is therefore *exclusively* to such practical concerns. These ideas are beneficial, in other words, only inasmuch as they might help us to relate to our world, to one another, and to the future with greater facility—only inasmuch as they help us, in other words, to answer the questions: "What can I know?" "What must I do?" and "What may I hope?"[73] It is only in pursuit of these practical questions, Kant argues, that we can speak meaningfully of *God*, the supreme *good*, and the *laws of nature*.[74] Any attempt to extend this discourse beyond this practical use of reason through the projection of these ideas onto or into the absolute nature of reality itself is necessarily to resurrect the kind of fanatical dogmatism or reductive scientism that his entire project is set against.

So, Kant concludes, "as exaggerated and contradictory as it may sound to say that the understanding is itself the source of the laws of nature, and thus of the formal unity of nature, such an assertion is nevertheless correct and appropriate."[75] "Nature," Kant writes, "is nothing in itself but a sum of appearances, hence not a thing in itself but merely a multitude of representations of the mind."[76] Similarly, God, he reasons, can only ever be understood as a "concept" or "ideal of pure reason" that is of practical moral use alone.[77] And since "reason does not furnish us with the objective validity of such a concept," Kant argues, we can never assert the actual existence of any divine power or celestial entity.[78] Indeed, according to him, we have "no concept of what [God may be] in itself," or any knowledge of whether any such God may actually exist independently from us; for, he writes, "reason's supposition of a highest being as the supreme cause is thought merely relatively, on behalf of the systematic unity of the world of sense, and it is a mere Something in idea."[79] "This being of reason," Kant makes clear, is nothing more than "a mere idea and is therefore not assumed absolutely and in itself as something actual."[80] As such, he concludes, "we do not have the least reason to assume absolutely (to suppose in itself) the [existence of the] object of this idea," for, like the natural world, it too is ultimately nothing more than the product of our own reasoning.[81] Finally, Kant argues, our concept of a "highest good," as we have already seen, must be understood to be likewise a product of "practical reason."[82] And, the function of this practical reason is simply "to produce the [idea of the] highest good through the freedom of the will."[83] For these reasons, Kant concludes, we can never be sure that our concept of the "highest good" accurately reflects any actual absolute moral value which may or may not exist independently of us. Indeed, for Kant, the very idea of an absolutely existent concept of moral value is logically contradictory, since value is established in and emergent from the nature of human reason. As we have seen, according to Kant the concept of the "highest good" is exclusively a product of reason and "can only be found," he argues, "in rational beings."[84] So it is that what was once seen as a set of separate, sacred, and absolute realities collapses as a result of Kant's critique onto the nature, operation, and function of human reasoning alone—and is thereafter understood as entirely immanent within and emergent from the structure of our being alone.

In this way, the concept of the absolute as it was understood and pursued in the history of philosophy prior to Kant—as an entirely independent and objective reality outside of and beyond the mutability of our own existence, world, and time, whether transcendent and divine or immanent and natural—became transfigured into an exclusively relative idea, something which was not representative of some presumed reality in-itself, but was instead viewed as a product of the structure and nature of human existence alone. So it was that Western philosophy lost its appeal to the absolute as the proper foundation of its truth claims, moral judgments, and existential hope. What resulted from this loss, as we have already seen in part, was the collective descent of Western philosophy into some form of ethical, social, and political quietism, relativistic nihilism, or fanaticism.

Kant and the Practical Problem of Universals

Of course, this was not what Kant intended to accomplish from his critique! To the contrary, Kant hoped to achieve precisely the opposite; namely, to provide a new and rational foundation for a universally acceptable conception of truth, value, and hope. Indeed, as he makes clear in his later political works, Kant thought that his metaphysics and ethics might establish the necessary conditions for the possibility of a new global "cosmopolitanism" and eventually a lasting and "perpetual peace" among all nations and peoples, provided, of course, that their inhabitants were as rational and observant of the moral edicts which he thought were deducible from the structures of reason as he conceived himself to be.[85] The problem, as we have already noted and the history of post-colonial philosophy testifies, is that Kant's conception of the "universality" of these structures is anything but. On the contrary, as a number of post-colonial scholars note, Kant's account of "human" rationality is decidedly regional—it is not only European, it is more often than not also gendered and racist. As a result, as Inder S. Marwah notes, "Kant's liberalism is closed to the forms of human difference that, arguably, make the most pressing claims on its universalism"; that is, those forms of being which are not afforded the privileges enjoyed by Kant or recognized by him as "normal" or "standard" modes of "rationality," most famously women, children, and people of color.[86] Indeed, Kant's analysis of the potential rationality—and therefore the moral, social, and political freedom—of women, children, and people of color, particularly in his early works, is notoriously provincial, narrow-minded, and tragically limited in scope, as has been extensively documented and commented on in the secondary literature.[87] These facts should already be enough to call into question the alleged universality of Kant's account of rationality, but the regionality of his claims is all the more apparent when we see how his conception of rationality was used in the colonial domination of people of color in the nineteenth and twentieth centuries.[88] Indeed, as David Harvey has meticulously and horrifyingly documented, when and where Kant's work was drawn upon to develop actual political policy and to direct practical action, far from establishing a "hospitable" and "inclusive" cosmopolitanism, its allegedly universal vision of peace, directly contributed to the marginalization, subjugation, and suffering of countless peoples.[89] Indeed, Kant's work was not merely *complicit* in the European conquest, colonial domination, and enslavement of other nations, it explicitly *justified* it; though, as Pauline Kleingeld notes, in his later works Kant seems to back down from some from his more controversial claims concerning the legitimacy of colonial action, not to mention racial and gendered norms.[90] Nevertheless, it is clear that Kant's claims of "universality" are, in the end, decidedly regional, leading many contemporary scholars to ask of his political projects: "whose cosmopolitanism?" and "for whose benefit?"[91]

If we are committed to retaining some concept of a universal moral value after Kant, then, it cannot be accomplished by reference to the allegedly universal operation of some virtual ideal alone, like human reason as detailed by Kant. The problem with such ideals, as should be clear from the above, is that it will either become complicit in some kind of practical humanitarian disaster; or result in a form of ineffectual social and political *quietism* that is incapable of acting in the face of these same disasters.[92] This is in fact precisely why, as we noted at the start of this chapter, so many thinkers after Kant have rejected his aspirations to an idealized universalism and have turned instead to the realm of what actually appears within the domain of the local, the singular, or the individual in order to ground a practical pursuit of the good. But, as we also saw there, the problem with this tactic is that by eschewing the universal it is no longer accountable to the critiques of others. As a result, not only do such projects tend toward the decidedly irrational, mystical, and even at times entirely fantastical, they also tend to resurrect precisely the kind of *fanaticism* which Kant's critique aimed to curtail and abolish from philosophical discourse, ethical judgment, and political activity. In recognition of the impasse each of these tactics face, it becomes all the more clear why so many after Kant have given up entirely on the concept of any sense of universal reality, truth, and value and have retreated into a self-justified and narcissistic *nihilism*, pursing nothing more than private follies and personal pleasures. Hence the history of Western philosophy's trajectory since Kant: either imperialism, quietism, fanaticism, and/or nihilism.

If we are to rescue the relevance of philosophical discourse for future generations, critique the tendencies of post-Kantian philosophy to imperialism, quietism, fanaticism, and nihilism, and establish a new foundation for a robust sense of reality, meaning, value, and truth, it is imperative that we re-inaugurate inquiry into the possibility of discovering some sense of the absolute, without, however, betraying Kant's analysis of the limits of human knowledge. Only thus can we secure both the relevance of philosophical discourse and, much more importantly, the possibility of developing from it a truly universal and practical sense of reality, meaning, value, and truth—one which doesn't risk resurrecting any form of dogmatism or fanaticism, or retreat into any form of quietism or nihilism. In order to explore the possibility of such a rationally accessible sense of the absolute, we must reexamine the limits of Kant's critique. Only thus can we discover whether and how it might be possible, through the use of reason alone, to move beyond the bounds of pure reason in order to discover again a noumenal sense of absolute reality and value. Only by critiquing Kant's critique in this way will it be possible to discover how and where a new sense of the absolute might be found and how we might establish a new philosophical account of meaning, value, and truth upon it. Fortunately, we are not alone in this quest. On the contrary, as we will see in the following chapter, this is a route which has already been well reconnoitered and thoroughly charted by a number of contemporary thinkers; namely the so-called "speculative realists"—thinkers like Quentin Meillassoux and Alain Badiou.

2

Absolutes within the Bounds of Reason

Speculative Realism and the Return of the Absolute

The Return of Speculative Philosophy

There is a certain irony to the Kantian project. In his attempt to rid philosophy of its hyperbolic tendency to metaphysical exaggerations of spiritualistic dogmatism and materialistic reductionism, and establish philosophy anew upon what he argues is the proper domain of rational inquiry, Kant inadvertently abolishes the one thing which had defined Western philosophical thinking since its inception: a robust sense of the absolute. As a result, philosophers after Kant could no longer ground their arguments upon any truly universal or actual sense of what is real, good, right, or true. They could not test their claims against the limits of some objective world or hope to discover some globally accepted concept of value, meaning, or justice. Such pretensions were unequivocally laid to rest by Kant's critique. After Kant, every claim made by philosophers had to be understood as framed within and structured by the architecture of human understanding alone. Indeed, according to Kant, every knowledge claim is always conditioned by, limited within, and reflective of the nature of the claimant. Kant seems to show us that every presumably absolute concept is ultimately entirely contingent upon the nature of the human who asserts it. In this way, Kant effectively abolishes the traditional aims of Western philosophy, namely, to discover and relate human reasoning to an absolute sense of reality by which meaning, value, justice, and truth might be secured. As a result, the history of Western philosophy after Kant has steadily devolved into a variety of quietisms, fanaticisms, relativisms, and nihilisms. Such is the tragic irony of the Kantian legacy in Western philosophy and beyond: it accomplishes precisely the opposite of what it aspires to.

Denied access to any real sense of the absolute by Kant, Western philosophers were forced to discover new ways to justify their claims and legitimate their aims: either (1) abandoning universal regulative concepts entirely in favor of ideas conceived of as nothing more than the play of different powers and claimants; (2) attempting to identify and define some new universal regulative concept located exclusively within the structures of human rationality, consciousness, or language alone; or finally (3) rejecting the strictures of rational discourse as defined by Kant in pursuit of an eccentric route beyond the limits of human consciousness into some presumed transcendental or ultimate sense of truth and reality. What inevitably results from each of these routes, however, is some version of precisely the kind of hyperbolic tendencies Kant hoped to purge from thought. So it is that philosophical discourse today is representative of some form of *nihilism*, ethical *quietism*, or dogmatic *fanaticism*. And as we saw in the last chapter, the inevitable consequences of each of these routes, particularly in the realm of ethics and politics, have been catastrophic.

To overcome these unintended and tragically ironic consequences of Kant's critique, it is incumbent on contemporary philosophers to recover some sense of the absolute without resorting to the kind of naive dogmatism or scientific reductionism which Kant aimed to abolish—without, in other words, abandoning the proper scope of rational investigation. Only in this way will some legitimate ground be established which is capable of resurrecting the traditional aims of philosophical inquiry and securing some truly universal sense of meaning, value, and truth. To this end, a number of contemporary thinkers have enjoined philosophy to learn to "speculat[e] once more about the nature of reality independently of thought and of humanity more generally" by "recuperat[ing] the precritical sense of 'speculation' as a concern with the Absolute, while also taking into account the undeniable progress that is due to the labour of [Kant's] critique."[1] What has resulted from this charge is a new aspiration to the absolute in contemporary philosophy in the form of what has been called *speculative realism*.

The central tenet of this new approach to the absolute, if any one tenet can be identified and agreed upon by its various proponents, is this: while Kant's critique was absolutely essential to pulling philosophy away from the fanatical dogmatism of its past and securing for it a firm foundation for any future validity, "the price to be paid for securing this basis [has been] the renunciation of any knowledge beyond how things appear to us."[2] The motivating aim of speculative realism is, in response to this renunciation, to discover a way in which Kant's critique can be accepted without having to pay that price—without, in other words, cutting off access to the idea of the absolute. Its aim is to restore philosophy's capacity to speak meaningfully of the absolute without abandoning or exceeding the limits of rational discourse established by Kant and resurrecting any form of fanatical dogmatism or scientific reductionism. Speculative realists agree that only by rediscovering some sense of the absolute within the limits of Kant's critique in this way can philosophy recover its value to the world and reanimate its critique of the kinds of fanatical dogmatisms, reductionistic nihilisms, and self-satisfied quietisms which have dominated philosophical and political discourse since Kant.

Correlationism and the Loss of Reality

The problem with the legacy of Kant's critique, these new speculative philosophers argue, is that "reality-in-itself [has become] cordoned off, at least in its cognitive aspects," from Western thinkers ever since.[3] After Kant, as Quentin Meillassoux puts it, "any philosopher who acknowledges the legitimacy of the transcendental revolutions—any philosopher who sees himself as 'post-critical' rather than a dogmatist—will maintain that it is naive to think we are able to think *something*... while abstracting from the fact that it is invariably we who are thinking that something."[4] As a result, Meillassoux suggests, philosophers after Kant have lost their connection to any sense of reality as an absolute object—one which exists independently of the bounds of human conception—and with it any meaningful sense of absolute or universal truth and value.[5] As a result of this loss, Meillassoux argues, philosophers in the West have stopped looking beyond themselves to consider questions of meaning, value, and truth. Instead, he claims, they have become obsessed with probing the nature and structures of human understanding and being itself in a bizarre existential form of navel-gazing. This tendency, he and his colleagues argue, has resulted in what they call a decidedly "anti-realist trend" in post-Kantian thought, a trend which, they argue, is exemplified in contemporary Western philosophy's "preoccupation with such issues as death and finitude, [its] aversion to science, [its] focus on language, culture, and subjectivity to the detriment of material factors, an anthropocentric stance towards nature, a relinquishing of the search for absolutes, and an acquiescence to the specific conditions of our historical thrownness."[6] As a result of this trend, speculative thinkers like Meillassoux argue that contemporary Western philosophy now resembles an "ethereal idealism" more than it does the kind of rigorous science it has aspired to be for the bulk of its history, and which Kant himself hoped to serve in his critique of that history.[7] As a result, they conclude, contemporary Western phi-

CHAPTER 2

losophy has lost its capacity to make any practical claims concerning the nature of meaning, value, and truth, much less engage with the products of the contemporary sciences, and, perhaps worst of all, provide any critical insights and recommendations to thoughtfully intervene on matters of imminent social and political concern. Hence, as we saw in the last chapter, contemporary Western philosophy's steady slide after Kant into quietism, nihilism, and fanaticism, not to mention its collapse into complete irrelevance both within and beyond the academy. All this, Meillassoux has convincingly argued, is the result of what he sees as the prevailing "correlationism" of Western philosophy after Kant.[8]

Meillassoux defines this *correlationism* as "the idea according to which we only ever have access to the correlation between thinking and being, and never to either term considered apart from the other."[9] Correlationism functions, he suggests therefore, "[by] disqualifying the claim that it is possible to consider the realms of subjectivity and objectivity independently of one another."[10] What it concludes, as he summarizes it, is "that we never grasp an object 'in itself,' in isolation from its relation to the subject."[11] As a result of some form or another of such a prevailing "correlationism" in post-Kantian philosophy, Meillassoux concludes, "contemporary philosophers have lost the *great outdoors*, the *absolute* outside of pre-critical thinkers: that outside which was not relative to us, and which was given as indifferent to its own givenness to be what it is, existing in itself, regardless of whether we are thinking of it or not; that outside which thought could explore with the legitimate feeling of being on foreign territory—of being entirely elsewhere."[12] After Kant, Meillassoux rightly asserts, every such concept of the absolute becomes "entirely *relative*, since it is—and this is precisely the point—*relative* to us."[13] "[This] means," Meillassoux suggests, "not only that the thing in itself is unknowable, as in Kant, but that the in itself is radically unthinkable."[14] For these reasons, Meillassoux identifies the correlationist tendency he sees as pervasive in all post-Kantian philosophy as "the contemporary opponent of any realism," since it claims "that there are no objects, no events, no laws, no beings which are not already correlated with a point of view, with a subjective access."[15] It is this tendency to anti-realism, which he sees as inextricable from the correlationist tendency of the bulk of post-Kantian thought, against which speculative realism in general and Meillassoux in particular mobilize their arguments, and with good reason!

Indeed, as Meillassoux convincingly argues, it is this loss of this concept of the absolute which results from the prevalence of correlationism in post-Kantian philosophy that has driven what he sees as philosophy's incapacity to keep up with, make sense of, and be relevant to the contemporary world. This is most obviously seen according to Meillassoux in how contemporary Western philosophy has lost its connection to, willingness to take seriously, and engage extensively with the products of the material sciences, where, he argues, statements are routinely made which "bear . . . explicitly upon a manifestation of the world that is posited as anterior to the emergence of thought and even of life—posited, that is, as anterior to every form of human relation to the world."[16] Post-critical philosophers may scoff at the apparent naivete of such scientific statements, Meillassoux thinks, but they do so at their own peril; for they can only maintain such a "sophisticated attitude" by blithely ignoring the great advances which have been made in the sciences since Kant, advances upon which the contemporary world in which they live is increasingly reliant.[17] In other words, Meillassoux argues, post-Kantian philosophers can only maintain their alleged superiority to the supposed "naivete of the sciences" by sacrificing their capacity to take seriously, and in turn be taken seriously by, the contemporary world, reliant as it is upon the technological products, medical breakthroughs, and increasingly nuanced understanding of the cosmos which the contemporary sciences have provided, despite their alleged "naivete." And so, Meillassoux thinks, by remaining faithful to the letter of Kant's critique, most contemporary Western philosophers have betrayed not only the spirit which motivated the entire history of philosophy before him, but even the spirit which motivated Kant himself; namely, the attempt to provide a solid foundation for a scientific account of the actual world in which we live. Meillassoux argues that as a result, most contemporary Western philosophers have become so disconnected from, ignorant of, and at times even scornful of the contemporary sciences that their work resembles more the kinds of idealized fantasies produced during the height of medieval Scholasticism, than it does the kind of rigorous engagement with reality envisioned by Kant. And as a result of the dominance of this "anti-realist trend," Meillassoux goes on to show, most contemporary philosophers are not only wholly ignorant of the astonishing developments and accomplishments in scientific research of the past 250 years, they are actually scornful of them! And it is this haughty ignorance, he thinks, which is the primary cause of their increasing irrelevance outside their own discipline, and in academia in general. Without some sense of a shared absolute reality, Meillassoux suggests, contemporary post-Kantian philosophy has, in a sense, lost its place in the world.

Even more consequential than the loss of prestige which has resulted from this anti-realist correlationism, Meillassoux thinks, is the way in which post-Kantian philosophy has aided in the return of various forms of dogmatic fanaticism within the social and political realm.[18] Indeed, according to him, the ultimate irony of Kant's critique is that "by forbidding reason any claim to the absolute," it cleared the way for an "exacerbated return of the religious" in public discourse.[19] In this sense, far from providing a firm foundation for a new, rational, and comprehensive understanding of the nature of reality, Meillassoux argues that post-Kantian "correlational reason [in fact] legitimates all those discourses that claim access to an absolute, the only proviso being that nothing in these discourses resembles a rational justification of their validity."[20] This apparent "de-absolutization of thought," Meillassoux claims, effectively "boils down to the mobilization of a fideist argument; but a fideism that is 'fundamental' rather than merely historical in nature."[21] And the result of this new form of fundamentalist fideism, he claims, has been a demonstrable increase in social and political sectarianism, nationalism, and ultimately violence, all forms of thought which Meillassoux follows Kant in identifying as ultimately *fanatical* in nature.[22] Indeed, according to Meillassoux, the increasing popularity of fanaticisms in the post-Kantian world is, tragically, "the effect of critical rationality, and this precisely insofar as . . . this rationality was effectively emancipatory; was effectively, and thankfully, successful in destroying dogmatism."[23] In this regard, Meillassoux argues, Kant's excision of the concept of the absolute from rational discourse, far from destabilizing and delegitimizing fanaticism, ultimately cleared the way for even more insidious forms of fanaticism. What's more, since philosophy thereafter is barred from accessing any form of actual absolute upon which in might establish a robust critique of such extremisms, it finds itself increasingly unable to respond to them in any meaningful or active way. Hence, the tendency toward relativistic *quietism* demonstrated by so many post-Kantian philosophical systems, as detailed in the last chapter.

According to Meillassoux, if contemporary philosophy is to overcome its tendency towards relativism and quietism and stem the rising tide of fundamentalism and fanaticism in the social and political arena, and reclaim in this way its relevance to public discourse, then it must reject its tendency toward "anti-realism," repudiate its correlationist assumptions, and discover a new route to a robust realism, one which is established upon a rationally justifiable account of absolute reality, truth, goodness, and justice. But all of this must be accomplished, he cautions, without losing the progress made by Kant's critique of dogmatic metaphysics. In other words, the ultimate task of speculative realism for Meillassoux is to rediscover some sense of the absolute without abandoning the critical assessment of the limits of rational inquiry which were secured by Kant. Only in this way, he thinks, might philosophy reassume it rightful place in the academy and the public sphere alike and overcome its complicity in the relativism, quietism, fideism, fundamentalism, and fanaticism of the post-Kantian world. This project hinges, according to Meillassoux, on the discovery of a new "non-metaphysical [sense of the] absolute"—an absolute which is discoverable, in other words, within the bounds of rational discourse, inquiry, and argumentation alone, but which is nevertheless truly absolute and not reducible to the structures of human understanding.[24] To show how and where such a discovery might be made is the ultimate task of speculative realism according to Meillassoux.

Speculative Realism and the Conceptual Power of the Material Sciences

"Against dogmatism," Meillassoux writes, "it is important that we uphold the refusal of every metaphysical absolute"; but at the same time, he counters, "against the reasoned violence of various fanaticisms, it is important that we rediscover in thought a modicum of absoluteness—enough of it, in any case, to counter the pretensions of those who would present themselves as its privileged trustees, solely by virtue of some revelation," lest we resign ourselves to quietism in the face of their atrocities.[25] With this cautioned aim in mind, Meillassoux's goal is "to refute every form of correlationism . . . by demonstrat[ing] that thinking, under very special conditions, can access reality as it is in itself, independently of any act of subjectivity."[26]

For Meillassoux, Kant's outline and survey of the limits of philosophical discourse and perhaps even of the nature and structure of reason are ultimately valid and of profound philosophical importance. However, he thinks that Kant's insistence that access to any robust sense of absolute reality should be excluded entirely from the products of rational inquiry is simply wrong. On the contrary, according to Meillassoux, the "absolute, i.e., a reality absolutely separate from the subject, *can* be thought by the subject," but only, he cautions, when the subject thinks in a very particular and specific way.[27] When rational thought is bound by these very "special conditions," Meillassoux argues, it is capable of rediscovering some "modicum of absoluteness," and in this way philosophy can renounce its tendency toward anti-realism and quietism as well as its complicity in new forms of dogmatisms, and mount an attack against the kinds of fanaticisms which have besieged public discourse since the publication of Kant's critique. In this way, he contends, contemporary philosophy might reclaim its relevance in and to the world. The "special conditions," Meillassoux suggests philosophers must follow to accomplish theme aims are that they think both (1) *speculatively* and (2) *materialistically*.

CHAPTER 2

By "speculative," thinking Meillassoux identifies "every type of thinking that claims to be able to access some form of absolute."[28] And by "materialistic," thinking Meillassoux indicates every kind of thinking that restricts itself exclusively to what is empirically evident or deducible from what is scientifically verifiable in the material world. From these definitions, Meillassoux suggests that "every materialism that would be speculative, and hence for which absolute reality is an *entity without thought*, must assert *both* that thought is not necessary (something can be independently of thought) and that thought can think what there must be when there is no thought."[29] By following an appropriately post-critical *speculative materialism* of this sort, Meillassoux suggests, philosophy should be able to deduce from the kinds of claims made by contemporary scientists some account of the absolute structure and nature of reality itself by speculatively "abstracting" our rational processes out of the equation.[30] By abstracting or, perhaps better put, *subtracting* the thinking subject from its products (i.e., the conclusions of the material sciences), Meillassoux maintains that philosophers should be able to "envisage an absolutizing thought that would not be absolutist," without betraying Kant's critique of the limits of rationality.[31]

What philosophy achieves through such a *speculative* abstraction of its subjective structures "out from" the rational products it achieves in and through the material sciences, Meillassoux claims, is precisely access to a sense of reality in its absolute form which nevertheless does not exceed the limits of reason or, consequently, require any extraordinary transcendental experience, eccentric leap of faith, or dogmatically affirmed and fanatically defended object of belief. On the contrary, what such a speculative materialism produces, he argues, is, for example, a concept of "absolute necessity that does not reinstate any form of absolutely necessary entity," and therefore does not reinitiate or justify any form of fanatical obedience to any actually existent transcendental object.[32] In this way, Meillassoux argues that a sufficiently rigorous mode of speculative materialism should be capable of achieving a new sense of absolute reality through which philosophy can renounce its anti-realist tendencies to relativism, nihilism, and quietism, and mount a robust and rationally justified critique of the kinds of irrational fideism and fanaticism which have flourished in the 250 years since Kant. As Alain Badiou, Meillassoux's mentor and most insightful interlocutor, argues, such a speculative approach to scientific materialism "allows thought to be destined towards the absolute once more, rather than towards those partial fragments and relations in which we complacently luxuriate while the 'return of the religious' provides us with a fictitious supplement of spirituality."[33]

In order to ensure that this mode of speculative abstraction is truly grounded in what is empirically and rationally justifiable and not productive of any kind of dogmatic idealism, Meillassoux argues that it must remain exclusively and entirely materialistic—bound wholly within the confines of what has been concluded by the contemporary sciences. Only by tethering itself to the products of the sciences in this way Meillassoux suggests can philosophy renew its ability to think alongside the sciences "that what comes before comes before, and that which came before us came before us"—can think, in other words, that an absolute world with an absolute sense of temporality exists "out there" beyond the realm of reason alone—without asserting that any metaphysical being or "thing" exists which secures that absolute reality.[34] What Meillassoux argues that "science reveals," and speculative materialism enables is, in other words, the concept of "a time that not only does not need conscious time but that allows the latter to arise at a determinate point in its own flux" without invoking the existence of some transcendent creator or guarantor of that reality.[35] By thinking speculatively through the mathematical and material sciences in this way, Meillassoux argues that philosophers gain the capacity to "think a world wherein spatio-temporal givenness itself came into being within a time and space which preceded every variety of givenness," even the givenness of some creative metaphysical power.[36] In and through this concept of an absolute temporality, Meillassoux argues that philosophers gain access to a concept of the absolute which does not require the assertion of any actually existent absolute thing that could demand or justify any form of dogmatic fidelity. By re-founding philosophy upon this sense of the absolute, he concludes, philosophers might reclaim a sense of absolute reality, ultimate meaning, and universal value without resorting to or resurrecting any form of fideism in some hyperbolic object, or relying on some merely virtual ideal which denies them access to any practical activity in its name. In this way, he argues, contemporary philosophy can renounce its anti-realist tendencies and overcome its complicity in relativism and quietism without risking any form of dogmatism, fideism, or fanaticism in the process. Meillassoux concludes that it is only through such a speculative approach to the products of the material sciences that contemporary philosophy can rediscover a sense of the absolute which would make all of this possible without betraying the limits of rational inquiry established by Kant's critique. To illustrate even more the kind of absolute temporality which he thinks is made available through a speculative extension of the products of the contemporary sciences, Meillassoux explores what he calls the *ancestrality* of "fossil-matter."[37]

The Challenge of the Ancestral and the Return of the Absolute

Meillassoux ascribes this "ancestrality" to any scientific statement that testifies to the existence of "reality anterior to the emergence of the human species—or even anterior to every recognized form of life on earth."[38] "Ancestrality" emerges for Meillassoux then from any "scientific statement bearing explicitly upon a manifestation of the world that is posited as anterior to the emergence of thought and even of life—posited, that is, as anterior to every form of human relation to the world."[39] Examples of such "ancestral statements" can be found, Meillassoux notes, in "statements . . . describing ancestral realities thanks to the radioactive isotope, whose rate of decay provides an index of the age of rock samples, or thanks to the starlight whose luminescence provides an index of the age of distant stars."[40]

What such ancestral statements make available, Meillassoux argues, is a concept of time which abolishes the correlationist tendency to see time as an exclusively subjective experience, one emergent from and grounded upon the structures of reason itself. Instead, Meillassoux contends, through reference to this concept of ancestrality we may posit time as an absolute thing-in-itself—a determinate part of the absolute reality of matter itself. Such a concept of time is only achievable, however, when we begin to take the conclusions of the contemporary sciences seriously and see in their statements the bounds of our rationality, and not the other way round. In other words, when we let science set the limits of what is cognizable rather than letting an account of cognition set the limits for what is achievable by science. In this way, Meillassoux concludes, the kinds of "arche-fossils" or "fossil-matter" which contemporary "astrophysicists, geologists, or paleontologists" study might open a path by which philosophers can think of an speak of absolute reality and truths anew—realities and truths like "the age of the universe, the date of the accretion of the earth, the date of the appearance of pre-human species, [and] the date of the emergence of humanity itself."[41] The concept of the absolute temporality which is referenced in such ancestral scientific statements thus represents for Meillassoux not only the death knell for correlationism and post-Kantian philosophy's tendency to "anti-realism," it represents for philosophy a new route to absolute reality itself which does not require the suspension of or betrayal of reason.[42]

For Meillassoux, "there is no possible compromise between the correlation and the arche-fossil: once one has acknowledged one, one has thereby disqualified the other."[43] By his read, by speculatively extending the concept of the absolute which he thinks is available in the contemporary sciences, post-Kantian philosophy is therefore granted a route by which it might overcome its tendencies to relativism and quietism without risking a return to any form of dogmatism, fideism, or fanatism. As such, Meillassoux claims that in reference to the robust sense of absolute reality which is granted us by the sciences, speculative philosophers might be able to reconstruct a new practical and actionable account of meaning, value, and truth that can counteract the tendency to fideism and fanatism in social and political discourse after Kant.

By thinking alongside the mathematical sciences in this way and abstracting from their claims some sense of the absolute, Meillassoux argues that contemporary philosophers can consider anew the possibility of "a world without thought—a world without the givenness of the world."[44] What he thinks the reality of arche-fossils empowers, in other words, is the possibility of conceiving of reality as radically outside of and absolutely independent from the structures of human consciousness—reality as it is in-itself, entirely free from the bounds of reason and emergent upon its own material ground. Indeed, according to Meillassoux, "if the ancestral is to be thinkable, then an *absolute* must be thinkable."[45] Through a speculative extension of the ancestrality of material nature which is provided by the modern sciences, Meillassoux concludes, contemporary philosophers can finally move beyond the predominance of the *cogito* in their attempt to secure a robust sense of reality and finally derive an accurate assessment of their values in reference to something which is empirically verifiable.[46] In this way, Meillassoux argues, post-Kantian philosophy are empowered "to take up once more the injunction to know the absolute, and to break with the transcendental tradition that rules out its possibility."[47]

Note that for Meillassoux, the concept of the absolute which is opened up through such a speculative abstraction of the concept of the ancestral is decidedly not dogmatic, virtual, religious, or spiritual in nature. Because it is grounded upon and emergent from the concrete material realities testified to in the research and "discourse of the empirical sciences," Meillassoux contends that the concept of the absolute referenced in his speculative realism is wholly material, and therefore not idealistic in any way.[48] Indeed, it is precisely for this reason, he argues, that his conception of the absolute does not betray the boundaries of rational inquiry; for, he claims, it does not require any hyperbolic leap of faith, or ecstatic experience of the "beyond," nor does it rely on any transcendental supposition or synthetic creation of any ideal concept. Precisely the opposite, in fact. According to Meillassoux, the absolute he asserts is fully manifest in and deducible from the structures of mathematical and empirical inquiry into material reality itself. The concept of the absolute which Meillassoux thinks is achievable through these methods is, he claims, attained exclusively by abstracting the thinking or researching subject out of the equation of its research and projecting the products of its thinking onto the nature of absolute material reality itself. This is for Meillassoux the "speculative" move of his philosophy, Through the products of the contemporary sciences, he argues, philosophy can discover anew a rationally justifiable, if speculative, account of "being whose *severance* (the original meaning of *absolutus*) and whose separateness from thought is such that it presents itself to us as non-relative to us, and hence capable of existing whether we exist or not."[49] Thus, while accomplished through the discourse of the material sciences, the sense of the absolute which Meillassoux thinks a speculative approach to philosophy can achieve is one which exists truly independently of and entirely outside of and beyond the bounds of reason alone. Indeed, he argues, the concept of the absolute provided via his speculative materialism, while accessed in and through the bounds of subjective reason, is ultimately entirely a-subjective, utterly inhuman, wholly irrational, and purely material.

For these reasons, Meillassoux contends that the kind of absolute that he thinks is achievable in and through his account of speculative materialism is not one which reflects or conforms to the structures of our being—nor does it correspond to our hopes, function to secure our sense of meaning, or confirm our sense that human existence must have some cosmic significance. On the contrary, it is an absolute which fundamentally confounds such sensibilities. Indeed, Meillassoux suggests that it is an absolute which refuses to confer any special status or significance upon our existence. In this sense, it is a "mute" absolute—one which declines to respond to our clamors, hopes, prayers, or cries of pain and remains silent and indifferent to our joy and suffering.

Nevertheless, according to Meillassoux, it is precisely the inhuman indifference and silence of the kind of material absolute which is accessed through speculative materialism that lends it such epistemic power in the evaluation and reassessment of our values and hopes. For, he argues, in its refusal to conform to our human expectations, desires, or rational understanding, this concept of the absolute forces us to radically reconceive of ourselves, our sense of reality, and our relation to the universe; and, in the wake of this reconsideration, to develop new senses of absolute meaning, value, and truth. Indeed, Meillassoux thinks that in light of the concept of the absolute accessed within the idea of ancestral temporality, all human knowledge, as well as every understanding of ourselves as human, not to mention our place in the universe, must be radically called into question. Nevertheless, he argues, this calling into question is not entirely negative. On the contrary, he suggests, its ultimate aim is to produce new understandings and conceptions of what is real, right, true, and good which might be operational for an entirely new metaphysics, ethics, and politics.

Measured against the kinds of absolutes which he thinks are achievable through a speculative extension of the nature of material reality granted to us by the contemporary sciences, Meillassoux argues that human beings must admit that they are decidedly not the pinnacle of creation or the culmination of some cosmic or ideal history. On the contrary, he argues, they must acknowledge themselves to be little more than a radically contingent and arbitrary continuation of a series of material accidents which have no special meaning or significance. What the concept of the absolute mobilized through his speculative materialism opens up, Meillassoux thinks, is the space to critically reevaluate the role and significance of human existence and its concerns within a more justifiable account of nature. More concretely, what Meillassoux thinks the concept of the absolute makes available through a speculative extension of the concept of ancestrality is a proper measure of the absolute insignificance of human hopes, beliefs, and endeavors—the realization that human beings, and every product of their history, are nothing more than an incidental epiphenomenon of cosmic coincidence and chance—a fluke of fortune. What such a concept of absolute temporality provides, in other words, he suggests, is a proper understanding of the radical contingency of our being and beliefs—indeed, the radical contingency of existence itself. For Meillassoux, it is this radical contingency which is the ultimate absolute which is discoverable from a speculative extension of the material sciences. And it is upon the "hard truth" of this radical contingency, he argues, that philosophers must redevelop their account of absolute meaning, value, and truth and mount their critique of every form of dogmatic metaphysics and fanatical fideism. Hence his reference to the absolute contingency of reality deducible from his conception of ancestrality as the ultimate *facticity* of reality.

Meillassoux and the Facticity of Absolute Contingency and "Unreason"

Meillassoux defines this "facticity" that he argues is deducible from the ancestral statements of sciences as that "real property whereby [we discover that] everything and every world *is* without reason, and is thereby capable of actually becoming otherwise without reason."[50] In this regard, *facticity* is for Meillassoux a property of what he calls the fundamental "unreason" of the cosmos. This unreasonableness of matter is for him *the* "ontological property" of the absolute structure of reality itself. It is therefore upon this fact that he thinks a speculative reconstruction of value and meaning might be built anew.[51] It is from this basic "property" then that Meillassoux thinks that the potentially absolute value of material reality might be established anew, as we will see in more detail in the following chapter.

What is entailed in this idea of the absolute unreasonableness of the cosmos, Meillassoux argues, is the demonstrable *fact* that "everything could actually collapse: from trees to stars, from stars to laws, from physical laws to logical laws; and this not by virtue of some superior law whereby everything is destined to perish, but by virtue of the absence of any superior law capable of preserving anything, no matter what, from perishing."[52] It is this materially manifest fact, which he thinks is accessible in the ancestral concept of time testified to by the contemporary sciences, which Meillassoux suggests is the ultimate and absolute foundation of a robust sense of reality. For him, in other words, the fundamental and absolute truth of the cosmos is that everything which is could be otherwise than it is—or indeed, could not be at all. It is this radical contingency—"the possible transition, devoid of reason, of my state toward any state whatsoever," which is for him the fundamental fact of existence upon which post-critical philosophy must found itself anew.[53] Indeed, according to Meillassoux, "if any absolute [is] capable of withstanding the ravages of the correlationist circle . . . it can only be one that results from the absolutization of [this] facticity."[54] In other words, the radical contingency of existence is not only "absolute," by Meillassoux's read, it is the basis for a new and robust sense of realism; one, moreover, which he thinks is sufficient to ground practical philosophy anew and therefore empower contemporary thinkers to counter the perils of the post-Kantian world.[55] Indeed, for Meillassoux, contingency "is not a fact which *might* be the case; [for] I cannot doubt the absoluteness of facticity without immediately reinstating it as an absolute."[56] So it is upon this unsettling, unreasonable, and wholly inhuman sense of the absolute that he thinks post-critical philosophy must found itself anew, reclaim the ambition of its history, and prove its relevance to the world again.

Emergent as it is through an entirely rational speculative abstraction of the products of the material sciences, Meillassoux contends that his conception of the absolute does not betray the basic insights of Kant's critique of dogmatic metaphysics. On the contrary, he argues, the absolute material fact of the irrational and contingent nature of the universe ultimately undermines the logic of dogmatism. For, he writes, "to be dogmatic is invariably to maintain that this or that—i.e., some determinate entity—must absolutely be, and be in the way it is, whether it is Idea, pure Act, atom, indivisible soul, harmonious world, perfect God, infinite substance, World-Soul, global history, etc."[57] "Conversely," he reasons, "to reject dogmatic metaphysics means to reject *all* real necessity, and *a fortiori*, to reject the principle of sufficient reason, as well as the ontological argument, which is the keystone that allows the system of real necessity to close in upon itself."[58] According to Meillassoux, then, the basic fact that the universe is unreasonable and radically contingent "uncover[s] an absolute that would not be an absolute entity," for it suggests "that every entity might not exist," whether conceived of as an "Idea, pure Act, atom, indivisible soul, harmonious world, perfect God, infinite substance, World-Soul, [or] global history."[59] For this reason, Meillassoux concludes, the absolute which he thinks is accessible through a speculative extension of the concept of ancestrality made available in the sciences does not empower a return "to dogmatism," nor does it encourage philosophers to "go back to being metaphysicians."[60] In this regard, Meillassoux argues, "on this point, we cannot but be heirs of Kantianism."[61] Nevertheless, he thinks, we must admit that in the material sciences some sense of the absolute appears upon which a new sense of noumenal reality can be accessed; namely, "the absolute truth of a principle of unreason," the inescapable fact that there is "no reason for anything to be or to remain the way it is; everything must, without reason, be able not to be and/or be able to be other than it is."[62] So, Meillassoux concludes, the kind of absolute which he thinks we achieve through a scientifically based speculative materialism is "the absolute necessity of everything's non-necessity"—"the absolute necessity," in other words, "of the contingency of everything."[63] This is, for Meillassoux, the only absolute which is thinkable after Kant without betraying the insights and aims of his critique. And, as we will see in more detail in the next chapter, it is upon this absolute that he contends that a new, and radically inhuman, sense of meaning, value, and truth can be established.

In light of this sense of contingency, Meillassoux concludes that in his account of the absolute "we are [indeed] thinking an absolute, but it is not metaphysical, since we are not thinking any *thing* (any entity) that would *be* absolute," rather, we are thinking a possibility, an absolute possibility that is nevertheless very real: namely, the imminent and inescapable contingency of everything.[64] Thus, while he argues that his speculative materialism remains within the limits of Kant's critique of pure reason, it nevertheless achieves something approximating Kant's hyperbolic noumenal *Ding an sich*, that which is deemed fundamentally inadmissible by the limits of Kant's critique, without asserting the existence of any actual metaphysical entity.[65] By establishing philosophy anew upon the hyperbolic and absolute fact that material reality is demonstratively contingent in the flow of time and forever subject to change rather than any static and eternally existing metaphysical object, Meillassoux thinks that contemporary thinkers can escape the vicissitudes of correlationism; eschew their fidelity to "anti-realism" as well as its corresponding tendencies to relativism, nihilism, and quietism; and discover a new, nondogmatic sense of absolute meaning, value, and truth upon which they can mount an actionable critique of fanaticism and fideism. In this way, Meillassoux argues, contemporary philosophers might reclaim the relevance of their history and pursue a new sense of absolute value, justice, and ultimately even hope.

The Possibility of Absolute Value, Justice, and Hope

Indeed, Meillassoux suggests that the real contribution of speculative realism to post-critical philosophy is this: to empower it to engage meaningfully once again with the products of contemporary science in such a way that it can arm itself against the kinds of social and political weaknesses and excesses which are all too apparent in the post-Kantian world: nihilism, quietism, fideism, and fanaticism. In many ways, this is the real aim of Meillassoux's project: to discover a new route through which the kinds of fanaticism and nihilism that Kant's critique aimed to abolish might finally be eradicated. Hence Meillassoux's claim that the kind of absolute suggested by his speculative materialism "furnishes the minimal condition for every critique of ideology, insofar as an ideology cannot be identified with just any variety of deceptive representation, but is rather any form of pseudo-rationality whose aim is to establish that what exists as a matter of fact, exists necessarily."[66]

Given the nature of the absolute provided in speculative realism, Meillassoux contends that philosophers should be able to argue convincingly that "there is no legitimate demonstration that a determinate entity should exist unconditionally," in reference to which social and political violence might attempt to be justified.[67] By granting reason access to an absolute which denies every pretense to this kind of transcendental legitimacy, Meillassoux contends that his speculative project fundamentally undermines the logic of every form of fanaticism manifest in the post-Kantian world. In this way, he argues, his concept of the absolute contingency of existence provides a sufficient foundation for a critique of every mode of absolutist logic, whether manifest in the fanatical devotion to one particular cultural order or the absolute resignation of the possibility of any universal sense of meaning and value.

Providing as it does a new foundation for a critique of every form of extremism, Meillassoux thinks that his concept of the contingency of existence equips contemporary philosophy to combat the kinds of logics which have been used to justify every form of social and political violence manifest in history since the publication of Kant's critique. Indeed, he contends that the kind of absolute which philosophers can achieve through a speculative extension of scientific materialism is sufficient to negate and reject every form of social and political injustice. In this way, Meillassoux argues that the sense of the absolute contingency of material reality which he thinks is won through science is essential for the development of a new and justifiable account of universally normative ethics and politics.

In fact, Meillassoux claims that one of the most useful extensions of his speculative resurrection of the absolute is how it can be used to establish a new account of universal value, justice, and even social and political peace. Indeed, he suggests that this should be "the goal of every philosophy" after Kant: namely, "the immanent inscription of value in being."[68] Hence Meillassoux's claim that "any philosopher worthy of the name aims at an immanent inscription of values. [And] this entails a new fervor for justice that must show how this requirement is not an illusion, a convention, or a submission to God and his earthly authorities," but is instead absolutely justified through a proper understanding of the universal facts of nature.[69] With this aim in mind, Meillassoux dedicates a significant portion of his work to showing how the absolute contingency of reality can be used not only to ground an effective critique of injustice, but to ground a productive and practically actionable sense of social and political hope. And for Meillassoux, this is the ultimate end of his speculative return to the absolute: to provide a firm foundation for a new account of absolute value and universal social and political justice.

Hence Meillassoux's claim that what "the factial permits us to resume . . . [is] the lost relation between being and value."[70] It accomplishes this, he argues, not by affirming what is the case in the world as it currently is, but the absolute possibility that the world might still be otherwise than it is. And this, as we saw in the introduction, is the classical foundation of the assertion of moral value; indeed, it is the very concept of the good. So Meillassoux makes the case that the absolute fact of the radical contingency of reality justifies a new sense of absolute hope—hope that things could be otherwise than, and better than they currently are.[71] In this regard, he suggests that his approach to the absolute contingency of reality provides a new foundation for not only hope, but for an account of a universal good, and through it the possibility of social and political justice. All of this is premised, Meillassoux contends, not upon the basis of any dogmatically asserted ideal, irrational faith, or purely virtual conception of value, but on what he claims is the indisputable fact of the radical mutability of material reality which is testified to in the natural sciences. For Meillassoux, the real power of the concept of absolute contingency which he thinks emerges from the concept of the ancestral which is operant in the material sciences is this: that it definitively proves that things were once different than they are now, and therefore that they might still be otherwise again, and perhaps even better, if not eventually perfect. It is upon the basis of the absolute possibility of radical change that Meillassoux justifies his radical sense of hope and moral value. Hence, his claim that through a speculative application of the absolute fact of contingency, moral "values return to life because they [can be] wagered on the being to come."[72]

In this way, Meillassoux claims, the radical contingency of material reality allows us to rethink the concept of absolute moral value anew as "not founded by the soil that sustains the human, but by the void that outstrips them."[73] "By seizing the radical contingency of worldly laws: a contingency that allows us to found ontologically the hope of justice," he concludes, "value [can be] inserted into a reality no longer identified with a determinate and perennial substance, but rather with the possibility of lawless change."[74] In this way, he suggests, the absolute fact of contingency empowers a rationally justifiable and universally applicable critique of injustices in the world as it currently *is* and opens a way in which we might legitimate what Meillassoux calls a moral *hope* in a future possible world *to come*.[75]

Such a moral hope, as Meillassoux defines it, "is a troubled certainty about possibility that protects us from the dogmatism of necessity, and which all subjects share once they associate the newly restored hope with their human condition."[76] The object of this hope, this *possibility*, as Meillassoux calls is, is justified in the materially assured fact of contingency. So it is, he argues, that through a speculative extension of this absolute fact contemporary philosophers can discover a new route to "the immanent binding of philosophical astonishment and messianic hope, understood as the hope for justice for the dead and the living."[77] Hope in the possibility of this just world at some point in the future, Meillassoux concludes, as radical, transcendental, and even messianic as it may be, is nevertheless not the product of a pure ideal or virtual projection of reason, and is not then a hope which is based on the assertion of some dogmatic truth which must be clung to in faith. On the contrary, he argues, it is speculatively and rationally extricable from the testimony of the sciences alone. In this way, the hope that Meillassoux asserts in the possibility of a just and good future world is not a resurrection of any pre-critical mode of thinking. Instead, he assures us, it is a post-critical rediscovery of the absolute power of that mode of thinking. Through his speculative extension of what he claims are the material facts of the universe as they are laid bare by the sciences he suggests that we can reclaim the power the pre-Kantian concept of the absolute which previously grounded our hope in discovering a final and ultimate sense of meaning, universal value, and transcendental justice without asserting the kind of metaphysical objects which had secured that hope in the past or risking in it the return of any sort of fanaticism.

Founded as it is on what he sees as the eternal possibility of change, Meillassoux's account of a new, absolutely founded sense of hope, universal justice, and perpetual peace is ultimately only aspirational for existence however, and not representative of how reality actually is. Indeed, he writes, "our aspiration to the Good is based once more on the knowledge of a world that allies with our hope."[78] The possibility of absolute justice is thus for Meillassoux "an imaginary Good, aimed at by an illusion for which only thinking beings are quieted. It is a Good at which one aims, perfectly inexistent in the world."[79] Nevertheless, he thinks, this "imaginary Good" is sufficient to ground anew an absolute vision of moral value by legitimating an universally defensible critique of the way the world currently is. By absolutely founding and justifying this critique, Meillassoux suggests, the radical contingency of reality empowers us to imagine a better world and to work toward making that world a reality without relying on any sort of dogmatic claim or fideist logic. In this way, he thinks, post-critical philosophy can finally overcome its relativism, nihilism, and quietism in the face of global humanitarian crises and reclaim its practical value to a world in need.

Metaphysics Naturalized?

The possibility of an absolutely justified sense of moral value and social and political hope is only achievable, Meillassoux contends, inasmuch as it is established on the firm foundation of a speculatively rational materialism which does not give up on the idea of the absolute, but does not give in either to the temptation to concretize that absolute as an ontological necessity. In this regard, Meillassoux suggests, it should be the aim of everyone committed to his project to reject the lure of classical metaphysics—to realize, in other words, that the only absolutely necessary being or reality which can be extracted from scientific facts is the fact that no being or reality is ultimately necessary. On the contrary, as we have seen, according to Meillassoux, every being is absolutely contingent. It is this absolute contingency, he thinks, which not only founds and justifies a new sense of value and hope, but further protects us against the return of every form of dogmatic metaphysics. And so Meillassoux seems to suggest that only inasmuch as we reject traditional metaphysics through speculative fidelity to the material facts testified to in the material sciences can we remain faithful to the one ultimate absolute truth discoverable therein; namely, that all things can change, disappear, and be made anew. According to him, what a scientifically empowered speculative reason accomplishes is to assert absolute laws without asserting any absolute being which guarantees or secures those laws. In this regard, Meillassoux argues, it provides a nondogmatic absolute ground upon which philosophical ethics can establish itself anew. This is why he concludes that if and when contemporary philosophers let the natural sciences guide and constrain their conception of the absolute, they can overcome the correlationist loop which has limited the effectiveness of their work for the last two centuries and can empower anew their engagement with the contemporary world and its problems. In this regard, Meillassoux's project closely resembles James Ladyman and Don Ross's work in their controversial book *Every Thing Must Go: Metaphysics Naturalized*.[80]

Like Meillassoux, Ladyman and Ross assert that much of contemporary philosophy "fails" in its "pursuit of objective truth, and should [therefore] be discontinued," at least, they caution, "as it is now practiced."[81] This, however, does not mean that they think that the project of pursuing the concept of absolute or objective truths in philosophy should be completely abandoned. On the contrary, it is their contention that contemporary philosophers should pursue instead a "truly naturalistic metaphysics."[82] Such a *naturalism*, they claim, "requires that, since scientific institutions are the instruments by which we investigate objective reality, their outputs should motivate all claims about this reality, including metaphysical ones."[83] Ladyman and Ross thus define the kind of naturalistic metaphysics they promote as "one motivated by currently pursued, specific scientific hypotheses, and having as its sole aim to bring these hypotheses advanced by the various special sciences together into a comprehensive world-view."[84] "We will argue," they state, "for a metaphysics consistent with and motivated by contemporary science."[85]

Only on the basis of such a naturalistic metaphysics, they claim, might contemporary philosophy begin to speak meaningfully again "about the general structure of reality" and overcome what they see as the "neo-scholastic" tendencies which they argue have dominated Western metaphysics since Kant.[86] With this goal in mind, Ladyman and Ross propose what they call a mode of "ontic structural realism."[87] "Roughly speaking," they claim, such a "structural realism is the view that our best scientific theories describe the structure of reality."[88] What their concept of "structural realism" proposes, in other words, is the idea that through contemporary science, philosophers can begin to conceive of reality anew as it is in and of itself, not merely as it accords with our folk intuitions or linguistic habits.[89] Such a scientifically guided structural realism, they argue, "is the only legitimate way of arguing for a speculative scientific metaphysics" because it is the only "ontological model according to which science is unifiable, and which explains the basis for such unity as it can produce."[90] Only by letting science guide metaphysical speculation through a naturalistic realism in this way, they argue, can contemporary philosophy hope to regain its status within the academy and the world at large.

In this regard, Ladyman and Ross affirm the basic project of Meillassoux's speculative realism. Interestingly, this symmetry is only furthered when we examine what they claim is discoverable through such a realistic approach to the natural sciences; namely, that the concept of necessary causation is unjustifiable and wholly unscientific. In its place they suggest that philosophers embrace a conception of reality that is more in keeping with the contemporary understanding of quantum uncertainty in physics.[91] On the basis of this claim, they argue, philosophers might abandon their outdated and "pseudo-scientific" beliefs in the deterministic necessity of the natural world.[92] Instead, they argue, philosophers should come to see reality as radically contingent. Indeed, they claim, this contingency is a "fundamental fact." Indeed, they assert, "if there are fundamental physical facts, if the world is not dappled—then at least some of these facts, those that are not explained by some of the others, are brute contingencies," and therefore, they conclude, also accept the absolute contingency of reality itself not to mention every meaning and value which we might ascribe to that reality.[93] Only by accepting such an absolute fact, they continue, might philosophers reconstruct and ground anew their classical projects. In this regard, Ladyman and Ross's account of philosophical naturalism works alongside Meillassoux's speculative materialism as a complementary attempt to achieve a sense of absolute reality after Kant in and through a reckoning with the testimonia of the sciences, particularly its assertion concerning the radical contingency of material existence. Both modes of naturalism seek to establish philosophy and its classical aims anew upon an absolutely justifiable account of universal meaning, value, and truth which they think is deducible from the scientific account of the radical contingency of the material world.

If we are to follow the suggestions of Meillassoux, Ladyman, and Ross, however, then it is essential that we examine whether their account of reality in its absolute form is truly accurate and representative of the testimony of the contemporary sciences. Much more importantly still, we must test whether this alleged "fact" is sufficient to absolutely ground and justify a new approach to ethics and politics, not to mention whether it is enough to ground a new sense of meaning and value that could overcome and counteract the tendencies in post-Kantian philosophy to relativism, quietism, nihilism, fanaticism, and fideism. To examine all this, it is essential that we understand better not only how Meillassoux's speculative ethics emerge from his "metaphysics" but how those ethics practically work in the actual world. It is also incumbent on us to make sure that his account of the reality of the material world from which he derives his metaphysics and his ethics is truly representative of the conclusions of the contemporary sciences. It is to these tasks that the next two chapters are dedicated.

3

Toward a Post-Critical Ethics

Meillassoux and Badiou on the Mathematization of Nature and the Possibility of Absolute Metaphysical and Moral Claims

Meillassoux on the Power of Scientific Discourse

The great contribution of speculative realism to contemporary philosophy is its resurrection of the possibility of speaking meaningfully of the idea of the absolute after Kant without returning to any kind of dogmatic metaphysics. By documenting how contemporary philosophers might access a robust sense of the absolute in and through the material sciences, speculative realism shows us how we might resume the mantle of our own history and pursue a defensible account of absolute truth, ultimate meaning, and universal value. In this way, speculative thinkers argue that contemporary philosophy can cast off the legacy of post-Kantian thought and the vicissitudes of the correlationist loop and the tendency toward anti-realism it initiated, tendencies which have hobbled philosophy's endeavors through a variety of relativisms, nihilisms, and quietisms. Speculative realism shows how contemporary philosophers might take up again their capacity to actively respond to and practically address the rise in fanaticism and fideism which has also appeared in post-Kantian social and political discourse. But, as we have seen, for this possibility to be realized, philosophers must learn to speculate boldly once again on the possibility of the absolute as it appears within what Quentin Meillassoux calls a set of "very special conditions."[1]

These "conditions," as we saw in the last chapter, are that philosophical rationality (1) restrict itself to thinking within the limits of that which is materially manifest alone (as examined in the natural sciences), rather than venturing into the realm of the ethereal or ideal; and (2) that it model itself on the kinds of inquiry which probe the nature of the material world (i.e., the sciences), rather than deducing its claims from what is asserted in faith or experienced in private ecstasy (i.e., dogmatism or fideism). According to Meillassoux, by limiting itself to what is entirely material and testified to in a rigorous scientific analysis of nature, and by modeling its speculation on the nature and products of that analysis, philosophy can rediscover a "modicum of absoluteness" upon which it can resume its pursuit of absolute truth, ultimate meaning, and universal value without risking any form of dogmatism or fanaticism. And so, Meillassoux concludes, through a scientifically established, purely materialistic speculative philosophy, contemporary philosophy might "envisage an absolutizing thought that would not be absolutist," and in this way might finally overcome the impotence and fragility of philosophical discourse since the publication of Kant's critique.[2]

Meillassoux's confidence in the value of the material sciences to these ends rests upon his assessment that some version of the absolute is not only achievable in and through science's methods, but has in fact already been achieved in its conclusions. For as we saw in the last chapter, according to Meillassoux, the concept of the *ancestral* is precisely a materially manifest absolute. In the ancestral, he therefore concludes, philosophers gain access to a conception of the absolute which is entirely free from and completely outside the bounds and schemata of human rationality. Hence his claim that "the discourse of empirical science . . . gives meaning to the idea of rational debate about what did or did not exist prior to the emergence of humankind, as well as about what might eventually succeed humanity."[3] When philosophy is constrained and guided by this discourse and not merely by the structure and nature of the reason that makes such a debate possible, Meillassoux is convinced that it can achieve a vision of reality "which, by definition, cannot be reduced to any givenness which preceded it and whose emergence it allows"; a vision of reality, in other words, which is entirely absolute and independent from human rationality, but which is nevertheless accessed in and through it.[4] It is for this reason, then, that Meillassoux thinks the contemporary sciences allow philosophers to accomplish through reason something that Kant claims is impossible: a speculative apperception of an absolute thing-in-itself. In their capacity to provide a justifiable foundation for the speculative assertion of a material world which existed before and is radically independent of human reasoning, Meillassoux insists that the sciences model how post-Kantian philosophers might develop a new sense of *realism*—a new way of speaking meaningfully of absolute truth, universal value, and the ultimate meaning of reality.

"To think science," Meillassoux writes, "is to think the status of a becoming which cannot be correlational because the correlate is in it, rather than it being in the correlate."[5] To think with science, in other words, is for Meillassoux to think radically beyond the constraints of the correlationist loop. It is only through and alongside the material sciences, he therefore concludes, that contemporary philosophy might rediscover its lost sense of the absolute, reinitiate its classical pursuit of meaning and value, and in this way reclaim its relevance to the world. After all, according to Meillassoux, the hard core of the "Copernican revolution" initiated by the modern sciences is not merely the displacement of human life from the center of the cosmos, but the "decentering of thought relative to the world within the process of knowledge," whereby meaning, value, reality, and truth can be reconceived entirely outside the bounds of human ways of being.[6] For Meillassoux then, what the modern sciences in effect provide to philosophy is nothing less than a model for how we might consider these concepts as existing independently of our own way of thinking and mode of being which is, nevertheless, achievable in and through a particular function of that way of thinking and mode of being.

Hence Meillassoux's insistence when contemporary philosophers are sufficiently guided by the discoveries of modern science and constrained by the regulations governing those research methods and discursive practices, they should be able to escape their post-Kantian tendency toward anti-realism and gain access once again to "the great outdoors, the absolute outside . . . : that outside which [is] not relative to us, and which [is] given as indifferent to its own givenness to be what it is, existing in itself, regardless of whether we are thinking of it or not; that outside which thought could explore with the legitimate feeling of being on foreign territory—of being entirely elsewhere."[7] What's more, these constraints do not require abandoning what Meillassoux thinks was accomplished by Kant's critique; namely, the abolition of dogmatic metaphysics and fideist systems of thought. For these reasons, he is convinced that when contemporary philosophers draw sufficiently from and begin to think alongside and learn from their colleagues in the material sciences, they might finally overcome their manifest tendencies toward quietism and nihilism without resurrecting any form of dogmatism, fideism, or fanaticism. In this way, he argues, philosophy can reclaim its proper place in the academy and beyond and reverse its slow descent into irrelevance.

Science and the Mathematization of Nature

For Meillassoux, the power of the sciences to rationally access the "great outdoors" of absolute reality in-itself as it exists outside the strictures of human reasoning rests upon their commitment to mathematics as a method of inquiry and understanding. According to Meillassoux, "science deploys a process whereby we are able to *know* what may be while we are not, and . . . this process is linked to what sets science apart: *the mathematization of nature*."[8] Thus, he argues, "it is precisely insofar as modern science is mathematized that it is capable of raising the question of a possible temporal hiatus between thinking and being—of constructing the latter as a meaningful hypothesis, of giving it meaning, of rendering it tractable—whether in order to refute it or confirm it."[9] Meillassoux thinks that it is only insofar as the material sciences are themselves constrained by the limits of mathematics then that they are able to separate the processes of their own rational inquiry from the nonrational products of their discoveries—to sever, in other words, the observer (*cogito*) from the observed (*cogitatum*). And, as we have seen, it is from this severance that he thinks the products of scientific inquiry can be legitimately speculatively postulated as expressions of an independently existing and absolute reality.[10] Mathematics is for Meillassoux, in other words, the blade by which the absolute is "cut free" from human reasoning. It is therefore exclusively in and through mathematical inquiry that philosophy might accomplish and achieve anew its aim to understand and draw upon a robust sense of absolute reality to provide answers to the practical questions and existential concerns of human wonder: what can I know, what must I do, and what must I hope.

For Meillassoux, "the specificity of mathematical language stems from its capacity to describe that which is independent of all thought."[11] Therefore, he reasons, when we think mathematically, we learn to think, as it were, in the language of the absolute—in the language of that which exists outside of and beyond language and thought. Through mathematics, in other words, Meillassoux claims that we can learn to give ourselves over entirely to the nature of reality as it exists outside of the bounds of the structures of human reasoning, and discover a way through those structures to think and speak meaningfully about reality in its own terms. This is the case, he argues, because "what is mathematizable cannot be reduced to a correlate of thought."[12] What mathematics accomplishes by his reckoning then is a way of formulating reality as it exists for itself and in its absolute form. Hence Meillassoux's conclusion that by emulating the mathematical procedures of the material sciences, philosophers can learn how to engage with the possibility of that which is not a product of human thought, is not dependent upon its structures, and is not ultimately reducible to a human way of being. In other words, what Meillassoux thinks that the kind of mathematization of the material world which is accomplished in the contemporary sciences provides for philosophy is a method by which it might rationally conceive of reality as an absolute, something which is wholly independent from and indifferent to us and yet, nevertheless, present for us.

"From its inception," Meillassoux writes, "the mathematization of the world bore with it the possibility of uncovering knowledge of a world more indifferent than ever to human existence, and hence indifferent to whatever knowledge humanity might have of it."[13] Hence his claim that it is only through "mathematical discourse [that we are] able to describe a world where humanity is absent; a world crammed with things and events that are not the correlates of any manifestation; a world that is not the correlate of a relation to the world."[14] By learning from and thinking through and alongside this scientific mathematization of nature, Meillassoux is therefore convinced that philosophy can achieve a concept of the absolute as something which is fundamentally "unreasonable," something which is, though available in and to human thought, nevertheless fundamentally contrary to and entirely independent of human thought.

According to Meillassoux, "the absoluteness [which is achieved in and through the mathematical sciences] expresses the following idea: it is meaningful to think (even if only in a hypothetical register) that all those aspects of the given that are mathematically describable can continue to exist regardless of whether or not we are there to convert the latter into something that is given-to or manifested-for."[15] Therefore, he reasons, what mathematics offers philosophy is the only means by which it can speculatively frame an account of reality as existing absolutely independently from the bounds of reasonability—an account from which, he adds, philosophers might extract a new sense of meaning, value, and truth which is not susceptible to the relativistic tendencies of post-Kantian philosophy, but lends itself instead to more practical application. Indeed, according to Meillassoux "it is by way of mathematics that we will finally succeed in thinking that which, through its power and beauty, vanquishes quantities and sounds the end of [the] play" which has marked post-Kantian philosophy and led to its increasing irrelevance in a world at war, and take up again our responsibility to meaningfully address and ameliorate that world.[16] For these reasons, he concludes, "it should be mathematics that constitutes ontology, rather than a discipline pertaining to another truth procedure, such as art."[17] And from this mathematical ontology, he suggests, a new ethics and politics too.

According to Meillassoux and his allies, if philosophy is going to make any headway in the contemporary world—if it is going to cast off the relativistic, nihilistic, and quietistic fetters which have bound its discourse since Kant, reclaim its original charge, and make any progress against the rising tide of fanaticism and fideism—then it must tie itself to the material sciences by adopting the language of mathematics and in this way begin to postulate alongside them a new account of the absolute structure and nature of reality. As Meillassoux puts it, "philosophy's task consists in re-absolutizing the scope of mathematics—thereby remaining, contrary to correlationism, faithful to thought's Copernican de-centering—but without lapsing back into any sort of metaphysical necessity, which has indeed become obsolete."[18] Only thusly, he argues, will contemporary philosophers be able to champion again the value and relevance of their work both within and beyond the academy.

Ladyman and Ross, for their part, as we saw toward the end of the last chapter, seem to agree with Meillassoux on this point, arguing that we must learn "to represent the world and reason mathematically—that is, in a manner that enables us to *abstract* away from our familiar environment."[19] Like Meillassoux, they argue that through mathematical abstraction, philosophy should be able to move beyond the folk epistemologies which have ensnared it since Kant and develop "some justified metaphysics."[20] For Ladyman and Ross then, while "scientific realists take it that appearances are caused by unseen objects and that the behaviour of these objects can be invoked to explain their appearances . . . the resources of the manifest image cannot be (directly) used for satisfactory representation in physics. Hence, mathematics has an ineliminable role to play in theories."[21] And so they conclude that mathematical models must be relied upon by philosophers if they want to develop a new metaphysics worthy of its name—a metaphysics, in other words, which can speak meaningfully of the absolute nature of reality and, even more importantly, of the possibility of any ultimate meaning and universal value within that reality.[22] And, in further concert with Meillassoux, Ladyman and Ross establish their confidence in the power of mathematics from their observation that "mathematics and science have undoubtedly borne fruits of great value."[23] So they conclude with him that in matters of metaphysical and ethical speculation, contemporary philosophers "should adopt the structural realist emphasis on the mathematical or structural content of [their] theories."[24]

Alain Badiou and the Mathematization of Ontology

Meillassoux is not, then, the only contemporary thinker who asserts the power of mathematics as the best means of developing a robust post-Kantian sense of absolute realism. In point of fact, he attributes his own confidence in the power of mathematics to this end to the work of his teacher and sometimes ally, Alain Badiou. Indeed, he openly confesses that "Badiou provided me with the mathematical soil needed for [the] development [of my own philosophical ideas . . . along with essential intellectual support for my desire to reactivate philosophy, in its most speculative aspect."[25] According to Meillassoux "the signal work of Alain Badiou—and primarily *Being and Event* . . . [is to show] the ontological pertinence of Cantor's theorem" to post-Kantian attempts to theorize the absolute nature of reality anew.[26] So it is to Badiou's account of the role and function of mathematics in the development of a new metaphysical and ethical realism that we must turn if we are to better understand how we might draw from mathematics a new sense of absolute meaning and value.

By Badiou's own account, the principal aim of his *Being and Event* is to suggest that if philosophy is to remain true to its founding principle by forwarding actual claims about the nature of reality, then it must "designat[e] amongst its own conditions, as a singular discursive situation, ontology itself in the pure form of mathematics."[27] For, according to him, mathematics "is precisely what delivers philosophy and ordains it to the care of truths."[28] According to Badiou then, only if and when philosophy takes mathematics as the model for its metaphysics can it approach the nature of existence as an absolute and derive from it a new sense of final truth, universal moral value, and ultimate meaning. For these reasons, he argues that mathematics must not be seen as merely *a* methodological procedure for philosophy, as if simply one among many. Instead, he argues, mathematics must be seen as "the *sole* discourse which 'knows' absolutely what it is talking about: being, as such."[29] Hence Badiou's claim that if philosophy is to reclaim its original aims and restore its relevance to the contemporary world, then it must not only learn to bind itself to the structures of mathematical analysis, endeavoring to constrain itself entirely within the limits of those methods and products, but it must discover how an operational metaphysics can be derived from the structures of mathematical reasoning itself and show how a practical ethics and actionable politics can in turn be developed from that metaphysics.

For Badiou, as for Meillassoux, the power of mathematics consists in its capacity to create a divorce between *what* it posits as a truth and the *one* who posits that truth—its ability, in other words, to abstract the knowing subject from what it knows. It is this power to divorce the known from the knower that establishes mathematics as a *universal* science according to Badiou, one which will yield the same results regardless of the subject who factors those results, or the time or place in which that factoring is accomplished. Hence Badiou's claim that "mathematics is the science of everything that is, grasped at its absolute formal level."[30] Inasmuch as mathematics operates in this universal and absolutely formal way, it expresses for Badiou a mode of human thinking that is not dependent upon or restricted by the cognitive faculties of the human's way or mode of being in the world. Instead, he argues, mathematics expresses a mode of thinking which allows the human being to think alongside the primordial material inhumanness within which it lives and from which it emerges. In this way, Badiou continues, mathematics provides a way in and through human thinking to that which exists utterly and entirely beyond it: the absolute reality of existence in and for itself. What Badiou thinks that mathematics grants to contemporary philosophy, then, is a path through which rational speculation can step beyond itself and achieve precisely what Kant thought impossible, a rational account of the thing-in-itself—noumenal reality as it exists in its own right.

Such a "pure presentation," Badiou writes, "abstracting all reference to 'that which' [something is]—which is to say, then, being-as-being . . . —can be thought *only* through mathematics."[31] By thinking alongside and through mathematics, he concludes, contemporary philosophers can surmount and escape the limitations of post-Kantian philosophy without resurrecting any form of dogmatic assertion or relying on any fideistic leap of faith. Hence his claim that through mathematics contemporary philosophers can rationally access the formal structure of something like the grounding "Being of beings," the absolute reality of existence as it exists in and for itself, and not merely as it appears to us through and according to the framework of human existence, reasoning, and understanding. Hence Badiou's further assessment that "mathematics is the guardian of being qua being," and is the path to a new and viable sense of metaphysical reality.[32] Badiou sums it thusly: "all that we know, and can ever know of being qua being is set out . . . by the historical discursivity of mathematics."[33] If contemporary philosophers hope to remain within the trajectory of their own history and speak meaningfully of the nature of absolute reality again, he thus concludes, "mathematics is our obligation."[34]

For this reason, he suggests that "the confrontation with mathematics is an absolutely indispensable condition for philosophy as such; a condition that is at once descriptively external and prescriptively immanent for philosophy."[35] To express this obligation, Badiou even goes so far as to formulate a basic axiomatic lemma equating mathematics with ontology, "mathematics = ontology," which he thinks must guide any mode of contemporary philosophy to assure its potential legitimacy.[36] According to Badiou's own assessment then, the primary goal of his philosophical work is "to integrate mathematics in all its rational force and splendor, particularly as regards the doctrine of being," into philosophy.[37] Hence, Meillassoux's reference to him as the principle source of his own confidence in the power and function of mathematics in the speculative assertion of a new sense of absolute reality.

By approaching philosophical questions concerning the nature of being mathematically, Badiou and Meillassoux argue that philosophy will be able to achieve once again the splendor and power of the absolute without resurrecting any form of dogmatic metaphysics or fideistic suspensions of reason. Badiou, for one, makes this claim explicit, arguing that what mathematization affords philosophy is nothing short of *the* path to "absolute truths"—truths, he goes on to suggest, by which it should be able to overcome its tendency toward nihilism and quietism and reclaim its effective and practical power in the world.[38] What Badiou thinks a mathematical approach to philosophy accomplishes, in other words, is a route out of the kind of correlational thinking which has hampered it since Kant. For, Badiou writes, in mathematics "you have the feeling of touching an external reality, in the sense that it's not just a fabrication of the mind."[39] For these reasons, he argues that "mathematics is a way of approaching the real, even the most elusive real."[40]

"What mathematics ultimately makes possible, how it offers itself . . . as a speculative resource to philosophers who want to go beyond contemporary relativism and restore the universal value of truths," Badiou concludes, "is what I'd call the possibility of an absolute ontology."[41] What's more, as he makes clear, it accomplishes this possibility without relying on, invoking, or asserting the existence of any kind of divine entity. Indeed, according to Badiou, "the mathematician was somebody who, for the first time, introduced a universality completely free of any mythological or religious assumptions and that no longer took the form of a narrative."[42] By binding themselves to the strictures of mathematical reasoning then, Badiou suggests, contemporary philosophers should be able to escape the limitations of post-Kantian philosophy without betraying the basic insight of Kant's critique of dogmatic metaphysics. In this regard, he thinks, they should be able to escape the modes of nihilism and quietism which have resulted from this critique without resurrecting any form of dogmatism or collapsing into any form of fideism. For these reasons, Badiou concludes that "mathematics provides philosophy with a weapon, a fearsome machine of thought, a catapult aimed at the bastions of ignorance, superstition, and mental servitude," and in this way, philosophy can mount a new and effective campaign against the myriad ethical, social, and political injustices which beset us today.[43]

CHAPTER 3

Regaining the Absolute through Mathematical Ontology

From this it would seem that mathematics provides the best, if only route through which speculative philosophers committed to accomplishing these tasks might achieve their aims. For, it seems, it is only through the kind of mathematical reckoning employed by the sciences that we can find a path back to absolute reality in reference to which we might establish a new universal account of meaning and value. To justify this confidence in the power of mathematics to this end, we only need to remind ourselves of all that the modern sciences have accomplished through mathematical reasoning in the last century alone—all that has been achieved with nothing more than basic arithmetic and a little patience.

With technology as rudimentary as a slide rule and a pencil, mathematical engineers were able to chart a path to our moon and launch the first astronauts into space. More recently, through only slightly more complex computational systems, contemporary physicists were able to accurately speculate about the fundamental building block of mass, long before it could be observed or measured experimentally. Indeed, every great leap forward in the empirical sciences for the last 200 years has been driven by mathematical speculation. Evaluated purely pragmatically, there is much to recommend the power of mathematics as the innate language of the universe in its purest and most absolute form. For these reasons, we might conclude with Galileo Galilei that

> the universe . . . cannot be understood unless one first learns to understand the language and know the character in which it is written. It is written in mathematical language, and its characters are triangles, circles, and other geometric figures; without these it is humanly impossible to understand a single word of it, and one wanders around pointlessly in a dark labyrinth.[44]

So it is in mathematics that we discover a truly *universal* language, one by which not only all human beings can relate to and understand one another, regardless of their individual, cultural, geographical, and historical differences; but through which every human being can relate to and understand that which is fundamentally and irrevocably nonhuman, and even inhuman. Indeed, when we understand not just any single arithmetical language, but the organizing principles of all mathematical languages, we discover behind them (whether the Latinate decimal system, Arabic algebraic calculus, or the Gallo-Runic, Central African, and Vedic duodecimal or dozenal base systems) a universal harmonic rhythm—a kind of musicality which can be communicated across human cultures and observable reality alike—a comity which allows, for example, a Western guitarist tuned in a heptatonic whole-tone scale to improvise along with an Indian sitar player's variable chromatic scale by way of the Persian pentatonic scale, all according to the same basic patterns and ratios that govern the blossoming of flowers in a Fibonacci spiral and the Voronoi tessellation of crystals across a plane.

It is this radical universality of mathematics which allows humans to connect further across cultures to the sheer material facts of reality itself, which is what Meillassoux, Badiou, and Ladyman and Ross all agree is the source of the epistemic power of mathematics as a royal road to absolute truth. For, they argue, through mathematics one finds a channel of communication between the relativity of any given human position and the absolute inhuman position of nature itself.[45] What's more, as they show, this channel is accessible in and through rational methods alone and does not, therefore, require any fideistic leap of faith or fanatical dogmatic assertion. So it is through the power of mathematics, we might conclude with them, that philosophy should be able to not only discover, but even formulate rationally the nature of that which is fundamentally un-reasonable or extra-rational: absolute reality in-itself.

For the speculative realist, it is this power of mathematics to connect what lies outside of and beyond the bounds of human reasoning (being itself) to what is inextricably constrained by human reasoning (our own being in the world) that assures its practical value to philosophers. By their account, the ultimate power of mathematics lies in in the fact that it provides a *universal* and *unifying* mode of thinking, in every sense of those two words: not only its *oneness* as an organizing language across various and diverse modes of being (i.e., human, nonhuman, and inhuman), but its truly *cosmic* scope as well. It is its *universality* that leads astrobiologists and exobiologists to suggest that if we ever discover some form of intelligent life elsewhere in the universe, whether organic or inorganic in form, our greatest hope for communication with it lies through mathematics and music—numbers and songs, which ultimately amount to the same thing, as Pythagoras first suggested.[46]

For Badiou, the universalizing power of mathematics is due to the fact that it "is concerned with, or latches onto, the most formal, abstract, universally quasi-empty dimension of being as such."[47] As such, he concludes, mathematics "is a thought process that bypasses the particularity of language."[48] For these reasons, Badiou argues that mathematical reasoning operates as a kind of primal democratizing power. Indeed, he claims that mathematics operates in such a way that it necessarily unites people by leveling the various historically contingent differences which separates them from one another (e.g., class, race, language, culture, etc.) in a single and shared common language and understanding of reality. But the unifying power of mathematics to this end extends well beyond the merely human, he thinks. Indeed, he suggests, it extends even into the realm of the absolutely inhuman and noumenal structures of absolute reality itself. In fact, it is from its capacity to unite the human to the inhuman, he claims, that the radical democratizing power of mathematics to unite humans to one another first grows. Hence Badiou's identification of "arithmetic as an instance of [a] stellar and warlike inhumanity," a power which, he claims, by overwhelming the particularity of any single human perspective, connects different humans to each other and unites diverse forms of material reality (whether sentient or not) to one another—from Kant's starry heavens above to the moral universe within.[49] For these reasons Badiou concludes that through mathematics contemporary philosophy might develop a new ethical, social, and political program by which it can overcome its tendency toward quietism and reengage the world. But, as he makes clear, and Meillassoux and Ladyman and Ross all agree, for this to occur, philosophers must learn to model their thinking on the kind of mathematical speculation demonstrated by and routinely practiced in the contemporary material sciences.

Meillassoux's Absolute—Contingency, Hyper-Chaos, and the Ethics of Hope

While all of these thinkers agree on these points, somewhat ironically, they disagree on the nature of the absolutes which they claim are discoverable through such a mathematical speculation. Thus, while each of them identifies the nature of the absolutes which they think are achieved via mathematics regarding the formal structure of reality as it exists in itself, and each also agrees that this reality is radically inhuman in nature, each thinker nevertheless differs in their account of the actual content of that reality, not to mention the practical meaning each derives from that content. These differences, aside from challenging their basic claim concerning the universality of mathematics and sciences, have profound consequences for what each thinks is the ultimate aim of contemporary philosophy: the reintegration of value into being—that is, philosophy's capacity to account for the final truth, universal moral value, and ultimate meaning of existence.

For Meillassoux and Ladyman and Ross, as we saw in the last chapter, what we discover by way of mathematics is the fundamental *facticity* of what Meillassoux designates the "absolute contingency" of existence and defines as the fact "of everything's capacity-to-be-other or capacity-not-to-be"—"the absolute necessity of everything's non-necessity."[50] According to him, "the fundamental criterion for every mathematical statement [is a recognition of the] necessary condition for the contingency of every entity."[51] The more we learn to philosophize mathematically, Meillassoux concludes, the more we begin to realize that underneath the apparent stability of existence lies a more profound and ultimately absolute instability. And, he reasons, it is in reference to this absolute instability that the final truth and ultimate nature of existence can be understood; and furthermore, that a new conception of universal moral value, ethical duty, and even social and political hope can be developed.

According to Meillassoux, then, what is revealed through the complete mathematization of the natural world is the fundamental fact that things needn't be the way they are—that, in other words, things could have been otherwise than they are and, therefore, might still become so in the future. This, he thinks, is the real power of mathematical speculation in contemporary ethics and politics: to practically demonstrate and definitively prove the radical mutability of existence. Meillassoux terms this absolute reality which he thinks is exposed through the mathematization of nature *hyper-chaos*. This hyper-chaos of reality, he claims, rests upon what he sees as the mathematically demonstrable fact that "there is no reason why a physical law endures, or persists, one day more, one more minute. Because these laws are just facts: you can't demonstrate their necessity."[52] It is the absolute contingency of reality which Meillassoux argues is revealed through mathematics, and which he thinks should function as a new ground for philosophical metaphysics, ethics, and politics. "Our absolute," he concludes, "is nothing other than an extreme form of chaos, a *hyper-chaos*, for which nothing is or would seem to be, impossible, not even the unthinkable."[53] What Meillassoux thinks mathematics grants to philosophy is the capacity to realize the factuality of the allegedly absolute contingency of being itself. Through mathematics, he claims, philosophers are able to access the "precise condition[s] for the manifest stability of chaos."[54]

What a complete mathematization of the natural world yields, Meillassoux summarizes, is a vision of reality as wholly contingent; indeed, a vision of reality in which "contingency alone is necessary."[55] And, he continues, it is through this new vision of reality that contemporary philosophers might overcome the history of correlationism which has hampered the relevance of their work for the last two centuries, and be empowered to escape their tendencies toward anti-realism, nihilism, relativism, and quietism. More importantly still, Meillassoux thinks that it is upon this

CHAPTER 3

vision of reality as wholly contingent that contemporary philosophers can erect a justifiable critique of every form of fanaticism which justifies its action through reference to the idea of absolute necessity.[56] In this way, on the basis of the absolute contingency of reality, Meillassoux suggests that philosophy might establish a new, absolutely founded sense of normative action. For Meillassoux, the idea of absolute contingency provides contemporary philosophy with definitive proof that the dogmatists are wrong—that the world does not have to be the way it is, but might instead be otherwise and better than it currently is. Armed with this apparent proof, he suggests that contemporary ethicists might absolutely justify their critique of every form of social and political absolutism, which he sees as emerging from dogmatic conceptions of reality as a product of metaphysical necessity. For Meillassoux, the alleged *fact* of the absolute contingency lays to rest the appeal to any and every other absolute. Moreover, he suggests, contemporary philosophers can justify in reference to this one absolute their practical hope in a future world to come, one in which the possibility of perpetual peace exists as a legitimate hope; for within a universe in which contingency reigns absolute, anything and indeed everything is possible, even perfection. Meillassoux goes so far as to suggest that the kind of normative order which could be established on the firm foundation of the absolute contingency of reality provides sufficient grounds for contemporary philosophers to critique even the apparent injustice of the laws of nature itself, laws which apparently demand our deterioration and ultimate demise. Such a critique of injustice, whether human or inhuman, as materially unnecessary, Meillassoux concludes, is made possible through the vision of the absolute he claims is revealed through the scientific mathematization of nature.[57]

"Even if natural laws have remained constant up until now," Meillassoux concludes, what the mathematization of nature shows is that there is "nothing in experience [that] can assure us that this will always be the case."[58] What mathematics shows us, he claims, is therefore that "the contingency of the laws of nature is not an absurd hypothesis, i.e., it is thinkable and unrefuted."[59] In the kind of hyper-chaos which he thinks is justified through the mathematization of nature, Meillassoux argues that we discover an absolute power which is thus "capable of destroying even becoming itself by bringing forth, perhaps forever, fixity, stasis, and death."[60] On this basis, he concludes, we might legitimately critique not only every existing moral, social, and political order, but even every natural and material reality and rationally justify our hope that everything could change and a more just and equitable world might eventually appear.

Meillassoux writes: "if facticity is the absolute, [then] contingency

TOWARD A POST-CRITICAL ETHICS

no longer means the necessity of destruction or disorder, but rather the equal contingency of order and disorder, of becoming and sempiternity."[61] After all, "contingency is such that anything might happen, even nothing at all, so that what is, remains as it is."[62] It is upon the basis of this alleged absolute contingency of reality, which he thinks is proven through the mathematization of nature in the material sciences, that Meillassoux argues that post-critical philosophers might rationally justify their hope in the eventual possibility of a perfectly just, absolutely good, and perpetually peaceful natural, social, and political order.[63] Since everything can always be otherwise than it is, he claims, it is not unreasonable to hope for and practically work toward the construction of this eventually perfect world, one in which all wrongs will be righted and every injustice abolished eternally. Indeed, Meillassoux claims, "the factial is an ontology that allows us to think [even] immortality directly as one possibility among others, but as a real possibility."[64] The absolute contingency of existence revealed through the mathematization of nature, he argues, "makes [even the idea of] universal justice possible, by erasing even the injustice of shattered lives."[65] Meillassoux concludes that in philosophy's pursuit of its ultimate goal of reinscribing value into being, "philosophy's main concern [should not be] with being but with [what] may-be"—in other words, with the possibilities contained in the absolute contingency of reality which he argues is proven through a complete mathematization of nature.[66]

Badiou's Absolute—The Transfinite Multiple and the Ethics of Fidelity

Whether or not such a "radical contingency" is actually "rationally proven" in and through the mathematical sciences is something we will examine in greater detail in the following chapter. But independent of this concern, there is another concern with the account of an allegedly practical and applicable ethics and politics which Meillassoux derives from his assessment of the absolute contingency of reality, a concern that Badiou calls a determinate ethical and "political weakness."[67] According to Badiou this problem is that Meillassoux's normativity empowers nothing more than hope. In this regard, he argues, Meillassoux's vision of an absolutely grounded ethics amounts to little more than an anticipatory desire for a future possible world, a world which he himself alternatively refers to as the "fourth World" or "the World of justice."[68] Unfortunately, according to Badiou, there is too little to draw upon from this account of justice to practically empower philosophers to directly address the actual injustices which exist in our *current* world—too little we can rely on to *actively* respond to the very imminent and real crises which face us here and now. For this reason, he concludes, Meillassoux's ethics and politics remains all too ideal and virtual to be of any real practical value, repeating, in effect, the same tendency toward quietism demonstrated by so many other post-Kantian normative systems.

As Badiou puts it, "there is a detachment from the present in [Meillassoux's ethics], a kind of stoicism of the present" which prevents it from giving us a "clear presentation or vision of the present."[69] As a result, he concludes, while Meillassoux's speculative ethics may be useful *negatively*, to justify a critique of the logic of the kinds of fanatical injustices which have proliferated after Kant, he thinks there is little in it that can be used *positively* to develop the kinds of action that we need here and now to build a more just and peaceful world. And so, Badiou argues, Meillassoux's ethics are ultimately useless—little more, in the final analysis, than a novel form of hopeful resignation or messianic faith; or, in other words, simply another kind of quietism. Hence his assessment that, despite his claims to the contrary, Meillassoux's ethics do not escape the tendencies of post-Kantian normative philosophy. On the contrary, Badiou concludes, if anything, Meillassoux's ethics amplifies and absolutizes this quietism.

For his part, Meillassoux seems to acknowledge as much, confessing that "the core of factial ethics thus consists in the immanent binding of philosophical astonishment and messianic hope, understood as the hope for justice for the living and the dead."[70] The problem with messianisms of this sort, of course, is that we face very real and pressing ethical dilemmas in the present world that cannot wait for some future possible world to be responded to. To restrict ethical action exclusively to a form of messianic hope in the face of the acute suffering of the present world, Badiou rightly concludes, is indeed merely to repeat the kind of quietism which has plagued post-Kantian philosophy in one form or another for the last 250 years.

In Badiou's opinion, the source of Meillassoux's problem on this front is that his ethics is established on a faulty metaphysics—a faulty understanding of the kinds of absolutes which are obtainable from the mathematization of nature accomplished in the contemporary sciences. To correct this error, Badiou proposes an entirely different account of the absolute and, from it, a radically different account of normativity—one which he claims not only more accurately reflects the conclusions of the kind of mathematization of nature achieved in the contemporary sciences, but which is, he argues, more effective at responding to the practical concerns of the contemporary world. In this way, the irony we referred to earlier becomes clear: while Badiou and Meillassoux agree that it is from an understanding of the mathematization of nature that something approaching an absolutely grounded ethics can be established, they ultimately disagree on the products of that mathematization and, therefore also, on the kinds of ethical systems which can be developed from them. For where Meillassoux sees mathematics confirming the "absolute contingency" of being, Badiou argues that mathematics proves the absolute "incompleteness" of being.[71] This "incompleteness," as we will see, grounds what Badiou sees as the moral imperative of all beings not merely to *hope* for change, but to actively *pursue* it; or put more concretely, to act in fidelity to their own singular incompleteness and the incompleteness of reality.

With Georg Cantor's set theory as his guide, Badiou argues that the real power of contemporary mathematics is to show philosophers that every supposed entity or object is not ultimately some coherent or unique substantial whole, consisting solely of itself; but is rather a complex assemblage that is composed of a set of multiple possibilities, each of which consists of a varying number of attributes, qualities, and phenomena.[72] What this means concretely, Badiou argues, is that every existent being is not, in the final analysis, some self-sufficient object emergent from and sustained by its own inner power, force, or material objecthood. Nor, he insists, is it part of some greater unifying whole, ultimate power, or cosmic nature from which it grows and upon which it depends for its reality and stability. Instead, Badiou argues, each existent being is merely a momentary confluence of a constantly varying set of finite possibilities.[73] In this regard, he suggests, each existent object, whether our own being, our culture, or our time and place in history, not to mention the various ethical and political dilemmas which we encounter therein, is ultimately nothing more than a complex "situation" or "event," each of which arises, he continues, from the confluence of a fluctuating set of differing transfinite possibilities.[74] By understanding this absolute *fact*, he argues, philosophers might develop an entirely new conception of absolute justice and universal normativity as a form of fidelity to the complexity and incompleteness of any given moment or event.

Thus, what Badiou thinks is granted through the mathematization of nature is a complete dismantling of the traditional concept of Being as the unifying essence of all beings—a concept which, he agrees with Meillassoux, is ultimately dogmatic and useful only to justify any number of injustices—and the construction of a new sense of being as event, and of value as a mode of being faithful to that event. Indeed, according to Badiou, "what set theory enacts . . . is that the one is not"—that, in other words, the concept of being is an empty concept, and is nothing more than the concept of the set itself—a purely theoretical container.[75] Thus, he argues, while "we admit the 'existence' of a category of sets ... it is contradictory to posit the existence of a set of all sets."[76] Likewise, he claims it is meaningless to posit the existence of some grand unifying essence. For these reasons, Badiou suggests, "the void [is] the proper name of Being."[77] This conception of the absolute void of existence, he thinks, is *the* revolutionary idea which philosophical ontology gains from mathematics and from which he suggests a more effective account of ethical responsibility might be established and developed.

According to Badiou, "the decisive break—in which mathematics blindly pronounces its own essence—is Cantor's creation. It is there alone that it is finally declared that, despite the prodigious variety of mathematical 'objects' and 'structures,' they can *all* be designated as pure multiplicities built, in a regulated manner, on the basis of a *void* set alone."[78] Therefore, Badiou concludes, if any absolutely grounded ethics is to be established on the basis of the complete mathematization of nature effected in the contemporary sciences, it must be upon this conception of the *void* or *absence* of any ultimate or final essence at the heart of set theory's reformulation of nature. "In set theory," he writes, "there exists an 'absolute' universe of reference, namely the cumulative hierarchy of sets, which is sutured to being *qua* being through the name of the void."[79] It is Badiou's conviction that "to preserve the absoluteness of truths without having recourse to any God, [contemporary ethics must] incorporate set theory, as a founding mathematical condition, into philosophy."[80] It is this idea of the absolute *absence* of any final or complete being which Badiou sees as the fundamental truth of set theory, and which he claims must be used to develop a new philosophical approach to absolute normativity and protect us from collapsing once more into the kind of quietism that Meillassoux's ethics appears to maintain and amplify.[81]

Badiou initiates this new approach to normativity by asserting a set of axioms which he thinks are deducible from Cantor's set theory and which, he claims, have a more practical ethical, social, and political import than Meillassoux's account of the absolute.[82] First, following what he sees as the primal void asserted by set theory, Badiou asserts that "there is no God. Which also means: the One is not."[83] A functional ethics, he claims on the basis of this axiom, cannot be extracted from the nature of any existent eternal or absolute being. Instead, he argues, it must be based precisely on the absence of any such primal or transcendental existence. The basis for a functional ethics must be extracted and deduced, he concludes, precisely from the *absence* of any such transcendental metaphysical entity. Following from this, Badiou asserts, in a second axiom, that existence must be seen as a collection of discrete attributes—or, in other words, a collection of *events*. "Every situation, in as much as it is," he writes, "is [therefore] a multiple, composed of an infinity of elements, each of which is itself a multiple."[84] From this, he claims, the possibility of moral value cannot be seen as emergent from any one way of being or event, but only ever in relation to some particular set of elements, beings, or events. Badiou reinforces this claim with his third axiom: that "considered in their simple belonging to a situation (to an infinite multiple), the animals of the species *Homo sapiens* are ordinary multiplicities."[85] The possibility of being an ethical animal of this sort, he argues, consists in acknowledging the multiplicity of any given situation, moment, or event in which some human being finds itself. As such, Badiou argues, fourthly, that "infinite alterity is quite simply *what there is*. Any experience at all is the infinite deployment of infinite differences."[86] From this, he suggests that there will never be any one, final, or universal concept of the right, true, and good. Instead, he argues, moral values and ethical truths can only emerge singularly from a constantly shifting and multiplying field of play within which any number of possible values and accounts of the good, right, and true is justified. What this means finally and fifthly, Badiou concludes, is that "there is not, in fact, one single Subject [or Truth], but as many subjects as there are truths, and as many subjective types as there are procedures of truths."[87] From this, Badiou suggests that "the only genuine ethics [can be] of truth*s* in the plural—or, more precisely, the only ethics is of processes of truth, of the labour that brings *some* truths into the world."[88] In other words, ethics, for Badiou, consists in learning to be faithful to the singularity of the truth of any given *specific* situation or event and is therefore not only fluid, but in actual fact constantly shifting and transforming.

Badiou summarizes his position thusly: "I shall call 'truth' (*a* truth) the real process of a fidelity to an event: that which this fidelity *produces* in the situation."[89] To be ethical, he argues, consists in learning to be faithful to this singular situation or particular truth which presents itself in any given way at any given moment. As such, he concludes, we can never hope to achieve any one ethics which holds for all or for all time. Instead, he thinks, we must endeavor to be attentive to the multiplicity of possible values and truths which appear from moment to moment, and event to event, and which differ from subject to subject. There are, in other words for Badiou, as many possible ethical procedures as there are subjects and truths: an infinity of constantly changing and shifting singular sets. For any philosophical ethics to be functional, Badiou argues, it must be attentive to this one absolute principle: that there is no ultimate singular principle for all. Ethics only works, he concludes, when it is developed to fit the singular set of circumstances from which it grows and to which it hopes to respond. For this reason, he insists, philosophical ethics, though emergent from the same universal *formal* procedure of mathematical reasoning, can never be universal in its *content*. Instead, Badiou maintains, ethics can only and must always be an *"ethics-of* (of politics, of love, of science, of art)"—an ethics of the particular event or truth in which one finds oneself at any given moment.[90] Any ethics grounded on the absolute void of being which Badiou thinks is thematizable as an absolute through a proper understanding of contemporary mathematics, would be an ethics which respects the singularity of any given event or truth.[91] Hence, his definition of such an absolutely justifiable ethics as an exhortation to "a principle of consistency, of a fidelity . . . , or [in] the maxim 'keep going!'"[92] "Only such a fidelity to the singular," Badiou suggests, can potentially "ward off the Evil that every singular truth makes possible."[93] It is only by reconceiving of ethics in this way, as a fidelity to the singularity of any apparent truth-event, that contemporary philosophy can resist what Badiou calls the "smug nihilism" of post-Kantian thinking and regain the ground which it has lost to quietism.[94] Thus, he concludes, it is "in mathematics that the maxim 'Keep going!' the only maxim required in ethics, has the greatest weight."[95]

The Dangers and Weaknesses of Speculative Ethics—Fideistic Messianism and Fanatical Authenticity

It should immediately be clear from all this that there is a problem at the heart of the claims of speculative realists. Not only do they assert contradictory accounts of what they claim is a universally defensible vision of the absolute, but they develop contradictory conceptions of moral value and ethical responsibility from it. What's more, both of these accounts of a new, absolutely justified conception of normativity contain within themselves the tendency to precisely the kinds of post-Kantian extremism that they claim to escape and overcome. Indeed, there is just as profound a danger and weakness to Badiou's conception of ethics as there is to Meillassoux's, though it comes from the opposite side. For it would seem, perhaps ironically, that Badiou's ethics contains within it the seeds of precisely the kind of danger which Meillassoux's ethics most strategically aims itself against; namely, the possibility of a return to relativism or fanaticism.

What else is Badiou's insistence on developing a fidelity to the singular if not a return to an even more insidious form of relativism or an opening to a fanatically defended assertion of one's own particularity? Indeed, when read through the lens of Meillassoux's critique of the logic of fanaticism, Badiou's definition of ethical responsibility as an absolutely justified fidelity to some determinate event or truth seems all too easily to fall into precisely the kind of logic which is employed by dogmatists and fanatics to defend their local truths, cultural values, individual experiences, or provincial history. Indeed, following Meillassoux's analysis, the call to fidelity at the heart of Badiou's ethics would seem to be nothing less than a renewal of precisely the kind of post-Kantian fideism which led to the melancholy record of sociopolitical horrors that has marked the last two centuries of global history, as we saw in chapter 1.

Within Badiou's framework, it does indeed appear far too easy to justify the pursuit of our own individual interests, experiences, truths, and desires over and above the interests of others, to define an ethics of any practical use. Indeed, what is this if not an amplification of precisely the kind of insidious, if not dogmatic, relativism which has already been affirmed by so many post-Kantian philosophers? In fact, what Badiou's conception of ethics seems to justify, if not demand, is a fanatical devotion to one's own being. In this regard, by providing an absolute ground for any number of concrete individual commitments, Badiou's ethics all too easily justifies any number of potentially evil acts, a possibility he seems to acknowledge when confessing that evil for him is a "(possible) effect of the Good itself," a perhaps excusable by-product of our attempts to pursue our own individual good.[96]

From this it should be clear that Badiou's account of ethics, like Meillassoux's, ultimately fails to overcome the basic antinomies of post-Kantian ethical philosophy—with each account giving way in one form or another to precisely the kind of quietism, relativism, or fanaticism it strives to overcome. And even more problematically, inasmuch as they fail to overcome this fundamental ethical antinomy in post-Kantian thought, each thinker promotes an ethical system which could, in its own way, become complicit in, if not demand, any number of actions which are demonstratively evil. But there is still another problem with each of their speculative projects; namely, they each propose a different and incompatible account of what they both claim to be a universal absolute that is obtainable from the mathematical sciences. What's more, as we will see in greater detail in the next chapter, neither of their accounts is actually justified according to the testimony of the contemporary sciences they purport to represent. The differences between their respective ethical accounts are, of course, due to the difference between their respective accounts of the absolute. But perhaps the failure of each of these ethical accounts is due to a more significant failure by Meillassoux and Badiou to take their own advice and attend carefully to the actual conclusions of the contemporary sciences. By failing to actually learn from these conclusions and focusing instead on the formal structure of scientific and mathematical reasoning, over and against the actual content of mathematical and scientific studies, these two thinkers cannot help but repeat the errors of the post-Kantian systems they so fervently strive to free themselves from.

If we are to take Meillassoux and Badiou's arguments seriously, it would seem that we must reject their respective accounts of the absolute, as well as the kinds of moral systems they think are deducible from it, and strive to learn from the conclusions of the actual sciences which they suggest are productive of a new ground for speculative philosophy. This, it would seem, is the only way we can be truly faithful to their project and potentially discover a new absolute foundation for a new metaphysics and ethics that can successfully escape the vicissitudes and frailties of other post-Kantian philosophies. To this end, it will be our goal in the following chapter to survey some of the conclusions of the mathematical sciences over the last 250 years in order to see whether any actual absolute can be discovered in the material structure of reality itself from which we might develop a new metaphysics and ethics. As we will discover there, what the complete mathematization of nature effected by the sciences has in fact shown, in contradistinction to both Meillassoux's "hyper-chaos" and Badiou's "primal void," is the demonstrable fact that nature does appear to be guided by a few definite, absolute, unchanging, and unchangeable ontological structures and material laws. If we are to follow the advice of speculative realism and discover through the mathematization of nature some new absolute foundation for philosophy's pursuit of a rational final truth, practical universal moral value, and actionable ultimate meaning to reality, then we must learn what these absolute structures and laws are.

4

The Science of Entropic Absolutes

The (Dis)Order of Nature

The Vacuity of Speculative Ethics

What we gain from speculative materialism is a new method by which contemporary philosophers might discover a new absolute ground for their claims concerning the nature of reality, metaphysical truths of existence, and the moral value of being, if not the final and ultimate meaning of it all, without betraying the limits of Kant's critique by resurrecting any form of dogmatism through the assertion of claims which can only be testified to in fidelity or maintained through hope. What figures like Meillassoux, Badiou, and Ladyman and Ross show is that through a speculative extension of the mathematization of nature as accomplished in the contemporary sciences, we can discover a route to what they think of as the "great outdoors" of absolute reality—which is nothing less than Kant's noumenal *Ding-an-sich*. In this way, they argue, philosophers might develop anew an ethics which is absolutely grounded upon a universal truth that is not reducible to any singular locality or particular way of being, nor requires any leap of faith into some transcendent metaphysical truth. Through a speculatively grounded ethics of this sort, they suggest, contemporary philosophers should not only be able to escape the correlationist loop which has mired post-Kantian philosophy since the publication of the critique, but they should be able to reclaim the trajectory and aim of their own history and in this way restore their relevance and value to the world at large.

Unfortunately, however, as we saw in the last chapter, every attempt to accomplish this task thus far has failed in one way or another. Indeed, as we saw there, however unintentionally, both Meillassoux and Badiou's normative systems inevitably revert into precisely the kind of nihilistic quietism or dogmatic fideism which they both strive to overcome in post-Kantian philosophy. From this, we concluded that while there may be some validity to the route they chart for philosophy to escape the straits of post-critical reasoning, neither Meillassoux nor Badiou are actually effective at navigating this route themselves. This failure, as we saw, was due to a larger failure in each of their projects; namely, the failure to follow their own advice properly and draw from the complete mathematization of nature (as effected in the contemporary sciences) in order to discover a new metaphysical absolute upon which philosophy might ground an account of ultimate truth, universal moral value, and final meaning. Indeed, as we saw there, and will see in more detail shortly, rather than attending to the actual products of the sciences they purport to respect so dearly, each thinker tends to focus instead on the formal methods of the sciences. In other words, rather than attempting to discover a new absolute ground for philosophical speculation within the actual conclusions of the mathematical sciences, each thinker attempts to extract some absolute from the procedural constraints of those sciences. As a result, each misses the actual absolutes which might appear within those sciences, and favor instead an abstracted account of the absolutization of the idea of science itself.

Indeed, one thing becomes immediately clear from a close reading of Meillassoux and Badiou; namely, that inasmuch as they tout their respect for and champion the work of contemporary mathematics and science, neither one of them engages with the actual products of those fields in any sustained way. Indeed, both thinkers spend much more time engaging the methods, procedures, and discursive forms of the sciences and mathematics than they do examining their actual output, results, or verdicts. In this regard, their work appears to tarry more with the *formal idea* of science and mathematics than with their *actual content,* as at least Badiou himself seems to admit.[1] This tendency to engage exclusively with the abstract power of mathematics and science rather than with the concrete data produced through that power is probably the unintended consequence of what excites both of them in the nature of mathematical speculation: its capacity to abstract from any particular set of data some universal form.

As we saw in more detail in the last chapter, according to both Meillassoux and Badiou, it is this capacity to speculatively escape the specifics of any particular framework in order to conceptualize reality in a more absolute and abstract form, which they claim is the critical power of mathematics—that power which both argue that philosophers must learn from. It should be no surprise, then, that by emphasizing this abstractive power, Meillassoux and Badiou at times overlook the specific and concrete products of the mathematical sciences—their capacity to create *actual knowledge* and reach *determinate conclusions* regarding the nature of existence. But *this* is, in the end, the real power of the contemporary sciences: their capacity to produce concrete claims concerning the nature of reality. Their use of mathematical abstraction is nothing more, ultimately, than a means to this end. For the contemporary sciences themselves, the value of mathematical abstraction lies exclusively and entirely in what it accomplishes; namely, an accurate and practical picture of the nature and structure of that which *is* in its absolute form. In this regard, the abstractive power of mathematics is like a finger pointing to the great beyond of reality itself. To focus on the abstractive power of mathematics in the way that both Meillassoux and Badiou do is to become distracted by the finger and to miss all of the heavenly glory that it indicates.

This tendency to focus on the abstractive power of the mathematical sciences over and against their actual conclusions explains, at least in part, the failure of the ethical systems of both Meillassoux and Badiou. For, as we saw in the last chapter, both of these systems draw more from the *idea* of the kinds of absolutes which are possibilized in the *form* of the mathematical sciences than from the *actual* material absolutes which are achieved in the *products* of those sciences. Inasmuch as they remain at the level of the idea of abstraction alone, both Meillassoux and Badiou's ethics are destined to fail—for, each repeats in its own way a problem which is essential to post-Kantian ethical thought, as we saw in chapter 1. As a result, neither thinker is capable of reaching any concrete conclusions regarding a truly *universal* and *practical* ethical claim. Instead, they merely repeat one of the problems which exists in the corpus of post-Kantian metaphysics and ethics. What their respective versions of the absolutization of the pure ideal of the sciences—rather than the actual material truths ascertained by them—ensures is that their projects suffer the same fate of every other post-Kantian system; namely, to ultimately collapse into some form of relativized nihilism, impotent quietism, or dogmatic fideism. By refusing to engage with the actual material products of the mathematical sciences, then, Meillassoux and Badiou's speculative projects are destined to remain within the limits of the Kantian system which they rightly note we must move beyond if we are to rescue philosophy from its tragic past.

What's more, by focusing their attention on the means of the mathematical sciences rather than their products, both Meillassoux and Badiou inadvertently betray the ultimate aim and intent of those sciences, which is not merely to describe a route to some form of absolute knowledge and truth, but to traverse that route and achieve and describe the absolutes that are discoverable at its end. Without engaging in any sustained way with the actual products of the mathematical sciences, then, Meillassoux and Badiou's praise for the sciences rings hollow, and appears to be little more than an exercise in empty encomium and pure rhetoric—a kind of poetic epideictic to the sciences as symbol, rather than an engagement with their products as a substantive demonstration of their power to discover the truth.[2]

Badiou for one seems to confess as much, admitting that he has faced "the mathematician's condemnation" for "borrow[ing] metaphorically from his vocabulary."[3] But perhaps this condemnation is deserved, for by dwelling exclusively on the discourse of mathematics and its language and forgetting, as a result, its content and concepts, Badiou appears to ignore not only the true aim of the mathematical sciences, but the very foundation of their claim to truth: the practical value of their actual products. By focusing on the mathematical sciences' discursive methods and languages rather than on the actual content and conclusions it has achieved, Meillassoux and Badiou not only betray the spirit of those sciences they claim to respect, they also betray the aim of their own account of the history of philosophy and the alleged method of their speculative projects; namely, to rely on the sciences to achieve some new, actual, absolute foundation for normative claims.[4]

We must remember, according to Meillassoux, that it is allegedly "by way of mathematics that we finally succeed in thinking that which, through its power and beauty, vanquishes quantities and sounds the end of [the] play" of language and poetry which has dominated philosophical discourse since Kant, and achieve thereby some new way to discover within existence some primal and absolute value.[5] Similarly, as we saw, Badiou continually praises mathematics' power to "interrupt . . . the poem" and "open . . . up the infinite possibility of an ontological text" from which we might draw arguments against the "smug nihilism" of post-Kantian philosophy.[6] Nevertheless, both thinkers appear to remain firmly entrenched within precisely such a metaphoric language game by failing to take seriously the products of the mathematical sciences over and beyond their discursive methods. It is only natural, then, that the normative systems these thinkers conceive of as a means of escaping the problems of post-Kantian philosophy ultimately succumb to precisely the problems they claim to evade.

If we are to successfully escape these dangers ourselves and travel the route to the absolute which speculative realism charts, then we must attempt to take seriously the actual products of the mathematical sciences by tying ourselves to the mast of the concrete data of their conclusions and not merely play within the abstractive means by which they achieve them. If we are to develop a functional post-Kantian ethics by speculatively exploring the moral significance of the material absolutes discoverable by the mathematical sciences, then we must first try to understand what concrete and actual absolutes have been posited by those sciences in the 250 years since the publication of Kant's critique. Only by attending to and genuinely engaging with the absolute laws of nature which have been discovered by the sciences can we hope to complete Meillassoux and Badiou's speculative project and escape the insular limits of a humanistic conception of the universe in order to speak meaningfully once more of the nature of absolute reality, universal moral value, and ultimate meaning and truth. Only in this way can we hope to develop an absolutely grounded normative system which might escape the dialectical antinomies of post-Kantian philosophy and reinaugurate philosophy's relevance to the world. To this end, we must endeavor to understand the actual absolutes which have been discovered by the contemporary mathematical sciences.

In Pursuit of a Material Absolute

We might initially consider biology, a field aimed at understanding and accounting for the order and structure of life, as the natural domain in which to begin this project. After all, it is there, we might think, that we are most likely to discover a unifying material principle which might establish some new, absolutely justified normative system capable of evaluating and regulating the activities of our lives. And indeed, the biological sciences have been consistently invoked throughout the history of modern philosophy to this end: to justify the nature of our moral sentiments, explain their origin, and thereby provide an apparently material guide for our ethical actions and duties. Thus, whether identified as the means to discovering some "natural law," as in the work of Aristotle and Thomas Aquinas, or as the mode by which we might understand the origin of our moral intuitions, as in Charles Darwin's *Descent of Man*, Dale Peterson's *The Moral Lives of Animals*, or Frans de Waal's *Primates and Philosophers: How Morality Evolved*, the biological sciences are a natural starting place for philosophers to pursue a possible link between the structures of material reality and the content of ethical responsibility. After all, we tend to think, there is something unusual and exceptional about the nature of living organisms, something which distinguishes them from other kinds of material entities and subjects them to the possibility of moral evaluation in ways that entirely passive and inanimate entities are not. Whatever this presumed *"elan vital"* might be, we tend to think that it grants to biological organisms a will, telos, value, and potentially even a purpose which other material objects simply do not have. As such, even when we think of living things as wholly material, we tend to think that they are special and unique, and not reducible to the laws which govern other purely material objects; or at the very least, make them subject to an additional set of laws and moral responsibilities that do not apply to other purely material things. Perhaps this explains the long-standing tendency of philosophers to turn first to the biological sciences to discover a material foundation for their pursuits.

The eminent physicist Erwin Schrödinger expressed the presupposition that seems to support this tendency beautifully: "living matter, while not eluding the 'laws of physics' as established up to date, is likely to involve 'other laws of physics' hitherto unknown."[7] These laws, he suggests, probably free biological organisms from the exclusive rule of determinate necessity which governs the world of simple material objects, and subject them to other kinds of laws like moral concern, ethical duty, and perhaps even the imperative to feel for, or even love one another. So it is that we tend to divide the natural world into two: one side, on which we slot all nonliving objects, and which we think of as entirely reducible to the principles and laws discovered and described by chemistry and physics; and another side, which we think of as consisting of living things of different levels of complexity, each operating according to its own set of principles and rules, and which we assume are not reducible to the laws of chemistry and physics alone, thus granting them some level of teleonomic meaning and moral potency.[8] And so those of us who are inclined to pursue a material foundation for philosophical questions most readily turn to biology, as the domain which studies this "other world," in order to discover a foundation for their claims.

The problem, however, is that this long standing quasi-dualistic division between organic and inorganic reality, a division which has been repeated throughout the history of the West and is still blithely maintained by the vast majority of philosophers today, is widely rejected in contemporary biology.[9] Indeed, the consensus of nearly every contemporary biologist is that there is no real or meaningful distinction between the organic and inorganic realms. As the contemporary physicist Sean Carroll put it, "at a fundamental level, there aren't separate 'living things' and 'non-living things,' 'things here on Earth' and 'things up in the sky,' 'matter' and 'spirit.' There is just the basic stuff of reality, appearing to us in many different forms."[10] This unity of material reality which integrates organic and inorganic objects is summed up nicely by Nick Lane, a leading biologist at University College London and author of *The Vital Question: Energy, Evolution, and the Origins of Complex Life*. By Lane's account "there is a continuum between non-living and living, and it is pointless to try to draw a line across it."[11] In point of fact, a significant share of biological research conducted over the past fifty years, as famously documented in Lynn Margulis and Dorion Sagan's classic *What Is Life?* has been dedicated precisely to mapping the continuum which exists between organic beings to inorganic objects with the aim of overturning the classical prejudice which has divided reality into two distinct realms.[12] To this end, Margulis and Sagan meticulously detail how organic life first emerged from inorganic matter, taking special care not only to show how every law which governs the realm of chemical exchanges is taken up and maintained in biological organisms, but how those same invariant laws which govern inorganic systems enable the development of and fundamentally structure the kinds of organic processes which define the nature and function of life. As a result of their work, it is now possible to show concretely and indisputably how every law which governs the operation of biological entities, potentially up to and including the expression of their moral sentiments, can be traced back to some more basic chemical law which governs the exchange of energy at the inorganic level.[13]

Drawing from and expanding this research, the contemporary biochemist Addy Pross has concluded that "there is no *elan vital*" which distinguishes living organisms from nonliving matter.[14] On the contrary, Pross assures us, "living things are made up of the same 'dead' molecules as non-living ones."[15] As such, Pross concludes, if we are to understand the basic function and apparent teleonomy of living organisms properly, then it is essential that we not only move beyond the false dualism which drives our tendency to turn first to biology to understand ourselves, but that we turn instead to the realm of inorganic chemistry to understand the nature and order of life. According to Pross, "[through] a newly defined area of chemistry, termed by Günter von Kiedrowski 'Systems Chemistry,' the existing chasm separating chemistry and biology can now be bridged, [such] that the central biological paradigm, Darwinism, is just the biological manifestation of a broader physiochemical description of natural forces."[16] "From a theoretical point of view," Nick Lane therefore concludes, "life is no mystery [and] it doesn't contravene any laws of nature."[17] Instead, as Pross shows and what areas of research like systems chemistry demonstrate is "that Darwinian theory, that quintessential biological principle, can be incorporated into a more general chemical theory of evolution, one that encompasses both living and non-living systems."[18]

We might justifiably reason from this that though any absolute law or truth which we might discover in our survey of the content and conclusions of the contemporary sciences must have some biological application and some import for the organic realm, it is not ultimately rooted in, original to, or exclusive to that domain. Instead, it will stem from the domain of chemistry. In this regard, rather than pursuing the absolutes we seek within biology, we may turn instead to the realm of chemistry. After all, as the Nobel prize-winning biologist (and eventual eugenicist, racist, and sexist) Francis Crick wrote: "all living things use the same four-letter language to carry genetic information. All use the same twenty-four letter language to construct their proteins, the machine tools of the living cell. [And] all use the same chemical dictionary to translate from one language to the other."[19] For these reasons, Crick concludes that "[a] living cell can be thought of as [little more than] a fairly complex, well-organized chemical factory."[20] So it is to chemistry and not biology that we might naturally turn to in our pursuit of some fundamental and absolute organizing law or structure upon which we might ground our speculative project.

But we must remember, the laws which govern the chemical exchange of energy and therefore structure the nature of the lives which emerge through them are not themselves original or exclusive to the realm of chemistry alone. Instead, they originate within and obey a higher order of necessity, one which is pursued within the domain of physics. Hence the Nobel prize-winning physicist Richard Feynman's conclusion that "the deepest part of theoretical chemistry must end up in quantum mechanics."[21] Indeed, for precisely these reasons, the contemporary biochemist Charles Cockell has argued in his landmark piece "The Laws of Life" that "life [itself] must be fashioned by the laws of physics."[22] Or, in the inimitable words of Feynman, "everything that living things do can be understood in terms of the jiggling and wiggling of atoms."[23] For this reason, many contemporary biochemists have turned in the last thirty years to physics in general, and quantum physics in particular, to discover the grounding principles which give rise to the processes they observe in their respective fields.

This transition in contemporary biochemistry to quantum mechanics has in fact given birth to a new subdiscipline called "quantum biology." Roughly defined, quantum biology is a field which attempts to understand and document the underlying laws of physics that govern the biochemical exchanges which define the nature of life. Johnjoe McFadden and Jim Al-Khalili, two of the pioneers of quantum biology, identify the axiomatic principle of the discipline thus: "Life," they write, "depends on quantum mechanics."[24] They maintain that it is only through a proper understanding of quantum physics that we can hope to understand the chemical foundation for life and explain the complex and unusual order of biological principles emergent from it, including its sense of teleonomic purpose and perhaps even moral sensibility. In the end, then, it is not to chemistry that we must turn in order to discover some absolute material principle upon which to found anew the classical pursuits of philosophy, but physics.

Of course, it has been a principal aim of theoretical physicists in the twentieth and twenty-first centuries to discover some grand unifying theory of existence which could reconcile the apparent conflict which seems to exist between the operation of matter at the macro level and its operation at the micro level. This pursuit is famously typified in the ongoing attempt to bridge the apparent divide which seems to separate the laws of general relativity, which govern the movement of larger bodies with absolute predictability, from the apparently chaotic dynamics of quantum bodies on the subatomic scale. And, as is well known, despite the great progress which has been made in advancing our knowledge of how matter operates at both levels, the discovery of some grand unified theory still eludes physicists today, though some progress has been made to this end in recent years.[25] Still, at this point there remains no immediately obvious way of reconciling these two systems into a single coherent theory, or explaining why the governing principles of motion at work at the subatomic quantum level apparently shift when they are aggregated to achieve an atomic scale.

While we do not currently have a reasonable explanation for this apparent disjunction, there is nevertheless nearly universal agreement among physicists today that however this apparent gap might eventually be bridged, it will not require a radical revision of the laws of physics which we have discovered to govern each of these realms independently. On the contrary, most physicists agree that their long sought-after grand unifying theory will eventually unite these two realms by exposing the more primal ground and conditions of every physical law currently agreed upon. Thus, while a full understanding of these underlying grounds and conditions is still out of our reach, and, as a result, a grand unifying system of physical matter is not yet in hand, most physicists agree that the laws of nature which govern the subatomic and atomic realms respectively, as we understand them today, are not only accurate, stable, and inviolable, they are moreover absolute. As a result, while physicists do not yet have a complete picture of the whole, they know enough of the fundamental operating principles of matter that we can expect to discover through their research any number of absolute, universal, and unchanging axiomatic grounds upon which we might mount the speculative project of philosophy anew.

Indeed, a number of such principles and grounds are not only currently at work in our contemporary models of the universe, they are routinely drawn upon to explain the operation of matter at every level. These absolute principles are in fact so universally accepted in the contemporary sciences that Frank Wilczek, a Nobel laureate in physics, has suggested that we could even treat them as a set of "fundamentals," not unlike those which populated the dogmatic principles of classical philosophy, though they have been derived, of course, from empirical observation and mathematical speculation, and not faith or tradition.[26] The status of the principles is due, he argues, to the enormous progress which has been made over the last fifty years in physics to prove that there are a few laws and structures which appear to govern the operation of material reality at every level, whether subatomic, atomic, chemical, or biological. So it is from within these principles that we are most likely to discover a new, nondogmatic absolute upon which we might found anew our pursuit of final truth, universal moral value, and ultimate meaning. Among the various universal and absolute principles which have been identified, none are more essential to and inextricable from the contemporary scientific account of reality than the laws of thermodynamics.[27]

Thermodynamics—the Underlying Mathematical Laws of the Universe

The formal study of the movement and exchange of energy as heat has been around since as early as the eighteenth century, when it was first developed to improve the efficiency of steam engines. But it wasn't until the early nineteenth century, when Nicolas Léonard Sadi Carnot, the "father of thermodynamics," defined the first of the underlying laws which govern the flow of heat (now counted as the second law of thermodynamics), that thermodynamics was formally established as a field of study and a more systematic account of energy exchange was developed. Thereafter, as a result of the work of J. Willard Gibbs, James Clerk Maxwell, and eventually, and most famously, Ludwig Boltzmann, the statistical methods necessary to measure heat exchange in both open and closed systems were clarified, and the formal laws of thermodynamics were defined and became what they are today. The field since then has progressed to the point that in recent years it is relied upon in nearly every scientific discipline to explain the nature of the transformation and operation of energy in and between its various forms, whether mechanical, acoustic, thermal, chemical, electrical, nuclear, or electromagnetic/radiant.[28] As a result, the laws of thermodynamics are used today to explain everything from the formation and eventual dissolution of stars, galaxies, and the universe as a whole to the emergence and evolution of life, not to mention its basic functions and even its eventual fate.[29]

Given the nearly universal application and use of the laws of thermodynamics in the sciences today, the eminent physicist Carlo Rovelli has proposed that the history of scientific development in the twentieth century can in many ways be recounted as little more than a history of the expansion and application of those laws. "In the course of the twentieth century," he writes, "thermodynamics (that is, the science of heat) and statistical mechanics (that is, the science of the probability of different motions) were extended to [even include] electromagnetics and quantum phenomena."[30] As a result of this extension, he goes on to note, thermodynamic principles have subsequently come to dominate nearly every branch of the material sciences.[31] So it is that the same basic laws which were first identified by Carnot in 1824 to improve the efficiency of steam engines have since come to be seen as the singular regulating principles of "*all* material systems," as Addy Pross puts it.[32] The universality of the laws of thermodynamics in material systems is so complete, in fact, that none other than Albert Einstein once noted that thermodynamics "is the only physical theory of universal content concerning which I am convinced that, within the framework of the applicability of its basic concepts, will never be overthrown."[33] Einstein's confidence in the profound constancy and universal power of thermodynamics was so great that he declared it the "firm and definitive foundation for all physics, indeed for the whole of natural science."[34] It is therefore within the laws of thermodynamics that we are most likely to find a candidate for the kind of absolute material principle upon which we hope to ground our project.

It is interesting to note, however, that these thermodynamic laws, though pioneered within physics, are themselves little more than the application of a statistical tendency within a large assemblage of atoms. In this regard, they are a perfect example of precisely the kind of theoretical mathematics, in particular statistics, which Badiou and Meillassoux think should guide philosophical inquiry. In fact, it is arguable that Ludwig Boltzmann's greatest insight was to see how statistical analysis might be applied to the seemingly random behavior of single atoms in order to perceive regularity in their apparent disorder and derive from it an effective set of descriptive laws which could be used to predict their behavior in aggregate. In this regard his work, which is now seen as an articulation of one of the most fundamental laws of material reality as a whole, is ultimately the product of arithmetics. This is only natural, as Erwin Schrödinger notes, for it is "only in the co-operation of an enormously large number of atoms [that] statistical laws [like the laws of thermodynamics] begin to operate and control [the] behavior of these *assemblées* with an accuracy increasing as the number of atoms involved increases."[35]

It was in fact this recognition which led Schrödinger to conclude that "all the physical and chemical laws that are known to play an important part in the life of organisms are [ultimately] of this statistical kind."[36] Hence the MIT physicist Max Tegmark's conclusion that ultimately the laws of physics are nothing more than expressions of simple mathematical principles extracted from and applied to observable reality. According to Tegmark, then, "our external physical reality is a mathematical structure."[37] From this he argues that we might come to see the very laws of nature as not only a product of material reality itself, but of mathematics—a conclusion which has led him to argue that mathematics is an ideal form and regulative order of material reality.[38] Hence his somewhat controversial conclusion that physics, however theoretical, should be seen less as a branch of the natural sciences than as a form of applied mathematics.

Erwin Schrödinger, for his part, seems to agree with Tegmark on this point, arguing that mathematics and physics are so inextricably bound to one another that any attempt to separate the two is not only impossible, it is meaningless—not unlike trying to separate water from its composite parts, hydrogen and oxygen. Indeed, according to Schrödinger, "an orderly and lawful behavior according to statistical physics [which is to say mathematics] *means* according to physics."[39] So it would seem that "the universe," as Graham Farmelo puts it, not only "speaks in numbers," but can in fact only be understood in and through numbers.[40] It makes sense, then, why Meillassoux and Badiou both suggest that philosophy must model itself on the mathematization of nature which they see at work in the material sciences if it is to discover an account of reality which can be declared absolute in any form.

Still, as we noted in our conclusion to the last chapter, we must be careful here to distinguish between the operation of mathematics as the *method* through which the nature of material reality is described and the actual *content* of that description. After all, while the universe may "*speak* in numbers," as Farmelo put it, very few physicists would go so far as to suggest that it is *composed* of numbers. Thus, though its structure can be modeled mathematically, as the preponderance of physicists agree, it is in fact composed of material energy in a variety of forms. We must be careful, in other words, to guard against confusing the signifier (mathematics) with the signified (matter). To conflate or equivocate between these two, as both Badiou and Meillassoux seem to do, would be to confuse the ideal reflection of an object with the actual object in-itself. Meillassoux and Badiou's failure to maintain this distinction is precisely what leads not only to their difference with one another, but to the collapse of their respective systems. Both thinkers offer, in lieu of an absolute extracted from the actual objects of the mathematical sciences themselves, an account of an absolute which is extracted from the idealization of the way in which those objects are achieved. Hence, for example, Meillassoux's insistence on the contingency of reality, a contingency which for him is based on the nature of mathematical speculation, rather than on the conclusions scientists have reached about the actual nature of the material universe itself—laws which are, as we will see shortly, anything but contingent. Thus, while we want to affirm with Meillassoux and Badiou the epistemological power of mathematics as the method of the material sciences, we must be careful to remember that the value of that power lies exclusively in how it can be used to discover, testify to, accurately describe, and clearly reflect the behavior and operation of physical reality itself. Only by insisting on this distinction can we ensure that we don't repeat the error made by Meillassoux and Badiou and incorrectly assume the perfect interchangeability of the sign for the signified. Only by maintaining this distinction will we be able to prevent ourselves from slipping back into some form of *idealism* (which identifies the absolute principle of reality with the rational operation of mathematics itself) and remain entirely within the realm of the realistically *material*.

The nature of and importance of this distinction is articulated beautifully by Peter Atkins, who writes that "despite all [the] varied applications of mathematics, they are not themselves laws."[41] Indeed, according to Atkins, mathematics "is not the stuff of the fundamental laws of nature, it is [merely] the *formulation* of a complex arrangement of the underlying fundamental physical laws"; it is not the actual arrangement or "substance" of those laws themselves.[42] Thus, while we want to follow the path outlined by Meillassoux and Badiou's advocacy of the power of mathematics as the ultimate epistemological tool in our speculative pursuit of the absolute laws of the universe, we must be careful not to repeat their failure and confuse the rules which govern the use of that *tool* with the rules which govern the *thing-itself*, rules which have been ascertained through the steady application of that tool. For, ultimately, our interest is not in the power or *potential* of the tool, but in the *actual* nature of the reality which can be excavated through its use: the absolute nature of the material universe itself.

Thus, while Meillassoux might think that the laws of the universe are ultimately contingent, since mathematical modeling can be used to demonstrate the possibility of other possible universes, empirical and mathematical physicists alike are united in their agreement that the laws which govern this, and any other possible universe, are anything but contingent; they are in fact unchangeable and inviolable. In fact, they argue, precisely against Meillassoux's insistence that there is no "superior law whereby everything is destined to perish," that there is in fact a superior law by which everything is destined to perish.[43] Indeed, this is precisely the conclusion of the absolute laws of thermodynamics as universally agreed upon by the contemporary mathematical sciences.

What's more, physicists agree, if these laws were changeable, then not only would they have already proven themselves to be so; but it is in fact their immutability which makes existence itself possible in any form, as we will see towards the end of this chapter. In this regard, Meillassoux's insistence on the radical contingency of the laws of physics on the basis of mathematical modeling amounts to a kind of *argumentum ad ignorantiam*. What's more, contemporary physicists are in universal agreement that no matter how else a possible universe may differ from our own, some laws and principles would have to remain absolute and unchangeable across them to even allow for the possibility of existence itself. And, among these principles, they suggest, are the laws which govern thermodynamic exchange. On this point, then, we must vehemently disagree with Meillassoux.

It is entirely understandable, though, how and why Meillassoux might be confused on this point. After all, as we have already noted, physical laws like the laws of thermodynamics are derived from statistical analysis. As such, they are derived exclusively from the aggregate movement of an assemblage of atoms in motion. Examined individually, each atom does indeed appear to operate independently from every other atom, wiggling and jiggling seemingly at random, without any governing order or principle.[44] It might be natural to conclude, then, that there is no universal law governing the operation of each atom and that chaos, chance, and contingency rule all. But when each of these seemingly random movements is examined as a part of a larger system and measured as a whole, their actions take on an absolute regularity and uniform motion that is describable according to the laws of thermodynamics. So, while it may seem that the regularity of atomic motion accounted for in the laws of thermodynamics is not in fact the result of some principle in atomic objects themselves, but is solely the consequence of the calculative system from which this regularity is derived; and it might seem reasonable, therefore, to conclude that the laws which are posited to explain and predict this synthetic regularity are exclusively a product of human reasoning and not representative of reality as it exists in its noumenal form—and therefore that the universe might be entirely unregulated and disordered, unstable and mutable, this is simply not the case. For the regularity which is observable en masse comes, in the end, not from the mathematical model itself, but from the aggregate nature of the atomic objects themselves when understood as inextricable from the material systems in which they appear and in relation to which they operate.

But again, Meillassoux's confusion on this point is entirely understandable. After all, none other than Ludwig Boltzmann himself suggested that the laws of thermodynamics might ultimately rest on little more than "sheer chance."⁴⁵ Indeed, a number of Boltzmann's biographers have speculated that it may have been his consideration of this possibility that led to his increasing depression towards the end of his life as well as his eventual suicide in 1906.⁴⁶ We might imagine him asking: "What is the meaning or purpose of living in a universe where even the most fundamental laws appear contingent and mutable and could shift at any moment?" After all, when abstracted from the actual realities it describes, the mathematizable nature of the universe does indeed seem to suggest a radical contingency in the laws which seem to govern it.

But, again, this is a conclusion which is only justified when we fail to distinguish properly between the mathematical map we use to understand the nature of the universe and the actual physical territory it surveys. For the flow of energy within the whole of a material system is ultimately entirely regular, predictable, and unchanging. Thus, while atomized from that system the building blocks of the universe may "justifiably be called orderless, lawless, unpredictable, and unexplainable," and perhaps even "capricious," as the physicist Joe Rosen has described this possibility; nevertheless, he and his colleagues assure us that even "the inherently orderless universe must possess (approximately) orderly, lawful aspects, which are the order, predictability, and laws we find in nature."⁴⁷ As such, Rosen concludes, while at some *theoretical* singular and isolated level we may want to affirm the apparent randomness of the founding structures of the universe, the *actual* material structure of the whole of reality is entirely constant, consistent, and predictable. Indeed, he writes, the apparent "lawlessness" of the foundation of the laws of the universe is nothing more than the consequence of the structural limitations of human reasoning and the mathematical methods we use to understand the universe, and not a structural reality of the universe itself.⁴⁸ Rosen goes so far as to suggest that behind the apparently random nature of nominal atomic motion there is more likely than not a hidden law which governs and regulates its apparent lawlessness. He even suggests that this "hidden order" is probably one further expression of the laws of thermodynamics operant at the subatomic level.⁴⁹ As such, he concludes that while the foundation of our lawful universe may *appear* lawless when mathematical systems are abstracted from the systematic material contexts in which they appear, ultimately the universe those systems describe as a whole is entirely lawful and entirely obedient to absolute physical laws.

Peter Atkins puts it this way: despite the apparent groundlessness of the laws of our universe, every contemporary scientist ultimately agrees that "the universe is a rational place and that even the origin of the laws it abides by are within the scope of human comprehension."⁵⁰ The absolute inviolability of the laws of the universe which we discover via mathematical analysis must be secured, Atkins suggests, by distinguishing the methods we use to understand the universe from the object of that study: the universe itself. Thus, while the method may suggest some *potential* contingency to the laws of nature, he ultimately concludes that there is nothing within the *actual* operation of those laws which supports this possibility. To the contrary, he goes to great lengths to show that everything which can be deduced from the universe itself attests to the absolute consistency, utter constancy, and complete stability of the natural laws which have been discovered to date. Hence our insistence that while Meillassoux and Badiou are right to identify the power of mathematics as an epistemological method of the sciences' account of the absolute nature of reality, we must break with the conclusions they derive from this fact; namely, that those laws are exclusively the product of mathematics, such that the operation of the material universe itself is seen as ultimately chaotic or void. While the mathematical/statistical methods used to determine the laws of the universe might suggest the *potential* contingency or emptiness of the reality of inviolable laws, there is nothing in the *actual* operation of material reality itself to support this claim. To the contrary, all that can be deduced from what is observed by the sciences and developed through mathematics is the absolute inviolability of the laws of nature, in particular the laws of thermodynamics.

Moreover, as John Bigelow has convincingly argued, all mathematical systems are derived from and find their ultimate ground in the physical reality of the consistent operation of the material universe itself.[51] So, he argues, the conclusions of mathematical analysis must ultimately be understood to conform to what is empirically true of physical reality itself. In this regard, he concludes, the substance and content of the scientific laws which are achievable through the operation and application of mathematics upon the observation of material reality—and not the theoretical contingency at work within the structure of mathematics alone, when it is abstracted and isolated from the physical systems of the world it attempts to model—should be seen as just as necessary as the actual reality from which they are derived.[52] In this regard, Bigelow argues, these laws can be treated as just as certain and absolute as the independent existence of physical reality itself. In this way, he claims, we might extract and deduce from the absolute laws which the mathematical sciences discover as the ruling structure of that reality (i.e., the laws of thermodynamics) a new absolute ground upon which we might develop other philosophical truths, and even perhaps a new account of ultimate meaning and universal moral value. It is to those laws, then, that we must now turn if we are to eventually discover these higher-order truths and discover a new ground for philosophy's classical projects.

The Absolute Law of Existence—Entropy and the Origin and Nature of Reality

At first glance, the content of the three basic laws of thermodynamics is relatively straightforward and easily understood. When those simple laws are applied to diverse systems, however, their meaning and significance becomes extraordinarily profound. The first of these laws, known as the law of the conservation of energy, states that energy, as motion, matter, or heat, can neither be created nor destroyed within a closed system, but can only ever change states within that system. Thus, while the total amount of energy within a system may appear to lessen as matter dissipates, motion slows down, and things cool off, the total amount of energy within that system is in fact always constant, albeit manifest in different forms. It is upon this law that Einstein famously established his equation governing the conversion of matter into energy, and it is upon this same law that we are able to predict the productive power of every heat engine, from the small machines which sputter away within our backyard mowers to the nuclear fusion which blasts away inside the heart of the star at the center of our solar system.

The second and perhaps most famous law of thermodynamics states that statistically, energy flows within any given system in such a way that over time it becomes evenly distributed across that system, moving generally from more organized and concentrated states to less integral and more dissipated ones. This tendency to disorder, known as entropy, means that every closed system tends toward a state of absolute energy equilibrium, where no one thing in the system will possess any more or less energy, whether as motion, matter, heat, and so on, than any other thing in the system. It is this law which physicists use to explain that, in the words of William Butler Yeats, "things fall apart," and that time moves in only one direction: towards disintegration—which is to say, energy distribution.[53] It is this law, moreover, which physicists use to explain the material difference between the past, the present, and future and which gives rise to what we experience as the "arrow of time." In fact, it is upon this law that the operant understanding of temporality itself is established in contemporary physics. As such, it is this law which guarantees that reality proceeds as it does, from one causal step to another; and that, in the words of Stephen Hawking, while we may reasonably expect a cup which has fallen from a table onto the floor to shatter into a number of smaller pieces with the movement of time, we cannot reasonably expect "[to] see broken cups gathering themselves together off the floor and jumping back onto the table" as time progresses.[54] The second law of thermodynamics assures us, to the contrary, that as the entropic disorder of a system increases, everything within that system will likewise "shatter" into increasingly smaller parts until everything in that system is relatively equal in energic size and all disequilibrium has been "destroyed." So it is from the regular governance of the second law of thermodynamics that our very understanding of the order and operation of existence itself emerges.

From this the third law of thermodynamics follows, which states that since entropy must necessarily increase within every closed system in the way outlined by the second law, the only logical end of this perpetual dissipation and collapse is a state in which every existent thing possesses the lowest total amount of complex energy possible, a state known as "absolute zero," and no further energy exchange or distribution is possible or necessary to achieve equilibrium. The ultimate expression of this state is a system in which there are no complex forms of energy at all, like material objects in motion, but instead only a low-level background radiation evenly distributed across a system. It is this law which enables us to know with absolute certainty that while energy can neither be created nor destroyed, in keeping with the first law of thermodynamics, it can nevertheless "burn out," as it were, and reach a state in which it has no effective mechanical power, demonstrate motion or change, or contain within itself the potential for any objective existence as we understand it.

Armed with these three basic laws, contemporary scientists have been able to speculatively construct a nearly complete picture of our universe and explain the origin, operation, and end of almost everything observable within it today, from the initial rapid expansion of the cosmos roughly 13.7 billion years ago, as testified to by the cosmic background radiation which fills all space; to the advent and evolution of life on our own planet around 3.5 billion years ago, as testified to in fossil matter; to the eventual explosion of the star around which our planet revolves in approximately 5 billion more years, an event which will eradicate any life still left upon our planet and erase with it any evidence that life ever existed there in the first place. The laws of thermodynamics have enabled astrophysicists to estimate the age of the cosmos and explain the nature of its sudden appearance and expansion—from an extremely dense, hot, and low entropic point in time/space to the ever-expanding and cooling state in which it exists today. The same laws enable them to account for the formation of all of the relatively less entropic material objects we find in the cosmos, like galaxies, nebulae, black holes, quasars, stars, planets, moons, meteors, asteroids, and even we ourselves. Not only can astrophysicists use the laws of thermodynamics to explain the accretion, nature, and celestial movement of such objects, they can even use them to predict their relative distribution within the universe, as well as the eventual collapse of all these things into relatively simpler energetic forms—all this using the same basic statistical models that Boltzmann pioneered in the nineteenth century to establish the constancy of heat dissipation across any given system.

Indeed, as have already seen in brief, it is from these same laws that the very understanding of the nature and operation of *time* itself, in which this expansion, distribution, and collapse will occur, is established. Hence Sean Carroll's conclusion that, ultimately, the "property of entropy is responsible for *all* of the difference between past and future that we know about. Memory, aging, cause and effect—all can be traced to the second law of thermodynamics and in particular to the fact that entropy used to be low in the past."[55] And it is from this same law that anything and everything that has, will, and can even *potentially happen* can be accounted for as an expression of the arrow and operation of time, as that wherein the very concept of *happening* itself occurs.

On a much smaller scale, Erwin Schrödinger has shown that it is the laws of thermodynamics which might govern, ground, and structure even the seemingly random nature of quantum systems.[56] His groundbreaking work to this end has developed more recently into one of the most dynamic areas of contemporary physics, "quantum thermodynamics," which was first pioneered by John von Neumann in his 1932 classic *Mathematical Foundations of Quantum Mechanics.*[57] There, von Neumann proposed a new model of entropic decay which was better equipped to predict quantum motion than Boltzmann's original atomic model. As a result of this work, most contemporary physicists agree that it will be through our increased understanding of the operation of thermodynamic principles at the subatomic level that the ultimate ground and condition for quantum laws and phenomena will eventually be explainable within the existing laws operant at the atomic level, and the long-sought "grand unified theory" of reality might eventually be discovered.[58] So it is to the laws of thermodynamics that most contemporary theoretical physicists turn in their efforts to discover and account for the founding principles which govern the order and operation of the entirety of material reality. In this way, from their relatively humble beginnings in applied mechanical physics, the laws of thermodynamics have steadily come to pervade and reign in nearly every field of contemporary physics, from the most practical to the most theoretical.

Within chemistry, through the innovative application of Willard Gibbs's analysis of the movement of energy in thermodynamic systems, Gilbert N. Lewis, Merle Randall, and eventually E. A. Guggenheim were able to determine and define the total set of laws which govern chemical reactions, laws which are still used and taught in chemistry labs across the globe today.[59] Even more famously, Marie Skłodowska-Curie used the laws of thermodynamics to identify and define the principles which give rise to radioactive decay in chemical structures and further showed how those laws allow us to predict with absolute certainty the slow dissolution and transformation of chemical elements into more basic elementary components through a process which could be described as a kind of entropic alchemy. And it is these same principles which were subsequently used to explain the emergence of every existent chemical compound and substance in the first few moments of our universe, as well as to predict their eventual dissolution into pure heat energy at the distant end of time.

Nowhere has the explanatory power of the laws of thermodynamics been more controversial and impactful, however, than in biology, where they have been increasingly relied upon in recent years to explain the basic nature and function of living organisms, as well as their initial development from inorganic matter and subsequent evolution into more complex forms. Such an application was first suggested by Erwin Schrödinger in his 1944 lectures *What Is Life*; but it was through the detailed lab work of Jacques Monod and others that the role of thermodynamic exchange in the evolution of living DNA self-replicators from mechanical RNA engines, and from that the explosion of complex life in its entirety, was clarified; and from that point on the application of thermodynamics truly flourished in the biological sciences.[60] As a result, thermodynamic principles are today the bedrock of every accepted scientific account of the nature, operation, and evolution of life.[61] Indeed, contemporary biologists are increasingly convinced that life is best understood as nothing more than a consequence of thermodynamic principles in certain conditions. For this reason, the biochemist Nick Lane has even gone so far as to define life as nothing more than a highly complex "dissipative structure," one which is, in the end, little more than "the visible product of sustained far-from-equilibrium conditions."[62]

Read through the lens of the laws of thermodynamics, most contemporary biologists agree that not only does complex life appear to be an effect of the dissipation of energy across a system; but, moreover, that all living things are ultimately best understood as highly complex and efficient agents of entropy—little more than an effective way in which energy can be broken down into its simplest structures and evenly dissipated and distributed across the cosmos. As the biophysicist Peter Hoffmann explains, "living systems are 'dissipative systems' because they continuously dissipate free energy into high-entropy energy."[63] This basic insight has inspired another contemporary biophysicist, Jeremy England, to model in his lab precisely how the dissipation of heat across a system in accordance with the second law of thermodynamics might lead to the self-organization of atoms into the kinds of structures necessary for the development of life, and to show definitively how the laws of thermodynamics can therefore be used to explain the evolution of life into more complex forms.[64] This work has led England to conclude that ultimately the only satisfactory explanation for the "why" of life is that it is the "aim" or teleonomic function of all life to aid entropy. Life, England argues, is little more than a kind of dissipation machine which uses its complexity to destroy other complex energetic forms by breaking them down, through consumption and metabolization, into simpler forms that can be more quickly dissipated and distributed across the system. In this regard, he concludes, life is nothing more than a product of and aid to the eventual dissolution of matter into heat and, through this, the eventual collapse and destruction of the universe as it currently exists in its steady march toward absolute zero.

As England puts it, "many of the properties of living things might be explainable as 'dissipative structures' that arise from a general thermodynamic tendency to reduce the rate of entropy production."[65] "Thus," he concludes, "the empirical biological fact that reproductive fitness is intimately linked to efficient metabolism now has a clear and simple basis in physics."[66] "Such a process," he writes, "must invariably be fueled by the production of entropy." Hence Sean Carroll's assessment that the "purpose" of life, from a material and scientific perspective in keeping with the application of the laws of thermodynamics, might, in the end, be nothing more than the conversion of matter to energy in the service of its dissolution and dissipation across a system. Indeed, he notes, the ultimate "purpose of life" might be summed up in a single word: *metabolism*, "essentially 'burning fuel.'"[67] This makes sense, he concludes, given the simple fact that living organisms, "like no other chemical reactions or combinations thereof, proceed by converting free energy into disordered energy."[68] Or, as Nick Lane, puts it, "life is not much like a candle; more like a rocket launcher."[69] Jeremy England has suggested that in fact there appear to be few agents of entropy which are more effective to this end than living organisms, few things that are as efficient as we are at transforming energy from a low entropic state, like matter, into a relatively higher entropic state, like heat, in such a way that it can be more quickly and evenly distributed across a system.

So it is through an application of the laws of thermodynamics in biology that we have finally discovered that life does not in the end violate or work against the laws which govern the inorganic physical universe, nor does it operate in obedience to what Erwin Schrödinger thought must be some other, higher set of laws. Life is not, in other, more poetic words, "a struggle against entropy," as Vaclav Havel put it.[70] On the contrary, everything that life is and does is perfectly explained according to the same basic principles which were first identified by Carnot, Gibbs, and Boltzmann as governing the order, operation, and efficiency of steam engines. Like them and every other heat engine which can exist, life is driven by the exchange of energy in absolute obedience to the laws of thermodynamics which necessitate the even distribution of energy across a system and between objects within that system. In this regard, life, in the end, is little more than an agent of entropy working alongside other existents toward the eventual end of everything—the absolute zero state to come. So it is that Peter Hoffmann concludes that "life does not exist despite the second law of thermodynamics; instead, life has evolved to take full advantage of the second law whenever it can."[71] Or, as Sean Carroll has it, "complex structures can form, not despite the growth of entropy but *because* entropy is growing. Living organisms can maintain their structural integrity not despite the second law but because of it."[72]

The Ultimate and Absolute End—Entropy and the Certainty of Annihilation

It is clear from this that the laws of thermodynamics are not only absolute and inviolable, but that they also explain everything which exists in our universe, from its origins to the emergence and operation of life within it. Indeed, the speculative power of the laws of thermodynamics is so great that they not only allow us to look backwards into our deepest past to explain the emergence of existing structures, but to look forward in time as well, to the ultimate and eventual end of every existent structure. Indeed, through the systematic application of the second law of thermodynamics, contemporary scientists can predict with a high degree of probability the eventual end of not only every living thing, but the very universe they inhabit too, all in accordance with the same entropic principles which can be used to explain the emergence of everything at the dawn of time and the operation of the living organisms therein in the meantime.

Within biology, of course, this end is already well known. All living things must die. This simple fact is an inherent and inexorable element of material life, structured and determined as it is by the second law of thermodynamics. Despite our best efforts and all of the ingenuity of modern science, death inevitably awaits every living thing. It is in fact this constant decay within and around us which is the very condition for the possibility of life, as we have already seen. What's more, it is this same constant decay which defines the nature of our growth and perpetuation in the meantime, fueling as it does our need to eat and work. So it is that the perpetual entropic decay which will eventually result in our complete collapse drives not only the final conclusion of life, it motivates its secret heart and ultimate essence as well. In this regard, entropic decay could in many ways be counted as the very cause, motivation, defining structure, and eventual end of all that we are and do. Thus, while we may hope, and perhaps even strive to delay the eventual arrival of our final end through diet, exercise, and the machinations of medicine, we must come to terms with the absolutely inescapable and assured fact that we will perpetually lose ground to the steady march of entropic decay, disintegration, and dissolution within us by the very nature of our existence, and indeed the very nature of existence and time themselves as thermodynamic consequents. As such, we can know with absolute certainty that our ultimate demise must eventually come; indeed, it is always already coming, despite our every attempt to keep it at bay. From the perspectives of the material sciences, this perpetual death is, as we have seen, integral to the very nature and definition of life as such. All of this is well understood and completely explainable according to the laws of thermodynamics. What is less known, however, is how much the second law of thermodynamics enables us to understand the nature, operation, and perhaps even the purpose of life in the meantime. Indeed, as we have just seen, every beat of our heart and pull of our lungs increases the effective dissipation of energy across our universe. In this regard, even the most complex life form is, from the perspective of the material sciences, little more than an incredibly efficient entropic engine. So it is that the second law of thermodynamics can be used to circumscribe the whole of our existence, from beginning to end, top to bottom, order to operation, aim to accomplishment.

Within chemistry, as we have already seen, the second law of thermodynamics can be used to explain the origin and formation of elementary particles in their current stable chemical structures and the conditions for the possibility of the construction of more complex compounds. It can also be used, however, to predict the eventual collapse of every such compound and element into its simplest energetic form, a process which will eventually result in nothing more than a homogeneous soup of elementary particles and low-level radioactivity. In fact, by measuring the extremely low-level radioactive output of even the most stable elements, chemists can speculatively predict the eventual entropic collapse of the entirety of chemical matter itself, and from this the eventual conclusion of chemical activity in a distant future, a time they refer to as the cosmological "dark era."[73] "In this bleak epoch," the astrophysicists Fred Adams and Greg Laughlin write, "the universe [will be] composed only

CHAPTER 4

of the smallest types of elementary particles and radiation of extremely low energy and long wavelengths. Protons [will] have long since decayed and no ordinary baryonic matter [will] remain."[74] So it is in accordance with the second law of thermodynamics in inorganic matter that chemists can predict that "in the far future, the universe [will] contain no complex structures," for "all conventional composite entities [will] have decayed away."[75] In that distant future, the cosmologist Lawrence Krauss notes, "matter will disappear, and the universe will approach a state of maximum simplicity and symmetry."[76]

This same process is what allows contemporary astrophysicists to predict the eventual end of the cosmos.[77] As the theoretical physicist Alan Lightman puts it, as a result of the entropic directionality assured by the second law of thermodynamics, physicists today know with absolute certainty that "the universe is relentlessly wearing down, falling apart, [and] driving itself toward a condition of maximum disorder."[78] As such, they can predict, in the words of the science reporter Philip Ball, that "eventually all the universe will be reduced to a uniform, boring jumble: a state of equilibrium, wherein entropy is maximized and nothing meaningful will ever happen again."[79] There is, of course, still robust debate among physicists about exactly *how* and *when* this eventual collapse will occur. The various positions in this debate hinge on whether the universe should be interpreted as an open or closed thermodynamic system, a distinction which depends in turn on whether the universe is still expanding at a constant rate or whether its expansion is slowing down and, if so, why, how, and what will happen once that expansion ends. In fact, in recent years a virtual cottage industry has cropped up in physics predicting which of these apocalyptic ends awaits our universe. However this debate will eventually be settled, though, nearly every contemporary physicist is in complete agreement that its end will eventually come in accordance with the laws of thermodynamics. Thus, while some cosmologists, like Lawrence Krauss and Glenn Starkman, argue for what has been called the eventual "heat death" of the universe on the basis of the "most recent cosmological observations," which, they argue, "suggest that [the] universe will continue to expand forever," other cosmologists, like Steven Frautschi, conclude the opposite, arguing that "heat death" will not occur and that a "big freeze" is more likely, a condition in which the "universe [will] 'die' . . . in the sense that the entropy in a co-moving volume asymptotically approaches a constant limit."[80] Whatever the actual case may be, all parties are nevertheless in complete agreement that the cosmos must, in accordance with the laws of thermodynamics, eventually come to a complete and total end. Thus, as the biologist Richard Dawkins has concluded, however it will happen, eventually, "finally, and inevitably the universe will [be reduced] into a nothingness that mirrors the beginning. Not only will there be no cosmologists to look out on the universe, there will be nothing for them to see even if they could. Nothing at all. Not even atoms. Nothing."[81] This eventual annihilation is guaranteed with complete certainty, given the absolute and universal reign of the laws of thermodynamics over and within existence, whether living or nonliving, organic or inorganic.

The Degenerative Essence of Existence and the Metaphysics of Decay

What we discover when we attend carefully to the actual products of the contemporary mathematical sciences is that nearly everyone is in complete agreement that there is at least one absolute law which governs the totality of reality regardless of form or size: the entropic principle of decay. From beginning to end, top to bottom, macro to micro, the laws of thermodynamics hold fast and determine all that is, all that can be, and all that will ever happen. Entropy is the absolute and inviolable law which governs the entirety of the material universe, from its origin to its annihilation. What this means concretely is that while the emergence of matter and life is perhaps *contingent*—indeed, it is just as likely that complex chemical compounds and organic structures do not emerge as they do—if any such emergence does occur, then it must *necessarily* happen according to the principle of entropy as it is outlined in the laws of thermodynamics. Indeed, for anything to happen at all, even the emergence of an empty universe with no matter or life at all, the directionality guaranteed by the laws of thermodynamics must be invoked. For it is only by virtue of entropy and in accordance with it, as we have seen, that the kind of temporality which must exist for something to happen at all is assured. Indeed, the spatiotemporal directionality inherent in the concept of "happening" or "event" is only possible through and according to the laws of thermodynamics. So it is that existence itself is only possible through an invocation of these laws. After all, there can be no-*thing* without the possibility of at least some implied change or movement between states for that *thing*, if only from non-being to being itself, not to mention within space or across time by that thing. And as the origin and governing structure of time, and therefore of change itself, the law of entropy holds fast over even the very concept of existence, since every form of movement and change, as we have seen, is statistically determined, by the second law of thermodynamics, as dispersion, dissolution, and entropy. So it is that entropy appears to be the one absolute constant which is necessary for any and every form of existence, even if only as a conceptual possibility. Indeed, for this reason, theoretical physicists agree that even in a multiverse model of reality in which many different possible universes are posited as speculative possibilities, each containing and operating according to its own set of laws, the one law they must all share in common is the second law of thermodynamics, the one law they hold which makes the very possibility of even a contingent universe operational.

Existence, it seems, whether actual and observable or conceptual and merely possible, is inherently bound to the *necessity* of entropic decay—a necessity that guarantees the disintegration, collapse, and ultimately the annihilation of every possible thing as well as the universe itself. Any speculative project that endeavors to be truly scientific must accept this absolute fact. So it is that any concept of being or value that it develops must conform to the entropic decay which defines the very possibility of existence itself. A truly scientific speculative philosophy must therefore develop an entirely new concept of being if it is to be properly material in form. When understood as emergent from and structured by the entropic thrust of reality, being can no longer be understood as the eternal purity of *stasis*, nor can it be accounted for as the dynamic transformation of perpetual *becoming*. Both of these conceptions have been proven utterly false by the developments of the material sciences in the last 250 years. Understood in light of the steady slouch of reality toward its own obliteration, being must be reformulated as something which is *unbecoming* in every sense of the word. This is the only logical conclusion for any scientifically informed and entirely materialist speculative metaphysics.

Within such a metaphysics, we must acknowledge that while at present living things may appear to proliferate and grow in complexity, ultimately this development is not an act of rebellion against or even a resistance to the inevitable entropic slide of matter towards absolute zero. On the contrary, this explosion in complexity is nothing more than the condition and operative actualization of the coming nihilation of matter which is assured by the third law of thermodynamics. Indeed, as we have seen, the growth and proliferation of complex life forms is the very *mode* in which this nihilation occurs. Living beings, in this regard, should be understood as nothing more than the *form* in which the dissipation, expiration, and ultimate extinction of being itself is accomplished.[82] So it would seem that a scientifically informed, speculative materialist metaphysics must conclude that living beings are ultimately nothing more than agents of oblivion, and being itself is simply the process of this coming obliteration.

The flow from being to nothingness is absolutely guaranteed by the laws of thermodynamics. Moreover, this flow defines the nature of reality at every level, from its *material* structure and *formal* organizing principles to its *efficient* driving force and *ultimate* teleological aim. In this regard, entropy might very well be read by a scientifically informed, speculative materialistic metaphysics as the ultimate *essence* of existence, in the Aristotelian sense: as the absolute principle, ground, and cause of reality itself. Such a nihilating account of the absolute is the only rational possibility for anyone who strives to build a scientifically informed and wholly materialistic metaphysics. Only by accepting this fact can speculative materialism successfully abandon the lingering traces of its correlationism and idealism and finally accomplish its aim of resurrecting an account of the absolute upon which the classical philosophical projects might be resurrected without inadvertently resurrecting any form of dogmatism.

To recognize and accept this scientifically informed and speculatively reasoned account of the absolute nature and structure of being requires rejecting Badiou's conception of the absolute void of being, upon which he mounts his claims concerning the quasi-sacred singularity and absolute freedom of every existent object, as well as his ethical injunction to "keep going." And it further requires rejecting Meillassoux's conception of the absolute necessity of contingency, upon which he justifies both his faith in the possibility of infinite change as well as his hope in a future possible world in which complete justice might be realized. Indeed, as we have just shown, these conclusions are epistemologically unfounded, resulting as they do from a logical equivocation of the rational *methods* employed by modern sciences in their mathematization of nature rather than the *actual products* of that mathematization. Inasmuch as both Badiou and Meillassoux are guilty of such an epistemic confusion, their work inevitably reverts to some version of precisely the kind of anti-realist *idealism* they hope to overcome in the history of post-Kantian philosophy. By failing to maintain this epistemological difference between method and content, both inevitably abandon the *materialism* they espouse as a solution to this anti-realism. As a result, the metaphysical conclusions drawn by both thinkers, extracted as they are from rational speculation on the *methods* of the sciences alone, rather than the *object* and *products* of the sciences, are unjustified according to their own parameters concerning the domain of justifiable speculative inquiry. In this regard, both of their systems are internally contradictory. Worse still, however, is the fact that their resulting metaphysics directly contravene what we have seen to be the actual conclusions of the contemporary mathematical sciences concerning the absolute nature of material reality. No wonder, then, that

CHAPTER 4

the ethical, social, and political conclusions they draw from their respective metaphysics so quickly collapse into some form of the relativism, nihilism, quietism, or fanatical fideism.

Against Badiou's assertion of the *void* or *absence* of any real metaphysical content in the absolute structure of reality, we have discovered through our survey of the contemporary material sciences a very determinate *presence* latent within every objective existent—a determinate and absolute structure which pervades the whole of reality in itself and unites and guides every being which exists therein toward a singular and absolutely inviolable aim: the utter annihilation and complete obliteration of the totality of reality. Far from ensuring the unique singularity and metaphysical freedom of each and every being, then, this metaphysical reality assures precisely the opposite: the cosmic unity and shared destiny of every existent *thing*, whether living or dead, organic or inorganic. For existence, as we have seen, from the perspective of a truly scientifically informed speculative metaphysics, must be understood as entirely determined and necessarily destined toward a relentless slide into cosmic annihilation and a perfect thermal equilibrium to come.

For this same reason, against Meillassoux's assertion of the *absolute contingency* of the present structure of material reality, we must affirm the *absolute necessity* of at least one element of reality: its inevitable and inescapable dissolution, dispersion, and eventual collapse in any and every form. Indeed, as we have seen, for existence to even be conceptually possible, according to what is empirically observable concerning material reality, it must be organized, structured, and absolutely determined by entropic disintegration; for it is this which founds the very idea of space and time, motion and change, and therefore being and becoming in the first place. To be at all, as we have seen, is necessarily to move toward nothingness, oblivion, and absolute emptiness. To be, in other words, is inexorably to unbecome, to unravel, and to dissolve. Thus, though we may affirm with Meillassoux that being itself may be contingent (after all, it is just as likely that there should be *nothing* rather than *something*, as classical metaphysics frames it), against Meillassoux, we must insist that inasmuch as any being can be said to exist (even conceptually), it must move inexorably towards its own decay and the destruction of everything else around it, as outlined in the second law of thermodynamics. At best, what we can deduce from this basic fact is not what Meillassoux calls the *absolute necessity of contingency*, but perhaps only the *contingency of absolute necessity*.[83] For, as we have seen, inasmuch as anything can be said to exist at all, it must be understood to have come into being at some determinate point in time and space and to occupy some definite amount of that time and space. And, as we have seen, any invocation of such a concept of becoming and spatiotemporal existence necessarily invokes some conception of the laws of thermodynamics that make change and a substances' spatiotemporal existence possible.

So it is, we can confidently conclude, that the only materially justifiable conception of being that we can maintain is the necessity of unbecoming—and the only metaphysics we can reasonably maintain is a metaphysics of decay. To maintain any other metaphysical conception of being—for example, as an eternally unchanging oneness, an infinitely becoming transformation, or an immaterial ideality—is necessarily to reject the observable facts of material reality itself; it is, in other words, to give way to the kind of anti-realist idealisms which have dominated post-Kantian philosophy. If we are to overcome this tendency, it is essential that we accept the irrefutable fact that being slouches by necessity toward absolute annihilation.

The only question that remains is how it might be possible to extract from this metaphysics of decay a new sense of absolute meaning, universal moral value, and ultimate truth. How, in other words, might we deduce some new sense of absolute moral value upon which we could establish a new model of evaluative judgment and normative ethics from this absolute law of reality? This will be the aim of the second half of the book. But in order to see how this project is even logically possible, it is incumbent that we first address the limits which have traditionally been placed upon this kind of endeavor. First, we must ensure that in drawing from the contemporary sciences as we do, we don't accidentally indulge in what Alan Sokal and Jean Bricmont infamously call "fashionable nonsense," and which they define as the misappropriation of scientific concepts for the development of obscurantist philosophical theories.[84] Secondly, we must examine how it might be possible to extract from our account of reality a sense of absolute moral value without committing the "naturalistic fallacy" which prohibits deriving a *prescriptive ought* from that which merely *descriptively is*. Only once we have addressed these two concerns can we proceed to the second part of this project and attempt to extract some moral meaning from the metaphysics of decay we have just articulated. It is to this aim, then, that the following chapter is dedicated.

5

The Value of Science and the Science of Value

Reevaluating the Moral Neutrality of Material Reality

Fashionable Nonsense?

If any material absolute exists upon which we can found a new, scientifically justified, speculative account of noumenal reality, ultimate meaning, and universal value, it is the entropic principle articulated in the second law of thermodynamics—that law which guarantees the complete collapse, dissolution, and eventual destruction of existence itself. As we saw in the last chapter, the validity of the principle of entropy is indeed truly absolute and universal. This principle is essential to the contemporary scientific account of reality as it *actually* exists at every level, and enables contemporary physicists, chemists, and biologists to understand everything from the formation of the tiniest subatomic particles to the eventual collapse of the largest astronomical objects, as well as the emergence, evolution, and expiration of every existent object therein, whether living or dead, organic or inorganic. But this same principle frames the limits of what is even logically *possible* within purely conceptual and virtual universes as well. Without the entropic thrust of reality, nothing at all could exist, either actually or possibly. For this reason, we concluded, not only does there appear to be a dissipative necessity embedded in the heart of all that is, but this degenerative necessity appears to be the very essence of all that is and all that could ever be—a material fact which, we concluded, demands the development of a new metaphysics of decay.

It is upon this absolute fact and from this metaphysics of decay that we must endeavor to found again and construct anew a speculative account of the classical aims of philosophy: to make meaningful claims about the absolute truth, universal moral value, and ultimate meaning of reality which are not only rationally justified and scientifically sound, but also practically actionable. Only in this way can we hope to overcome the limits of the correlationist tendency toward anti-realism which has dominated Western philosophy since Kant's critique of dogmatic metaphysics. It is only upon such a scientifically valid account of the absolute structure of reality that we can hope to overcome the latent relativism, nihilism, quietism, and fanatical fideism of Western philosophy and restore its relevance both within and beyond the academy.

There are, however, a few possible objections which we must respond to first if we are to accomplish this aim. The first of these is the suspicion that by relying upon the conclusions of science and mathematics as we do, we might be committing what the mathematician Alan Sokal and the physicist Jean Bricmont have infamously called an "abuse of science" in the service of some form of "fashionable nonsense."[1] This is an especially relevant concern because one of the thinkers that we have drawn upon to make our case is Alain Badiou, who receives no small rebuke from Sokal and Bricmont for his attempts to develop a formal ontology from set theory and to extract from it a justification for his revolutionary politics.[2] So before we try to derive some sense of the universal meaning and value of existence from the scientific account of entropy we have just outlined, it is essential that we first address those who, like Sokal and Bricmont, might be suspicious of the validity of our engagement with the sciences. In this way, we might distance this project from those who, like Badiou and perhaps Meillassoux, tout a respect for the sciences in theory but, more often than not, tend to abuse them in practice.

It was, of course, the aim of Sokal's now infamous "hoax," and his subsequent book (coauthored with Bricmont) outlining the motivations for this hoax, to "show that famous intellectuals . . . have repeatedly abused scientific concepts and terminology: either [by] using scientific ideas totally out of context without the slightest justification . . . or [by] throwing around scientific jargon . . . without any regard for its relevance or even its meaning."[3] The source of this problem, they argue, is not that philosophers and social scientists engage with or draw from mathematics and the material sciences. Nor is it the fact that they very often interpret incorrectly the nature and meaning of the claims and conclusions of scientists and mathematicians. To the contrary, Sokal and Bricmont laud such attempts at cross-disciplinary work and go to great lengths to emphasize its importance to the future of the academy. In fact, they take specific occasions in their book to highlight what they see as particularly good examples of this kind of cross-disciplinary work.[4] The aim of their critique of the kind of "fashionable nonsense" they think has run rampant in the humanities and social sciences is not, then, to inhibit scholars from "extrapolating concepts from one field to another."[5] Their aim is exclusively to curb those "extrapolations [which are] made without argument," especially when the latter rely on what they call "mystification, deliberately obscure language, confused thinking, and the misuse of scientific concepts."[6] For these reasons, as Sokal and Bricmont make clear, they "are not attacking philosophy, the humanities, or the social sciences *in general*."[7] "On the contrary," they repeat throughout their work, "these fields are of the utmost importance."[8] Nor, they insist, do they aim "to prevent anybody from speaking about anything."[9] Instead, they emphasize, the sole aim of their work is to call out, correct, and curtail what they take to be "the repeated *abuse* of concepts and terminology coming from mathematics and physics" within the humanities and social sciences.[10] What Sokal and Bricmont hope to accomplish, in other words, is to ensure that if and when mathematical or scientific concepts are borrowed by other disciplines, their use is wholly justified, their content is expressed clearly and unpretentiously, and their contextual origin is acknowledged and explained thoroughly. As such, Sokal and Bricmont conclude, their "criticism does *not* deal primarily with errors" in the use of such concepts, so long as those errors are made in good faith, with sufficient justification and due diligence to their original use and meaning within the scientific and mathematical literature from which they were borrowed.[11] Instead, as they make clear, the principal aim of their criticism is the *misuse* of scientific and mathematical concepts. And, as they document, this misuse occurs whenever scientific concepts are used either "irrelevantly" and unjustifiably, metaphorically or "poetically," or when they are cut free from their original disciplinary context and meaning.[12] To combat the tendency toward such misuse, Sokal and Bricmont modestly suggest that "when concepts from mathematics or physics are invoked in another domain of study, some argument ought to be given to justify their relevance" and some modicum of care should be paid to ensure that this use is faithful to the original meaning and the disciplinary context from which they're borrowed.[13] Only in this way, they suggest, can philosophers and others guard their use of scientific and mathematical concepts against the possibility of falling into either obscurantism or sheer nonsense. In deference to this humble request, it is incumbent that we test our own use of scientific and mathematical concepts against Sokal and Bricmont's account of the kind of abuse they hope to purge from the academy.

The Varieties of Epistemic Abuse

Sokal and Bricmont identify four primary ways in which they think the misuse and abuse of scientific concepts most often occurs. Let us address each one in turn and measure our use of mathematical and scientific concepts against their standard. First, Sokal and Bricmont note, this abuse appears when an author "hold[s] forth at length on scientific theories about which [they have], at best, an exceedingly hazy idea."[14] This is, of course, as they openly admit, always a danger when someone works across disciplines and attempts to draw from a body of knowledge in which they are not an expert. Indeed, errors are likely anytime one strives to work outside the strict disciplinary boundaries which circumscribe the various territories of the academy. But remember, it is not Sokal and Bricmont's aim to curtail such inter- or cross-disciplinary work. They are not concerned with what they consider to be the good faith errors which might arise from such attempts to transgress intellectual borders and disciplinary boundaries. Rather, their concern is with errors which occur when someone acts *as if* they were an expert in a field in which they have no formal training and, despite their lack of knowledge and experience, proceeds to "riff" or "theorize from" what they have only ever studied at a glance. Sokal and Bricmont's concern, in other words, is with errors which arise from a failure to rely sufficiently on the testimony of the proper experts from the field in which they are drawing. They are not concerned with "good faith" errors which might occur when a scholar from one field misinterprets, misunderstands, or unintentionally misrepresents the testimony of experts from within mathematics or science. The heart of their critique is concerned instead with those who fail to engage with or don't sufficiently try to understand the claims of the experts in the field from which they're borrowing. Sokal and Bricmont's concern is in other words what we might call a *fallacy of inappropriate authority*—an error which occurs when one fails to rely sufficiently upon the testimony of *appropriate* authorities concerning the claims one is making, and relies instead on the testimony of others who are not qualified to comment expertly on those claims. This tendency to either establish oneself as an expert on something one has no formal training in or to rely on the testimony of others who have no formal training in that field is, according to Sokal and Bricmont, one of the primary sources of the kind of "fashionable nonsense" they hope to eliminate from the academy.

To guard against this possibility, I have tried to rely as extensively as possible on the relevant primary and secondary literature in the fields from which I've drawn—contemporary biology, chemistry, and physics—and to let those who have a much deeper understanding of the concepts in question speak for themselves, as it were. Hence the emphasis in the last chapter on the testimony of relevant and contemporary experts in biology, chemistry, and physics on the origin, nature, and role of the laws of thermodynamics within those fields. By highlighting the testimony of the appropriate experts in this way, my account and use of the concept of entropy does not betray the reasonable use limits established by Sokal and Bricmont in their critique. Thus, while I may inadvertently commit some minor error in this account, any such error should not stem from an appeal to inappropriate authority, or result from a failure to engage with the proper experts on the subject at hand. On this front, at least, we can rest assured that we have not yet crossed into the realm of the kind of "fashionable nonsense" rightly decried by Sokal and Bricmont. On the contrary, we have merely followed the aims of the bulk of modern philosophers: to learn from the research and conclusions of the modern sciences in order to inform and enrich our understanding and account of the nature of reality.

The second most common cause of the kind of "fashionable nonsense" Sokal and Bricmont hope to curtail occurs when, they note, "concepts from the natural sciences [are imported] into the humanities or social sciences without giving the slightest conceptual or empirical justification."[15] This, of course, is a much easier concern to settle. Indeed, the first three chapters of this work are dedicated to outlining our reasons for turning to the sciences to discover a new and universally acceptable account of the absolute nature of reality. As we have (hopefully) extensively shown by this point, if our goal is to discover some way in which we might overcome the limits of Kant's critique of dogmatism and establish within the limits of rational argumentation and research a new speculative account of absolute reality, then science and mathematics provide the best model, as Meillassoux and Badiou have convincingly argued. Indeed, as we have seen, perhaps the greatest accomplishment of the contemporary sciences has been their capacity to enlarge the limits of human understanding and account for the nature of reality as it exists in its own right, outside of and independent from the limitations of human ratiocination. It was for this reason that we concluded with them that if any account of reality as it might exist *for-itself*, and not merely *for-us*, is to be achieved, it will be through the radically inhuman abstractive power of the mathematical sciences alone. If we are to discover some absolute ground upon which we might reestablish a philosophical account of meaning, value, and truth without resurrecting any form of dogmatic metaphysics then it must be upon what has been discovered in and through the mathematization of nature accomplished in the contemporary sciences. Our use of and reliance upon the testimony of the sciences is therefore wholly justified and extensively documented. Indeed, it is essential to the very nature and success of our project. On this front too, then, we are not guilty of what Sokal and Bricmont see as one of the primary causes of the kind of "fashionable nonsense" they hope to drum out of the academy.

This justification of our survey and use of the products of contemporary mathematics and science is also germane to what Sokal and Bricmont account for as the third most common cause of the kind of abuse they decry; namely, the "display . . . [of] superficial erudition by shamelessly throwing around technical terms in a context where they are completely irrelevant."[16] As we have just seen, our use of the technical terms we've borrowed from the history of science is neither irrelevant nor immaterial to the task at hand, nor are they used to effect some pretentious erudition. Not only is our use of these terms essential to our argument, but moreover, that use is as nuanced and clear as it can possible be, is contextualized within the proper disciplinary fields from which it is drawn, and is supported by the testimony and work of the appropriate experts in those fields. Indeed, given the integral role of these terms in my argument, I have paid special attention to avoid "shamelessly" adopting or haphazardly exploiting their meaning or use. Instead, I have endeavored to describe these terms as simply as possible and to remain as faithful to their original meaning and contextual use within the existent scientific literature as possible. Thus, while I am indeed interested in extending the potential reach and implication of these ideas into the realm of metaphysics, ethics, and eventually politics, this extension is neither irrelevant nor unjustified since, as we saw in greater detail in the last chapter, the laws of thermodynamics are in fact used by contemporary scientists to account for the conditions for, emergence, nature of, and ultimate telos and end of the whole of material reality, both organic and inorganic. It stands to reason, then, that these laws might also be used to account for the behavior and actions of any and every entity therein, up to and including ourselves. So while my use of "entropy" and other terms in the following chapters is original, and perhaps even unorthodox, this use is neither unjustified nor irrelevant. On the contrary, as should already be clear, if any justifiable sense of the absolute is to be obtained upon which a new account of ultimate meaning, universal moral value, and practical ethical responsibility can be established, it will only be through the operation and conclusions of the contemporary sciences.

It is this commitment to properly understanding and faithfully rendering the scientific account of these ideas that further protects us from falling into the fourth and final source of abuse identified by Sokal and Bricmont; namely, the "manipulat[ion] of phrases and sentences that, are in fact, meaningless," a practice which displays an "indifference to meaning" and results in what they call merely "poetic" use.[17] It is this general indifference to meaning, perhaps more than every other form of epistemic abuse they document in their book, which is the hard core of Sokal and Bricmont's critique. Indeed, as they repeatedly note, the greatest single cause of the kind of "fashionable nonsense" they observe in the humanities and social sciences is the transformation of scientific concepts which have a literal, narrow, and specific meaning into nothing more than empty signifiers which are employed purely metaphorically or wholly analogically.[18] It is precisely this sort of metaphorical "indifference to meaning" which they identify in Badiou's use of set theory in his own work, a criticism which echoes the one we detailed in the previous chapter.[19] On this front, then, I wholly agree with Sokal and Bricmont and have endeavored, as is evidenced in the last chapter, to distance my engagement with the mathematical sciences from Badiou and Meillassoux's own involvement with them. Indeed, as I detail there, my critique of Badiou is precisely that he fails to engage with the *actual products* of the mathematical sciences, and focuses instead merely on their *ideal formal methods*, a focus which, as I have shown, he openly confesses is purely "poetic."[20]

In contrast to Badiou's merely "metaphorical" use of mathematics, my own use of the concept of entropy as the absolute law of material existence is anything but symbolic, lyrical, poetic, or analogical. It is instead a *literal* and epistemologically *narrow* invocation of a scientifically established *fact* which is based wholly and exclusively on the testimony of the sciences regarding the statistical tendency of energy to distribute itself over time in pursuit of thermal equilibrium. It is from this simple, mathematically derived material fact of reality that my metaphysical claims concerning the unbecoming of being are established and justified. And it is from this same literal and narrow use of the concept of entropy that I think we might develop a new sense of absolute meaning, universal moral value, and therefore normative ethics and political justice in the chapters to come. In this regard too, then, I am not guilty of the accusations brought by Sokal and Bricmont against the humanities and social sciences in their account of "fashionable nonsense." On the contrary, my attempt to absolutely ground the classical pursuits of philosophers anew upon the laws of thermodynamics and the necessity of entropic decay is an earnest attempt to take seriously the most up-to-date scientific accounts of the ultimate ground, motivating cause, structuring nature, teleonomic aim, and final end of material reality as it is understood by those most equipped to discover and detail it in its absolute form: scientists and mathematicians. As such, it should be clear that my attempt to rely on the great discoveries of mathematical and scientific research is not without reason and is entirely in good faith. Indeed, it is accomplished with the greatest respect for the original contextual significance and meaning of these ideas.

Having dispelled the possible criticism that my invocation of the laws of thermodynamics is a form of what Sokal and Bricmont call "fashionable nonsense," I can now turn to another conceptual obstacle potentially blocking this endeavor to derive a new foundation for moral and political philosophy from the metaphysics of decay which we developed from the scientific concept of entropy. This obstacle is the long-held assumption that the natural world is, on its own, morally neutral and that, as such, no *prescriptive ought* or moral value can be derived directly from that which merely *descriptively is* and exists simply as a matter of fact. The logical foundation for this claim is the assumption that the material world, which is described so accurately by the mathematization of nature accomplished in the material sciences, has no immediate ethical significance and cannot, therefore, be used to ground any normative or prescriptive judgments. If we are to see how some sense of absolute value, and therefore a universally actionable account of normative ethics and political justice, might be derived from our scientifically informed speculative metaphysics of the unbecoming of being, we must address this assumption and the limitations upon philosophical reasoning which it has justified: the nature of the "naturalistic fallacy."

Against the Alleged Moral Neutrality of the Natural World

The modern assumption that value is an intervention upon or extraneous judgment regarding the otherwise moral neutrality of the natural/material world is summarized neatly in Shakespeare's famous quip that "there is nothing either good or bad, but thinking makes it so."[21] Of course, neither this sentiment nor this line is original to Shakespeare. It was in fact lifted, nearly word for word, from Michel de Montaigne's *Essays*, which Shakespeare drew throughout his work.[22] But in all fairness to Shakespeare, Montaigne himself borrowed the phrase from Epictetus's *Discourses* and *Enchiridion*, where it appears virtually identically.[23] For his part, Epictetus appears to have derived his wording from an observation in Seneca's *Letters* where, in turn, the concept is attributed to Socrates, whom Plato has attribute it to Parmenides.[24]

Whatever its original source, this distinction between the world of things and the world of value has been widely shared and often repeated throughout the history of Western thought. Indeed, some version of it can be found in nearly every major period of Western philosophical history from Parmenides onwards. Take, for example, the logical justification of both Augustine and Aquinas's subtle distinction between what one might mistakenly call a natural evil, like sickness and disease, and what both thinkers suggest is a more proper understanding of moral evil, inclusive exclusively of human vices, like inordinate desire and malice.[25] A similar epistemic distinction can be found in the early modern era in the virtual debate between Rousseau and Voltaire on the level of moral culpability which might be assigned to various city planners, architects, and civic leaders following the devastation of the 1755 Lisbon earthquake which killed nearly 50,000 people, while exonerating "nature itself" for its role in the carnage.[26] Later on in the modern period, we find a similar distinction invoked by Immanuel Kant to argue for the apparent moral neutrality of the natural world in support of his claim that ethical responsibility cannot be assigned to anything (or anyone, for that matter) which does not have the capacity to rationally and freely choose for itself.[27] Later still, Jeremy Bentham suggests that we must distinguish between the objective natural world and the moral world of sentient subjects in order to justify the use of the material objects of the natural world for the benefit of the lives of those moral subjects. As a simple object, he argues, the natural world bears no intrinsic worth. Its moral value, he concludes, is therefore entirely established in its use for human satisfaction.[28] More recently still, as we will see in greater detail later, Friedrich Nietzsche draws upon a distinction of this sort to argue that our traditional estimation of the moral significance of nature has less to do with the "reality of things" than with our "opinions *about* things"; though, as we will see in chapter 8, Nietzsche is exceptional in this regard for thinking that some moral value does still exist inherently in the natural world, even if it is not the value which we traditionally esteem within it and ourselves.[29] And even more recently, Martin Heidegger employs a version of this distinction in his account of the mere "equipmentality" (*Zeughaftigkeit*) of tools (*Zeug*) which, he claims, are merely "at-hand" (*Zuhanden*) for *Dasein*'s use and concerns (*Sorge*) in contrast to *Dasein*'s lived mode of being-in-the-world (*in-der-Welt-sein*).[30]

From this brief survey, it should be clear that some version of the classical distinction between the alleged moral neutrality of the natural/material world and the moral concerns of human beings pervades the history of Western thought. And, of course, this distinction is not unique to academic philosophy alone, it permeates popular social and political discourse as well. Perhaps the most ubiquitous example can be found in the popular American political slogan which declares that "guns don't kill people, people kill people"; a statement which assumes that objective pieces of metal can bear no culpability in the epidemic of gun-related deaths which plagues the United States today. The responsibility for such atrocities, the argument goes, lies solely in the hands of the presumably free moral subjects or agents who use guns to commit them. It is this same assumption which has fueled the transformation in debates over possible gun regulation in American politics which shifts the focus of the discussion from questions concerning the sale and possession of firearms themselves to issues surrounding the moral status or mental health of potential gun owners. Indeed, one of the most common talking points on this topic is the repeated phrase that the only thing which can stop a "bad guy with a gun" is a "good guy with a gun," an expression which clearly restricts moral power to the gun-wielding subject alone and not the material and objective existence of the gun itself. The assumption here, as should be clear, is that guns, by virtue of their entirely objective material nature, cannot bear any moral culpability or complicity in ethical concerns. Such culpability and concern, it is believed, is the exclusive domain of moral agents and subjects alone.

Whatever its form and however it has appeared, whether in the sophisticated arguments of Western philosophers or the sloganized stickers of car drivers across the United States, the underlying premise of the claim remains the same; namely, the assumption that material reality, as purely *objective*, is totally *passive* in questions of ethical concern and is therefore entirely morally *neutral*—that, in other words, natural objects, left entirely to themselves and guided by nothing more than the blind mechanics of the universe, have no intrinsic ethical value or moral worth. Every ethical dilemma that such a purely material *object* might become embroiled in, the reasoning goes, is ultimately attributable exclusively to the moral *subject* or ethical *agent* alone—the one who employs, uses, or puts that material object in motion. To obfuscate this distinction and attribute ethical value or moral worth to a purely material object, the argument concludes, is to commit the *naturalistic fallacy*, i.e., to violate the logical distinction which maintains an absolute division between *natural descriptive facts* of that which merely *is*, and *ethical values* or *prescriptive moral judgments* of that which we think *ought to be*.

The Logical Foundations of the Naturalistic Fallacy

The concept of the naturalistic fallacy is traditionally attributed David Hume, who in book III of his *Treatise of Human Nature* (1739) critiques those who would assign moral praise or blame to anything which is purely *natural* or entirely a *matter of fact*—something which, in other words, is exclusively a product of matter in motion and is not the exercise of any free will or active choice of a thinking and judging moral agent.³¹ According to Hume, it is an error to think that the actions of such naturally "inanimate beings" are "susceptible [to] moral beauty and deformity."³² For, Hume argues with the tradition, "morality consists not in any . . . *matter of fact*, which can be discover'd by the understanding . . . but [rather in] *perceptions in the mind*."³³ As such, he suggests, a practical concept of virtue and "vice entirely escapes you, as long as you consider the object" a source of moral worth in its own right.³⁴ In order to develop an effective model of moral responsibility, he concludes, philosophers must try to draw a line separating their judgment concerning that which "is and is not" (i.e., natural reality) from our sentiments concerning that which "ought, or ought not [to be]" (i.e., moral reality).³⁵

In Hume's account, the establishment and maintenance of this division in philosophical reasoning is essential if it is to progress beyond the dogmatic assumptions of the classical and medieval world. For "nothing can be more unphilosophical," Hume writes in support of his claim, "than those systems which assert that virtue is the same with what is natural and vice with what is unnatural."³⁶ Since it is "impossible . . . that the character of natural and unnatural can ever, in any sense, mark the boundaries of vice and virtue," he concludes, moral philosophers must work to establish and maintain a firm boundary between those natural facts which describe that which *is* and their moral judgments concerning what they *think should be* or *ought to be* the case.³⁷ Only thusly, he argues, will philosophy be able to accurately account for the world as it is, and not merely as we believe it to be; and in this way, develop a better understanding of the world and clear the way for a more nuanced account of morality and ethics. It is from this distinction that the contemporary account of the naturalistic fallacy grew until it was finally and fully articulated in G. E. Moore's *Principia Ethica* (1903).³⁸

Though Moore's ultimate aims in the *Principia Ethica* are wholly different from Hume's, he pursues those ends by insisting with Hume on the radical distinction between the nature of material objects as a *matter of fact* and moral judgments as a *matter of value*. By emphasizing this distinction, Moore aims to overcome what he sees as the irrational assumption that moral judgments can be justified with reference to some definite or natural reality which exists inherently in the world of material objects. In this regard, Moore's work grows out of and works to affirm Kant's distinction between *phenomena* and *noumena*. Against the kind of naive naturalism which Moore sees as limiting the full application of Kant's critique in moral philosophy, he argues that value claims should only be made in reference to the semantic context in which they appear (i.e., the thought world of the judging subject who issues them). For this reason, he argues, moral judgments, unlike matters of fact, should be regarded as "simple," "non-natural," and as such "non-analyzable" and "indefinable" in natural terms.[39] According to Moore, any attempt to define value as a complex reality that is emergent from the natural world itself, or to analyze those values as a product of nature itself, is to commit what he calls the "naturalistic fallacy."[40]

Against this fallacious tendency, Moore insists that moral philosophers distinguish between what he claims are the natural properties of observable reality, on the one hand, and the evaluative properties which can be attributed to observable reality through mental processing or judgment alone, on the other hand.[41] To exemplify this distinction, Moore suggests that while something like the property of mass belongs to an object naturally, properties like its taste, not to mention the kinds of judgments we might make about those properties (i.e., "sweet" or "delicious"), are the result of exclusively mental processes, and should not be seen as belonging properly to or inherent in material objects themselves.[42] Thus, he argues, whereas the proper domain for the study of the former is the empirical sciences, the latter can only be understood within the confines of the metaphysical beliefs and ethical judgments of the conscious subject alone, which is to say, the semantic field of understanding and not the natural world itself.

In this regard, the basis of Moore and Hume's respective accounts of the absolute distinction between matters of fact and matters of value lies in their shared conviction that no moral *ought* can be observed within the domain of natural or material objects. Indeed, they rightly suggest, no matter how closely an empirical scientist may study any naturally occurring material object, they will never find any prescriptive *should* within that which merely *is*. For these reasons, Moore and Hume conclude, a distinction must be maintained between the natural properties of material objects and the moral judgments we make concerning those objects' potential value, lest in our confusion we fall back into the superstitions and folk beliefs of our dogmatic past and undo the great progress achieved by Kant's critique. Moore and Hume argue that when contemporary philosophers fail to recognize or maintain this epistemic divorce between nature and judgment, and insist on attributing values like "goodness" or "pleasantness" to natural or material objects themselves, they not only risk committing this naturalistic fallacy, they also risk carrying philosophy backwards into a past which is not only irrational but morally dangerous. Hence Moore's assessment that "the naturalistic fallacy always implies that when we think 'This is good,' what we are thinking is that the thing in question bears a definite relation to some one other thing," as well as his insistence that such a naturalistic fallacy should be avoided at all costs.[43]

To prevent this, Moore argues that moral philosophers should acknowledge that the concept of value cannot be reduced to or identified with any natural or supersensible reality.[44] Value, he argues, must come to be seen instead as entirely a product of some relation or "state of affairs" which exists *between* a thinking and judging subject and the natural world, rather than as existing in any inherent properties or observable realities manifest within the natural world itself.[45] Values, he concludes in other words, should not be seen as having any intrinsic meaning in any world which might lie outside the conceptual frame or semantic field of understanding of the thinking, speaking, and judging subject. For the meaning of such values, as Moore makes clear, is entirely circumscribed by and contained within the semantic context of the thinking, speaking, and judging subject. Any attempt to abstract values from this context and import them into the natural world itself, Moore determines, is both rationally unjustifiable and epistemologically dangerous. On these grounds, he insists that philosophers reject every form of this naturalistic fallacy and strive to rid themselves of the temptation to look to the natural or material world to justify and ground their moral claims. In this way, the classical distinction dividing the natural/material world from the world of moral value and ethical judgment became solidified within Western thought, and our hope that any moral claim might be rationally extracted from some account of the absolute nature of reality itself was relegated to the backwaters of philosophical debate.[46]

It might seem from this, then, that our attempts to extract some ethical principle from the absolute law of thermodynamic decay must necessarily transgress the limits placed upon philosophical reasoning by Hume and Moore, commit a naturalistic fallacy, and, in this way, potentially resurrect some form of naive folk belief or superstitious dogmatism. As I will show, however, this is not necessarily the case. To the contrary, I think it is possible to rationally justify the deduction of an absolute moral value from the natural fact of entropic decay while upholding the basic assumptions which underlie and inform Hume and Moore's claims. To do so, however, we must first refamiliarize ourselves, in brief, with the nature of the classical moral values which have traditionally been attributed to the natural world in the Western tradition. Through a short survey of the origin and nature of those values (i.e., good and evil), I will show how the apparent absence of moral *oughts* in the natural world, that observation upon which Hume and Moore establish their distinction between matters of fact and matters of value, does not necessarily lead to the conclusion that the natural world is devoid of moral value. On the contrary, as we will see, it can lead to the opposite conclusion; namely, that the natural world contains within it a moral potency wholly its own—one which is, however, as we will see, contrary to what Hume, Moore, and indeed the whole history of Western philosophy assumes to be the natural basis and foundation for moral judgements. When the nature of this moral potency is properly acknowledged, as I will show, it allows us to ascribe an absolute moral value to the nature of reality precisely as it is described by the material sciences. But to see how this might be the case requires first refining our understanding of the classical moral values of the West: good and evil.

Reconsidering the Moral Value of the Natural World

As we have seen, the foundation of Hume and Moore's argument for the distinction between *matters of fact* and *matters of value* lies in their entirely correct recognition that no *ought* immediately appears within any purely descriptive account of that which merely *is*. On this account, Hume and Moore are demonstratively right. The natural sciences will never discover any intrinsic "good" or moral imperative from their empirical survey of the material universe. Approached purely materially, the natural world of objects is entirely devoid of any inherent ethical injunction. From this, it might seem logically necessary to conclude, with the reigning moral intuitions of Western philosophy, that material reality is both entirely passive and value-neutral, neither good nor bad in itself. The prevailing wisdom which accepts the limits placed upon philosophical reasoning by the naturalistic fallacy is founded on this conclusion. And so, both Hume and Moore affirm in one way or another Shakespeare's maxim that "there is nothing either good or bad, but thinking makes it so."

The problem, however, is that the demonstrable absence of such ethical edicts within nature does not necessarily imply the absence of any moral values at all, much less the moral passivity of the material world. On the contrary, this conclusion can only be reached by way of its own logical fallacy; namely, by equivocating between the absence in the natural world of any ethical *prescription* (*oughts*) and the absence of any moral *value* at all (e.g., good and evil). By confusing these two epistemologically distinct concepts, those who insist on the moral neutrality of the material universe on the basis of the apparent absence of any apparent ethical prescriptions therein fail to see that this *absence* testifies to the *presence* of another moral value altogether. Put another way, the simple fact that there are no apparent ethical *oughts* in the natural world does not necessarily mean that the material universe is devoid of any moral *value* at all. On the contrary, it may be precisely this empirical fact which evinces a wholly different category of moral order in the natural world. By failing to recognize this possibility, philosophers who maintain the impossibility of deriving moral meaning from the natural world compound their equivocation between moral prescriptions and moral values with an appeal to ignorance by deducing from the demonstrative absence of moral prescriptions (or goods) within the natural world the logical absence of any moral value whatsoever. And they compound this with a fallacy of presumption, specifically a false dilemma which assumes, against the evidence, that the material and objective world is purely passive and therefore unworthy of the kind of moral agency ascribed to conscious subjects, a problem we will address more in the following three chapters.

In order to see how the apparent *absence* of ethical *oughts* might testify to the *presence* of an inherent *moral value*, and, in this way, how we might overcome the equivocation and appeal to ignorance maintained by the majority of thinkers in the history of Western thought, it is sufficient to provide a few precising definitions of the primary moral values outlined within that history. For, as we will see, not all moral values have been accounted for *positively* therein. On the contrary, the definition of at least one of the primary moral values maintained by the canon of Western thought has traditionally been established *negatively*—not by virtue of that which *appears* or *is*, but precisely by virtue of that which *does not appear* or *is not*. This value, of course, is *evil*.

The idea that evil is not a positive phenomenon in its own right but a *negative* one is most commonly attributed to Augustine of Hippo. And indeed, Augustine does argue throughout his writings that "evil has no positive nature," but instead manifests entirely *negatively* through the loss, absence, or privation of some positive good.[47] But most scholars agree that this idea is not ultimately original to Augustine but is an adaptation of an argument he found in Plotinus who, some suggest, derived it from Aristotle and possibly Plato.[48] Whatever its true origin, perhaps the most famous and complete articulation of this argument can be found in Thomas Aquinas who, drawing from all of these sources, defined evil succinctly as a *privatio boni*, a privation or deprivation of the good—an absence, in other words, of some moral force which he thought *should* or *ought to be* present in all that is.[49] In this regard, for Aquinas, evil appears anywhere some *good* or *ought* is not.

This definition is, of course, not exclusive to these ancient or medieval thinkers. On the contrary, it has held sway throughout nearly every subsequent period in the history of Western thought. As a result, some version of Aquinas's account of the privative nature of evil can be found in the moral claims of any number of subsequent thinkers. Take, for example, Leibniz's account of the metaphysical evil from which moral evil grows in his famous *Theodicy* as "imperfection."[50] Or consider Kant's account of evil in *Religion within the Boundaries of Mere Reason* as something which naturally results from the failure of the rational subject to operate in accordance with the edicts of reason, whether through frailty, impurity, or wickedness.[51] Take as a further example Hannah Arendt's claim that evil results from a "sheer thoughtlessness," a condition she defines as a refusal to consider the effects of one's actions upon the body politic.[52] Wherever one turns in the history of Western philosophy, one finds some account of evil as a fundamentally *negative* phenomenon, something which appears where some *good* or *ought* should be, but demonstratively *is not*. In fact, it is exceedingly rare in the history of Western thought to discover a thinker who maintains the possibility of evil as a *positive* phenomenon in its own right, as something which exists independently of the good by virtue of its own ontological power.[53] Instead, evil has almost exclusively been defined and identified in Western moral philosophy as that which appears where some determinate *good* or *ethical injunction* is absent.

It is strange, then, that Hume and Moore should assume so readily that the impossibility of identifying any natural *good* or *ought* in material reality must necessarily lead to the conclusion that the natural/material world is devoid of moral value and is therefore somehow morally neutral. Indeed, for the bulk of the history of Western philosophy, this demonstrative *absence* could have been used as evidence for precisely another conclusion entirely; namely, the conclusion that the material world is fundamentally evil! Far from testifying to the moral neutrality of the natural/material world, then, the demonstrative absence of any inherent moral good or prescriptive *ought* therein might just as easily be read through the lens of the traditional definition of moral values which has been maintained throughout the history of Western philosophy as evidence of the primal and inherent evil of the natural world. Indeed, it is precisely for this reason that Plotinus and any number of Gnostic thinkers after him reach this very conclusion and argue that material existence in an inherent moral evil which must be resisted in order for any good to be achieved and which must escaped entirely, eventually, if one is to ever achieve any lasting sense of peace.[54] Given this fact, Moore and Hume's assumption of the absence of any prescriptive *ought* or *good* in a purely scientific description of the natural/material world is not only logically problematic, it overlooks the very real possibility that the material world might demonstrate an entirely different moral value altogether, namely evil.

In order to see how this chain of reasoning might be developed, it is instructive to briefly examine the work of Emmanuel Levinas, one of the most profoundly original moral thinkers of the twentieth century, and those from whom he drew in the development of his moral claims. For according to both Levinas and his teacher, Martin Heidegger, the sheer moral indifference of the natural/material world to any form of good, that same empirical fact upon which Hume and Moore founded their insistence on the moral neutrality of the natural world, lends itself more immediately to the conclusion that the material world is a form of natural evil. Through a brief analysis of Levinas's phenomenological account of moral values and the moral philosophies of his interlocutors, we will see all the more then how it might be possible to speculatively derive an absolute account of moral value from the universally valid metaphysics of decay we developed in the last chapter, provided we interpret the value of the material world as wholly evil.

The Moral Meaning of Absence

Drawing from his exhaustive familiarity with the history of thought, Levinas argues that the absolute nature of material existence, identified by him as that which simply "*is*," or "being in general," is anything but morally neutral.[55] To the contrary, following the traditional account of evil as a privative moral force, Levinas argues that the natural world, which he identifies with the "brute sensible datum of the empiricists," should be read as the very essence of evil itself.[56] Indeed, Levinas even goes so far as to suggest that every concrete and particular moral failure in human agents might ultimately stem from their complicity in the indifference of the natural world to human concerns and well-being. Such moral failures result, in other words, when we treat each other with the same indifference that the material universe treats us.[57] In this regard, Levinas suggests, the material universe could be seen as the metaphysical ground and logical condition for the possibility of every manifestation of ethical, social, and political evil between and among human beings. According to Levinas, if we treat others with the same indifference with which the world treats us, or we justify or model our actions toward one another on what appears in the material world, devoid as it is of any inherent good or natural ethical edicts, our actions are not morally neutral, but necessarily evil. And so, Levinas concludes, we might extend our moral responsibilities to one another into our understanding of the natural/material world itself in order to see it not as a morally neutral force, but as a primarily evil force; indeed, the ground, condition, model, and even possible cause of our moral failures. Following this line of reasoning, Levinas suggests that the demonstrative absence of any ethical good in the natural world (i.e., its indifference to everything, even that which it grounds and conditions) should not be read as a morally neutral fact. Instead, he argues, it should be seen as evidence for its evaluation as a moral power: namely, evil.[58]

For Levinas, the same evidence used by Hume and Moore to argue for the moral neutrality of the material world is actually evidence for of the conclusion that the natural world is a morally evil force. Indeed, according to Levinas, lacking those inhibitions and injunctions which constitute the heart of any ethical order between humans, and operating instead blindly and indifferently to every ethical order which we strive to maintain, the most logical conclusion we can draw from the history of Western philosophy concerning the material world is that its indifference is "evil in its very quiddity."[59] For these reasons, Levinas maintains that the *privation* of ethical concern in the natural world is ultimately a *positive* ontological and moral fact. Hence his assessment that being itself should be evaluated as "evil, not because it is finite but because it is without limits"—because, in other words, it is without those limits, prescriptions, and prohibitions which circumscribe and define the nature of the good.[60]

Lacking such ethical limits, Levinas concludes, the material universe must be interpreted as the positive expression of a negative moral force: evil. In this regard, Levinas seems to suggest that though it manifests as an *absence* of ethical concern, evil is, in the final analysis, not an ontological *privation*. On the contrary, he argues, evil manifests precisely where *there is* something which exists so excessively that it exceeds any ethical precepts which might limit it or inhibit its natural indifference. In this regard, for Levinas, evil exists precisely where there is only or exclusively some empirical *thing*—where, in other words, there are no ethical demarcations to define or limit the thinghood of that thing—or put another way, where there is *nothing* to inspire that thing toward some good or moral injunction. Such a totalizing *thingness* is for Levinas the essence of the kind of absolute indifference he identifies with evil. In this way, Levinas identifies the pure materiality of the natural world—devoid as it is of any original ethical ordering within it, anything which would naturally propel it toward some natural good or limit its activity in deference to that which it creates—as the origin and source of, if not the inspiration and model for, the moral horrors that humanity itself is capable of. For Levinas, when we act in accordance with the ethical indifference of the material universe, we make way in human activity for that primary evil which exists inherently within the cosmos itself—the natural ontological necessity of material beings indifference to itself and everything else.

This argument, that the ethical privation of the material universe, though ethically *negative*, might be the *positive* expression of an all together different ontological and moral order, is of course not original to Levinas. On the contrary, Levinas developed his ideas on this matter from the work of his former mentor and friend Martin Heidegger, who proposes a similar account of the nature, origin, and operation of evil in his 1936 lectures on the philosophy of Friedrich Schelling. Heidegger begins his remarks there, drawing from Schelling, with the observation that there is an obvious problem with the traditional conclusion of Western philosophy that there is "nothing existent and nothing depressing and nothing burdensome" in the apparent absence of any ethical order within reality.[61] For Heidegger, this lack, while an ontological consequence of some form of "not-being-present," is not necessarily "nothing" at all.[62] On the contrary, he insists, this lack is "not nugatory; but, rather, something tremendous, the most tremendous element in the *nature of Being*"; it is nothing less, he concludes, than evil itself.[63] For this reason, Heidegger argues that though the ontological power of the natural world might appear in and through some form of moral privation, this privation should not be interpreted as evidence of the *absence* of anything at all, any moral value or way of being. Instead, he claims, this absence must be understood as "something positive" in its own right; namely, evil in its absolute form.[64]

"Evil," Heidegger concludes, "as a *lack* is something [which therefore is] *existent*."[65] Indeed, he suggests, evil exists precisely in the ontological power and indifference of nature itself to that which it creates. As such, he argues, evil, though apparent in the *absence* of moral concern within nature, should in fact be seen as a *positive* expression of the ontological potency of the being of nature itself—being, in other words, manifest in its primal form.[66] So Heidegger insists that we should not confuse the absence of any ethical order in the natural world with the pure privation of any ontological power or moral force at all. On the contrary, he suggests, it is precisely the fact of this ethical absence which is the *positive* expression of the ultimate moral and ontological nature of material reality itself: namely, evil.

Heidegger's claims about the moral value of existence are themselves derived from Friedrich Schelling's rereading of Augustine's account of evil in his *Philosophical Investigations into the Nature of Human Freedom* (1809).[67] There Schelling insists that while we may indeed follow the traditional interpretation of evil as the *lack* or *absence* of any ethical order in the material universe, we must nevertheless see it as a *positive* power, force, or expression of the ontological nature of material reality in its own right.[68] Hence Schelling's claim that "the ground of evil must lie . . . not only in something generally positive but rather in that which is most positive in what nature contains . . . primal will," which for him is the essence of material reality itself.[69] From this, Schelling concludes that while evil is certainly expressive of a privative moral order, appearing as it does where no good is to be found, "it is [nevertheless] necessary that a kind of *being* is in evil."[70] Thus, for Schelling, while evil manifests as an ethical void, it is not properly understood an ontological absence. Instead, he argues, it is the most *positive* expression of the true nature of material reality in its absolute ontological form. In this regard, as Schelling makes clear, moral evil is inherently bound to the order and operation of the metaphysical structure of the existence of natural world itself. And, he concludes, if that structure is not corrected or mediated by the subject's active attempts to limit or resist the natural trajectory of material reality through ethical intervention, the force of nature will eventually "pervert the temperance contained in the [subject's] good into distemperance" and compel it to act in accord with its inner will; i.e., to do evil.[71] In this way, he thinks, without active ethical resistance to nature, human subjects will become complicit agents in the natural evil of the material world and engage in morally reprehensible acts. For Schelling, then, it is ultimately the natural ontological power of the material world itself which conditions and motivates evil acts between human agents. For these reasons, he concludes that the material world, inherently devoid as it is of those ethical structures which human rationality attempts to place upon it, is not morally neutral, but is in fact the essence of evil itself. In other words, Schelling thinks that the metaphysical structure of reality contains within itself an ethical potency: namely, the absolute necessity of evil.

For Schelling, it is this capacity of material nature to unsettle every ethical code or order that human reason and judgment may attempt to erect within, place upon it, and contain it within, which justifies his evaluation of the natural world as a morally pernicious force. Hence his claim that the "interpretation of Platonic matter" as morally indifferent, lacking any observable ethical structures in itself, while "completely correct," is nevertheless not sufficient to conclude that matter is morally neutral. On the contrary, he claims, it is more logical to conclude that precisely the opposite is the case; namely, that "matter is originally a kind of being that resists [the good] and for that reason is an evil being in itself."[72] Moral evil, Schelling concludes, must be understood to "come from ancient nature" and grow from the sheer indifference of nature to every attempt by human subjects to establish, maintain, and corral it through some rational ethical order.[73] For this reason, Schelling argues that though evil may appear as a privation within nature, and in this sense is indeed a *negative* phenomenon, it is at the same time the most *positive* expression of the absolute form of the metaphysical reality of matter in its own right. For, as we have seen, according to Schelling, material reality is precisely that realm wherein every *ought*, established as it is through the operation of human reason and judgment, not only disappears, but is necessarily challenged and disrupted.[74] Far from evincing some moral neutrality, then, this absence of every *ought* in the empirical world lends itself more properly to the conclusion that matter contains within it a positive moral force in its own right: evil.

Borrowing from Heidegger's interpretation of Schelling on this matter, Levinas similarly defines the evil acts of human agents as the result of a "natural propensity" that is inherent to material existence itself—a propensity, as he defines it, to operate alongside nature in a way that is utterly indifferently to the human order of ethical concerns. Levinas therefore echoes Schelling when he concludes that the practical consequence of acting in accordance with material reality and becoming complicit in its operation, or justifying or modeling our actions on the basis of what is evident in an empirical survey of the material universe, is evil.[75]

Still, Levinas suggests, in further agreement with Schelling, that "evil remains always an individual's own choice"; for, as Schelling argues, while this propensity and possibility necessarily exists in every subjective agent by virtue of its material existence, the material world alone "cannot make us evil."[76] On the contrary, both thinkers agree, the material world merely provides the grounding condition and model (i.e., the essence) for whatever evil acts we might commit. Hence Schelling's conclusion that, in the end, "every creature falls due to its own guilt."[77] Nevertheless, as we have just seen, for Schelling, Heidegger, and Levinas together, the condition for the possibility of this guilt lies in the ontological structures of material reality itself, given the natural absence of any ethical *oughts* or prescriptive concerns therein—a fact which, they suggest, works to confound and flummox any attempt to apply prescriptive ethical edicts therein. Hence their collective conclusion that in order to be ethically responsible or achieve some semblance of good in the world, we must learn to resist the natural ethical disorder of the material universe and should strive to make and maintain critical ethical distinctions and limits, even, and perhaps especially, when these are challenged by the indifference of the material universe itself.[78]

In this way, the traditional ontological status of moral values is inverted by these thinkers such that the *absence* of ethical limits in the material universe itself is interpreted as evidence for the *presence* of its ontological and moral power; and the good, rather than being defined as a natural extension of what is, becomes defined by them as the attempt of human subjects to *negate* or *resist* this primal ontological and moral power. This inversion supports the interpretation of the metaphysical structure of reality as an absolute evil. Following their arguments, we might indeed conclude that the good only arises as a possibility from the natural world inasmuch as one is capable of interrupting, breaking with, or disturbing the primal ethical indifference of the material universe. Insofar as we fail in these endeavors to negate the positive force of nature, the primary moral propensity of the world will reign and evil will take the day. So it is that we discover a way in which we might interpret the descriptive absence of any ethical *oughts* or goods in the material structure of the universe itself as logical cause to interpret it as possessing its own positive moral value; namely, evil.

Science and the Absolute Reality of Moral Evil

Following this survey of the traditional account of evil as an ethically privative force and the interpretation of that absence as the natural expression of a positive moral force in the ontological structure of material nature, it should be clear that our attempt to derive a moral value from a scientific account of the empirical facts of nature is neither naive nor a betrayal of philosophical reasoning. On the contrary, as we have seen, there is sufficient reason in the history of Western philosophy alone to interpret the apparent absence of such ethical prescriptions as evidence for the interpretation of reality as a moral evil. This is a conclusion which is only supported further when we consider what we discovered in the last chapter concerning the metaphysical nature of material reality; namely, that the essence of the material universe is to destroy itself and to unsettle, disrupt, overturn, and dissolve every form of determinate distinction, whether ethical, social, political, or even ontological, that might exist in it. When read through Schelling, Heidegger, and Levinas's critiques of the traditional definition of evil as a moral privation, what else are we to conclude about the blindly destructive force that inheres within the very essence of material reality itself, other than the fact that matter is evil?

From what we have seen, there is sufficient reason to derive a positive moral value from the purely descriptive account of reality given to us by the contemporary sciences. Indeed, the history of Western philosophical thought itself seems to justify our attempt to extract a moral significance from the absolute law of entropic decay, so long as we acknowledge with it that no ethical edicts or prescriptions are empirically observable therein. The key to our argument lies in realizing that this demonstrable empirical absence of any ethical order within the entropic

CHAPTER 5

thrust of material reality is not cause to conclude its moral neutrality. On the contrary, it is the very evidence for our interpretation of material reality as a morally pernicious force—a positive ontological force which aims to destroy every moral order; nothing less than evil itself. Only when we invert our moral expectations regarding the nature of the material universe in this way and begin to see it not as the source of our sense of the good, but as the condition for the possibility of every form of moral evil, can we see how we might extract an ethical meaning from the metaphysical structures of material reality without betraying the limits of philosophical rationality.

It is from this evaluation of the natural moral order of the material universe in its own right as the cause and condition of evil in the world that we might reestablish and derive a new absolute and universal account of ethical action, moral responsibility, and perhaps even political action. When we learn to see in the entropic drive of the material universe toward complete annihilation not a morally neutral force, but precisely the opposite—as a fundamentally destructive force, one which operates in absolute indifference to every structure it gives rise to, whether ethical, social, political, or even ontological, nothing less, in other words, than the classical account of evil itself—we discover a firm foundation upon which we might resurrect a new account of ethical judgment, political action, and ultimately even goodness itself, only now understood negatively as that which endeavors, however futilely, to resist the expression of the entropic will or destructive indifference of the material universe by erecting and establishing some form of moral order within it, however ineffective it is destined to be. In this way, we move ever closer to our goal: to reestablish the classical philosophical pursuit of an absolute account of ultimate reality, universal moral value, and final truth. In order to see how our account of the absolute structure of reality as unbecoming, as well as our interpretation of it as a moral evil, might ground such a determinate and actionable ethics and politics, we must first examine how it is possible to account for ethical responsibility at all within our account of reality. It is to this end that the following three chapters are directed.

6

Moral Value and Absolute Necessity

Baruch Spinoza's Metaphysical Monism

Entropic Moral Monism and the Question of Ethical Responsibility

By taking seriously the classical definition of evil as a privative moral power while, at the same time, recognizing that this moral power emerges from a positive ontological element immanent within material nature itself, we discover a route by which we might reevaluate the apparent lack of any moral good or ethical *ought* within that which merely descriptively *is* as evidence for the presence of another moral value altogether, one upon which we might reestablish an absolute account of ethical normativity anew. Indeed, as we saw in the last chapter, the apparent absence of any *ought* in the natural world is not necessarily evidence for the moral neutrality of matter. On the contrary, it might also be read as evidence for the abject moral indifference of the material universe to any and every ethical prescription and judgment. And as we saw, the absence of this care for, concern over, or deference to our well-being, ethical judgments, and our social and political structures is anything but light and easy, or free from existential or moral significance, as Heidegger notes. In fact, this absence weighs upon us with a very definite moral weight, one which threatens to overwhelm us entirely, grind down our ethical, social, and political structures, and reduce us to a "state of nature," as Hobbes called it. Indeed, as we saw previously, the very structure of the universe, as an inexorable entropic unbecoming, is not only indifferent to our ethical, social, and political structures, it actively works to destroy them. The mute indifference of matter to the suffering and destruction it grounds and necessitates by virtue of its obedience to the laws of thermodynamics is not, then, cause to interpret it as a morally neutral force. On the contrary, this great indifference and active drive to destroy all that it creates and gives rise to justifies our interpretation of it as an inexorably and inherently pernicious power—nothing less than evil itself. The destructive indifference of matter to itself is in fact the very cause of every moral harm we suffer. It is therefore the ultimate ground for what we saw in the introduction as our most primal moral sentiments: our outrage at, ethical horror over, and existential dread in the face of matters of fact. Why continue to persist, then, in maintaining the claim that the material universe is a morally neutral force, or even more improbably, a morally good one? Why insist on denying our primal moral intuitions in response to the great indifference of matter? Why not admit the logical extension of these intuitions and conclude that the material universe is an ethically malevolent force; that it is nothing less than *evil* in its very essence? The benefit of admitting this logical possibility—a possibility which, as we have just seen, is not only rationally justifiable and historically supported, but also more representative of the testimony of both our moral intuitions and the conclusions of the empirical sciences—is that we gain a new absolute foundation for our moral judgment and, therefore, potentially a new ground for a universally actionable normative ethics. In this way we might rescue post-Kantian ethics from its steady slide toward nihilism, quietism, fideism, and fanaticism and restore the practical function of philosophical speculation to the world.

Granted, this absolute moral ground is not the one traditionally established by natural law theorists in order to found and justify their own pursuit of these aims. On the contrary, it is its inverse. In this regard, any ethics we develop from this natural law would likewise have to be developed inversely, deriving its imperatives not categorically from the primal goodness of the universe, but disjunctively from its primal malevolence. Nevertheless, as the only rationally defendable absolute moral fact which can be derived from the apparent absence of ethical structures, edicts, or prescriptive *oughts* in a materialistic and empirical account of the universe, there is a way in which we might build a new conception of universal normativity from our evaluation of material reality as evil. But before we can explore the nuances of such a disjunctive or negative account of ethical normativity, we have to see how it might be possible to account for ethical responsibility within the kind of wholly material and ethically monistic account of the universe we have put forward—that is, a universe wherein only one metaphysical and moral power is acknowledged. The problem, in other words, is to show how it might be possible to maintain an account of ethical responsibility within a system which is the expression of only one thing: the necessary operation of matter itself, evaluated as a moral evil. How is it possible to conceive of moral action within a system which appears, by virtue of its ontological and moral monism, to eliminate the possibility of *free choice* or *autonomous will*, much less the good as a properly existent possibility? We must answer this question if we are to develop any practical and actionable normative ethics and politics from the metaphysics and ethics of decay which we established in the previous two chapters.

Free will has, of course, traditionally been seen as the ultimate condition for the possibility of moral agency by the bulk of Western philosophers. Indeed, it is in no small part this assumption which underlies the classical distinction which we explored in the last chapter between the moral value of subjective agents, on the one hand, and the presumed moral neutrality of the inhuman and entirely materialistic world of presumably passive objects, on the other. In order to continue the line of argumentation which we initiated there and develop from our account of the moral value of matter as wholly evil a practical and actionable account of ethical normativity, it is essential that we examine how it might be possible to account for ethical responsibility within an entirely materialistic metaphysical and ethical monism. To this end, this chapter will address two problems. First, picking up from the last chapter, we will question the inherent dualism of the classical Western division of the world into two realms, the first consisting of presumably active moral subjects and the second consisting of purely passive inhuman objects—that division which underlies our conception of the possibility of free will. And second, this chapter will show, through an analysis of Baruch Spinoza's metaphysical and ethical monism, how it might be possible to rethink the nature of ethical responsibility in an entirely materialistic monism without invoking an account of free will. In this way we will show how it might be possible to develop a new, universally valid, and practically actionable account of ethical normativity from our entirely materialistic account of the universe evaluated as absolutely evil.

Ontological Dualism of the Problem of "Free Will"

The arguments which maintain "free will" as the condition for the possibility of moral responsibility are well known. In order to be held morally responsible, the classical argument claims, one must first be a sufficiently capable moral *agent*—that is, one must have the ability to think, to choose, and to act according to one's own judgments. It is this *agency* which defines the *will* which, philosophers have traditionally argued, is one part of the necessary condition to be considered morally praiseworthy or blameworthy. Without evidence of such an active *agency*, we think, someone or some thing cannot be held morally responsible for their actions. This is why we do not typically hold the same ethical standards for so-called "moral patients," for example, children, animals, or those suffering from a mental impairment, as we do for those who are deemed to be full moral agents, that is, those who are in complete possession of their will. Unless someone's will is sufficiently developed in this way, the classical argument goes, they cannot be considered the source of their own activity and therefore cannot, or at least should not, be held fully morally responsible for their actions. It follows from this that since the material universe is traditionally seen as purely objective, possessing no apparent will or active agency, it likewise should not be considered a moral agent, nor should any inherent moral value or responsibility be ascribed to it. Hence the standard conclusion of philosophers that any and all ethical value which might be attributed to the material universe should be seen as nothing more than a product of whatever acting or judging agent uses a material object or sets it in motion.

Secondly, and following this argument, philosophy has traditionally taught that in order to be held fully morally responsible, one must not only be able to *will*, think, choose, and act, but one must be sufficiently *free* to will, think, choose, and act as they see fit. No matter how developed one's will is, the argument goes, unless someone has the *freedom* to order their will freely, and is perhaps even free to control their actions according to the impetus of their will, they cannot be held fully responsible for the moral consequences of those actions. So it is that if someone is compelled against their will to act in a certain way, either through verbal coercion or physical force, then traditionally they are not seen as fully responsible for their actions, nor are they considered entirely worthy of the guilt or blame those actions may merit on their own. Only a fully *willing* and sufficiently *free* subject, the argument goes, should be considered a proper bearer of ethical responsibility; for only such a *freely willing agent* is sufficiently capable of both *choosing* for itself and *acting* upon those choices. Hence, again the classical claim that since the material universe demonstrates no apparent *freedom* to *act* in any way other than is dictated by the laws of nature, it cannot and should not be held responsible for any moral harm it may cause, or be praised for any moral good it may bring. On the contrary, we are told, the actions of the material universe (and their moral consequences) should be seen as "acts of God" or simply as passive happenings—nothing more than the happenstance of "luck" or "fate," and not bearing any moral weight or significance, regardless of its effects on us. Any value we might want to attribute to the natural world and its processes is inappropriate, the argument concludes, for the only proper bearer of such a moral evaluation is a truly *free* and fully *willing* agent. Hence, again, the alleged moral neutrality of the material universe.

It is from precisely this chain of reasoning that the "problem of evil," or "theodicy," arises in Western philosophy. When natural disasters occur or viruses invade our bodies, we are told that it is illogical to blame the material universe itself. Instead, we are told to blame whatever freely willing moral agent has caused or allowed those disasters to occur, through either action or inaction. And if no immediate agent appears to whom we can attribute this causal impetus, then it is only natural that we should turn our attention to whatever transcendent deity or divine maker we believe first crafted the universe and set it in motion in such a way that natural disasters and deadly viruses can occur. But to whomever we address our dismay over such events, we are taught that if our dismay is to remain rational, then it should be directed toward a freely willing agent and not some apparently passive material object. And so we are cautioned against blaming the earth itself when it destroys our cities or the viruses themselves when they multiply within our lungs, but the one who has framed such fearful conditions within existence or perhaps the one who could have, but failed to limit the effect of these maladies upon us. Unless some active agent can be found who is both somehow *free* from the laws of the material universe and also capable of directing their *will* against the mechanistic causal chain which dictates the movement of the natural world, we have been taught, we cannot rationally assign any moral praise or blame.

It should be clear from this line of argumentation that what underlies this classical philosophical assumption concerning the primacy of *free will* in the assignment of moral value is a version of the dualism we called into question in chapter 4—the unjustifiable belief that there must be some concrete difference which separates organic, living and willing beings, from inorganic, merely passive and purely inactive, material objects. Since, as we saw there, such a distinction is no longer defensible in light of the testimony of the contemporary empirical sciences—and, indeed, appears to be nothing more than an irrational holdover from an earlier period of metaphysical dogmatism—then we must further call into question the arguments which are supported by this dualism; namely, the ideas that (1) it might be possible to be *free* from the laws and activity of the material universe, that (2) this *freedom* is a necessary condition for the possibility of being held morally praiseworthy or blameworthy, and that (3) the material universe has no demonstrable *will* inherent to its operation which would warrant moral praise or blame. Unless we can unsettle each of these assumptions and show how the material universe might display some primal *will* that could be held morally accountable for the product of its actions, even if it is not *free* to act otherwise than or against the laws which govern it, then it will be impossible to extend our earlier argument against the dogmatically upheld ontological dualism of Western moral philosophy, justify our judgment of the natural material world as a moral evil, and develop from this a new, universally valid and practical account of ethical normativity and political action.

Fortunately, we are not alone in these tasks. On the contrary, a number of thinkers in the course of Western philosophy have already questioned these assumptions in their own attempts to cast off the pervasive dualism of Western thought. The most famous of these is Baruch Spinoza's development of a wholly original metaphysical and moral monism. Through an analysis of this monism, we can discover a way in which we might develop an account of moral responsibility from the monism which we established in our metaphysics and ethics of decay in the previous chapters.

Will and Material Law in Spinoza's Monism

The fundamental claim of Spinoza's monism is famously summarized by his logical equivalence between God, which he defines as the absolute primal power of reality, and nature, which he defines as the totality of material existence—or as the axiom goes, *Deus sive Natura*, "God or Nature."[1] In this simple phrase Spinoza expresses what he sees as the perfect unity of the causal and determining *agency* which sets reality in motion, and the observable mechanistic *laws* which perfectly and completely govern the operation of that reality. This perfect unity between the mechanistic laws of nature and the agency of any presumable divine will is the axiomatic foundation of Spinoza's monistic metaphysics and ethics.

With this singular claim, Spinoza not only calls into question the traditional Western distinction between purely passive material *objects*, on the one hand, and the activity of a supposedly freely willing *subject*, on the other; but also the idea that the latter could be held morally responsible without assigning any moral value or ethical agency to the former. For according to Spinoza, *agent* and *object*, and therefore *freedom* and *necessity*, alike must be seen as coexisting interdependently within one system and, as such, inextricably cohering within one other as divergent expressions of that system. In this way, he thinks, whatever is attributable to one must likewise be attributable to the other. Indeed, according to Spinoza, this unity of reality is so perfect that the very idea of some actual separation or proper distinction between these two expressions or modes of being is almost entirely meaningless. And as he makes clear, this apparent division is the result of a limited interpretation and understanding of the whole by one of its parts.[2] It is not something, in other words, which testifies to the final truth of reality itself, but rather to the limitations of our understanding of the unity of reality. So it is, Spinoza argues, that when a proper philosophical understanding of the totality of reality is achieved, these distinctions will disappear and a full understanding and affirmation of the whole will emerge. The aim of Spinoza's work is to facilitate this understanding and affirmation through what he sees as the logical proof of the unity of reality. Through a full understanding and accounting of Spinoza's metaphysical monism, then, we will see how it might be possible to maintain a perfectly material account of reality, like the one given to us by the contemporary material sciences, while still upholding the possibility that some sense of moral value might be speculatively extracted from it and a new account of ethical responsibility might be developed from it.

Given what he takes to be the metaphysical oneness of reality, Spinoza argues that there is no epistemologically meaningful concept or ontologically unique nature separating the activity of a *willing* agent from the activity of an apparently purely *passive* material object in such a way that the former might be deemed somehow *free* from the laws which govern the latter. He insists, to the contrary, that since logically there can be only one reality, whatever is attributable to any subjective agent within that reality must also be attributable to any objective entity in that reality. For this reason, Spinoza claims, both *subjective will* and *objective existence*, and, as such, *moral freedom* and *material necessity*, must be understood as different but equal expressions of one singular and total metaphysical reality. As such, Spinoza not only attributes a form of *will* to the operation of material nature, but he also denies the possibility that any meaningful sense of *freedom* can be achieved from the laws which govern the operation of nature. As such, he argues, to hold something like freedom to be a necessary condition for the attribution of moral value and ethical meaning would be to fundamentally deny the logical possibility of those things. But since such concepts obviously exist, Spinoza reasons, it is much more logical to simply hold that no such freedom is needed to maintain the possibility of moral value and ethical responsibility. Indeed, Spinoza insists that not only is it possible to attribute a *will* to the order and operation of nature, it is possible to assert the moral value and ethical activity of that will without affirming the possibility of freedom.

To show how this might be possible, according to Spinoza, we must first recognize that by definition *all existent things*, whether organic or inorganic, living or nonliving, conscious or unconscious, are all equal expressions of *one unified absolute being* (i.e., nature, or God). When the logical necessity of the oneness of being/reality is acknowledged, Spinoza contends, then everything which is attributable to that being/reality can be seen as inhering within and belonging to every other existent object of that reality. In this way, he suggests, the artificial distinctions which have traditionally been invoked in Western philosophy to separate beings from one another by kind, such as free, active, living, and so on, will naturally be overcome and a more robust understanding of the totality of reality will emerge. The key to achieving such an understanding, Spinoza argues, is to recognize that something like human *will* is ultimately nothing more than a singular modality or expression of the primal movement of material reality itself.[3] In other words, Spinoza shows that while something like human consciousness and agency appear to be unique in its form, they are ultimately nothing more than the expression of a more primal *conatus*—a natural tendency or striving—that is immanent in material nature itself and which expresses itself equally in the activity of the subject and in the physical dynamics of simple material objects, all according to the laws of nature. Each, according to Spinoza, is an expression of the same basic *will* which he thinks suffuses all of reality and which, he claims, is the primal essence of existence. Through such a radical monism, Spinoza challenges the prevailing assumptions of Western metaphysics while demonstrating how they might be overcome without the concepts of moral value or ethical responsibility. Indeed, on the basis of his logical equivalence of primal agency (i.e., God) and material reality (i.e., nature), Spinoza extends the operative limits of moral value and ethical responsibility. By showing how every existent material object can and indeed should be seen as alternatively and simultaneously the expression of a kind of *willing* agency; and vice versa, that every expression of a subjective desire or agency can and should be seen as a modality of an objective material principle or *law* in nature, Spinoza opens the door to an ethical evaluation of matter itself.

To make his logical equivalence all the more clear, Spinoza defines human consciousness, the traditional subject of ethical responsibility, as "part of the infinite intellect of God"; or, as we have seen, an expression of material nature itself.[4] Indeed, it is due to this equivalence that one of the most famous elements of Spinoza's ethics naturally follows; namely, that any subjective agency (i.e., mind) must be seen as entirely immanent within and perfectly identical to its material nature (i.e., body). And so, Spinoza thinks, against the prevailing dualism of Western philosophy, any expression of subjective agency can be seen as ultimately an expression of the *idea* of God within material reality. The apparent distinction of such an agency from *material* reality, he concludes, is only *ideally* possible and not an expression of the nature of *actual* reality. Spinoza argues that as a logical consequence of this perfect equivalence of matter and form—i.e., nature and God, mind and body, law and will, necessity and freedom—every material object must likewise be understood as an expression of some conceptual and ideal form, that is, divine will. Hence his claim that

> what we have proved so far is very general and pertains no more particularly to human beings than to other individual things, all of which are animate, albeit in different degrees. For of every single thing there necessarily is in God an idea, of which God is the cause in the same way as he is the cause of the idea of the human body. Therefore, whatever we have said about the idea of the human body, we must necessarily say about the idea of any thing.[5]

For Spinoza then, the movement of every material body, whether it is the flight of a star through space in obedience to the material laws of nature or the operation of the human mind in accordance with the ideal laws of reason (i.e., logic and mathematics), perfectly expresses one absolute willing reality, either interpreted ideally as divine or understood materially as nature. In this regard, the *operation of will* becomes interchangeable for Spinoza with the *order of natural laws*. Likewise, he reasons, the empirical movement of any material object can be read simultaneously and alternatively as either the expression of a purely material *nature* or the expression of some ideal *will*. All of existence, Spinoza insists, is therefore entirely and purely natural and totally material while, simultaneously, perfectly ideal and essentially divine. Whether some material movement in nature is seen as the product of the activity of a conscious subjective agent, in accordance with the rational activity of the mind, or appears as the effect of the operation of the laws of nature upon a purely material object, each for Spinoza is ultimately the same thing; namely, an expression of the same singular being/will of reality, either interpreted ideally, as a product of the *conatus* of God, or interpreted materially, as an effect of the order of *nature*. Nevertheless, he argues, both are ultimately one and the same in essence. In this way, Spinoza argues that the concept of will can and should be extended into the operation of material nature itself so that it becomes subject to the same moral judgments and ethical categories as the subjective agent.

Equating as it does ideal reality with nature, Spinoza's monism enables us to ascribe to the movements of the material world, bound as they are by natural laws, a kind of agency or will. At the same time, it allows us to see that what we call active will or consciousness is nothing more than the expression of a natural force or material principle that works according to the laws of physics, one which is not, therefore, free in any meaningful sense of the word. In this way, Spinoza's monism, by overcoming the artificial distinction maintained in Western metaphysics between willing subjects and passive objects, allows us to cast off the assumption that something like freedom must exist to maintain the possibility of concepts like moral value and ethical responsibility.

The Illusion of Freedom

Note that Spinoza's monism entails that some form of will be granted to all material objects such that their activity should no longer be seen as random, but purposeful. It also requires that the natural laws which we understand to determine and define the order and operation of material objects with absolute regularity be extended to govern, guide, and rule over the operation of the ideal realm of mental activity in such a way that every intention and rational act cannot be seen as free from nature, but rather as a consequence of causal necessity. And so, Spinoza insists, inasmuch as the material world can be said to display an active and purposeful will, human agency can be said to operate in perfect obedience to the laws of nature. This is why he argues that everything which is governed absolutely by the laws of nature, from the heavenly spheres circulating above us to the tectonic plates trembling beneath us, not to mention the viruses replicating within us, must be seen as the expression of a purposeful will that is immanent in material reality itself. And at the same time, he suggests that every mental activity of a subjective agent, from the most rational and logical deduction to the most passionate and spontaneous emotional expression, must be seen as operating according to the absolute laws of necessity that govern material reality. This perfect symmetry follows logically and necessarily from Spinoza's monistic equivalence of ideal and real as God and Nature, mind and body, and so on.

The problem, as Spinoza details in sections IV and V of the *Ethics*, is that the particular modality of nature which finds expression in us as consciousness grants us the power to mistakenly think of ourselves as somehow unique, separate, distinct, and independent from the laws of nature which govern being in its material modes.[6] As a result, Spinoza notes, humans tend to mistakenly think of themselves as somehow *free* from or *outside* of the material laws of physical reality. It is this confusion which is the source of the historical tendency to ontological dualism in Western metaphysics. Nevertheless, he insists, "human beings are mistaken in thinking they are free."⁷ "This belief," he notes, "consists simply of their being conscious of their actions but ignorant of the causes by which they are determined."⁸ Indeed, he concludes, the apparent freedom of subjective and conscious will is an error which must be excised from our thought if we are to properly understand the nature of our being and the perfect unity of being as a whole, as well as our ethical responsibility to both.⁹

According to Spinoza, when we transcend the limitations of the first-person perspective and ascend, through pure logic, to an objective understanding of the nature of the whole of being—which is precisely what he hopes to engender in his readers through his geometric method of argumentation—we will begin to realize that "there is no absolute or free will in the mind; but [instead] the mind is determined to will this or that by a cause, which is also determined by another cause, and this in turn by another, and so on *ad infinitum*."¹⁰ In just the same way that a rock is determined to fall by the laws of physics, the trembling of the earth's mantle is determined by the principles of geothermal cooling, and the replication of a virus's RNA in the DNA of a living cell is determined by its biochemical code, so too are human cognition and rational consciousness entirely determined by the mechanistic laws of nature. As such, Spinoza concludes, human agency, as a conscious and willing expression of nature, is entirely bound and causally determined by the same laws of matter which govern the order and operation of every other thing. For Spinoza, then, the subject's relationship to itself and its world, which it experiences as a free will, is ultimately no different in kind than the relationship which any material object has with the world; for example, the gravitational relationship a celestial body has with the mass of other nearby bodies, a relationship which we understand to be ruled entirely by the laws of nature. As a result, he concludes, the former should not be seen as any more "free" in its actions than the latter. For, he insists, the same primal *conatus* which sets the celestial bodies in motion and maintains them along their course is the same primal *will* that manifests in the machinations of the human mind. As such, Spinoza argues that the operation of every conscious subject must be understood to be just as determined, and even theoretically predictable, as the movement of every material object in motion. Each, he thinks, obeys absolutely and operates in perfect accordance with the will or *conatus* of God/nature. Each falls, as it were, according to its own singular nature along its own preestablished course toward its own inevitable end. And so, Spinoza argues, "nothing in nature is contingent, but everything is determined to exist and to operate in a specific way by the necessity of the divine nature."¹¹

In this way Spinoza challenges the prevailing ontological dualism of Western metaphysics and empowers us to endow the material universe with the same kind of activity and agency which has traditionally been reserved for human subjects (i.e., willing beings) alone. Moreover, he shows us how this ascription requires a complete rejection of the concept of freedom as it has traditionally been understood in the West. Nevertheless, and this is absolutely essential to our argument, Spinoza insists that the ontological impossibility of freedom does *not* eradicate the concepts of moral value or ethical responsibility. On the contrary, he argues that it is precisely the causal and mechanistic determinism of the system of nature which establishes a conception of moral value and ethical responsibility, and this in turn infuses the whole of nature with worth. To understand how this is the case, however, requires radically reconceiving the nature of moral value and ethical duty. This re-conception of the *value* of nature and the mode of ethical responsibility is in many ways the real aim of Spinoza's *Ethics*, as is indicated by its title. Indeed, Spinoza's metaphysical monism is in many ways the preliminary work which he must accomplish in order to redefine moral value and ethical responsibility so that they can fit within a more scientific understanding of nature as wholly determined. So it is that the concluding parts of his *Ethics*, sections IV and V, attend nearly exclusively to a redefinition of moral value and duty which escapes the limitations of ontological dualism and its assumptions about the conditions for the possibility of ethical responsibility (i.e., free will).

Necessity, Ethical Duty, and Relative Value

Spinoza begins his analysis of the possibility of ethical responsibility within his metaphysics by defining the concepts of good and evil as categories of human understanding.[12] Goodness, as he famously identifies it, indicates a mode of conscious understanding which recognizes, acknowledges, and affirms the deterministic *conatus* or will of nature.[13] Inversely, he argues, evil is a mode of understanding or being which is ignorant of, refuses to accept, or attempts, however futilely, to resist the determining will of nature.[14] Since, by his definition, goodness begins with a recognition of the laws of nature, Spinoza further defines it "as that which we certainly know to be useful to us"; that which, in other words, helps us to transcend our individual perspective and acknowledge ourselves as we truly are: an inexorable part of the whole of material being itself.[15] And conversely, Spinoza further defines badness or evil "as that which we certainly know hinders us from becoming possessed of any good"; i.e., that which further entrenches us within the limited perspectives of our individual existence and, as a result, further promotes the illusion that we are free from the whole of material reality.[16]

On the basis of these definitions of good and evil, Spinoza goes on to outline his account of ethical responsibility as the duty which every existent thing has immanently within itself, by virtue of its very being, to affirm perfectly the predetermined course which nature has set out for it. What this duty entails for the subjective agent, he argues, is for each of us to learn, through rational deduction, to progress beyond the limited perspective of the *individuum* in order to achieve a transcendental perspective of the whole of nature and to affirm fully the necessity of that nature within us. More concretely, what this ethical responsibility demands from us, Spinoza thinks, is to recognize, accept, and perfectly assent to the fact that we are *not free* but are, in fact, absolutely *determined* to be the way we are and to act in the ways that we do—that, in other words, things cannot be otherwise than they are. It is our ethical responsibility, Spinoza concludes, to learn to act and think in a way which helps us to consciously accept and willingly affirm the ruling principle and governing forces of nature within and over us: the absolute law of reality which governs all that is, all that we are, all that we do, and all that we will ever be. In other words, to borrow language from Nietzsche's succinct articulation of Spinoza's morality, the ultimate expression of ethical responsibility within this system is to learn to love our fate: to affirm in our will the absolute rule of the laws of nature.[17]

Given his definitions of good and evil, not to mention his account of ethical responsibility, Spinoza has often been mischaracterized, like Nietzsche after him, as a kind of moral relativist.[18] While it is indeed a mischaracterization, this interpretation is not without cause. After all, Spinoza does initially define good and evil as exclusively categories of human understanding—little more, at first glance, than the product of a finite and limited understanding of the whole—a perspective which, he further argues, must be transcended through logical analysis if we are to achieve a proper understanding of the full nature of the perfect unity of the whole of being itself. It would seem from this that once such an understanding of the whole is achieved, concepts like good and evil might ultimately disappear. What's more, Spinoza argues that more often than not, the concepts of good and evil that we maintain in the meantime are tied to our own self-interest. As he notes, "we do not endeavor anything, we do not will anything, we do not seek or desire anything, because we judge it to be good; on the contrary, we judge a thing to be good because we endeavor it, will it, seek it and desire it."[19] What is this if not further evidence of Spinoza's apparent moral relativism? From these two claims alone, in fact, one might understandably conclude that for Spinoza, not only are the concepts of good and evil wholly human, finite, and limited, something to eventually be overcome; but they are moreover solely products of human desires and nothing more, therefore, than a reflection of one mode of nature, rather than a manifestation of absolute reality of nature as a whole. After all, as Spinoza writes, in concert with the history of thought before him, "as concerns good and bad: they too indicate nothing positive in things, considered, that is, in themselves. They are simply ways of thinking or notions which we form by comparing things with each other."[20]

It stands to reason, then, that the casual reader of Spinoza might think that he rejects entirely the idea of absolute moral value in favor of a kind of moral relativism wherein ethical evaluation becomes little more than a purely human endeavor, one which, moreover, must be transcended if we are to properly understand the full nature of reality. Indeed, it was in large part such an understanding of his work which inspired his first readers to decry his *Theological-Political Treatise* as "a book forged in hell," and to denounce Spinoza as a crass agent of immoralism and atheism.[21] Such misunderstandings, while not without cause, are wholly incorrect, however. For, as the careful reader of Spinoza will note, statements of this sort appear almost exclusively in sections III and IV of his *Ethics*, entitled "Of the Affects" and "Of Human Bondage," respectively. In these sections, it is Spinoza's sole aim to catalog the everyday activity and quotidian understanding of human consciousness, to diagnose their origins, and ultimately, to dismiss them. In these sections, the everyday and limited understanding, account of, and nature of good and evil operant in quotidian human interactions is indeed critiqued by Spinoza as little more than products of human desire and self-interest.

But—and this is essential to a proper understanding of Spinoza's work as a whole—these ways of thinking are identified by him as "bound" and limited; as something, in other words, which must be overcome in order to achieve a proper understanding of the fullness of reality. There is, however, a fifth section to the *Ethics* where Spinoza explores what "freedom" from such a limited perspective might entail. If Spinoza were indeed a moral relativist, then we might reasonably expect section V of his *Ethics*, which details a mode of thinking that is not "bound" by the finitude of everyday human understanding but which perfectly affirms the absolute nature of reality, to abandon moral considerations altogether. But, in point of fact, precisely the opposite is the case. Indeed, it is here, in the final section of his *Ethics*, that Spinoza makes his most original arguments concerning the nature of moral value and ethical responsibility, as part of his account of the proper nature of the totality of absolute reality itself. So the interpretation of Spinoza as a moral relativist must be rejected vociferously. Indeed, and entirely to the contrary, as we will see, Spinoza has much more in common with a moral absolutist than with a moral relativist. The key difference between him and other moral absolutists, however, lies in his claim that the source of absolute moral value is not some transcendent power, one which is asserted in faith, but rather something immanent within the nature, order, and operation of material reality itself.

The Highest Value and Acquiescence

As Spinoza makes clear in the final sections of his *Ethics*, when we have fully transcended through geometric logic the limited perspective of human understanding and everyday morality wherein reality is understood as contingent, beings are judged as separate and distinct from one another, and moral values are applied according to the individual perspective and nature of each being—when, in other words, we achieve a comprehensive understanding of the totality of reality as a single, coherent, whole, and entirely necessary absolute being—then we come to see moral value as an intrinsic quality of being itself, and not merely a contingent element of human judgment. Spinoza goes on to argue in section V of the *Ethics* that when the relative perspective of human understanding is transcended, we discover what he calls the highest or greatest virtue, which he terms *love*.[22] According to Spinoza, love is an expression of the highest virtue which comes from a perfect understanding of the unity of reality. In this regard, he sees love as the affective consequence within us of a complete affirmation of the absolute value of the nature of existence.[23] To achieve this greatest or highest virtue, he argues, we must come to understand ourselves and every other part of the universe as *sub specie aeternitatis*, "from the standpoint of eternity"; as part, in other words, of the oneness of an infinite, eternal, and absolute being—a oneness, moreover, which is, as we will see, good in itself.

"Insofar as our mind knows itself and the body from the vantage of eternity," Spinoza writes, "to that extent it necessarily has cognition of God, and knows that it is in God and is conceived through God."[24] By acknowledging the perfect unity between our existence and the being of the divine, Spinoza argues, we can come to understand that all that is, has, can, and will eventually exist to be absolutely immutable, entirely necessary, and an essential and inexorable expression of the perfect and eternal being of God/nature. This recognition, he argues, allows us to affirm the material universe as it is, along with all that has, can, and will happen within it as an essential and necessary part of the whole of reality; as something which cannot, by definition, be other than it is. In this way, he thinks, finite beings can discover a way in which they can greet the universe, replete with all of its apparent ills, as the expression of an eternal goodness and a source of transcendental joy.[25] Indeed, according to Spinoza, when we understand the universe through the lens of his metaphysical monism, we can begin to "find a pleasure in it which is accompanied by the idea of God as its cause."[26] This, for Spinoza, is the very definition of true love: the perfect affirmation of the absolute necessity of nature as an expression of a divine being.[27] Only through love of this sort, Spinoza concludes, can any individual modality of the whole achieve what he calls the highest affects: blessedness and perfection. And it is through this love and its accompanying affects, he argues, that the incomplete and imperfect moralities of a limited and "bound" human consciousness can be transcended, and a more full, complete, and perfect morality that is representative of the whole and absolute nature of reality can be achieved. "If joy consists in passing to a greater perfection," he concludes, absolute "blessedness must surely consist in the mind's being endowed with perfection itself."[28] Spinoza argues that anyone, insofar as they accept their fate, in perfect assurance that the order of nature understood as a divine order, can achieve moral goodness and take full expression of their ethical responsibility—that is, to own and affirm their fate within that order—and thereby achieve the highest virtue, love, which is for him the source of a transcendental joy.

According to Spinoza, ethical responsibility is fulfilled when we realize that everything which is and which could ever be, even those things which we may initially think of as bad or evil, are actually, when viewed *sub specie aeternitatis*, rightly part of the absolute necessity and ultimate perfection of reality itself—in other words, they are absolutely good, by definition. Blessedness, he argues, is simply the natural result of realizing this absolute and complete moral truth that is immanent in material reality as God or nature. "The more proficient anyone is in this kind of cognition," Spinoza writes, "the better he is conscious of himself and of God; i.e., the more perfect he is and the more blessed."[29] For these reasons, Spinoza argues that when it is considered rightly, the universe can be seen as something which is *not* devoid of value, but which is suffused with absolute moral value in itself—something which is morally perfect and absolutely good; a material expression of the perfect goodness of the divine will itself. As a result of this, he thinks, the possibility of achieving perfect joy and utter blessedness lies immanent within every being at any given moment. All we need to do in order to acknowledge, affirm, and become one with this goodness is to transcend our limited perspectives, which fail to understand the whole and, through the operation of logic, align our wills with the absolute necessity and perfect goodness of the laws of nature as the material expression of the divine will of God. In this way, Spinoza concludes, we will come to see the perfect goodness of reality as it is, come to love it as it is, and come to experience the perfect blessedness of the transcendental joy of all that is.

This, in the end, is the ultimate aim of his *Ethics*: to free his readers from the bondage of their false belief that the only values which are achievable are those which present themselves through the limited and finite perspective, judgments, and actions of any particular human perspective; and to show his readers instead that the whole of reality shines with an immanent and absolute value which places an inescapable ethical demand upon them and on every other existent thing; namely, to obey perfectly the necessity of natural laws as the expression of a perfect and divine will. For Spinoza, insofar as we accept this ethical demand—this moral fate, as it were—and affirm the absolute moral value of nature, we can know the absolute good of reality itself, practice the highest good of loving that reality, and experience the blessedness of perfect joy as a consequence and reward of our perfect affirmation of and assimilation to nature. Insofar as we persist in the illusion of our individual freedom from nature, however, and attempt to exercise control over ourselves and nature, we will fail to understand the perfection of nature in and around us and will respond to the necessity of nature with resentment, a decidedly bad condition. Only when we transcend the limited bonds of our finitude and recognize that all that we are is entirely determined by the absolute necessity of the perfect unity of material reality, then, Spinoza promises us, we can overcome this resentment, reconcile ourselves to the nature of reality, and find in this accord, finally, perfect peace. Hence Spinoza's claim in the proof and the scholium of proposition 42, the last of his *Ethics,* that lasting peace is the ultimate reward which awaits those who achieve a proper understanding of the whole of reality and fulfill their inescapable ethical duty to affirm in their will the perfect necessity of nature. "[A] wise person," he writes, "insofar as he is considered as such, is scarcely moved in spirit, but being conscious of himself and of God and of things by some eternal necessity, he never ceases to be, but always has possession of true contentment of spirit."[30] This is for Spinoza the essence of true joy, complete blessedness, and perfect love—to affirm what is absolutely necessary in and through us by virtue of the nature, order, and operation of material reality as an expression of the perfect will of God.

From this it should be clear that moral relativism does not have the final word in Spinoza's *Ethics*. On the contrary: in the final analysis, Spinoza accounts for moral value as an absolute fact which is grounded in and emergent from the immanent nature of material reality itself. What's more, his account of the absolute necessity of nature, far from relieving people of any ethical responsibility or duty, demands that they learn to affirm in their *will* the absolute value of being as a perfect good—a demand, he thinks, which can only be satisfied when we transcend our limited and individual perspective through the operation of reason in order to achieve an understanding of reality as a species of eternity. Thus, Spinoza insists that even though a human being has no real freedom to speak of, since each of us is ultimately a modality of the perfect unity of the totality of material reality as bound by the laws of nature, nevertheless, every person, as well as every material object, has an inexorable ethical duty to obey and affirm the absolute moral value of existence expressed in the order and operation of the laws of nature. Spinoza defines the ultimate expression of this ethical responsibility as *acquiescentia*, which is usually translated as "contentment," but is perhaps better and more directly rendered as "acquiescence."[31]

For Spinoza, the aim of ethics is to learn to *acquiesce*—to obey, affirm, and find peace in the absolute necessity of material reality as the expression of a perfect and divine will.[32] By learning to surrender ourselves wholly to the laws and operation of nature as absolutely necessary, Spinoza argues, we achieve the greatest good: to affirm the divine as wholly and perfectly good.[33] Spinoza concludes that by acquiring an absolute perspective on existence, and (through affirmative acquiescence) aligning our individual wills with the will of God at work in the operation of the cosmos, we can participate in the absolute goodness and the eternal blessedness of reality as an expression of the divine.[34] Hence Spinoza's identification of *joy* as the affect which accompanies the fulfillment of our ethical responsibility to the necessity of reality.[35]

Joy, for Spinoza, is the natural consequence of learning to submit wholly to, become perfectly subservient to, and completely align ourselves with the absolute necessity "of God and of things."[36] Joy is, in other words for Spinoza, that which results from surrendering to and acquiescing fully to the necessity of nature, as God. By relinquishing the illusion of our independence from nature and instead acceding fully to and complying perfectly with the necessity of material nature, Spinoza assures us that we may become reconciled to what he terms the "glory" of reality.[37] For these reasons, Spinoza sees in the *acquiescence* to nature the ultimate ethical imperative required of all beings. Only through such an acquiescence, he claims, might we finally discover through thought "a way" to salvation by recognizing within ourselves the perfect and absolute goodness of reality as a whole, understood as a species of eternity.[38]

The Blessedness of Eternity

It should be clear from this that Spinoza's account of good and evil as apparently relative terms, in sections III and IV of the *Ethics*, is solely a means to the end of his final arguments in section V, where he identifies material reality, understood *sub specie aeternitatis*, with an absolute moral value, namely perfect goodness. Spinoza's alleged moral relativism thus appears to be, in the end, a sort of ladder which he uses to ascend beyond the bondage of the limited and finite perspective which traps human consciousness in its everyday understanding of reality, so that we may ascend through it to a higher understanding of moral value and ethical responsibility wherein the whole of existence is revealed to be the expression of an absolute moral value: perfect goodness in itself. In this regard, it is utterly improper to read Spinoza as a precursor to the kinds of post-Kantian relativism which plague us today. Instead, it is more accurate to read his work as a creative reinterpretation and secularization of the kind of natural theology espoused by Augustine, Maimonides, and Aquinas.[39] In this regard, Spinoza's work is a perfect model for what we hope to achieve here: a way of accounting for an absolute moral value within an entirely nondogmatic account of reality as wholly material and entirely unified—an account of reality which, as we have seen, is best achieved today in and through the mathematical sciences.

When Spinoza is understood in this way, as a secularized and nondogmatic reinterpreter of natural theology, his claims about the absolute value of material reality can be better understood, as can his claims that this absolute value is only visible to the one who has come to see nature *sub specie aeternitatis*. Whereas for classical dogmatic natural theologians this eternity is assured by the being of God, for Spinoza this eternity is a natural quality of material reality itself. When the eternal nature of the cosmos is understood as all there is and all there can be, Spinoza argues—in affirmation of the logic of the natural theologian in reference to God—its order and operations can be affirmed as absolute necessary and perfectly good. From this perspective, he claims, in further affirmation of his natural theologian predecessors, all that is can be affirmed as an expression of a perfect and absolute goodness, a conclusion which he initially teases in the preface to section IV of the *Ethics*.[40] This follows logically for Spinoza, since goodness is defined as the result of a perfect obedience to the absolute will of nature, and every natural object cannot but obey its own nature. It follows from this that all of existence must, in light of its natural eternity, be part of the good for Spinoza. It is only from our own limited perspective, or *sub specie durationis* ("from the standpoint of time"), that we may evaluate certain things as evil; that is, as somehow not conforming to what we think of as our limited and personal wills or relative "good." But, thinks Spinoza, when we understand the perfect unity of the whole and learn to align our wills to the perfect necessity of it, then we can come to see, *sub specie aeternitatis*, that everything is part of and a servant to an absolute good, even that which appears to be evil from the limited perspective of the individual will and the finite perspective of time.

From this, it becomes clear that while the concept of good is indeed an absolute value for Spinoza, the concept of evil is solely a form of "imperfection" for him, one which results from the failure to see things properly; that is, in light of the perfect necessity and eternity of being. In this regard, and in further affirmation of the tradition of natural theology, Spinoza does not see evil as something which is ultimately real. Instead, he argues, evil exists purely as a category of human understanding, one that is bound entirely within the limited and finite framework of an individual consciousness which has failed to comprehend the totality of reality *sub specie aeternitatis*. Evil thus exists for Spinoza solely as a product of an understanding of reality *sub specie durationis*, that is, from the standpoint of our own limited personal perspective. For Spinoza then, while the concept of goodness which arises within a bound consciousness is indeed ultimately incorrect and worth rejecting, it nevertheless has some logical basis as a correlate and incomplete understanding of reality as it actually is and can be understood *sub specie aeternitatis*. Evil, he argues, on the other hand, does not have a similar logical correlate *sub specie aeternitatis*. In this regard, unlike goodness, Spinoza argues that evil has no real essence or proper being. Instead, he argues, it is exclusively and entirely a product of human understanding—an illusion which arises from a faulty rendering of the activity of nature as contingent, random, and changeable. Evil, in other words for Spinoza, is simply the result of a failure to properly understand the necessity of nature as the expression of a perfect will. In this regard, like his predecessors, Spinoza sees evil as the consequence of a privation of human understanding and not something which has any real existential content on its own.

By contrast, Spinoza sees goodness as a proper reflection of the ultimate reality of nature understood from the absolute perspective, and containing therefore an actual and real ontological power. Indeed, as we have seen, Spinoza argues that nature itself *is* good. Indeed, being is for him ultimately an absolute good. Hence his claim that our relative goodness can only be achieved in and through our perfect affirmation of and acquiescence to nature, as well as his account of ethical responsibility as demanding our acquiescence to nature. Indeed, for these reasons, in further extension of the claims of his predecessors in the natural theological tradition, Spinoza concludes that nature is ultimately an expression of absolute goodness and that every apparent evil is not only the product of a finite, limited, and false judgment, but a judgment which can only be corrected and resolved by a more complete understanding of the "fullness of time," wherein every tear shall be wiped away and all broken things will be made whole. Such is Spinoza's reinvention of the classical apologia for the absolute perfection of the divine in nature, only now without reference to any dogmatic existence or transcendental object. Indeed, for Spinoza this conclusion is simply the logical consequence of a proper understanding of the immanent and natural necessity of material reality understood from the perspective of the totality of existence.

It should be clear from this that Spinoza's monism, while denying the possibility of free will, does not do away with the concepts of moral value or ethical responsibility. To the contrary, his metaphysical monism affirms the existence of a single and absolute moral value that is immanent within and inextricable from material nature itself. As a consequence of this equivalence between nature and morality, Spinoza thinks that every existent object, whether conscious or unconscious, actively willing or passively willing, is bound by an absolute ethical responsibility to affirm the necessity and moral value of nature. Thus, he concludes, while no existent thing is ultimately *free* in any meaningful sense, all things are nevertheless beholden to an absolute moral value immanent within material reality itself and are ethically *responsible* for the affirmation of that value. Indeed, he argues, all existent things *should* learn to affirm in their subjective will, inasmuch as they have one, the *laws of nature*. And, Spinoza concludes, it is only by acceding to and loving wholly the absolute necessity of material reality in this way, that we can be called virtuous and experience the eternal blessedness of true joy and lasting peace.

Such an affirmation is, of course, much easier for simple material objects, where the will of nature (operant in and through its mechanical laws) is expressed unconsciously, than it is for consciously willing subjects. For, as Spinoza notes, simple objects are, by virtue of their very being, always already in perfect union with the laws of material nature. Thus, they are always already in perfect union with the good. Things are much more complicated for conscious willing subjects within this system, as Spinoza notes. For, as he explains, given the nature of the modality of our being, it is all too easy for us to be led astray by unproductive illusions like the concept of free will, the idea of ontological individuation, and the concept of metaphysical dualism. As a result of these illusions and others, Spinoza thinks that human subjects tend to think of themselves as unique, outside of, other than, and distinct from the totality and necessity of nature. And when we are taken in by such illusions, flowing as they do from the natural limitations of our consciousness, he argues that we will judge the world according to our own individual interests and attempt to change it to suit our own particular being and will. It is in this way, Spinoza argues, that the concept of evil is born and exists exclusively within us as a product of our incomplete judgment and understanding. Things are evil, we think, inasmuch as they fail to affirm our individual being or conform to our particular will. The source of our false understanding of the evil of the world, Spinoza assures us, is the result of a failure to see that we are not ultimately individual or singular. Indeed, according to Spinoza, our individual being and particular will are nothing more than the expression of a modality of the one singular will of nature, the same will that drives the course of those things and events which we think harm or oppose us. And so, Spinoza concludes that their operation cannot ultimately be opposed to us, for the will of nature cannot be opposed to itself. Its operation must instead, by the nature of the monism of the whole, be in affirmation of itself, even if in doing so it frustrates our momentary hopes and dreams. When we come to understand the unity of the whole of reality, however, we can surmount such limited interpretations, cast off our misjudgment of certain events as evil, and come to affirm everything that happens as part of the necessity of nature and the ultimate goodness of reality understood *sub specie aeternitatis*.

For Spinoza, the illusory nature of concepts such as free will, metaphysical dualism, and the moral reality of evil lies in the fact that they have no ontological power. It is for this reason that he holds that they have no epistemological validity. On the contrary, they arise, he claims, as a consequence of faulty and limited understanding of reality perceived *sub specie durationis*. Thus, he concludes, when we come to understand reality as it actually is, and view it *sub specie aeternitatis*, such concepts necessarily wither and fade away. Indeed, Spinoza assures us, within the scope of eternity, every illusion and apparent evil which results from our misunderstanding of reality will prove itself, through a proper understanding of the perfect necessity of the absolute unity and eternity of being, to be an expression of the ultimate and final good of the operation of nature. It is solely due to our limited understanding, as he makes clear, that we perceive apparent evils in the operation of nature. And so, he argues, we must transcend the limitations of these perceptions through reason in order to see that the logical consequence of a proper understanding of the wholeness of reality as one is the realization that there can only be one absolute moral value: namely, goodness. When we realize this, Spinoza concludes, we can come to affirm all that happens as not only necessary, but as wholly good. And through our recognition and affirmation of this ultimate and final goodness, he assures us, we will be at peace with nature and participate consciously in its goodness, which is the essence of joy. Spinoza argues that it is our ethical duty to see and affirm the truth of reality *sub specie aeternitatis*, and acquiesce to the absolute necessity of its laws, in order to achieve the blessedness promised us by its divine order and operation. When we learn to act in perfect complicity with the necessity of nature—as do the heavenly spheres above us, the tectonic plates beneath us, and the viruses inside us—Spinoza thinks that we will become perfect agents of the necessity of nature and servants to its moral goodness. And ultimately, he claims, this is the sole aim of our understanding of nature: to become properly responsible to its absolute and immanent ethical power—its perfect goodness

It should be clear from this how Spinoza's materialistic monism, while dispelling the concept of free will, nevertheless affirms the idea of absolute moral value and ethical responsibility. For Spinoza, as we have seen, free will is not a condition for the possibility of ethical responsibility and moral judgment. On the contrary, for Spinoza, free will is an illusion which inhibits the proper exercise of our natural ethical responsibility to nature as well as our capacity to properly acquiesce to its moral perfection. For Spinoza, then, the real condition for the possibility of ethical responsibility is not freedom, but our recognition and affirmation of the absolute necessity and perfect causal power of nature. Indeed, he claims, only in acquiescence to the absolute necessity of material reality can we properly attend to our ethical duty within the inherent moral order of nature. Only in and through such a perfect acquiescence, he concludes, can we come to know and affirm the absolute goodness of existence and participate joyfully in its eternal blessedness. Hence his designation of acquiescence to nature as a mode of love and as the highest virtue of ethical duty. Only in and through such a loving affirmation of and perfect obedience to the will of nature, Spinoza concludes, will we align ourselves with the absolute moral value of existence itself and achieve perfect goodness. In this way, Spinoza provides an insightful model for how we might speculatively extract a concept of absolute moral value and even ethical responsibility from an entirely materialistic and monistic account of the cosmos—like the one granted us by the contemporary mathematical sciences. But, as should be clear already, in order to use Spinoza's ethics to guide us in this task, we must make some critical breaks with his account

CHAPTER 6

of the order and operation of reality, and what he takes to be its ultimate and absolute value.

Spinoza's Misplaced Optimism

There is a fundamental problem with Spinoza's account of the absolute goodness of nature in his secularized version of medieval natural theology. While his account does provide a metaphysical system which allows us to break with some of the assumptions that ground the alleged "moral neutrality" of objects, it does so only by asserting yet another ungrounded assumption; namely, the inherent goodness, virtue, or blessedness of nature. And this assumption is in turn supported by still another assumption; namely, that it is the natural trajectory of the universe, either by divine decree or fortunate accident, to affirm itself *eternally* in such a way that everything which happens can be interpreted and redeemed in light of eternity (i.e., *sub specie aeternitatis*). Indeed, as we have seen, according to Spinoza, it is only from the standpoint of the eternity of nature that the moral harm and suffering we endure in existence is redeemable as a good. Only when such things are evaluated in the scope of this presumed eternity, he argues, can the slings and arrows of our outrageous misfortune which pierce our flesh and haunt our minds be celebrated as expressions of a perfect goodness, and become transformed into a pathway to perfect joy, eternal blessedness, and lasting peace—rather than how they are actually experienced from the perspective of our finite and limited understanding, as the cause of our pain, terror, and dread. As Spinoza makes clear, outside these parameters, when understood and interpreted solely within the duration of our finite and limited experience and time in existence, such things cannot be understood as good, but only as evil.

The heart of Spinoza's argument for understanding and interpreting nature as absolutely good, and therefore as a source of perfect blessedness, hinges on his account of material reality as an expression of eternity. The potential goodness of any material object, natural fact, or accident of history, whether it is the rock which strikes us, the earth which crumbles beneath us and destroys our homes and cities, or the virus which infects our bodies and undermines our health, rests for Spinoza on its participation in and affirmation of the eternity of reality— the fact that every moment, event, or happening is a modal existence of infinity. Whatever apparent "evil" we may appear to suffer in time, *sub specie durationis*, Spinoza argues, is only redeemable as good if it can be asserted, *sub specie aeternitatis*, as an expression of the absolute necessity of an eternal reality which can only affirm itself forever. So it is that Spinoza suggests that even amidst their suffering, people who have come to understand the necessity of existence *sub specie aeternitatis* can find joy in their misery and achieve peace and blessedness in the midst of their torment. In this regard, Spinoza's ethics appear to be little more than a novel reinterpretation of the dogmatic claim that "for those who love God, all things work together for good."[41] In light of and from a proper understanding of eternity, he and his allies from the natural theological tradition assert, even the most horrendous events of human history can come to be seen as episodic adventures in the expression of a perfect and eternal good.

The blessedness of reality thus hinges for Spinoza on the claim that the universe is eternally self-affirming—that, in other words, the underlying will of the universe is to maintain itself perpetually. The problem, however, as we saw in chapter 4, is that this is simply not the case according to the best and most complete accounting of the universe provided to us by the contemporary sciences. To the contrary, as we have seen, given the absolute reign of entropy over reality, the ultimate will or aim of the universe is to destroy itself entirely—and what's more, it uses every existent thing within it to accomplish this self-annihilation as quickly and efficiently as possible. Indeed, as we have seen, even the apparently creative acts of the cosmos are ultimately a function of this obliterative and dissipative trajectory. Not only do complex objects come to be in complete accordance with the absolute necessity of entropic destruction, but the development of even more highly organized structures emerge solely to accelerate this end. And so reality is demonstratively *not eternal*, but is in fact *absolutely finite*. Indeed, as we affirmed in our metaphysics of decay, its very essence is to unbecome and destroy itself. To acquiesce in and affirm the laws of *this* universe as it actually operates in perfect obedience to the absolute necessity to dissipate and collapse is therefore to make ourselves complicit not in eternity, but in finitude and an imminent nihilation of all that is. Hence, to affirm in our will the order and operation of material reality as it actually is would be to become the willing servants of a cataclysmic machine, one which would use our acquiescence to destroy others, itself, and ourselves in the process. It would amount, in other words, to our becoming agents of oblivion—agents of what we have argued is absolutely evil.

There is no *aeternitatis* (eternity) in relation to which we might reassess the destructive trajectory of this process and its consequent horrors in such a way that our universe could be counted as good and our participation in it a virtue. There is only the abject suffering of the concrete and finite *durationis* (temporal duration) of material reality itself. If we are to follow the logic of Spinoza's monism, then we must wholly reject his evaluation of the absolute value of existence as a good. Instead, we can only interpret reality as we actually know it to be through the testimony of the contemporary sciences as the expression of a destructive will that works indifferently to obliterate everything which it creates and evaluate it, therefore, as an evil in itself.

We must remember that, according to Spinoza, we can only affirm the operation of reality as good *sub specie aeternitatis*. It is only from "the standpoint of eternity," in other words, that our temporal suffering can be redeemed as a means to some ultimate end and final blessedness. It is only in the light of eternity that Spinoza thinks the universe can be counted as an absolute good—one which merits our acquiescence. If that same universe is restricted exclusively to the realm of the finite and is interpreted entirely *sub specie durationis* (from the standpoint of time), emerging as it does from finitude and working entirely in accordance with ultimately and final collapse, then it would seem that any suffering we endure therein would no longer be redeemable, nor could it be counted as a path to some perfect benevolence, lasting peace, or salvific joy to come. Quite the contrary: in a universe that is entirely circumscribed by finitude and aimed solely toward its own destruction and the destruction of everything in it, every agony which we endure as a consequence of its drive toward this obliteration could only be counted as a moral horror—something which is unredeemable and unjustifiable—in others words, as absolutely evil.

How are we to evaluate a universe which seemingly requires and necessitates the tragedies it causes as anything but the expression of an absolute evil? What sort of universe is this in which we find ourselves if it is not the worst of all possible worlds? How else are we to hold the manifest will of material nature ethically responsible for the harm it causes, without concluding that it is morally blameworthy? Indeed, how are we to account for the unconscious operation of the destructive will of nature, entropically driven as it is by an absolute trajectory toward decay in the service of a final and complete obliteration, if not as a force which is wholly malevolent, in the Spinozistic sense of the word? Is this a universe to which we should give ourselves in perfect acquiescence? Or is it one which we should endeavor to reject in moral outrage, even if impossibly and futilely, given the totality of its reign as a metaphysical singularity? If we were to follow Spinoza by equating the natural universe with the divine, then we would have to evaluate God as a perverse and malicious entity, one who creates and exists solely to maim, torture, and ultimately destroy itself in and through its creation. And how are we to evaluate the reign of such a cruel deity otherwise than as an absolute tyrant and evil dictator?

From these brief excurses, it should be clear that while we may discover in Spinoza's monism a model for how we can maintain a system of moral evaluation and ethical responsibility within an entirely materialistic and monistic account of reality, if we are to apply that system to what we have learned about the actual order and operation of the universe, then we must ultimately break with Spinoza's account of the absolute moral value of reality, as well as his account of the ethical duty which arises from it. Whereas Spinoza, operating under the illusion of eternity, sees the value of reality as wholly good and our ethical duty to it as one of perfect acquiescence, we ourselves, operating as we do under the actual reality of a metaphysics of decay, must see that value as entirely evil, and conclude that it is our duty to resist its destructive indifference, no matter how impossible and fruitless our resistance might ultimately be.

Interestingly, this is precisely the conclusion of Arthur Schopenhauer who, like us, sought to draw from Spinoza's monism a way of reconceiving the idea of absolute moral value and ethical duty after Kant in an entirely materialistic system which denies the possibility of free will. But whereas Spinoza maintains, in his optimism, the absolute goodness of reality in service to eternity, Schopenhauer, like us, sees the nature of the universe in light of the suffering it necessitates in its operation, as entirely unjustifiable. Indeed, according to Schopenhauer, given what we know about the nature of the material universe as it really is, we can only conclude that Spinoza's metaphysics is far too optimistic, "and therefore false."[42] In order to speculatively develop what we have learned from Spinoza within a more realistic account of the nature of material reality as it actually is according to the testimony of the contemporary sciences, it is therefore incumbent on us to examine Schopenhauer's reformulation of Spinoza's monism, and understand his turn away from the latter's "false" and unjustifiable optimism in order to develop what might be a more accurate and appropriate form of moral pessimism.

7

The Monstrous Will of Nature

Arthur Schopenhauer's Ethical Monism

Schopenhauer's Critique

In many ways, Schopenhauer's project can be read as an extension and revision of Spinoza's attempt to challenge the prevailing metaphysical and ethical assumptions in the West.[1] Like Spinoza, Schopenhauer endeavors to dismantle what he sees as the reigning dualism of Western metaphysics. What's more, he attempts to accomplish this task by developing a metaphysical monism which unites subjective experience and objective material reality in a single coherent ontological unity. Furthermore, following Spinoza's lead, Schopenhauer aspires to use his account of this metaphysical monism to ground a new account of moral value and ethical responsibility which doesn't rely on any concept of the absolute freedom of the will from the laws of nature. In these endeavors, Schopenhauer and Spinoza are nearly perfectly aligned. Where Schopenhauer breaks with Spinoza, however, is in his account of the order and operation of nature, his assessment of nature's primal moral value, and his definition of our ethical duties in light of that value. It is the nature of this break which makes Schopenhauer's work of such vital importance to our own attempt to speculatively develop an absolutely grounded account of moral value and ethical normativity from what we've learned through the contemporary sciences concerning the absolute unbecoming of being. Through an analysis of Schopenhauer's metaphysics and ethics, we will therefore move one step closer to the final aim of this work: to see how a scientifically informed speculative metaphysics might ground a new account of absolute meaning, universal moral value, and ultimate truth.

Following Spinoza, Schopenhauer sees the fundamental problem with the West's long-standing metaphysical dualism as the fact that it simply does not stand up to any real logical scrutiny, much less the testimony of the sciences. To the contrary, he argues, it relies on the unjustifiable assertion of the existence of some "spiritual" reality which must exist "beyond the empirical world." In this regard, Schopenhauer concludes, the West's metaphysical dualism inevitably preserves, whether intentionally or unintentionally, some element of precisely the kind of dogmatic fideism which Kant sought to eliminate. And so, Schopenhauer argues that if we are to remain faithful to the insights of Kant's attempt to awaken philosophy from its "dogmatic slumber," then this metaphysical dualism must be eliminated, and with it any concept which arises from it (e.g., the idea of the absolute freedom of the human will). To make such an extension of Kant's critique palatable, however, Schopenhauer argues that it is necessary to show how concepts like moral value and ethical responsibility are not ultimately dependent upon this dualism or its corollaries, but can in fact be reestablished all the more firmly without them. It is to this end that the bulk of Schopenhauer's early works are dedicated.

In those works, as Schopenhauer makes clear, the key to this task lies in developing a new metaphysics which "does not, like all previous ones, float in the air high above all reality and experience, but [which] descends to this firm ground of actuality where the physical sciences receive the learner in turn."[2] Only through the development of such a scientifically established metaphysics of actuality, Schopenhauer argues, can we establish a new *terra firma* for the concept of absolute moral value and ethical responsibility. To this end, he sought to develop an entirely new metaphysics that could serve as "a common point of contact with the physical sciences" and, by drawing from them, aid Kant's aim to rid philosophical rationality of every lingering trace of dogmatic fideism.[3]

Given his deliberate attempt to affirm and complete the Kantian critique in this way, it might surprise someone unfamiliar with Schopenhauer that he begins this project with a calculated attack on Kant's own metaphysical claims. But for Schopenhauer, this is the only natural way to start, for he thinks that if there is any part of the Kantian project which has not yet overcome its own allegiance to dogmatism, then how can we rely upon its analysis of the limits of reason to carry philosophy beyond its past? And as Schopenhauer makes clear, there are certain elements of Kant's work which, despite his best efforts to the contrary, are still all too faithful to dogmatic metaphysics. One particularly consequential example of this lingering trace of dogmatism in Kant's work, Schopenhauer argues, is his insistence on the absolute distinction between the realm of subjective *phenomena* and the domain of objective *noumena*. While, as we have seen, Kant asserts this distinction in order to establish the proper boundaries which circumscribe the limits of philosophical rationality precisely to distinguish his work from dogmatism, in actual fact, Schopenhauer claims, this distinction is established upon one of the grounding assumptions of dogmatic metaphysics; namely, the dualistic division of reality into two realms—the absolute realm of the thing-in-itself and the wholly subjective realm of our own ratiocination. For this reason, Schopenhauer argues, if the aim of Kant's critique is to be accomplished, ironically, Kant's metaphysics must be abandoned. Only by breaking with the lingering traces of dogmatism which justify this distinction, Schopenhauer argues, can we actually be faithful to Kant's project as a whole: to excise dogmatic irrationality from philosophical speculation. In this regard, while Schopenhauer's work decisively breaks with a number of Kant's most significant claims, he nevertheless envisions it as a continuation of the Kantian project. As he put it, "Kant introduced seriousness into philosophy, and I continue it."[4]

The Crypto-Dogmatism of Kantian Dualism

In Schopenhauer's reading, the core insight of Kant's work, the one which he wants to affirm and maintain above all else, is the argument that "cognition and matter (subject and object) exist only relative to one another and constitute *appearance*."[5] For Kant, as we have seen, it is only through the inextricable entanglement of knower and known that reality exists for us. The effective power of this claim is to abolish what Schopenhauer thinks is the artificial distinction between active conscious subjects on the one hand, and passive unconscious material objects on the other. Understood in this way, he argues, Kant's work paves the way for a metaphysics which unites moral subjects and material objects in one coherent and monistic metaphysical system. In other words, Schopenhauer suggests that Kant's analysis of the structures of perception lay the epistemological groundwork for the completion of Spinoza's attempts to overcome the Western insistence on dividing the world in two and to develop a new metaphysical monism.

Indeed, according to Schopenhauer, Kant's account of the nature of phenomenal reality provides the best way in which existence might be conceived of as a coherent whole. It accomplishes this, he suggests, by commingling agency and objecthood such that any *known* material object can be said to possess some element of the *knowing* agent who constitutes it; and, vice versa, every *knowing* subject can be said to possess within itself the essence of the material object which it constitutes as *known*. Such a commingling of knowing agent and known object, Schopenhauer argues, allows us to envision reality as a metaphysical unity—the expression of a single primal will which interpenetrates both the knower and known alike. Hence his conclusion at the beginning of book II of the first volume of *The World as Will and Representation* that through Kant we might begin to envision in *nature* some underlying elemental or universal agency upon which a coherent metaphysics of reality can be developed.[6] According to Schopenhauer, it is only through the development of such a monistic metaphysics that we can escape the last vestiges of dogmatic thinking in the West; namely, its insistence on some form of dualistic thinking.[7] What's more, he thinks all of this can be done, following Spinoza's lead, without sacrificing a robust account of moral value and ethical responsibility.

However, as Schopenhauer makes clear, this is not the position that Kant himself takes in his own account of his metaphysics. On the contrary, according to Schopenhauer, Kant uses his insight to reinforce precisely the kind of metaphysical dualism which, Schopenhauer at least thinks, is a holdover from and vestigial trait of philosophy's dogmatic past. Hence his claim that in order to be faithful to the aim of Kant's critique, he must critique Kant himself. Indeed, according to Schopenhauer, it is only by radicalizing Kant's insights concerning the intermingling of knower and known beyond its originally intended meaning, and speculatively developing from this insight a new metaphysical monism which unites reality as one, that we can be faithful to the heart of the Kantian project to cleanse philosophy of every trace of dogmatic logic. For Schopenhauer, in other words, it is only by betraying Kant's metaphysics that we can be true to his epistemological aims.

According to Schopenhauer, the problem with Kant's interpretation of his own epistemological insight is his assumption that it is possible that the kind of agency which he identifies with the life of the subject could spontaneously emerge from its own activity; that is, from that ratiocination of the knowing subject alone. By Schopenhauer's read, Kant's account of the life and activity of the subject is not sufficiently grounded in any actually manifest force, power, or activity which appears in the world itself. As such, he suggests, the power to know which is identical with the rational life of the subject in Kant appears as something *sui generis*, separate, distinct, and unique in the world as the product of its own activity, and not, like everything else observable therein, as the causal product of something other than or outside of itself As a result, Schopenhauer argues that the knowing subject appears in Kant as something which is entirely ontologically unsupported and exists absolutely independently from the rest of reality. What this account of the nature and genesis of subjective agency entails, Schopenhauer therefore concludes, is a reinvention of the underlying claims of classical dogmatism; namely, the assertion of an absolutely existent metaphysical object that is entirely sufficient unto itself and independent from and outside the operation of the rest of material reality—something, in other words, which is free from the bounds and limits of the principle of sufficient causation: that is, God. In this regard, Schopenhauer argues, Kant's account of the nature and genesis of subjectivity, not to mention the entire metaphysics he develops from it, remain wholly dependent on the logic of dogmatism in its assertion of a new kind of divine power: the rational agent or knowing subject.

By defining the ground of subjective agency as its own operation in such a way that it exists as a metaphysical product of the synthetic extension of its own structures and powers, Schopenhauer argues that Kant's metaphysics does not ultimately free itself from or reject the logic of dogmatism. Instead, he claims, it reinforces it at a new transcendental level by transferring the nature and power of the dogmatic conception of the divine onto the nature, structure, and operation of the rational subject. In this regard, he concludes, Kant's metaphysics relies upon, maintains, and elevates the classical logic of dogmatism and, in so doing, reasserts the dualism inherent to that dogmatism, further dividing the world between that which exists in actual fact and according to the principle of sufficient reason, and that which exists by virtue of its own ideal nature and is free from the strictures of logical necessity.[8] In other words, Schopenhauer argues that by defining the nature and origin of subjective agency as he does, Kant necessarily restricts it to the realm of the ideal alone, thereby cutting it off from the rest of what actually exists and can be testified to by reason and or empirical evidence. In this way Schopenhauer suggests that Kant reasserts the claims of classical dogmatism, only now at the level of transcendental subjectivity, and, as such, invokes, albeit in a novel way, an unjustifiable form of metaphysical dualism.

As a result, Schopenhauer argues that despite its aims and its profoundly important and original insights, Kant's work ultimately fails to escape the trappings of dogmatism and, if anything, doubles down on them. For these reasons Schopenhauer argues that if philosophy is to finally disentangle itself from the logic, structure, and content of dogmatic metaphysics, then it must reject Kant's account of the nature and origin of subjectivity.[9] To this end, Schopenhauer proposes a new metaphysics which he thinks will fully unite subjective agency and rational will with the nature of objective reality in such a way that each might be understood as co-constituting and mutually informing its other, and, thereby, providing the sufficient causal ground for the existence, operation, and nature of its other. Only through the development of such a metaphysical monism, Schopenhauer argues, will the last traces of dogmatism be overcome in the West and a new absolute ground for an account of moral value and ethical responsibility be developed which will unite philosophical reasoning with the insights of the empirical sciences. To this end, Schopenhauer endeavors to use Spinoza to overcome what he sees as the vicissitudes of

Kant's epistemology; and vice versa, to use Kant's epistemology to update, enliven, and expand what he sees as the limitations and irrational justifications of Spinoza's metaphysical optimism.[10]

According to Schopenhauer, by establishing the ground of subjective agency within its own operation alone, Kant breaks with the principle of sufficient reason, a principle which both Schopenhauer and Kant agree is necessary in order to eliminate the kind of *deus ex machina* mysticism which critical philosophy stands against.[11] And so Schopenhauer argues that the ground of subjective agency must be established in some-*thing* which exists entirely outside of and beyond its own mental activity, some-*thing* which is material and natural in the absolute structure of reality itself. But Schopenhauer warns us that whatever form this *thing* may take, it must be seen as wholly natural and immanent and not some sort of divine power, transcendental ideality, or immaterial subjectivity. For, he argues, to establish the ground of subjective agency in some transcendental power of this sort would be to reassert the dogmatic error which he thinks philosophy must free itself from in order to secure its rationality and legitimacy. To guard against this danger, Schopenhauer suggests locating the grounding condition for the agency of the willing subject within the noumenal realm of reality in-itself. This can be accomplished, he argues, merely by extending the power and agency of the subject to will and to know into the natural objecthood of *things-in-themselves*.[12] In this way, Schopenhauer argues, the power of the subject can be sufficiently grounded by the nature of absolute reality itself. But, as should already be clear from this, to make this claim requires not only radically reconceiving the nature of the noumenal *thing-in-itself*, it requires reconceiving the nature of the interaction and engagement between the noumenal realm and the phenomenal realm. What's more, it requires re-envisioning the nature, order, and operation of every other purely material thing which arises on the basis of this noumenal reality as an equal expression of this primal will. It is in service to these tasks that Schopenhauer's own version of monistic metaphysics is developed.

The Absolute Will of Reality

Schopenhauer's argument that subjective consciousness is not the condition for the possibility of its own agency, but is grounded upon and conditioned by a more primal agency that is immanent within the structure of reality itself, proceeds by (1) challenging his readers to reconceive the nature of the *thing-in-itself* as an active agent; and (2) attempting to heal the divorce maintained by Kant between phenomenal reality and noumenal reality. Through these two concomitant steps, Schopenhauer argues, we begin to see how a subjective will might emerge as the conscious expression of the agency of absolute noumenal reality itself. Following this line of reasoning, Schopenhauer concludes against Kant that not only is it possible to *know* the nature of absolute reality, but that how and what we know is an expression of that absolute reality, in one form or another. In this way, as we will see, Schopenhauer's metaphysics lays the foundation for the reformation of absolute value and ethical responsibility after Kant without relying on any form of dogmatic logic.

To develop his transformation of Kant's metaphysics, Schopenhauer begins by drawing from Spinoza to identify a primal unconscious and asubjective agency or *will* within the noumenal thing-in-itself. "The core and principal point of my theory, its metaphysics proper," Schopenhauer writes, is "that paradoxical fundamental truth, the truth that what Kant called the thing-in-itself as opposed to mere appearance (more definitively called representation by me), and considered absolutely unknowable ... is nothing other than that with which we are immediately acquainted and precisely intimate, that which we find in our innermost selves as will."[13] This primal will is, for Schopenhauer, "the only thing-in-itself, the only truly real thing, the only original and metaphysical thing"; and, he goes on, it is what "give[s] to everything, whatever it may be, the power by means of which it can exist and have effect," so that it embraces "not only the voluntary actions of animal beings, but also the organic drives of their living bodies, even the form and nature of their bodies, and further the vegetative growth of plants, and finally even the inorganic realm of crystallization and any original force anywhere that manifests itself in physical and chemical appearances—indeed gravity itself."[14]

For Schopenhauer, then, in further affirmation of Spinoza's metaphysics, everything that exists, whether manifest in a subjective consciousness or a simple material object, is ultimately an expression of a primal natural will. "Nature," Schopenhauer concludes, "is th[is] will."[15] Indeed, as he make clear, everything in material reality is nothing other than "the mere visibility of the will."[16] The activity this will displays in its unconscious movement, he reasons, while perhaps different in *form* from the activity of a subjective agent, is ultimately then no different in *kind*. To the contrary, Schopenhauer claims, the same basic kind of will that we experience within ourselves as our conscious agency must "be attributed to the inanimate, the inorganic" as well.[17] For these reasons, he argues, it is wrong to see material objects as somehow absolutely different than or entirely separate from subjective agency. According to Schopenhauer, the difference which separates them from our kind of being is only one of degree or expression, and not ultimately of ontological nature or form. For this reason, he argues that material objects should never be seen as purely passive *hyle* (matter) that are exclusively acted upon by some subjective agent who exists otherwise than and beyond them. In fact, Schopenhauer labels such accounts of reality as simply "stupid."[18] Against such accounts then, he proposes that material objects and knowing subjects alike be seen as equal expressions of a single primal will or vital agency which is essential to the whole of nature. In this way, he argues, we must come to see every element of reality, from the activity of consciousness to the activity of matter, as all part of one contiguously related primal agency. This is what he means by the *will* of nature. As the primal ground for all of reality, Schopenhauer identifies this primal will as the "absolute" essence of reality.[19]

According to Schopenhauer, by identifying the activity of the material world with the operation of an absolute and primal will in this way, we can escape the "false oppositions between spirit and matter" which he thinks are constitutive of the dogmatic dualism of Western metaphysics.[20] Against this "Cartesian division of all things into spirit and matter," Schopenhauer suggests that reality should be understood as the expression of "will and representation"—the former informing what we have traditionally interpreted as "matter," and the latter identified with what we have traditionally interpreted as "spirit."[21] In Schopenhauer's account, this distinction between will and representation is therefore a distinction between two expressions of the same single reality—the former manifesting as a pure, direct, and unconscious expression of that reality, and the latter appearing as an alloyed, indirect, and conscious expression of that reality. The difference between them, therefore, is for Schopenhauer merely a matter of expression, and not a matter of substantive ontological categories. The apparent difference between the phenomenal realm of the knowing subject and its known world and the theoretically noumenal realm of things-in-themselves is not therefore absolute, but merely relative, merely a matter of perspective, as it were. Indeed, he argues, both conscious subjects and unconscious material objects alike are equally expressions, as we have seen, of the same one absolute reality which is the will of nature only either perceived directly in being or indirectly through representative knowing. Thus, where objective materiality is, according to him, the "mere visibility of the will," subjective consciousness is the representation or reflection of that visibility in another mode of the will of nature.

CHAPTER 7

The Necessity of Nature

In this way, Schopenhauer argues that subjectivity and objectivity can finally be united in a single coherent metaphysical system, each equally grounded upon and emergent from the primal agency of absolute reality itself. "I first posit will as a thing in itself, something completely original," Schopenhauer writes, "second the body as its mere visibility, objectivation; and third, cognition as merely a function of a part of this body."[22] Through an understanding of this monistic continuum which pervades the whole of reality despite its appearance in different forms, Schopenhauer suggests we might overturn the long-standing ontological dualism of Western metaphysics and finally awaken it from the lingering traces of dogmatism.[23] What's more, he argues that in and through such a metaphysical monism we might establish a more meaningful link between what science accounts for empirically/objectively regarding the nature of reality and what we experience phenomenally/subjectively of that reality. Through such a metaphysical monism, Schopenhauer concludes that we should be able to achieve, finally, a single coherent account of reality which unites in one system the empirical sciences accounting of the simple activity of objects in motion through space, like "the force of gravity in a stone," with absolute certainty with the seemingly much more complex activity of conscious "thinking in the human mind," through whatever laws govern the cognitive apparatus, such that a similar modicum of certainty might also be achieved.[24] Indeed, Schopenhauer thinks, one of the strengths of his post-Kantian revision of Spinoza's monism is that it provides a way in which the apparently objective sciences can be coherently wed to what we think of as the purely subjective sciences to yield a single metaphysical system which allows us to achieve the same level of absolute certainty in our accounting of the order and operation of both. All of this can be achieved, according to Schopenhauer, when we acknowledge that these apparently divergent realms are ultimately nothing more than distinct expressions of the same single primal *energeia*—the will of absolute nature itself.

Indeed, Schopenhauer suggests that his version of Spinoza's metaphysical monism allows us to understand how the same causal mechanical laws which we know to govern the movement of purely material objects in the empirical world might also function within and govern the subjective experiences and reflections of conscious subjects in our experience of and reflection upon that world. In this way, he thinks, his monism might finally complete the promise of the Kantian project: to provide a philosophical foundation for the scientific account of the world as a whole, and not merely as an objective appearance. By defining the operation of subjective consciousness as the complex recursive expression of the same *energeia* which is at work in the mechanistic movement of purely material objects, Schopenhauer argues that his metaphysical system coherently integrates the modern scientific account of reality into a Kantian account of the structures of subjectivity. In this way, he suggests, every law which has been established in and through the scientific study of the material world can be transcendentally assimilated into philosophical reflection on the nature and operation of subjectivity, and ultimately, as we will see, even into moral evaluation and the exercise of ethical responsibility.

Hence Schopenhauer's claim that "the law of causality stands firm *a priori* as the universal rule to which all real objects in the external world without exception are subordinated."[25] Following his insistence on the validity of this and every other natural law, he argues that his metaphysics provides a way in which we may finally see that "everything that happens, from the greatest to the smallest, happens necessarily," while maintaining some of our traditional philosophical concepts like subjective experience, moral value, and ethical responsibility.[26] Indeed, he argues that unless philosophy admits that all that we are and all that we do as conscious agents is alike in kind to the movement of material objects observable in the external world, then those concepts will have no real rational foundation or empirical validity and we will be bound within the constraints of dogmatic irrationality forever. If we are to finally overcome the influence of dogmatic thinking in philosophy and develop a fully rational metaphysical foundation for these concepts, Schopenhauer suggests that we must accept the scientific view of the world that "causality governs all . . . alterations," changes, and movements, whether they appear directly as "cause in the narrowest sense of the word, or [indirectly] as stimulus," as is the case in animal sensibility, or whether they appear "as motivation," as is the case with the conscious life of the human subject.[27] Whatever form in which it appears, Schopenhauer claims that his monistic account of the one primal will of nature enables us to acknowledge that the same basic laws which govern the material world must also govern us as well, though in less distinct and direct way. So it is, he concludes, whether it is expressed directly, in the movement of objects through space, or indirectly, in the representative power of conscious subjectivity in our minds, everything which is must operate in perfect obedience to the laws of causality which define the nature and operation of existence as a whole accounted for as an expression of a single absolute *energeia* or *will*.

From this conclusion, Schopenhauer argues that if philosophical reflection is to have any future validity, it must concede that "the entire empirical course of a human life, in all its events great and small, is as necessarily predetermined as the course of a clock."[28] In this regard, he maintains that we must come to see that "the human being is, like all objects of experience, an appearance in time and space, and since the law of causality is valid *a priori* for all objects and so without exception, he too must be subordinate to it."[29] For these reasons, he concludes moreover that "it is definitely neither metaphor nor hyperbole, but a quite dry and literal truth, that just as a ball cannot start into motion on a billiard table until it receives an impact, no more can a human being stand up from his chair until a motive draws or drives him away; but then his standing up is as necessary and inevitable as the ball's rolling after impact."[30] In fact, Schopenhauer even goes so far as to suggest that "one can visualize human behavior as the course of a planet which is the result of the tangential force given to it and the centripetal force acting from its sun."[31]

For Schopenhauer, then, subjective thought and rational reflection, as merely one expression of the primal will of nature, which expresses itself directly in the movement of material objects, should not be seen as operating outside of or free from the laws and principles which govern the movement of those objects. On the contrary, he maintains, subjective thought and rational reflection must be understood as operating in perfect obedience to the same laws of nature which govern the order and operation of material reality (as accounted for by the empirical sciences), only in a way which is harder to perceive, obscured as it is by the way that their reflection expresses indirectly the will of nature.[32] Despite this potential obscurity, however, Schopenhauer insists that we should not be fooled into thinking that subjective thought and action can ever be free from nature. While we may only know our dependence on and obedience to the causal laws of nature indirectly and obscurely, he thinks, we must nevertheless acknowledge that the absolute necessity of nature rules over and within us, just as it does outside and beyond us. As such, Schopenhauer concludes, "that undeniable pronouncement of self-consciousness 'I can do what I will' contains and decides absolutely nothing about the freedom of the will."[33] On the contrary, he argues, in conscious activity we "merely come to experience what we are" as it is absolutely determined by the one will of nature.[34]

What a recognition of this primal unity of reality entails, Schopenhauer continues, is a complete repudiation of the concept of *free will*—the recognition, in other words, "that a *liberum arbitrium* does not exist at all."[35] Unless we reject the concept of free will in its entirety, Schopenhauer maintains, we will remain beholden to the same remnants of dogmatic dualism which he thinks plagues Kant's critical philosophy; for according to Schopenhauer, "under the presupposition of free will each human action would be an inexplicable miracle—an effect without a cause."[36] If philosophy is to become truly critical and cast off its dogmatic past, he concludes, it must jettison completely the concept of *"liberum arbitrium indifferentiae* [which] under the name of 'moral freedom' [has become] a most precious doll of philosophy processors," and accept as absolute law the universal mechanical causality of nature as an expression of the single *energeia* or will of reality.[37] According to Schopenhauer, only by smashing the idol of free will entirely and destroying with it its implied metaphysical dualism through the hammer blow of a full and proper understanding of reality as it is accounted for in a scientifically informed materialistic monism might we finally accomplish the ultimate aims of Kant's critique: to achieve a fully rational and scientific accounting of reality as a whole. Thus, he concludes, "instead of trying to discount the basic truth of fatalism with frivolous babble and silly excuses, [philosophers] should attempt to understand it properly and clearly and to recognize that it is a demonstrable truth which provides an important datum for comprehending our highly enigmatic existence."[38]

The Moral Value of Necessity

The real originality and genius of Schopenhauer's dispute with the ontological dualism of Western metaphysics and its dogmatic insistence upon the idea of free will is to show how a concept of absolute moral value and ethical responsibility might be speculatively extracted from a materialistic monism which necessitates the absolute reign of mechanistic causality. This is, of course, the ultimate aim of his work: to dispel what he sees as the false belief "that the world has a mere physical but no moral significance."[39] According to Schopenhauer, this belief "is the greatest, most ruinous and fundamental error, [a] real perversity of the mind" which must be dismissed from the outset to ensure that his version of monistic materialism isn't misinterpreted as reductive or lose one of the most significant phenomena of subjective experience: the sense of good and evil.[40] Hence Schopenhauer's insistence that we must reject such "moral materialisms" with the same vehemence with which we reject dogmatic metaphysics.[41] With this aim in mind, he dedicates the bulk of his work to showing how an account of absolute moral value and ethical duty might be asserted within a purely materialistic and monistic account of nature.

Against the kind of purely reductive "moral" materialism which discounts the concept of moral value as a "folk" concept, Schopenhauer insists that "what is most important, indeed, what alone is essential in all of existence, that on which everything depends, the actual meaning, the turning point, the point of it all (if I may say so) lies in the morality of human actions."[42] According to him, if we are to develop a valid metaphysics which insists on the materialistic monism of reality, it is essential that we discover a way in which the activity of will can be evaluated as a *moral* force and still be bound by ethical duties, despite its apparent lack of freedom. Hence his claim that "the only metaphysics that is actually and immediately the support of ethics is the one that is originally ethical and already constructed out of the material of ethics, will."[43] In this way, Schopenhauer's critique of the metaphysical dualism of the West further advances our ongoing critique of the alleged "moral neutrality" of material objects. Indeed, according to Schopenhauer, if all of reality is to be united under one governing moral principle, then the moral value of existence must not only be grounded and supported by that principle, it must also be extended to include every existent object which is ruled by that principle. As such, Schopenhauer argues that the totality of reality must bear a moral meaning and ethical significance such that every existent object, human and inhuman alike, bears an inherent moral value. In this regard, his work affirms Spinoza. But where Schopenhauer diverges from Spinoza is in his account of the nature of that value. For, as Schopenhauer makes clear throughout his work, the moral force of reality is not in support of any ultimate or final absolute good; but, just the opposite, it is an expression of and perpetually in service to an absolute *evil*.

Schopenhauer reasons it thusly: if it is according to some natural will that a rock should fall in such a way that it can injure; or alternatively, if it is the will of nature that the earth's mantle should shift beneath our cities in such a way that it causes their destruction; or, finally, if it is the will of nature that viruses should replicate within our bloodstream such that we grow ill and die and suffer in the meantime; then it would appear as if the will of nature is not only indifferent to but directly opposed to our well-being and flourishing. What's more, Schopenhauer argues, it would appear from this that our suffering and extinction are absolutely necessitated by the will, order, and operation of nature. Indeed, he reasons, given its pervasiveness in all that we experience and do, it would seem that suffering is "the closest and most immediate goal of our life."[44] In fact, Schopenhauer argues that suffering and misery not only appear to be necessitated by the will of nature, they appear to be inherent and inescapable facts and consequences of that will. For this reason, Schopenhauer concludes, quoting the author of the *Theologia Germanica*, that it is entirely proper "to identify the world with the devil," inasmuch as we understand that "the evil spirit and nature are One, and where nature has not been overcome, there also the evil foe has not been overcome."[45] Indeed, according to Schopenhauer, if something "is bad, it is natural, and precisely because it is natural, it is bad."[46]

On this basis, Schopenhauer calls for a reevaluation of the natural laws of the universe. Since by his account, the causality of nature necessarily entails the misery and suffering of all beings capable of representing that nature within themselves through sensation or reflection, it is entirely logical to conclude that nature and all that it entails, from the simplest atom to the most complex human action, should be evaluated as an expression of an absolute and "radical evil."[47] Hence Schopenhauer's conclusion that "the existence of evil is already woven together with that of the world," such that the ultimate cause and "origin of evil, of the monstrous, nameless evil, of the horrible, heart-rendering misery in the world," is nothing other than the existence of the world itself: its own inner nature and will.[48] Indeed, Schopenhauer argues that it is entirely justified to conclude that "the world is simply hell, and human beings are on the one hand its tortured souls and on the other hand its devils."[49]

Following this evaluation of the natural world as the expression of a primal and absolute evil and the identification of subjective consciousness as the most complex expression of that will, Schopenhauer asserts that the whole of nature is evil and that human beings, as the most complex expression of that nature, are the worst of all natural objects. Indeed, he writes, "the human being is at bottom a wild, horrible animal."[50] In fact, Schopenhauer argues that as that expression of the will of nature which can reflect upon and develop nature through representation and use, human beings are "the evil animal *par excellence*, [for] man is the only animal which causes others pain for no other purpose than causing pain."[51] From this, Schopenhauer concludes that human beings are both the most effective agents and the ultimate victims of the moral malevolence of the will of nature. In this regard he suggests that human beings "resemble lambs playing in the meadow while the butcher already makes his selection of one or the other of them with his eyes"; all the while, he insists, we remain unaware of "what disaster is being prepared for us now by fate—illness, persecution, impoverishment, loss of limb, blindness, madness, death and so on."[52]

Given the variety of sufferings which necessarily await us in one form or another by virtue of the order and operation of the will of nature, Schopenhauer reasons that we "can conceive of our life as a uselessly disturbing episode in the blissful calm of nothingness," as, in other words, "a chore to be worked off," hopefully sooner rather than later.[53] Existence for Schopenhauer is therefore nothing less than evil itself, an evil curse which we can only hope to counter through absolute negation—which is to say the realization of perfect oblivion. For, he thinks, the more we are aware of and capable of participating in the operation of existence, the more we must both suffer and contribute to the moral harm it necessitates. By contrast, he argues, the less we participate in or contribute to the function of the will of nature, the more morally perfect we become. This equivalence between existence and evil, on the one hand, and nonexistence and goodness on the other, is for Schopenhauer the only logically justifiable moral system which can be established from a proper understanding of the function of nature as a primal will which necessitates suffering according to causal laws. Once we properly understand that nature itself not only creates the conditions for the possibility of suffering and harm, but necessitates it, can we realize the moral truth that nature is inherently evil, and the only good which we might achieve within it is through its negation.

From this, it should be clear how Schopenhauer's work supports our evaluation of the entropic thrust of nature as that governing principle and essence of all reality which, in its operation, necessitates our decay and suffering, as well as our evaluation of it as an absolute moral evil. Indeed, Schopenhauer's account of the nature and operation of the will of nature fits perfectly with what we have seen to be the contemporary scientific account of the trajectory of material reality toward absolute degradation and disintegration. For, as we have already noted, the inescapable law of entropic decay guarantees that all of nature is slouching inevitably toward its own annihilation and that everything which exists contributes, by its very nature, to that final end. What's more, as we saw, the more complex a thing is, the more efficient an agent of entropy it must necessarily be, since entropy is driving the development of such complex mechanisms as the efficient means to its ultimate end. In this way we can affirm Schopenhauer's conclusion that human beings, as one of the most complex material forms, might at the same time be both the "tortured souls" of existence and the terrible "devils" which haunt it.

From Schopenhauer's perspective, reality has an inbuilt and inherent telos, an unconscious drive or urge to disintegrate, exterminate, obliterate, and eradicate itself by enlisting all that is—and most of all we human existence—to accomplish this aim. It is precisely this impulse and trajectory that Schopenhauer identifies as the monstrous will of nature—a will which he thinks unites all existent things, from the smallest and simplest atoms to the most complex moral objects, human beings, and grants them an inherent moral value: evil. In this way, Schopenhauer's monism provides a model for how we might morally evaluate it all according to what we concluded concerning the inherent and essential unbecoming of being from our speculative extension of the observations of the contemporary sciences.

In a world entirely ordered by and necessitating destruction, wherein certain beings must reflect, experience, and suffer that destruction as harm, what else are we to conclude than that the function of the laws of nature is to ensure, as Schopenhauer put it, that "misfortune generally is the rule"?[54] What the absolute rule of the laws of thermodynamics guarantees is the absolute fact that, as Schopenhauer put it, "today is bad and it will get worse every day—until the worst arrives."[55] A world that is built upon and entirely obedient to the absolute order of entropic decay is, within Schopenhauer's framework, an entirely evil world—something which should be rejected as morally repugnant.

If we are to follow Schopenhauer's conclusions in our own attempt to erect an absolutely grounded normative system upon this evaluation of the inviolable laws of nature, then we must see how we might extract an account of ethical duty from his evaluation of reality as an absolute evil. After all, as Schopenhauer argues, it is only from a proper understanding of the absolute evil of existence that "an objective, unveiled and naked exposition of the ultimate ground of all moral good conduct" might be developed.[56] But how is a coherent account of "moral good conduct" to be envisioned within such a system—how, in other words, might we conceive of ethical responsibility and goodness in a universe which is entirely evil and predicated upon, determined by, and aimed at our suffering and ultimate destruction? This is, in many ways, the fundamental conflict driving Schopenhauer's own attempts to develop a robust account of ethical responsibility. And it is in his answer to this question that Schopenhauer believed he had achieved the crowning accomplishment of his work.[57] For according to him, what a recognition of the absolute maliciousness of existence empowers is not the evacuation of ethical responsibility but precisely the opposite: the exigency of an account of moral responsibility aimed at strategically countering the moral harm of the universe by alleviating, however futilely, the suffering it necessitates.[58] It is only through the development of a model of ethical responsibility which demands that the subject strive to resist, negate, and counter the effects of the absolute evil of the universe that Schopenhauer thinks any semblance of the good might be accomplished.

Ethical Responsibility in an Evil World

According to Schopenhauer, while the material world and everything which exists in it is absolutely determined by the operation of the malevolent will of nature and is therefore necessarily evil, human beings need not be willing participants in or wholly complicit to its malicious activity. Indeed, Schopenhauer suggests while we can never escape our essential participation in the order and operation of that will so long as we are alive, we need not cooperate with it fully. On the contrary, he argues, given the way the will of nature manifests in us, as a recursive and indirect representation of reality, we contain the capacity to develop an awareness of and compassion for the suffering of the world which we participate in and contribute to. Through the development of this awareness, Schopenhauer thinks, it is possible for us to cultivate an active hatred for and desire to resist the will of nature and to act in such a way that minimizes our participation in that will and that alleviates the suffering which results from our participation with it. According to Schopenhauer, while such endeavors can never liberate us fully from the operation of the will and the evil it necessitates in and through us, if they are strategic enough and vigilantly pursued, they can nevertheless effect a "relative freedom" within us from the system.[59] While this "relative" ethical freedom cannot exonerate the conscious subject from their participation in the moral harm of existence, or exculpate it fully, therefore, from its complicity in the suffering of the world, it is enough, nevertheless, he thinks, to constitute some approximation of the good, and establish, in this regard, an effective aim for ethical behavior. Though this diminution of our moral culpability is the only semblance of the good we can hope to achieve in an utterly evil world, Schopenhauer argues, it is enough to develop a new model for ethical responsibility. Thus, while he maintains that it is impossible to ever free ourselves entirely from the moral harm which is necessitated by being a part of the natural world—which is for him absolutely evil—he nevertheless thinks that this exercise of the "relative freedom" of subjective representation is enough to achieve some "relative good." This relative good is accomplished, Schopenhauer claims, first through the development of our awareness of the absolute evil of existence; that is, through the recognition of our inextricable participation in the evil of being. The second step comes, Schopenhauer continues, through a commitment to diminish our complicity in the order and operation of existence, by striving to withdraw from existence, as much as possible, and counter its effects when and where we can; in other words, by striving to resist the evil will of nature in and around us and to lessen its effects on us and in others. This is the sum total of ethical responsibility for Schopenhauer. Given the absolute moral value of the universe, Schopenhauer thinks, it is our absolute moral duty to exercise the "relative freedom" of our consciousness to take ownership of and responsibility for the harm we cause in the world, and to commit ourselves to lessening the effect of that harm as much possible. This conscientiousness negation of the order and operation of nature within and through us is the heart of ethical duty for Schopenhauer; hence his identification of the "relative" freedom of consciousness as a mode of "transcendental" or moral freedom.[60] Only by acknowledging and taking ownership of this "fact of consciousness," he argues, can we discover a way in which we might conceive of ethical responsibility within this metaphysical and moral monism.[61] Hence his conclusion that ethical responsibility "depend[s] entirely on the capacity for abstract representations, concepts," a capacity which he thinks empowers conscious subjects to become aware of, free themselves relatively from, and actively strive to diminish and palliate the effects of the absolute and abject horror of existence, both within themselves and within others.[62]

Note that according to Schopenhauer, the potential to exercise this "relative" moral freedom does not assure the moral worth of conscious subjects. On the contrary: as we have already seen, according to Schopenhauer, as the most effective agents of the malicious will of the cosmos, human beings are not only prone to *participate* in the suffering and ruination which is inherent to existence, they are generally wont to *advance* its monstrous enterprise day by day. Indeed, according to Schopenhauer, within the subject the "rational and vicious can combine very well, and it is only though their combination that great, far-reaching crimes are possible."[63] Thus, while Schopenhauer identifies the exercise of rational subjectivity as the condition for the possibility of ethical goodness, he does not see subjectivity itself as a candidate for or a guarantor of moral worth. As an existent thing, it too, he thinks, is ultimately an inherent evil. In fact, as that faculty of nature which is most capable of becoming aware of, reflecting upon, and employing the will of nature, Schopenhauer sees subjective rationality as capable of rising to the highest expressions of evil. Hence his claim that the worst demonstrations of the potential evil of the natural universe are to be found in the actions and aims of the human subject. Nevertheless, he thinks, it is this same power that grants to the human subject the potential to effect a critical distance from the moral harm of the universe, discover its cause and nature, recognize its moral worth to be absolutely evil, and subsequently endeavor to counter it.

For Schopenhauer, the aim of ethical responsibility is therefore precisely this: to utilize the representative power of the most powerful instrument of nature, subjective consciousness, to negate and neutralize the operation of the will of nature within itself and, in this way, lessen the effects of that will within itself and the lives of others. When a fully willing subjects uses the power of their consciousness in this way, Schopenhauer concludes, they actualize the possibility of what he calls "free justice and genuine loving kindness," or *compassion*.[64] Hence Schopenhauer's conclusion that the height of ethical duty is to cultivate "compassion; which wills someone else's well-being."⁶⁵ This, he thinks, is the only ethical injunction which can be deduced from the moral value of the cosmos as absolutely evil: to act in such a way that the will of nature is resisted in our own actions and in the passive experience of others.

Schopenhauer defines moral *compassion*, which he sees as the duty of every conscious subject, as "the wholly immediate sympathy, independent of any other consideration, in the first place towards another's suffering, and hence towards the prevention or removal of this suffering, which is ultimately what all satisfaction and all well-being and happiness consists in."⁶⁶ Inasmuch as someone successfully employs their reason to cultivate such a compassion for the suffering of the world, Schopenhauer argues, we may call them *just*.⁶⁷ Schopenhauer concludes that such a limited justice, aiming as it does to "help everyone to the extent that [we] can," is the best and only good we can ever hope to achieve from this wretched existence.⁶⁸ Schopenhauer identifies this limited and provisional sense of justice, achieved as it is exclusively through compassionate service to others in the hope of alleviating their suffering, as "the first and the fundamentally essential cardinal virtue."⁶⁹ "Compassion," he concludes, "is the sole non-egoistic incentive, is also the only genuine one."⁷⁰

Given the purpose of acts of compassion, Schopenhauer identifies the ultimate aim of his account of ethical responsibility as primarily *negative*.⁷¹ Indeed, according to him, "the first degree of the effect of compassion . . . [is] *to obstruct* those sufferings about to be caused to others that arise out of myself in consequence of the anti-moral powers that dwell within me."⁷² The primary aim of acts of compassion as Schopenhauer envisions it is, in other words, to discover a way in which the activity of the will represented in consciousness can be used to develop a "defensive shield" from our actions, one which aims to protect both ourselves and others from the full effects of the will of nature.⁷³ Schopenhauer therefore defines justice and goodness as exclusively *privative* moral forces—possibilities which are only achievable by dialectically opposing and effectively negating the positive moral value of what actually is: nature as an absolute evil.

For Schopenhauer, goodness is not something therefore which exists in its own right. On the contrary, he argues that goodness can only be conceived, like the freedom which makes it possible, as a "relative value"—one which can only be approximated when we use the power of our will to soften the malevolent blows of nature upon its creatures—or, framed alternatively, when we learn to use the destructive power of nature against itself. Hence his conclusion that "right is the negative, as opposed to wrong which is positive."⁷⁴ Schopenhauer reasons that it is our ethical duty to work *negatively* in this way, to counter and strive *against nature*, through the cultivation of compassion and the accomplishment of justice, something which he thinks can only be achieved through the alleviation of the suffering and moral harm which nature causes. So it would seem that for Schopenhauer, the sum total of our ethical duty is to strive to say "no" to the will of nature and to work, however futilely, to reduce the harm it necessitates.[75]

"Existence itself," Schopenhauer argues, "[is] something that should not be," from an ethical perspective.[76] Inasmuch as we exist, he continues, we are bound to do evil and "[a] happy life is impossible" for us.[77] Nevertheless, he maintains that because of the way in which the will manifests within us, we can strive to be good by "fight[ing] against overwhelming odds for something that benefits everyone."[78] The height of ethical responsibility, Schopenhauer therefore concludes with Shakespeare's Hamlet, lies in committing ourselves wholly to this fight—to this futile attempt to "take up arms against a sea of troubles; and by opposing end them."[79]

Schopenhauer's Ethical Quietism

Following his definition of goodness as an exclusively relative value, one which strives to oppose or at least dilute the primal moral harm of existence, Schopenhauer sees the ethical duty of conscious agents fulfilled not in what someone tries *to do*, but instead in what they strive *not* to do. For Schopenhauer then, in contrast to Kant, the best way to deduce our ethical duties from the absolute moral value of the universe is not categorically, or for that matter hypothetically; but rather, *disjunctively*. Given the nature of the cosmos, he claims, it is our ethical responsibility to work to divert, reject, or lessen the natural trajectory and effect of nature upon itself. We might imagine, therefore, that the kinds of moral maxims which could be developed from Schopenhauer's ethic's would be framed negatively, not as moral *oughts* but as moral *ought nots*. Indeed, Schopenhauer even suggests that it may have been this primal ethical insight which inspired the authors of the Ten Commandments to articulate their ethical code as a series of "shalt nots," rather than as a series of "shalts."

In this spirit, Schopenhauer drafts a number of possible moral prohibitions for his readers. For example, he enjoins us to act *not* out of cruelty to anyone or anything.[80] Following this prohibition, Schopenhauer famously mounts one of the first arguments in the history of Western thought for the inherent rights of animals, though his compassion on this point did not ultimately result in a commitment to stop eating them.[81]

CHAPTER 7

Nevertheless, Schopenhauer argues that even if we must rely on animals for sustenance, we *should not* cause them any more suffering than is absolutely necessary in the process, nor, he notes, should we ever "degrade animals to things."[82]

Another of Schopenhauer's ethical prohibitions of this sort can be found in his surprising insistence that despite the inherent evil of existence, we should *not* commit suicide.[83] This injunction follows from Schopenhauer's identification of the "relative goodness" which he thinks can be achieved from acts of subjective rationality, a relative good which, as he notes, cannot be achieved if we are dead. After all, he argues, if it is the will of nature to destroy us, and it is our ethical duty to oppose that will, then it follows that we have a moral imperative to hold out against nature for as long as possible, and not to hasten it to its inevitable end by committing suicide. Thus, Schopenhauer argues, it is our moral duty to resist the temptation to commit suicide, an action which, by any measure, acts alongside the malevolent will of nature to destroy. And, as he makes clear, it is only by opposing this will that we can hope to do some relative good while alive. Thus, while suicide may appear to be a relative good, taking us entirely out of the equation of nature and freeing us entirely from its grasp as it does, Schopenhauer concludes that we must not give in to its false promise and should instead resign ourselves fully to our fate, only in such a way that reduces the effect of that fate on the world.

From this it should be clear how Schopenhauer's account of moral goodness as a negative capacity might help us to conceive of the possibility of ethical responsibility in a morally monistic system. It is our duty, we might say, following Schopenhauer's account of the moral value of nature, to reject and resist, however impossibly, the dissipative will of the universe: to strive, however futile our efforts must ultimately be, to lessen the suffering of others and to offer compassion to those who are doomed to misery by its trajectory. Unfortunately, what Schopenhauer's account of morality gives to us in this way, it takes away from us in another. For, as should be clear from his definition of justice, there is an inherent quietism to Schopenhauer's account of ethical duty, one which only sinks us deeper in the mire of post-Kantian moral reasoning that we detailed in chapters 1 and 2.

Thus while Schopenhauer's ethics enable us to know what we should *not* do, they don't help to instruct us on what we *should*. For this reason, while they might help us to conceive of how ethical responsibility might be maintained and re-envisioned in an absolutely evil universe, they don't help us to see how we might *actively* respond to the suffering we see in the world today. So, though we may use Schopenhauer's ethical monism to evaluate the trajectory of existence as a moral evil, and define ethical responsibility negatively therein, as that which can be deduced from the absolute value of the universe disjunctively, we cannot use it to construct a *positive, practical,* or *active* ethics which energetically strives to escape the potential quietism of post-Kantian moral philosophy. For this reason, we must move beyond Schopenhauer if we are to accomplish the ultimate aim of this work: to escape the vicissitudes of post-Kantian moral and political philosophy and empower it again to a mode of normative thinking that can actively and practically respond to the problems of our world.

Frederick Beiser summarizes this limitation well: "Schopenhauer's teachings in the final chapters of *Die Welt als Wille und Vorstellung* is that we should deny our will and resign ourselves to the evil and suffering of the world."[84] Thus "rather than striving to create a better world," Beiser notes that Schopenhauer's philosophy tells us that "we should renounce our will to live and attempt to escape the world in religious and aesthetic contemplations."[85] If we want to discover a way to justify our active pursuit of a "better world," on the basis of our identification of its absolute moral value, then we must renounce Schopenhauer's quietism and embrace a more positive, practical, and active ethics, without, however, losing the heart of his metaphysical and ethical insights. This, of course, is precisely what Friedrich Nietzsche, Schopenhauer's most insightful reader and eventually his greatest critic, attempted to accomplish in his own work, particularly his early work. It is therefore to an analysis of how Nietzsche tried to overcome Schopenhauer's quietism that we must now turn if we are to discover how a practical and active normative system might be built from our assessment of the absolute evil of this universe governed entirely as it is by the metaphysics of decay.

8

The Specter of Nihilism

Friedrich Nietzsche's Moral Naturalism

Nietzsche and the Specter of European Nihilism

There are few thinkers who understand the consequences of Kant's critique of metaphysics and ethics as deeply as Friedrich Nietzsche. In many ways, Nietzsche was the first to fully assess the effects of Kant's critique upon philosophy and to recognize that rather than securing a firm rational foundation for scientific claims, it effectively undermined the possibility of making any absolute claims whatsoever. Hence Nietzsche's assessment that the inadvertent consequence of Kant's subversion of the logic of dogmatism was the complete collapse of every sense of the absolute good, right, or true. This is part the meaning of Nietzsche's now infamous assertion that after Kant "God is dead! God remains dead! And we have killed him!"[1] After Kant, Nietzsche claims, every "god," whether human or divine, becomes little more than a hollow idol to be sounded out by the hammer of critique.

One of Nietzsche's greatest insights into the power and effect of Kant's critique is his analysis of and attempt to respond to the consequences of this "death of god" in European philosophy: his diagnosis of the advent, rise, and eventual domination of nihilism in scholarly thought and public opinion alike. By Nietzsche's reckoning, it is Kant's "faith in the categories of reason" that is the direct "cause of nihilism."[2] According to Nietzsche, by reducing ethical value to the operation and structure of human reasoning alone, Kant's philosophy effectively devalues "the highest values" of humanity in such a way that a general "feeling of valuelessness" pervades and a sense that "existence has no goal or end" dominates the ethical, social, and political imagination.[3] In this regard, Nietzsche traces the origin of what has subsequently been called the "postmodern condition" in the West to Kant's account of the centrality of the subject in the production of meaning and value; his prohibition against the absolute or independent reality of these objects of human hope. As a result, Nietzsche declares, it became rationally impossible to find "any comprehensive unity in the plurality of events," to such an extent that any experience we might have of such a unity had to be judged as "not 'true'," and logically "false."[4] More than anything else then, Nietzsche concludes, this is the ultimate legacy of Kant's critique: the sense that "there simply is no true world" outside of and beyond "a perspectival appearance whose origin lies in us."[5] In other words, Nietzsche suggests that the practical consequence of Kant's critique is the general sense that reality as we know it, both ontologically and morally, is ultimately just a reflection of our own inner nature, rather than a representative of any absolute reality which might exist "out there," as it were.[6] It is this sense that, within a properly rational accounting of reality, all of our dearest truths, highest values, and hopes for an ultimate meaning might ultimately be nothing more than a reflection of our own most nature and not a representation of the structure of existence itself that Nietzsche sees as the source of the nihilism he thinks haunts the West after Kant and which he attempts to counter in his own work. Indeed, the principle aim of Nietzsche's work is precisely to defeat this sense that no absolute meaning, truth, or value can be found immanent within existence itself.

The great irony of Nietzsche's diagnosis of the effects of Kant's critique is, of course, that he, much more than Kant, is generally identified as the principal author, ultimate origin, and greatest advocate of European nihilism. Indeed, Nietzsche is popularly referred to as the father of all subsequent "moral relativists," despite the fact that it is his express aim not merely to diagnosis the origin and nature of such relativisms, but to overcome them. The irony of this bizarre inversion was not unknown to Nietzsche himself, who seems to enjoy his rather inappropriate infamy. Indeed, he jokingly references this unseemly reputation throughout his published works. Take, for example, the preface to the 1886 edition of *Human, All Too Human* where he refers to himself as an "old immoralist" who is accustomed to "speaking immorally, extramorally," and carrying philosophy "beyond good and evil."[7] Such appellations, while not entirely accurate, as Nietzsche comically notes, are not entirely without cause, however. After all, as he freely admits, it is his aim to maintain the spirit of Kant's critical philosophy by "posing questions with a hammer" in order to "soun[d] out [the] idols" of dogmatism which remain in our metaphysics and ethics and to prove them "hollow," empty, and devoid of meaning.[8] And, famously for Nietzsche, chief among these idols are what he takes to be traditional concepts of "good and evil" when they are conceived of as transcendental truths and eternal categories.[9] Indeed, following the line of argument which began with Kant, Nietzsche makes clear that these concepts only have meaning "in regard to human beings," and are not therefore representative of the structure of reality itself.[10] What's more, he argues, "perhaps even here [in the context of the human, they] are not justified in the way in which they generally get used" and are perhaps best abandoned entirely, along with whatever metaphysical systems have been used to maintain and justify them.[11] In fact, Nietzsche continues, it would be best if we were to jettison every metaphysical system entirely, given the complicity of metaphysics in the dogmatisms of the past and the way in which those systems have been used to justify the rule of those who would assert their power over us.[12] For this reason, Nietzsche concludes that if it is truly the aim of critical philosophy to uproot the terror imposed by dogmatic fanatics, then every metaphysical system must also be pulled up by the roots and burned as an infectious species which threatens to choke out the native power of what actually is.[13] In this regard, Nietzsche is perfectly aligned with Kant's critique. Indeed, it is this alignment which motivates his desire to trace the origins of the classical conceptions of good and evil to various power relations in the dogmatic history of Western philosophy in order to show that they do not arise spontaneously, or express some final or ultimate truth, but are simply a product of human reasoning. Where Nietzsche breaks with Kant, however, is in his evaluation of the possibility that some other sense of the absolute truth, value, and meaning of existence might be found, not in some transcendental or eternal ideal, but rather in the immanent dynamism of material reality itself.

Given the origin and nature of our classical values, however, Nietzsche concludes with Kant that they are, in the end, products of human invention—little more than figments of the imagination or empty signifiers which he likens to elements of a dream which he and Kant alike are trying to awaken us from.[14] Against such metaphysical fantasies, Nietzsche argues that what Kant's critique proves is that "nothing good, nothing beautiful, nothing sublime, nothing evil exists in itself."[15] As such, he concludes, all of our ethical systems are established upon metaphysical illusions and must, like them, be awoken from, abandoned entirely, and relegated entirely to the realm of fantasy. Hence, Nietzsche's declaration that following the collapse of every traditional metaphysical system through Kant's critique "there is no longer a Thou Shalt; morality, insofar as it was a Thou Shalt, has been as thoroughly destroyed by our way of viewing things."[16] Ethical evaluations of this sort, Nietzsche proclaims, are no longer meaningful after Kant—they are simply relics of an extinct dogmatism which is best burned upon the refuse heap of history in order to clear a way for the growth of new ideas.

This affirmation and amplification of the consequences of the Kantian critique on traditional metaphysics and morality in Nietzsche's work has been alternately celebrated and reviled. But according to Nietzsche, this attempt to complete the true aims of Kant's critique is only a prelude to his real aims. By his account, the real aim of his work is to establish a new account of reality, and through it, perhaps strangely, a new ethics—one which can recover our sense of absolute truth, value, and even meaning, only not in reference to any metaphysical structures, but in reference instead to the immanent nature of material reality itself. Thus, while Nietzsche follows Kant in his critique of the traditional concepts of good and evil as *things-in-themselves* and, in this sense, might indeed be seen as a kind of moral relativist, his ultimate aim is to move in and through this relativization of classical morality to develop a new conception of absolute moral value from a scientific account of the natural world. In this sense, rather than being counted as a moral relativist, Nietzsche is perhaps best understood as a precursor to the kind of absolute speculative materialism pursued by Badiou, Meillassoux, and myself. The crucial difference between Nietzsche's work and Kant's thus becomes clear: while both thinkers critique the classical accounts of absolute moral value, Kant suggests that this critique entails abandoning the concept of the absolute altogether while Nietzsche argues that this critique invites us to rediscover a modicum of absoluteness within a new domain; namely, the scientific account of material nature itself. Thus, while Nietzsche wants to affirm the aims of Kant's critique of the classical account of moral value, like Schopenhauer before him, he ultimately breaks with the conclusions of Kant's critique. For where Kant's critique abolishes the possibility of absolute value in toto, Nietzsche thinks some sense of the absolute might still be achieved from a fully scientific accounting of the natural world. Hence his claim that the ultimate aim of his own critique of traditional morality and metaphysics, unlike Kant's, is to initiate a "revaluation of all values"—in other words, to reassess the foundation, nature, method, and possibility of the evaluation of the absolute truth, moral value, and ultimate meaning.[17] So while Nietzsche confesses that he intends to carry philosophical reflection "*'Beyond Good and Evil'* . . . this does *not* mean 'Beyond Good and Bad.'"[18] On the contrary, as he makes clear, the aim of his critique is to "create new values."[19] By carrying philosophy "outside" the bounds of classical dogmatic morality, Nietzsche aims not to deepen the problem of post-Kantian nihilism, but to *overcome* it.[20]

This is in no small part the meaning of Nietzsche's infamous assessment that human existence itself "is something that must be overcome," and, to this end, that we must endeavor to cultivate within us an "overman," someone who is free from the bounds of traditional reasoning and classical dogmatic morality.[21] Hence Nietzsche's equivalence of the "death of God" in traditional metaphysics and dogmatic morality with the advent of a new way of being—a way of being natural, being ethical, and, as we will see, being joyful . "Dead are all gods," Nietzsche writes, "now we want the overman to live."[22] In striving to overcome "good and evil" and the traditional metaphysical grounds for these values, Nietzsche is no evangelist for atheism or advocate for nihilism then, as so many of his critics and fans might suggest. On the contrary, Nietzsche's announcement of the "death of God" and his intention to carry philosophy "beyond good and evil" are almost exactly the opposite: they are an invitation to discover new, nondogmatic absolutes and natural moral values upon which new ways of thinking, being, and acting may be established. Nietzsche's aim in doing away with the classical concepts of "good and evil" is not therefore to clear a space for some form of radical nihilism, but rather to make it possible to develop new ways of conceiving of and relating to the possibility of the absolute as it announces itself in a fully scientific accounting of the immanent power of material reality itself.

In contrast to the dogmatic moralities of the past, the nihilisms of post-Kantian philosophy, or the critiques of those moralities which sermonize from the heights of some new transcendental absolute or abstract rational structure, Nietzsche forwards a new natural morality, which is "coming and going to be," as a way of thinking that flows directly from what he thinks is most immanent and *positive* in us.[23] This new account of a scientifically grounded absolute morality grows, he argues, from a full accounting and proper understanding of what is vital in and essential to our natural material nature. Given his hope that a new morality can be discovered in a complete accounting of nature, Brian Leiter identifies Nietzsche not as a moral nihilist, but as a *moral naturalist*—someone who "aims to offer theories that explain various important human phenomena (especially the phenomenon of morality)."[24]

Nietzsche's Scientific Naturalism

According to Nietzsche, his attempt to overcome the limitations and effects of Kant's critique was initially inspired by his reading of Schopenhauer's own critique of Kant, which, as we saw in the last chapter, established a new account of the moral value of nature through a scientifically informed understanding of the order and operation of material reality. Nietzsche appears, at least initially, to have followed Schopenhauer almost to the letter in this endeavor. Indeed, in his earliest works he goes so far as to conclude with Schopenhauer that all that can be developed from a proper understanding of the absolute nature of material reality is an ethics of resignation and a politics of pessimistic quietism.[25] Famously, however, Nietzsche's allegiance to Schopenhauer's pessimism shifted around 1876, as he confided in a letter to Cosima Wagner in December of that year. "I have to confess," he wrote to her of his developing convictions, "[of] a difference that I have with Schopenhauer's teaching, a difference that developed quite gradually, but of which I have suddenly become aware. In terms of almost all his general claims I do not take his side."[26] From that moment onward, Nietzsche grew increasingly critical of Schopenhauer throughout his works to the point in his mature works of not only fully repudiating him, but openly mocking him as well. Note, for example, his conclusion that Schopenhauer's pessimism is a "cancerous ill of old idealists and habitual liars" which must be rejected entirely if we are to embrace the full expression of the natural world as the ultimate source of our power, being, and value.[27] Thus, while Nietzsche's attempt to ground a new account of moral value in a fully scientific understanding of the natural world and to develop from this a new ethics is entirely Schopenhauerian in direction, its conclusions, as we will see, differ dramatically from Schopenhauer's. It is for this reason that his work is so essential to our attempt to affirm Schopenhauer's assessment of the potential absolute moral value of material reality without, however, giving in to the kind of ethical and political quietism it seems to demand.

Interestingly, as Nietzsche's differences with Schopenhauer grew, he found a new and growing appreciation for Spinoza, an admiration which resulted in his declaration in 1878 that in Spinoza he had found "the purest sage" to have ever lived, and a mentor worthy of his own aims.[28] Indeed, according to Nietzsche, Spinoza's ethics are for him "the most effective moral code in the world."[29] Hence Nietzsche's assessment in 1881 that in Spinoza he had finally found a precursor to his philosophical project. "I am utterly amazed, utterly enchanted!" he wrote in a letter to Franz Overbeck that same year. "I have a precursor, and what a precursor."[30] Over the course of the next few years, the influence of Spinoza's naturalistic optimism slowly overtook the influence of Schopenhauer's scientific pessimism in Nietzsche's work, though the legacy of Schopenhauer's thought was never fully erased. Still, it is from Spinoza that Nietzsche ultimately drew to argue that a new sense of moral value and ethical responsibility could be developed from a scientific accounting of the natural world. Nevertheless, even these later works are clearly inspired by both thinkers. For, according to Nietzsche, following Spinoza and Schopenhauer before him, in order for an account of moral value to have any real validity, it must be grounded upon and grow from a speculative rendering of the actual powers of the natural world as they are revealed in the modern sciences.

CHAPTER 8

Nietzsche's assessment of the power and value of the modern sciences to this end is rooted in his view that what they accomplish, unlike the metaphysical and moral dogmatisms of the past, is nothing short of "the imitation of nature in concepts."[31] According to Nietzsche, this power of the sciences to imitate and reflect nature directly stems from their capacity to account for nature in a way that is not dependent on what he sees as the ideological lens of tradition, community, or culture. Indeed, he claims, what makes the sciences so effective is their capacity to dissociate us from these "all too human" interpretive frameworks, sentimental filters, and dogmatic interpretations and to show us instead nature as it actually is, purely and objectively, in its profound inhuman indifference, as radically free from, outside of, and superior to all of our interpretive and evaluative mechanisms.[32] Indeed, Nietzsche notes, "[s]cience has taught and continues to teach us to experience the earth as small and the solar system even as a mere dot."[33] From science's revelations of the objective and inhuman scale of reality, Nietzsche concludes, we gain a proper estimation of our significance in relation to the cosmos as a whole, and not merely as it appears to us, as Kant would have it.

Following what he takes to be the principal revelation of the modern sciences regarding our place in the cosmos, Nietzsche asks: if our solar system is but "a mere dot," imagine how much more insignificant our evaluations of that solar system and its products are. By showing us the complexity and enormity of the natural world, Nietzsche thinks that the sciences reveal to us the relative impotence and meaninglessness of our traditional metaphysical concepts and moral ideals. This, then, is the hermeneutical and critical power of the sciences according to Nietzsche: they force us to abandon these old systems and frameworks and embrace a new, inhuman, and cosmically expansive way of thinking and being, one which is more reflective of the way the world *actually* is, as opposed to how we *think* it might be or *believe* it should be according to our traditional metaphysical frameworks and moral judgments. For these reasons, Nietzsche argues that the ultimate aim of the Kantian critique can only be fulfilled in and through a reckoning with the modern sciences. And more importantly still, he thinks that it is only through the perspective provided by the sciences that the nihilism initiated by Kant's critique of classical dogmatic metaphysics and morality can be overcome and a new, natural approach to reality as it actually is can be developed such that a new sense of the possible moral value of existence can be created.

Like the speculative realists who were inspired by this project, Nietzsche attributes science's power to strip away our old ideals and confront us with the inhuman facts of reality as they actually are to its dependence on mathematics as a method. According to Nietzsche, "our knowledge has become scientific [only] to the extent that it is able to employ number and measure . . . All other 'values' are prejudices, naivetes, misunderstandings."[34] Nietzsche concludes that "mathematics is the only means to a general and final knowledge of humanity."[35] Hence his injunction that we should "introduce the subtlety and rigor of mathematics into all sciences."[36] Indeed, Nietzsche argues that if any understanding of existence as it actually is, outside the bounds of our human reasoning and metaphysical traditions, is to be achieved in a way that is productive of a new natural moral value, then we must endeavor to understand the world exclusively from this mathematical perspective. Only through such a mathematical rendering of the world, he argues, can we discover a new and valid sense of absolute value. For these reasons, he concludes that the question of value must ultimately be framed as "a purely scientific problem" if we are to overcome both dogmatism and nihilism in one go and discover in this way a new path to a naturally justifiable account of ethical responsibility.[37]

Indeed, Nietzsche suggests that at its root, the problem with traditional accounts of moral value (as good and evil) is that they derive these values from a metaphysical structure which can only be achieved through human means alone: either faith, in the case of classical dogmatism, or rationality, in the case of what Nietzsche sees as Kant's nihilism. By contrast, Nietzsche sees his own account of moral value as emerging from an account of reality that is achievable through an entirely inhuman rendering of what actually is in the world itself as it is accounted for by the empirical sciences. According to Nietzsche, sciences' reliance on mathematics grants it this power to break with human renderings and to present the natural world as it actually is in all of its inhuman truth—to think and speak, in other words, with and in the language of the cosmos itself. Hence Nietzsche's insistence that in order to overcome both classical dogmatism of the past and post-Kantian nihilisms which have resulted from the critique of those dogmatisms, we must turn to the mathematization of nature accomplished in the natural sciences to find a new way of thinking and being which is in line with the true structure of reality.

To make this all the more clear Nietzsche likens the values which are upheld in traditional "popular morality" to a murky "pseudoscience" against which, he thinks, the striking power of the actual sciences appear as the break of light at dawn.[38] Hence his further comparison of his rejection of these classical moral values to the scientific repudiation of magic. "I deny morality," Nietzsche writes, "the same way I deny alchemy, which is to say I deny its presuppositions."[39] If we are to overcome the presuppositions of traditional moralities, he argues, we must replace the metaphysical grounds from which they grow, whether dogmatic or critical, with a thoroughly mathematical and scientific accounting of the immensity of nature in its absolute form. "If only we had been taught to revere these sciences," Nietzsche suggests, we would already have a sense of absolute value such that dogmatism and nihilism would never have arisen in the first place.[40]

Nietzsche therefore argues that any account of reality which is not founded on a proper scientific account of the world must be entirely rejected in order to clear the way for a new and entirely mathematizable "metaphysics in the future."[41] Only on the basis of such a scientific and mathematical future "metaphysics," Nietzsche thinks, can any useful conception of moral value appear which clears the way for a new, absolutely grounded and scientifically defensible account of ultimate truth, practical ethical responsibility, and final meaning. It is Nietzsche's aim to use the mathematical and scientific rendering of reality to "awaken such [a] faith" as was once inspired by the metaphysical dogmatisms of the past; for, he assures his readers, the only valid "final [and] definitive foundations have been given in them on which henceforth all future generations of humanity will have to settle and to build."[42] Only on the basis of these "definitive foundations" which he thinks are secured by mathematics and the material sciences, Nietzsche claims, can a new "higher morality" be established.[43] In this regard, his aims are perfectly in accord with those of Spinoza, Schopenhauer, and the speculative materialists who come after them all. And, for these reasons, an analysis of Nietzsche's work is essential to my own attempt to scientifically ground philosophy's development of a new account of absolute truth, universal moral value, and ultimate meaning.

For Nietzsche, the ultimate power of science's abolition of our metaphysical pretenses is to clear the way for our discovery of the great "silence" of nature in response to our traditional questions about the nature of truth, value, and meaning.[44] By revealing and amplifying this silence, he argues, the modern sciences help to reveal that our belief in a "moral world order" is unfounded and nothing more, in the end, than a hopeful "delusion."[45] By awakening us from this delusion, Nietzsche thinks, the modern sciences empower us to see the emptiness of our long hoped for "moral world order," and to celebrate its absence as the appearance of the "beautiful chaos of existence" itself.[46] Only by learning to recognize, appreciate, embrace, and indeed celebrate, the primal immorality of this "chaos" in nature, he thinks, can we discover a new route to the absolute and develop from it a new sense of truth, value, and meaning. For these reasons, Nietzsche concludes that in the sciences we not only find the power necessary to cast off every trace of the metaphysical and moral dogmatisms of the past, but we further gain the capacity to escape the transcendentally grounded nihilisms which have replaced them in the present; and in this way to discover a new path to a more naturally grounded account of absolute truth, moral value, and ultimate meaning.

What science teaches us, Nietzsche makes clear, is the irrefutable fact that "there is [. . .] only one realm, that of chance events and stupidity," a realm governed exclusively by the drive of a blind mechanistic will. It is here, in the "one realm" "of chance events and stupidity," that he thinks we must discover a new, firm foundation for an entirely inhuman and absolute sense of truth, moral value, and existential meaning.[47] With this aim in mind, Nietzsche dedicates the bulk of his mature work to showing how an account of truth, moral value, ethical responsibility, and ultimate meaning might be extracted from a reformulation of Spinoza's metaphysical monism which equates God with nature. Where Spinoza's monism begins with the assertion of *Deus sive Natura*, Nietzsche's own monism is established on the equivalence chaos and nature—*Chaos sive Natura*.[48] It is upon operation of this primordial natural chaos, which he thinks it testified to in the modern sciences, and not some outdated faith in a relic of our dogmatic past (God), that Nietzsche's "revaluation of all values" grows.[49]

The Moral Value of Chaos

According to Nietzsche, what we realize through a scientific accounting of the world as fundamentally chaotic is that nature has no inherent order, purpose, or telos—that, in other words, it cannot be interpreted as affirming any of our traditional dogmatic or transcendentally established accounts of moral value—or "good and evil," as they are classically conceived.[50] What a scientific rendering of nature shows is the fact that nature is entirely indifferent to and fundamentally neutral with regard to any presumably eternal and transcendentally constant values. "How," Nietzsche therefore asks, "could we reproach or praise the universe! Let us beware of attributing to it heartlessness or unreason or their opposites: it is neither perfect, nor beautiful, nor noble, nor does it want to become any of these things."[51] Against such attributions, Nietzsche enjoins to recognize nature simply as it *is* rather than evaluating it according to our fixed ideas concerning what is good or evil. In contrast to such static and otherworldly ideals, Nietzsche sees the world testified to in the sciences as not only radically indifferent to our human evaluative categories, but also as perpetually changing and thus continually evading the limits of whatever judgment we attempt to impose upon it on the basis of these categories. By showing us concretely the fact that nature is dynamically indifferent to these ideals, Nietzsche argues that the modern sciences not only empower, but practically *demand* that we cast off the trappings of our traditional moral values, even our pessimistic ones, and develop in turn an entirely new set of values which are as dynamic as the chaotic power of nature itself. Indeed, Nietzsche argues, through a proper understanding of nature's chaotic dynamism, as he understands it to be revealed in the modern sciences, "there are no sins in the metaphysical sense; but, in the same sense, no virtues either; that this whole field of moral conceptions is continually in flux."[52] What we can discover from a proper understanding of the chaotic dynamism of nature, Nietzsche therefore concludes, is that "whatever has value in the present world has it not in itself, according to its nature—nature is always value-less—but has rather been given, granted value, and we were the givers and granters!"[53]

What Nietzsche thinks that the sciences prove, in other words, is that our traditional concepts of good and evil do not come from nature itself, but are exclusively products of human evaluation alone. Within a properly scientific rendering of the chaotic dynamic of nature, Nietzsche therefore concludes, "there is no difference in kind between good and evil actions, but at most in degree."[54] Indeed, Nietzsche claims that when they are rendered through this scientific accounting of nature, we might begin to see that even what we experience as "evil drives are [in fact] just as expediently species-preserving and indispensable as the good ones—they just have a different function."[55] Therefore, Nietzsche thinks, it is from a proper understanding of the scientific accounting of nature that we can finally discover that not only are our popular and traditional understanding of moral value "wholly ungrounded in the reality of things," and "solely the consequence of opinions about things," but so too is Schopenhauer's pessimistic evaluation of things.[56] For these reasons, Nietzsche argues that the categories of good and evil, however they are derived and justified, must be seen as ultimately and entirely a product of our limited perspective in such a way that "if humanity no longer considers itself evil, it will cease to be so."[57] In this way, Nietzsche repudiates both the traditional bounds of moral thinking as well as Schopenhauer's pessimistic revaluation of nature. The virtue of science and mathematics, Nietzsche suggests instead, with Spinoza, is that they can free us from such false evaluations by forcing us to reckon with the radical indifference of the universe to these categories. In this regard, Nietzsche thinks, the real power of science lies in how it can "teach the human being to cease being human"—to cease to conform, in other words, to socially constructed and culturally contingent moralities.[58] Thusly, he argues, the sciences provide a way in which we might achieve a new understanding of ourselves—one that is more true to the dynamism of nature itself—and develop from this new and more natural understanding an alternative set of values which might more accurately reflect the chaotic power of nature itself.

Nietzsche's praise of the power of the sciences to break down our traditional accounts of good and evil is not then a prelude to any future nihilism. On the contrary, it is a preface to the formation of new values—values which are grounded in a scientific account of nature as it *actually* is and not as we might *idealize* through our classical dogmatisms and transcendental rationalities. Indeed, as Nietzsche makes clear, the aim of his embrace of the scientific account of the universe is not to destroy the concept of value itself, but to clear the way for the development of a truer sense of value, "[to] begin to naturalize humanity with a pure, newly discovered, newly redeemed nature."[59] It is to this task that Nietzsche dedicates his last works.

The "Essence" of Nature—the Will to Power

Nietzsche begins this task by identifying what he sees as the "essence" of nature, if such a term can still be used in Nietzsche's naturalistic and scientifically inspired rejection of traditional metaphysics. Drawing from his early Schopenhauerian convictions, Nietzsche identifies the primal power of the natural world as a kind of chaotic *will*—one which he famously identifies as a "will to power."[60] "The world seen from inside," he writes, "the world determined and characterized on the basis of its 'intelligible character'—[is] precisely 'will to power' and nothing else."[61] Everything which is, Nietzsche argues, whether organic or inorganic, is an expression of this primal will to power. "This world," he summarizes, "is the will to power—and nothing besides."[62]

What Nietzsche identifies in this "will to power" is not some metaphysical first principle or ideal transcendental structure. It is instead, he claims, a logical extension or speculative deduction from the wholly scientific and empirically verifiable material fact that the natural world is bound by the "law of the conservation of energy."[63] According to Nietzsche, this law entails that "change belongs to the essence" of material existence. This is the foundation of Nietzsche's Spinozistic equivalence between nature and *chaos*. As the expression of the "law of the conservation of energy," Nietzsche sees the universe as perpetually re-creating itself, eternally transforming, and forever becoming. "Will to power," is

Nietzsche's way of identifying this relentless will to self-transformation and chaotic dynamism, which he thinks is the inner "essence" of nature as accounted for in the modern sciences. It is this, he argues, which the sciences force us to recognize—the fact that in its dynamic self-actualization, nature is not static and hence will never conform to any set of eternally existent concepts or ideas, like the dogmatic conception of good and evil.

In contrast to such ideas, Nietzsche claims that the "new world-conception" that is granted through a scientific understanding of reality in accordance with the law of the conservation of energy is of a world which "becomes, it passes away, but it has never begun to become and never ceases from passing away [but rather] it maintains itself in both—It lives on itself: its excrements are its food."[64] "Will to power" is simply Nietzsche's term for what he thinks of as the modern sciences' demonstration of this eternal dynamism in nature, operating as it does in conformity with the first law of thermodynamics. The will to power is thus, for him, a simple expression of the fact that in the scientific rendering of nature, existence is "thought of as a certain definite quantity of force and as a certain definite number of centers of force."[65] What Nietzsche hopes to convey in the phrase "will to power" is nothing more, then, than the idea that the cosmos can be understood as a "monster of energy, without beginning, without end; a firm, iron magnitude of forces that does not grow bigger or smaller, that does not expend itself but only transforms itself" over time.[66]

This model of existence as perpetually changing and devouring itself, Nietzsche concludes, is of a

> sea of forces flowing and rushing together, eternally changing, eternally flooding back, with tremendous years of recurrence, with an ebb and a flood of its forms out of the simplest forms striving toward the most complex, out of the stillest, most rigid, coldest forms toward the hottest, most turbulent, most self-contradictory, and then again returning home to the simple out of this abundance, out of the play of contradictions back to the joy of concord, still affirming itself in this uniformity of its courses and its years, blessing itself as that which must return eternally, as a becoming that knows no satiety, no disgust, no weariness.[67]

Nietzsche's will to power is simply an account of the world which he thinks the modern sciences describe—not the world as we rationalize it, wish it were, think it ought to be, or hope it still might become, but as it actually *is*, eternally becoming, ever changing, and forever creative—an infinitely transformative power or *energeia*. This, he thinks, is what is testified to in the first law of thermodynamics. Only by reconceiving of existence through it, Nietzsche argues, as a dynamic and eternally becoming *will to power*, can we come to understand reality and ourselves properly and discover therein some new account of absolute truth, value, and meaning which is scientifically justifiable and universally valid. It is only by embracing this dynamic account of reality which is given to us by the sciences, Nietzsche concludes then, that philosophy can hope to overcome the dogmatisms of the past without giving way to some form of nihilism. To this end, he asserts, "every other representation [of the world] remains indefinite and therefore useless."[68]

By speculatively extracting from the first law of thermodynamics the perpetually transformative and creative power of nature, Nietzsche surmises that existence must be, by definition, eternally recurring—perpetually recycling itself indefinitely into ever new forms and modes.[69] Indeed, he writes, "the law of the conservation of energy demands eternal recurrence."[70] And so, he concludes, a proper understanding of nature requires that we see "the world as a circular movement that has already repeated itself infinitely often and plays its game *in infinitum*."[71] It is from this account of reality as the expression of an eternally recurring creative will that Nietzsche develops his own version of metaphysical and moral monism.

According to Nietzsche, the *will to power* expresses "a more primitive form of the world . . . in which everything is still locked within a powerful unity, which then branches off in the organic process and takes shape . . . as a kind of life of the drives in which all the organic functions are still synthetically bound to each other with self-regulation, assimilation, nutrition, excretion, metabolism—as a pre-form of life."[72] For this reason, Nietzsche defines the "will to power," which he sees as the true nature of being, as the source of "all effective force" in nature, whether manifest in the force of our own human activities and meaning-making, or expressed in the irrational vital evolution of nature's creatures, or apparent in the silent drift of the celestial bodies in their orbits.[73] Indeed, Nietzsche claims, as the "essence" of all that is, the will to power is nothing less than "the essence of life."[74] Thus, he argues, "if [something] is a living and not a dying body . . . it will have to be the incarnate will to power, it will grow, spread out, pull things in, try to get the upper hand—not due to some morality or immorality, but because it *lives*, and because life simply *is* will to power."[75] And so Nietzsche concludes that "where life is, is there also will; but not will to life, [but] instead . . . will to power."[76]

CHAPTER 8

The Necessity of Will and the "Illusion" of Freedom

Since it is the inner essence and primal power of existence, Nietzsche argues that every part of our living being must at some level be an expression of the *will to power*. Indeed, he claims that *all* that *is*, whether overtly or covertly, in one way or another expresses and works according to the inner urge of reality toward dynamic chaos and eternal transformation. Nietzsche thus cautions us against thinking that living things have any real freedom in themselves, whether to define their own being, make coherence out of the chaos of their existence, or resist the inevitable collapse of every current order into disorder. In nature, he argues, "there are only necessities."[77] Therefore, he assures us, everything which is, including human beings, must at some level conform to the demands of being's trajectory toward anarchic mutation, that process which he thinks is assured by the will to power in nature, according to the first law of thermodynamics.

Given that the will to power is the one and only essence of all that is, Nietzsche concludes, in harmony with Spinoza and Schopenhauer's materialistic monisms, that the concept of free will must be rejected as an "illusion" in subjective life.[78] Indeed, he claims that a properly scientific understanding of the human as a natural object and expression of the will to power entails that "no one is responsible for his actions, no one for his nature."[79] The manifestation of the illusion of free will, Nietzsche suggests, is even ultimately the result of a causal chain of material factors which are driven by the inner necessity of the will to power. Hence, Nietzsche writes, "the agent's delusions about himself, the assumption of free will, is itself a part of this still-to-be-calculated mechanism."[80] "All actions" and experiences, Nietzsche concludes, even those which appear to be freely willed, "must first be made possible mechanically before they are willed."[81] Thus, Nietzsche argues, all that is, and all that can, does, and will happen in reality must be determined by the mechanistic necessity of nature's primal drive to perpetually re-create itself according to the law of the conservation of energy. If we are to maintain any sense of ethical value or "responsibility" in such a system, Nietzsche therefore argues, in further accord with Spinoza and Schopenhauer, we must recognize and affirm the absolute necessity of the will to power in nature and in turn reject what he calls the "error of free will" in our account of that responsibility.[82]

"A person is necessary," Nietzsche writes, "a piece of fate, a person belongs to the whole, a person only *is* in the context of the whole," and "there is nothing outside the whole."[83] Until we understand a person's being as bound and determined by the laws which govern the whole of nature, Nietzsche concludes, we cannot establish any viable system of ethical responsibility with which we might hope to practically guide human activity. Since for Nietzsche "all meaning is will to power" and must necessarily come from and conform to that will, any account of ethical responsibility must conform to our understanding of the will to power and accept its absolute causal power over all we are and do.[84] Only by crafting an ethics which accepts the absolute authority of this natural necessity within reality, Nietzsche maintains, can "we begin to redeem the world" with a new sense of moral value and ethical responsibility.[85] With this goal in mind, Nietzsche poses the fundamental question from which his redemption of ethics and his re-formulation of moral value grows: "Ought we to become as you [nature] are now, pale, shimmering, mute, prodigious, reposing above oneself? Sublimely above oneself?"[86] For Nietzsche, our capacity to derive some "ought" from that which merely is rests on our response to this question.

Nietzsche's Ethics of Affirmation

If any new set of values is to be derived from a properly scientific account of the natural world, Nietzsche argues that it must come through fidelity to the absolute necessity of nature and the profound silence of the cosmos in response to our questions concerning our own meaning and value. According to Nietzsche, then, the profound indifference of the universe to our traditional conceptions of morality should not be seen as a rejection of the question of value entirely, but as an invitation to invent a new and more natural sense of value. Indeed, he argues, these new and more natural conceptions of moral value can only be achieved once we learn to see in the indifference of nature not just a negative and destructive power, one which is capable of overturning our traditional account of value and meaning, but a positive and creative power as well, one that is capable of inspiring an entirely new set of values and meaning. Only through such a reformulation of the inherent and chaotic power of nature, Nietzsche thinks, can we learn to approach the indifference of the universe not with repugnance (which he thinks is the tack taken by Schopenhauer's pessimism), but with a "sacred yes-saying" that can carry our "spirit" from being "lost to the world" to a new way of being that can "win its own world."[87]

It is to this end that Nietzsche enjoins us to embrace the apparent indifference of the universe to our traditional moralities not as a solely nugatory force, but also as an invitation; indeed, as the very condition for the possibility of our discovery and reinvention of a sense of absolute meaning and ultimate values.[88] The indifference of matter to our traditional conceptions of good and evil should not inspire us to give up on the concept of absolute value, as it does in most post-Kantian traditions. Instead, Nietzsche argues, it should drive us to create entirely new values which are more reflective of the eternally transformative power of the cosmos as chaos. Indeed, Nietzsche claims, the indifference of the will to power in nature should be embraced as a "life-affirming drive," and perhaps even as a value-affirming power, as we will see.[89]

It is this possibility of discovering, creating, and affirming a new moral value which gives birth to Nietzsche's exhortation that it is our sacred duty to "be natural"; to embrace the will to power in us and the whole of nature as a fundamentally creative force which, through its indifference to our traditional values and rational conclusions, invites us to likewise be indifferent to the idealities of the past and to be faithful instead to what actually *is* eternally in nature itself: chaos, dynamism, and change.[90] For Nietzsche, the indifference of nature to us invites us to "no longer bury your head in the sand of heavenly things, but to bear it freely instead, an earthly head that creates a meaning for the earth."[91] It is through this affirmation of the natural world as it actually is (in its radical indifference) rather than as we think it ideally might or should be (aware of us and working for our good) that we will discover what he argues is the only scientifically justifiable path to a re-creation of value and meaning. Hence Nietzsche's definition of the *overman*, that version of ourselves which he thinks might come about through a properly naturalized and scientific account of existence as wholly natural and material, as "the meaning of the earth," as well as his claim that in order to find meaning and value anew we must "remain faithful to the earth and not believe those who speak to you of extraterrestrial hopes."[92]

In order to understand ourselves anew and develop from this understanding a new set of values, Nietzsche argues that we must "begin to naturalize humanity with a pure, newly discovered, newly redeemed [understanding of] nature" as is provided by the mathematization of nature accomplished in the modern sciences.[93] For, he thinks, the account of the cosmos that is provided by these sciences models a possible set of new moral values and ethical imperatives. Indeed, Nietzsche suggests, there appears to be an inherent "ought" within the indifference of nature as it is described by the sciences. According to him, we *ought* to "become hard," like nature itself; that is, we must "dare . . . to be immoral like nature," and become as indifferent to the categories of morality and rationality which he inherent from our dogmatic past as nature itself is to them.[94]

We should learn, in other words, he argues, to be faithful to the chaotic dynamism of nature itself which cannot be tamed by such static idealities. This dynamic indifference to any and every ideal is the only *ought* Nietzsche thinks is immanently extractable from the nature of matter itself: the imperative to, like nature, become eternally self-transformative and creative—rather than to cling to any particular form, value, or idea which is asserted in or maintained by the history of Western philosophy. Against such values, Nietzsche thinks we should embrace the ever-changing, ever-morphing nature of reality as it actually is, according to his interpretation of the first law of thermodynamics. Only by embracing this natural drive to transform and create, and by paying no heed to the traditional prohibitions and limitations which have historically hindered us from doing so, does Nietzsche think we might finally overcome the legacy of dogmatism and nihilism and discover a new sense of absolutely justifiable moral value and a superior ethical way of being in the world. So it is only through such an ethical fidelity to what he thinks is the scientific account of nature that Nietzsche argues that we might develop "the courage to [reclaim our] natural drives" and give ourselves over to the imperative to create, regardless of what may be destroyed in the process.[95] By learning to embrace this drive to perpetual transform ourselves and to "[say] yes to life, even in its strangest and harshest problems," Nietzsche concludes, we can rescue ourselves from the specter of nihilism which has haunted the Western world since Kant.[96]

For Nietzsche, in other words, the only way that ethics might be reclaimed and redeemed after Kant's critique is by unequivocally affirming the hard facts of nature, not as we wish nature were or hope it might still be, but as it actually is, as it is revealed in the sciences—cold, indifferent, and eternally changing; but also vital, invigorating, and creative. By embracing these same qualities in ourselves, in our thoughts and conduct alike, Nietzsche thinks, we might develop a new ethics and a more natural moral code. Hence, Nietzsche's assertion that the essence of his ethical system is to "say yes" to nature, to embrace the absolute necessity of nature to change in accordance with the first law of thermodynamics. To be moral in this way, he concludes, is "to learn more and more how to see what is necessary in things as what is beautiful in them."[97] It is from this conclusion that Nietzsche coins what he sees, borrowing from Spinoza, as the one true and highest commandment of his new ethics: *Amor fati*, to "love fate."[98]

"My formula for human greatness," Nietzsche writes, "is *amor fati*: that you do not want anything to be different, not forwards, not backwards, not for all eternity. Not just to tolerate necessity, still less to conceal it . . . , but to love it."[99] According to Nietzsche, to love fate is to love the absolute necessity of what happens to us by virtue of our participation in the natural will to power—to actively and enthusiastically surrender ourselves to it and celebrate all that it accomplishes in, through, and to us.[100] In order to love our fate in this way, Nietzsche thinks, we must cast off the old evaluative grids which we have traditionally relied on to judge the world, in which we celebrate some of what fate brings us as "good" while mourning the rest as either morally neutral or, worse still, "evil." In contrast to this old humanistic and dogmatic sense of value, Nietzsche thinks we must reject every category of human judgment, and, by moving beyond these ideas of "good and evil," embrace *all* that happens within and to us as part of the absolute necessity of nature. This, for Nietzsche, is to embrace and love the whole of reality as it actually is. But, in order to embrace reality in this way, Nietzsche thinks, we must first learn to glorify the necessity of nature as an expression of an eternally creative and transformative power. So it is, Nietzsche suggests, that such a glorification of nature is the condition for the possibility of his new sense of ethical value.

To exemplify his new conception of morality as an eternally creative activity, Nietzsche often elevates the artist as a sort of ethical ideal. This hagiography of the artist in Nietzsche's work is founded upon his estimation that in order to be a true artist, one must reject the conventions of any given time and commit oneself to a primal creative urge to reframe the world in new and original ways. Thus, Nietzsche encourages his readers to "learn from artists" in order to achieve moral perfection.[101] Like the artist, Nietzsche claims, only someone who strives to respond to the creative drive within them and, in service to it, cast off every convention and restriction which might inhibit or curb their own growth and transformation, can be called truly moral. In this regard, Nietzsche thinks, aesthetic creativity and moral perfection proceed in the same manner: through a fearless acceptance of a dynamic power within, throughout, and beyond us. Only by becoming a conduit for this creative power, Nietzsche argues, can we create great art and in turn embrace and reflect the primal value of nature. It is only through such a cultivation of our creative power that we can be said to act responsibly to the demands of nature and achieve something resembling ethical virtue from nature.

Insofar as we embrace the path of nature like the true artist does, Nietzsche thinks we might develop a new, more virtuous way of being that is situated "beyond" traditional concepts of good and evil, and act in a way which affirms the absolute value of nature itself. The fundamental test in Nietzsche's account of ethical responsibility, then, is to ask whether we have been "faithful to the earth" or, alternatively, whether we have abandoned what is natural by judging and resenting the necessity of nature (i.e., fate) to perpetually unsettle our current mode of being and thinking in pursuit of its eternal transformation and re-creation of itself.[102] Only if we can answer this question with a "sacred yes," Nietzsche claims, can we be sure that we have acted in such a way that affirms the absolute value of nature, and thus be assured of our ethical virtue. On this basis and this basis alone, Nietzsche suggests, we might possibly resurrect the term "good" to indicate an action which fully and freely embraces the will to power and rejoices in its chaotic and unpredictable consequences.[103] In this same way, he suggests, we might reclaim the term "evil" to designate any action which rejects the primal value of nature and judge, strives against, negates, or resents that which is necessitated by the will to power (i.e., fate), a subtle repudiation of Schopenhauer's whole system.[104] Nietzsche sums up his new account of moral value and naturally established ethics, against Schopenhauer's, thusly: we *should* pursue "a triumphant Yes-saying to [ourselves]" and to the necessity of nature; and we *should not* accept any "morality [which] from the start says NO to an 'outside,' to a 'different,' to [the] 'non-self,'" to the chaotic power of nature in its absolute form.[105]

Nietzsche develops what he sees as the one natural moral prohibition, that "*ressentiment* should be what is forbidden most rigorously," for, he reasons, this feeling of resentment is "to desecrate the earth" and "is the most terrible thing."[106] According to him, this *ressentiment* is the natural consequence of retaining the evaluative schema of classical metaphysics and morality, which unjustifiably account for human beings as somehow standing outside of and beyond the necessity of nature and, therefore, capable of judging it from some transcendental position "on high," as it were. Hence Nietzsche's claim that *ressentiment* flows from the false "belief in free will [which] provokes hatred, vengefulness, malice, an entire degradation of the imagination."[107] With this claim Nietzsche positions Schopenhauer's work, along with classical metaphysics and morality, as precisely what must be overcome in order to embrace a new natural morality. In order to be truly "good," Nietzsche concludes, every trace of any such judgment of the natural world must be eradicated in favor of a fully scientific account of nature as entirely determined by its own eternally creative power. Only by letting value flow from this natural creative energy, he thinks, rather than coming from outside of it and standing in judgment over it can we hope to escape dogmatism, nihilism, pessimism, and quietism alike and rediscover a more natural and scientifically supported sense of practical value and active meaning in nature and for ourselves.

It is this chain of reasoning then which led to Nietzsche's eventual break with Schopenhauer's pessimism. For Nietzsche, the weakness of Schopenhauer's ethics is that, while rejecting the possibility of free will, it nevertheless holds that the only good which we can gain from existence comes from directing the power of reality against itself in mournful acts of compassion. Indeed, as we saw in the last chapter, such acts of compassion, aimed as they are at negating what he sees as the primal evil of nature, are for Schopenhauer the sum total of ethical responsibility. Moreover, as we saw, these acts are only possible according to Schopenhauer if we cultivate within us rationally justified hatred of nature. In this regard, Schopenhauer's "good" is precisely what Nietzsche identifies as "evil"; namely, a cultivated resentment and rejection of nature which arises from the belief that nature must somehow be opposed or escaped.[108] For these reasons, Nietzsche concludes that not only does Schopenhauer's pessimism fail to develop a useful ethics from its engagement with the scientific account of nature, it conceals within itself a covert belief in the metaphysical possibility of freedom and, as a result, ultimately promotes yet another form of nihilism.[109] As such, Nietzsche argues, Schopenhauer, and indeed every form of pessimism thereafter, must be entirely repudiated and rejected as little more than a novel form of Kantianism.[110]

In contrast to what he sees as Schopenhauer's life-denying pessimism, covert metaphysics, and ultimately nihilistic ethics, Nietzsche asserts his own ethics as fundamentally "life-affirming."[111] In contrast to what he identifies as the affects which accompany Schopenhauerian pessimism—"annoyance, abnormal vulnerability, inability to take revenge, the desire, the thirst for revenge"—Nietzsche identifies the affects of his own morality, drawing from Spinoza, as *joy*.[112] Indeed, he claims, by learning to love fate, we learn to take joy in the necessity of nature and to draw upon its tumultuous and creative transformative power to celebrate all things. On this point, Nietzsche follows Spinoza even further by defining joy as that which "wants the eternity of all things, wants deep eternity."[113] According to Nietzsche, then, when our individual will becomes "unharnessed from its own folly," from the folly of its individual desires, hopes, dreams, and *ressentiments*, and instead aligned perfectly with the will to power in nature through *amor fati*, it can "become its own redeemer and joy bringer."[114] And so, he concludes, we might rediscover a profound sense of natural value and meaning by giving ourselves over to the natural laws of the cosmos and in this way overcome the strictures of post-Kantian nihilism without resurrecting any form of dogmatic metaphysics. Through a full immersion in and ethical affirmation of the primal power of nature as the one absolute value of reality, Nietzsche suggests that one can cultivate within themselves an "immense capacity for letting new galaxies of joy flare up!"[115] Thus, Nietzsche concludes, by responding appropriately to what we discover through science to be the true nature and value of reality and resigning our individual will to the will of nature, "you yourself may be the eternal joy in becoming."[116]

Nietzsche's Misguided Optimism

In this way, in his mature works Nietzsche overcomes the Schopenhauerian pessimism of his youth by embracing a version of what we have identified earlier as a kind of Spinozistic optimism. Indeed, according to Nietzsche in his final unpublished manuscript, the greatness of Spinoza's ethics was its capacity to achieve "such an affirmative position" in response to the material fact that "every moment has a logical necessity" and must not only *be* the way that it *is*, but "*should* be constituted that way."[117] In emulation of Spinoza's discovery of such a primal *ought* within what which *is*, Nietzsche crafts his own version of a naturalistic ethics. Indeed, in many ways, Nietzsche's ethics of affirmation (i.e., *amor fati*) is nothing more than a post-Kantian reinvention of Spinoza's ethics of acquiescence (i.e., *amor dei*).[118] Following the logic of Spinoza's ethics on this point, Nietzsche thinks it is likewise our absolute ethical duty to cede our will to the necessity of the material world and to derive value and joy from what he claims is its eternal creative power and infinite potentiality.

The problem, however, as we have already seen, is that though it is perhaps faithful to what he understood to be the testimony of the sciences of his day, Nietzsche's account of the nature of reality is no longer justifiable according to the current model of reality provided by the contemporary mathematical sciences. Thus, while it may accord perfectly with the first law of thermodynamics as it was articulated in the late nineteenth century, Nietzsche's metaphysics and ethics fail to account for what we now know of the second, third, and fourth laws; namely, that all matter and energy must perpetually dissipate, degrade, and eventually collapse, not in pursuit of eternal re-creation, but in pursuit of ultimate annihilation and perfect thermal equilibrium, a state in which no further change, transformation, or creation can occur. Thus, while Nietzsche's ethics may indeed be faithful to the best science of its day, it is nevertheless inaccurate. As a result, we must conclude that, like Schopenhauer's assessment of Spinoza, it is hopelessly optimistic.

Indeed, in direct contrast to Nietzsche's claim that the material world is eternally creative, contemporary science has shown that the only absolute necessity of nature is that it move inexorably and inevitably toward its own destruction, and the eventual obliteration of itself and everything else. In this regard, nature is not ultimately an affirmative or creative force, but a radically negative and nihilating force. It follows from this that Nietzsche was not only wrong to see in nature a purely creative and infinitely enduring power; he was also wrong to deny it any inherent aim, trajectory, or telos—that is, to think that it was ruled by nothing more than chaos. Against such a naive optimism, the contemporary sciences have proven definitively that the laws of nature do indeed operate with a very particular goal and absolutely invariable teleological aim: the evacuation of energy and heat by any means necessary. Thus, against Nietzsche's conclusion that we must see in the natural world an eternally recurring and chaotically generative force, the contemporary sciences prove the cosmos to be definitively finite; indeed, they show it to be progressing steadily toward its own expiration at an increasing rate and with a predictable and demonstrable end. Moreover, as we have seen, all of what we might call nature's "creative potential" is aimed solely and entirely at accomplishing this end as efficiently, effectively, and expediently as possible. The universe's creative drive is therefore nothing more than an expression of its ultimate annihilative aim. Existence is not, then, as Nietzsche would have it, a dynamically protean becoming, but a regulated entropic unbecoming—a passageway to an absolute void at the end of history. What's more, as we have shown, this unbecoming does not call for the eradication of every metaphysics, but rather the absolute justification of a new metaphysics of decay—a new metaphysics which can and should serve as a firm foundation for the extraction of new absolute values and a practical ethics. We cannot help but conclude that Nietzsche's call for the end of metaphysics as well as his apparent optimism in the creative power of nature is, like Spinoza's before him, entirely unjustifiable.

In a universe governed absolutely by the entropic principle alone, we should not affirm with Nietzsche a positive ethics which celebrates the power of nature as the source of a new absolute meaning and value to be embraced, celebrated, and enjoyed. On the contrary: ordered as it is toward a singular and absolutely obliterative end, we can only conclude with Schopenhauer that in nature we discover a force which must be negated, rejected, and resisted with every ounce of our being if we are to achieve any semblance of creativity and goodness. Against what is ultimately Nietzsche's starry-eyed optimism, his hope to find joy in the power of nature, we must reassert a more profound account of pessimistic skepticism, one which recognizes that the height of ethical duty is the futile attempt to extract the individual from becoming too complicit in the order and operation of cosmic destruction. To maintain a Spinozistic or Nietzschean optimism in light of the contemporary account of reality is to cling to an ideal which is no longer justifiable—to resurrect, in other words, a new dogmatic assertion of a some concept of the good which the order and operation of nature itself denies and contradicts.

If we are to derive some actually justifiable account of ethical responsibility from what we now know to be true of the destructive power of nature, then we must follow Nietzsche's advice and acknowledge the fundamental facts of reality; but this in turn requires breaking with what

Nietzsche took those facts to be. In other words, we must acknowledge, against Nietzsche's claims to the contrary, that ultimately and in essence nature is wholly bent on destruction. This, in turn, requires breaking with Nietzsche's Spinozistic evaluation that some natural sense of "goodness" might be speculatively derived from a scientific rendering of nature. Instead, we must return to some form of Schopenhauer's pessimistic evaluation of nature as an absolute evil.

For, as we have seen, an accurate scientific account of the power of nature cannot embrace Spinoza's assertion of *Deus, sive Natura*, nor can it assent to Nietzsche's secularized rendition of it which would assert *Chaos, sive Natura*. If any such equivalence is to be derived from what we know of the true order and operation of nature it could only be the much more Schopenhauerian conclusion: *Monstrum, sive Natura*. If we are to develop a new system of ethics from what we have speculatively extracted from the contemporary sciences concerning the absolute moral value of being as unbecoming, then we must acknowledge the monstrous fact that nature is aimed entirely and exclusively at obliteration in such a way that it necessitates our suffering. Only through a pessimistic reckoning with this fact can we hope to construct a naturally grounded and scientifically justifiable account of ethical responsibility.

The question remains, though, how it might be possible to accomplish this without giving in to the kind of quietism which, as we saw in the last chapter, seems to flow directly from Schopenhauer's pessimism. If we are to develop from his pessimistic evaluation a new account of absolute truth, universal moral value, ethical responsibility, political justice, and eventually ultimate meaning, then we must discover some new way of developing a more positive account of ethical duty from the material facts of reality than is found in Schopenhauer's metaphysics and morality. To this end, it is instructive to examine those pessimisms which both informed and emerged in response to Schopenhauer's. In this way we might finally see how and where a more active account of ethical responsibility can be developed from a pessimistic evaluation of the natural world as absolutely evil. This will be the aim of the following and final chapters of this book.

9

The Ethical Potency of Pessimism

Schopenhauerian Negation, Buddhist Renunciation, and the Political Activism of Philipp Mainländer

The Hope of Ethical Pessimism

Any metaphysics which hopes to have some practical import in the contemporary world must be compatible with and grow from the account of reality given to us by the contemporary sciences. And it is the consensus of the modern sciences, from physics to chemistry and biology, that the universe is governed entirely and absolutely by the laws of thermodynamics. These laws not only explain the emergence of existence as it is, they determine the nature of its structure, define the parameters of its operation, and account for every iteration of its appearance, from the movements of the simplest forms of matter to the dynamics of the most complex organic and living subjects. But these same laws also guarantee that everything that is must necessarily dissolve in such a way that the entirety of existence will eventually cease to be. Indeed, as we have seen, it is precisely the universe's trajectory toward this coming nihilation which conditions and motivates the development of more complex entities in the first place. What's more, this nihilating drive necessitates the suffering and eventual death of every living and sentient thing it creates. If there is any one natural law which we might identify as the absolute ground of being and potentially its meaning and value, it is the entropic necessity which directs the whole of reality toward its own destruction.

Entropy rules all. It conditions, provokes, regulates, and directs the totality of our existence and defines the quality of our experience of it, without exception. In light of the absolute rule of this one law, being appears to be nothing more than the efficient means by which the perfect oblivion of nothingness at the distant end of time is achieved—a fact which gives rise to what we called our "metaphysics of decay." Every specific being within this metaphysics is, in turn, little more than an agent of ontological extermination—a transitory object employed in the accomplishment of the coming void—and none more so than us. Indeed, as we saw, the sole purpose, aim, and end of all that is, especially complex living organisms, is to aid this ongoing desolation. Unfortunately, for every being endowed by this process with consciousness, these facts guarantee that a melancholic pallor shades our existence and we are bound by necessity to suffer. If we are to define an ethical system which is grounded upon, consistent with, and therefore useful to the contemporary world as a consequence and expression of that necessity, it must acknowledge, grow from, and be consistent with these fundamental facts. Only on the basis of such a naturalized and scientifically informed metaphysics of obliteration that accepts the inherent nature of suffering as an inexorable quality of sentient existence can a realistic and practical normative system be established which might empower us to act meaningfully in the face of our miserable fate and instruct us how to secure some semblance of good from our wretched lot.

This requires first, however, as we have seen, breaking decisively with the naturalisms of the past. Against those naturalisms which either: (a) have given up on moral absolutes entirely and concluded, on the basis of the apparent absence of moral value in nature as it is observed by the empirical sciences that reality must be morally neutral in essence, or (b) which have insisted on clinging to the dogmatic assertion that nature must be, against all evidence to the contrary, somehow, impossibly an eternal good; we have argued the opposite; namely, that the moral indifference of nature which arises from the apparent absence of any *ought* or *should* within it is evidence for its evaluation as an absolute evil. This obvious fact, when coupled with what the contemporary sciences have testified to regarding its inherently destructive aim, not to mention the suffering it necessitates in conscious beings along the way, is sufficient cause to justify our evaluation of existence as an absolute evil—indeed, as evil in its very essence, aligning perfectly as it does with the classical definition of evil provided by the history of Western thought. In light of these facts and this reasoning, any ethical naturalism which continues to insist, without cause, reason, or evidence, on the moral neutrality of the world, let alone its inherent moral goodness, must be considered simply another relic of the metaphysical and moral dogmatism of the past. If we hope to escape this dogmatism without giving into the myriad problems of other post-Kantian ethical systems and to discover in the natural world an absolute metaphysics and ethics which does not require any fideistic leap of faith, but which is bound instead entirely by the laws of rational deduction and the testimony of the empirical sciences, then it can only be through the development of our meta-

CHAPTER 9

physics of decay and an accompanying naturalistic ethics which acknowledges the horrifying truth that reality is and can only ever be an absolute moral evil.

From this we concluded at the end of the last chapter that it can only be by means of some form of ethical pessimism that contemporary philosophy might reclaim its pursuit of the absolute and outline a new sense of ultimate truth, universal moral value, practical ethical action, and final meaning which might make it relevant to the world beyond the academy once again. We have yet to see, however, how we might develop such a robust account of ethical responsibility and sociopolitical activism from metaphysical and moral pessimism—one that does not ultimately give way, at least, to some form of moral quietism. To address this problem, we must further analyze the nature and function of pessimism in the history of thought. The best place to start this analysis is, of course, with Schopenhauer himself, the so-called father of Western pessimism. By examining the roots of Schopenhauer's pessimism and the fruits which it bore we might discover a way in which we can embrace his moral evaluation of reality without giving way to his quietism.

The Value of Entropic Pessimism

As we have seen, metaphysical pessimism does not necessitate, as Nietzsche mischaracterized it, a denial of the ethical potency of nature. On the contrary, it's foundation is the affirmation of a wholly different value immanent in the absolute structure of nature itself; namely, nature's existence as an absolute evil—an evaluation which it justifies in reference to the indifferent and destructive power of nature, one which necessitates the degeneration and eventual extinction of all that it creates and the experience of that deterioration and annihilation within sentient beings as suffering. In this regard, ethical pessimism is wholly distinct from the kinds of metaphysical and moral nihilisms which Nietzsche sought to eliminate from philosophical discourse. But the assertion of this absolute value is nevertheless wholly distinct from other post-Kantian attempts to reclaim the absolute, for its assertion is entirely non-dogmatic. Instead, this pessimism is established on the most up-to-date scientific rendering of existence. The great insight of ethical pessimism is that it is possible to identify within this completely descriptive scientific account of the world the presence of an absolute moral value. The originality of ethical pessimism lies in how it inverts our expectations concerning the first principle of moral evaluation and discovers in this essential function of reality a new moral value upon which might give way to a new account of normative ethics and political action.

In light of the scientifically informed evaluation of nature as an absolute evil, ethical pessimism argues that moral responsibility might be defined anew, not positively, but negatively; as a *resistance* to and *rejection* of the innate trajectory of nature. This, as we have seen, is the essence of Schopenhauer's own moral pessimism; the idea that the *possibility* of goodness only emerges in dialectical opposition to what is positive in nature itself: pure evil. But it was precisely for this reason that Nietzsche argued that his pessimism appears to be inherently bound to a kind of ethical quietism which can at best hope to negate the malevolence of being as something that is entirely unbecoming, in every sense of the word, by reducing ones participation in it.

Frederick Beiser's analysis is right, Schopenhauer's "pessimism and ethics depend on his metaphysics. His pessimism holds that life is suffering because it is the product of an insatiable and incessant cosmic will; and his ethics holds that we achieve redemption only when we recognize our identity with all other things."[1] But is it possible to actively redress the suffering necessitated by the structure of being and actively pursue some semblance of goodness and justice without renouncing and withdrawing entirely from the structure of reality itself? Is it possible, in other words, to find some modicum of redemption through the negation of being while still being an active participant in it, and therefore necessarily a part of its insatiable and incessant drive toward destruction, decay, discontent, and suffering; or, in a word, evil? It is in answer to this question that the success of this project hinges.

Interestingly, this assessment of pessimism as the most scientifically informed ethical system and, therefore, of the apparent logical necessity of removing oneself from existence in order to achieve some passing hope in the possibility of goodness, seems to have been the reluctant conclusion of none other than Ludwig Boltzmann himself, the principal architect of the laws of thermodynamics as we know them today. Indeed, despite his expressed disdain for Schopenhauer, whose work he likened to a kind of "spiritual migraine," Boltzmann argues that the ontological principles of moral pessimism were undeniable, given what he had discovered concerning the absolute law of entropic decay over and within existence.[2] Indeed, some have even speculated that Boltzmann's suicide in 1906 may have resulted from his pessimistic assessment of the fate of our universe and the dismal prospects it set for the possibility of goodness.[3] Whether or not this interpretation of the reasons he chose to end his life is correct, it is clear that Boltzmann felt that any attempt to correctly evaluate the nature of the cosmos must begin with an acknowledgement of the indisputable fact that, by virtue of the entropic principle of reality, nature is inherently finite and constantly working toward its eventual end in such a way that everything which exists must become an accomplice to its inevitable destruction. Unless moral philosophy takes into account this fundamental fact, Boltzmann suggests in one of his last lectures, it will be destined to break apart upon the hard truth of reality itself. For this reason, Boltzmann concludes that philosophy must ultimately make a pessimistic assessment of the nature and value of existence if it is to square itself with the testimony of the sciences. Hence his suggestion in these same lectures that we should be wary of any philosophical system that insists on viewing the natural world as a benevolent power which promises the progress, regeneration, or perfection of any individual or any social or political order.[4] Against such optimistic naiveties, Boltzmann argues that the only philosophical systems which can hope to have any validity in light of the discoveries of contemporary science are ones which accept the fact that the universe is working blindly and tirelessly toward its own destruction and is busy corralling every existent object to the accomplishment of this eventual end. Hence Boltzmann's conclusion that even though "philosophy gets on my nerves," when he attempts to "analyze the ultimate ground of everything," he is forced to admit with Schopenhauer that "everything finally falls into nothing," and that this fact presents a predicament which "can be quite ominous if one values one's life."[5] It is of course this very predicament which motivated Schopenhauer's own ethical pessimism.

Schopenhauer's Ethics of Negation

For Schopenhauer, as we have seen, the real problem of moral philosophy is not the supposed division between *fact* and *value* as it is asserted by Hume and later by Moore. On the contrary, for Schopenhauer, existence, by virtue of its destructive indifference, is always already imbued with an intrinsic and inherent moral value. Hence his claim that a proper metaphysics "is originally ethical and already constructed out of the material of ethics."[6] The real problem of moral philosophy for Schopenhauer, then, is not how to deal with the apparent lack of moral value within a purely scientific account of the natural world. The real problem, he thinks, is how to deal with the incontrovertible fact that only *one* moral value appears within such an account of nature: namely, *evil*. By Schopenhauer's account, then, the real problem of moral philosophy is not the so-called *is/ought* distinction maintained in the naturalistic fallacy, but rather the traditional account of *good* and *evil* maintained in the history of philosophy. More to the point, the real problem of moral philosophy for Schopenhauer is how it might be possible to extract and define some account of goodness within an entirely monistic ethical system which insists on everything being evil. In other words, the real question for normative philosophy, he thinks, is how it might be possible to define the ethical pursuit of something like goodness without collapsing back into some form of dogmatically asserted metaphysical dualism; without, in other words, asserting, without evidence, that there may be other forces at work within reality which are somehow otherwise than being as it is testified to by the sciences. This, for Schopenhauer, is the ultimate question which contemporary moral philosophy must answer if it is to be of any practical use and value to the world.

According to Schopenhauer, "all finitude, all suffering, all the misery the world contains, belongs to the expression of what it wills; it is so because the will wills it so."[7] Hence his claim that "incurable suffering and endless misery are the appearance of the will, of the world."[8] For Schopenhauer, all the suffering and misery we endure are not merely *accidental* or *incidental* to the nature of existence. On the contrary, they are for him the very *form* in which existence as an absolute evil appears to those beings which are capable of representing the nature of reality in themselves. Suffering and misery are therefore the perfect reflection of the essential nature of existence within those beings, he thinks. Indeed, he concludes, they are the very *affect* and *experience* of the absolute moral fact of reality—the fact that it is ethically reprehensible to be. As such, he argues, suffering and misery are not something which can be avoided, eschewed, or escaped easily, either by moral luck or earnest endeavor. They are instead, he suggests, necessary and inevitable to being itself. As such, he thinks, suffering and misery are inseparable from the very nature of conscious existence itself, as the expression of the malevolent will of nature within a subject. For these reasons, Schopenhauer concludes, "the world in all the multiplicity of its parts and forms," and indeed even "existence itself as well as the mode of existence," should be understood as not merely occasionally malevolent, but as essentially, inescapably, and necessarily so.[9] Evil, in other words, is for him the true moral form, the absolute nature, and the ultimate reality of existence itself.[10]

For these reasons, Schopenhauer concludes that evil is not the result of some moral failure within us. Nor, he thinks, is it the result of some moral accident or unlucky happenstance. On the contrary, he argues, "the responsibility for the existence and condition of this world [as evil] can only be borne by the world itself, and no other; for how could anyone else take it upon themselves?"[11] Evil, which is experienced by the subject as suffering and misery, is for Schopenhauer then a necessary and unavoidable fact of reality. For this reason, Schopenhauer concludes that the moral arc of the universe bends exclusively and entirely toward evil. This fact guarantees, he thinks, that as long as we exist, we are bound to misery and suffering, both to experience it and to contribute to it. Indeed, it is this fact more than any other, which leads to his claim that the more capable a being is of representing and understanding nature, the more it will be a victim of the moral horror of existence and the more it will also be an agent of that horror in the experience of others. Hence his assessment of human subjects as "on the one hand [the world's] tortured souls and on the other hand its devils."[12] For Schopenhauer, "if you want to know what humanity, morally considered, is worth overall and in general, just look at the fate of humanity overall and in general. It is want, misery, sorrow, trouble and death."[13] This evaluation of human beings as the "worst of all creatures" follows directly from his assessment of our capacity to represent more fully and completely the malicious power and malevolence of the will of nature.

Though it is perhaps perfected in human beings, Schopenhauer insists that this capacity for moral evil is nevertheless "absolutely essential to [all] life."[14] It is indeed for him *the* moral value of life in general. The evil acts of more complex rational beings, he concludes, are therefore merely the natural consequences of their participation in and capacity to express the moral fact of reality itself. For Schopenhauer then, all existent entities are the efficient agents of the evil of existence. Thus, he reasons, while the "human being is always inclined to do wrong as soon as the opportunity exists and no outside force restrains him," it cannot help itself by virtue of anything in its existence.[15] To the contrary, Schopenhauer argues, it is the natural inclination of everything in existence to contribute to the moral harm of reality itself. So, he concludes, when we act in such a way that "affirms the will to life" within us, we necessarily become complicit in the absolute evil of our existence.[16] Indeed, Schopenhauer suggests, such affirmations of the will to life, as affirmations of the will of nature within us, are the "inner essence of evil."[17]

It follows for Schopenhauer then that if any hope of goodness is to be maintained in such an apparently monistic moral system, it can only come through some modification of the direction and consequence of the malevolent will of nature in us—some attempt to use that will's dynamic power to oppose, resist, or negate its primal effects. Since Schopenhauer thinks that it is the sole trajectory of the will to cause suffering and destruction, the possibility of some form of this "goodness" can only be defined dialectically and negatively as that which attempts to bend the destructive power of the will against itself in the attempt to establish some kind of "counterbalance" to its malevolence.[18] The possibility of goodness thus emerges according to Schopenhauer solely in reaction to and in negation of the primal evil of the universe. Goodness is only possible, in other words, Schopenhauer thinks, as an intentional "self-abolition and negation of the will."[19] For this reason he argues that the possibility of goodness "is [exclusively] a relative thing . . . because its essence is to exist only in relation to a desiring will."[20] Hence Schopenhauer's claim that there is no such thing as an "absolute good."[21] The only absolute moral value which exists in itself, as he makes clear, is evil. Goodness appears for him only in the negation of this absolute value.

Since any semblance of the good in such a monistic metaphysics of morals can only be achieved negatively in this way, by turning the destructive potency of nature against itself, Schopenhauer defines the good exclusively as a secondary quality—one which is achievable only insofar as we are successful in perverting the will of nature against itself. Goodness, in other words, he thinks, is merely a variation in the expression and representation of the one will of nature. It is a possibility that is actualized, Schopenhauer claims, when the malicious power of nature is used to temporarily negate, suspend, or lessen its own deleterious effects. If any goodness is achievable for Schopenhauer, then, it can solely be accomplished by providing fleeting relief from the otherwise incessant onslaught of moral harm necessitated by nature. Such momentary mitigations of the otherwise absolute horror of reality are for him the only good we can ever reasonably hope to accomplish. For this reason, he concludes, we can never expect goodness to achieve anything final or decisive in reality. As an exclusively dialectical and ephemeral possibility, such passing alleviations of the absolute misery of existence must eventually fail and give way once again to the absolute reign of the malicious will of nature. Nevertheless, Schopenhauer concludes, these evanescent respites are worth fighting for if only because they are the best we can hope to achieve while alive—the most we can hope to do, in other words, while still a part of and therefore a necessary accomplice to the evil regime of existence. As such, he concludes, the creation of such fleeting eddies of moral respite should not only be our focused ethical aim; the pursuit of these momentary respites define for him the moral potency and final meaning of our being. For Schopenhauer, the only hope for the good that we can reasonably hope to achieve from this wretched life is the possibility that we might accomplish, however fleetingly and ineffectually, some alleviation of the moral and practical harms which we must both suffer and contribute to by virtue of our participation in the will of nature.

According to Schopenhauer, this hope exists exclusively for human beings who can not only become aware of the truth of reality through the exercise of their reflective powers, but who can further use those powers to create new and inventive ways of directing the will of nature against itself. Thus, while Schopenhauer views human subjects as the "tortured souls" and "devils" of reality, he also thinks that it is exclusively within them that the possibility of some relative freedom from reality and therefore some relative good might be accomplished within reality. Indeed, inasmuch as we have the power to become complicit in nature's destructive will, he maintains, we also have the power to turn that will against itself. Therein, he suggests, lies the moral potency and ethical duty of human reasoning.

It is essential to understand Schopenhauer's account of ethical responsibility, however, that we remember that goodness never appears as an independent or absolute moral value in his system. On the contrary, it remains always and exclusively a relative value that only exists, by his reckoning, solely in and for human beings themselves (and perhaps other sufficiently sentient beings) in as much as they are capable of negating the power of being itself and, in this way, lessening its capacity to use them for ill. Evil, as we have seen, is for Schopenhauer in the end the only actual moral value which exists in and for itself. Thus, whereas evil exists within the thing-itself of nature, goodness exists exclusively for him as a category of rational deduction; it only "exists," he argues, inasmuch as it can be said to exist at all, as a subjective possibility which lies entirely within the structure of human representation. Goodness, in other words, is exclusively a category of perception and action for Schopenhauer, and never an absolute reality in its own right or a natural phenomenon in the world itself. Indeed, Schopenhauer argues, "since the will to life is the sole metaphysical entity or thing in itself . . . the will to life itself cannot be suppressed by anything except cognition."[22] And so, he argues, goodness exists as a possibility for human beings solely in their capacity to think rationally and act according to their reason against the manifestly malevolent will of nature.

"In human beings," Schopenhauer writes, "the will can achieve full self-consciousness, clear and exhaustive cognition of its own essence as it is mirrored in the whole world."[23] Inasmuch as this mirroring is cultivated, he argues, human "cognition makes possible an abolition of and self-negation of the will."[24] It is through such a negation of the will by rational cognition that the possibility of goodness emerges. By becoming aware of the operation of the will of nature in this way, human subjects can learn to "abolish . . . the essence that grounds appearance (while appearance itself continues in time) [so that] it can generate a self-contradiction within appearance and in so doing present the phenomena of holiness and self-denial."[25]

What we might call goodness, or what Schopenhauer at times, somewhat facetiously, calls "holiness," thus exists for him exclusively when "willing comes to an end with . . . cognition"—when, in other words, "cognition that has arisen by grasping the Ideas—becomes a tranquillizer of the will and the will freely abolishes itself."[26] This negation of the will, Schopenhauer argues, which is accomplished in and through the subject's own cognition is the only way that something like goodness might be definable within an entirely monistic ethical system where reality is identified with moral evil. Hence his claim that it is through the negation of the will that "the only thing that can give everlasting contentment, the only thing that can redeem the world" might be achieved.[27] Indeed, he argues that if anything resembling a *summum bonum* (highest good) is to be achieved within his moral monism, it can only be accomplished by the conscientious attempts of human subjects to negate the power of the will of nature through acts of rationally justified compassion.[28]

Compassion, Asceticism, and the Possibility of Inner Joy and Heavenly Peace

As we have already seen, Schopenhauer thinks that this active self-negation of the will, which presents the possibility of some semblance of moral good, is achieved only through rationally justified acts of *compassion*.[29] Compassion, as the concrete expression of a negation of the will which strives exclusively toward its own survival, is for him the only moral virtue which can be achieved, given his evaluation of nature as an absolute evil.[30] By cultivating the power of the will as it manifests in consciousness against its natural material tendency to self-perpetuation and affirmation, Schopenhauer suggests that we can direct our power to care for others and actively alleviate the suffering which that same nature necessitates. Since these are attempts to negate, resist, or reject the natural trajectory of the will, Schopenhauer identifies these acts of compassion as ontologically negative. Indeed, he writes: "the same source that gives rise to all goodness, love, virtue and nobility . . . ultimately emerges [from] what I call the negation of the will to life."[31]

Since the inner essence of such relatively good acts is negative in this way, Schopenhauer reasons that the ultimate expression of moral perfection in the individual is the complete renunciation and abolition of the will in pursuit of some version of ego death.[32] This attempt to abjure and eliminate the expression of the will of nature and to achieve, through this, the inner promise of death while still alive is exemplified for Schopenhauer in the commitment of various saints and holy persons to practical acts of *asceticism*.[33] Schopenhauer defines asceticism as a "deliberate breaking of the will by forgoing what is pleasant and seeking out what is unpleasant, choosing a lifestyle of penitence and self-castigation for the constant mortification of the will."[34] As such, he reasons, "the inner nature of . . . asceticism [is] the negation of the will to life," and this, as we have seen, is the essence of goodness for him.[35] Schopenhauer views the ascetic as someone who attempts to negate the will to life in all its forms by renouncing its insistence that we enjoy and perpetuate our lives, and thus rejects the will's desire to consume, grow, and rule all. Consequently, Schopenhauer sees the life of the ascetic as the only moral ideal toward which every human should ultimately strive. Indeed, he argues, only through such an ascetic attempt to negate life in every form will we discover "the complete resignation and holiness that comes from goodness once it attains its highest degree."[36] Schopenhauer concludes that it is through the negation of the will of nature in this way, first through compassion and ultimately through asceticism, that human beings can hope to effect some semblance of good while alive and attempt to redeem themselves and the world and gain "inner joy and true heavenly peace."[37] Indeed, for Schopenhauer, it is only through a diligent resistance to the inner will of nature that we can exercise our relative "freedom" from and, in this way, find some modicum of "tranquility" within the nightmare of existence.[38]

For Schopenhauer, the ultimate aim of all moral acts is to achieve this tranquility, or this pacification of the will of nature, through *negation*, first within ourselves, then in the lives of others, and finally throughout the natural world itself. In this way, he argues, we might slowly, from moment to moment, direct the power of the will of nature against itself in anticipation of and in practice for the eventual total respite of nonexistence to come. It thus becomes clear that for Schopenhauer, the ultimate aim of every moral act is this gradual "melting away [of the world] through the abolition of the will, [eventually] leaving only empty nothing before us."[39] This is Schopenhauer's own rendition of the infamous Platonic maxim which posits philosophy as a preparation for death. The goal of philosophical ethics, Schopenhauer agrees with Plato, is to slowly prepare the human subject to see the nothingness of death as morally superior to any and every form of existence.

By practicing the negation of the will through acts of rationally motivated compassion which spring from a properly scientific understanding of the world, Schopenhauer thinks that we may come to know this modicum of peace, embrace it with all that we are, and act in accordance with it. Hence Schopenhauer's final words at the end of *The World as Will and*

Representation: "for those in whom the will has turned and negated itself, this world of ours which is so very real with all its suns and galaxies—is nothing."[40] For Schopenhauer, the sum total of ethical responsibility in an absolutely evil world is this: the deliberate attempt to reconcile and commit ourselves in the hope for a possible perfect peace to come through the final and ultimate negation of our own life, the lives of others, and eventually the whole of nature in a final and complete nihilation of existence which leaves only the undisturbed purity of absolute nothingness.

The Buddhist Renunciation of Being

Schopenhauer's argument that it is only through a negation of the will in pursuit of the purity of absolute nothingness that some semblance of the "good" can be achieved is, of course, profoundly influenced by his understanding of the Buddhist scriptures, which had only just been translated into German when he was a student.[41] Indeed, Schopenhauer has nothing but praise for the moral teachings of Buddhism, writing that "there has never been and will never be a [system] that is bound up so strongly with a philosophical truth" as Buddhism.[42] The moral perfection of Buddhism emerges for Schopenhauer from what he takes, whether accurately or inaccurately, to be its assertion that "existence is . . . an evil and the world [is] a scene of misery in which it would be better not to appear."[43]

Whether Schopenhauer's pessimistic rendering of the teachings of Theravada Buddhism, the only school with which he seems to have been acquainted, is ultimately accurate or representative of its own understanding of itself has been hotly debated.[44] But however one comes down on this debate, it is clear that what he admires in Buddhism is what he sees as the profound ontological and moral pessimism of its core tenets, and its capacity to extract a practical ethics from this pessimistic evaluation of existence. Indeed, according to Schopenhauer, it is this pessimistic core to the teachings of Buddhism, as he understands it, that he thinks makes it so foreign to the "European mind . . . brought up in optimism."[45] What Schopenhauer thinks the "European mind" has to learn from Buddhism is not only its appreciation of the fundamental predicament of existence, but, even more importantly, the Buddhist belief that the best means to surmount and escape that predicament is not through some transcendental leap of faith or dogmatic hope in the possibility of another realm of existence, but rather the disciplined and practical rejection of being. For Schopenhauer, as we have seen, this rejection is achieved through an inner negation of the will of nature in us, understood as the expression

CHAPTER 9

of the absolute evil of existence. And, as he understands it, this is also the primary aim of Buddhist ethics: the liberation from suffering through the extinction of the conscious egoic will. What's more, as Schopenhauer correctly notes, this pursuit can only be initiated according to Buddhist ethics by giving up hope that salvation from suffering can come from anything or anyone other than the self. On this note, at least Schopenhauer's understanding of Theravada Buddhism is correct.

Indeed, one of the core teachings of early Buddhist thought in the Theravada tradition is that for someone to have any hope of resolving or redeeming the inescapable suffering of existence, they must reject every transcendental or otherworldly account of reality.[46] This position is articulated concisely in the "Sabba Sutta" or "Discourse on the All," as recorded in the *Saḷāyatanavagga* of the *Saṃyutta Nikāya*, or the *Connected Discourses of the Pali Canon*, one of the primary texts of Theravada Buddhism. There, Siddhartha Gautama, the first historical Buddha, instructs his students in the totality of what he calls "the all," which is to say, the full extent of reality and existence as he understands it.[47]

"The all," the text reads, consists entirely in this: "the eye and forms, the ear and sounds, the nose and odours, the tongue and tastes, the body and tactile objects, [and] the mind and mental phenomena."[48] "This," Gautama concludes, "is called the all"; it is entirely and exclusively the sum of the content of our body and mental perceptions—nothing more, nothing less.[49] Reality, according to the early Buddhist teachings, is the sum total of concrete phenomena and the perceptions and perceptual structures which structure the nature of that phenomena. Indeed, the text maintains, there is *nothing* outside of or beyond such concrete appearances. Hence Gautama's conclusion that if anyone promises to teach "another all" beyond that which is immediately apparent in and through our mental and bodily perceptions, it "would be a mere empty boast on his part, [for] if he were questioned he would not be able to reply."[50] Indeed, the early Buddhist teachings in the "Tevijja Sutta" of the *Dīgha Nikāya*, or *Long Discourses of the Pali Canon*, suggest that "the talk of that man [would] be stupid." The text compares this mode of discourse to the empty and meaningless praise of a lover who rhapsodizes over "the most beautiful girl in the country," but who cannot say what she might looks like or what her voice might sound like, for they have never actually seen or heard anyone as beautiful as they have imagined and hoped for in their romantic fantasies.[51] In a similar way, the text suggests, anyone who would hold out hope for what they "do not know and see . . . cannot possibly be right."[52] Gautama instructs his students to reject such transcendental teachings or fantasies of a perfect realm beyond this one as the basis for their hope in or pursuit of liberation. Instead, he teaches, they should restrict their understanding of reality to the realm of what is phenomenally apparent and to the nature of phenomenality itself; for therein, he concludes, lies the "root of all things" and therefore too, the only legitimate path to the liberation from those things.[53] In this regard, the teachings of early Buddhism as documented in the Pali Canon, like those of Schopenhauer, assert that reality is nothing more than a relation between an apparently material *world* and our phenomenal *representations* of that world. Between and through the interrelations of a presumably material *world* and the perceptions of a conscious *I*, both agree, arise the sum total of reality.

This claim is in fact one of the core tenets of early Buddhist philosophy. This doctrine, known as *pratītyasamutpāda*, or the "interdependent arising of existence," holds that all of reality appears through a mutually co-constitutive play between the seemingly inner life of a perceiving subject and the apparently outer life of the objective world in such a way that neither the world nor the self can be fully separated or individuated from its other without assuring the mutual destruction of both. This metaphysical structure is perhaps most clearly articulated in the *Vedanāsaṃyutta*, where Gautama teaches that

> just as heat is generated and fire is produced from the conjunction and friction of two fire-sticks, but when the sticks are separated and laid aside the resultant heat ceases and subsides; so too, [all sense perceptions] are born of contact, rooted in contact, with contact as their source and condition. In dependence on the appropriate contacts the corresponding feelings arise; with the cessation of the appropriate contacts the corresponding feelings cease.[54]

As a result of the conjunction and contact of *perceiver* (representation) and *perceived* (world), early Buddhist thinkers teach that reality as we know it is fundamentally impermanent (*annica*)—forever waxing and waning with our perceptions and the passage of time. As such, the totality of reality as we know it, the argument goes, is "subject to destruction, subject to vanishing, subject to fading away, subject to cessation."[55] And, for this reason, they conclude, reality is fundamentally and inexorably *finite*—it is always and forever on the brink of its own annihilation. This is the fundamental fact of existence, according to early Buddhist philosophy. Note, however, that for early Buddhism this fact has no inherent value. It simply *is* the nature of reality. These are the inescapable constraints of being, according to early Buddhism. Nevertheless, the first Buddha teaches, at least according to the interpretation of the Theravada tradition, that it is from this fundamental fact that the possibility and the eventual nature of moral value appears within existence; a value, moreover, which imbues that existence with a specific existential and ethical quality.

Indeed, early Buddhism teaches that our experience of existence comes precisely from the way in which we attach value to phenomenal appearances and cling to them in the hope that we might somehow make them permanent. This is why early Buddhist philosophy teaches that our *attachment* or *clinging* (*upādāna*) to these appearances is the source of the "whole mass of suffering" (*duḥkha*) which defines our experience of existence.[56] As a result of our attachments, Gautama teaches, the simple fact of the impermanence of existence is experienced negatively. Thus, while not intrinsic to the nature of reality itself, the useless suffering which results from the mode in which we relate to existence grants our experience of it a moral weight.[57] Hence the argument laid out in the first of the four "noble truths" of Buddhism as documented in the *Saccasaṃyutta*: "the noble truth of suffering," which states that to exist is to suffer.[58] Suffering and misery, early Buddhism concludes, are therefore fundamentally constitutive of and inextricable from our experience of being.

This is an argument which is rendered beautifully in the "Ādittapariyāya Sutta," or "Fire Sermon," of the Pali Canon. There Gautama describes "the all" of reality as "burning . . . Burning with the fire of lust, with the fire of hatred, with the fire of delusion; burning with birth, aging, and death; with sorrow, lamentation, pain, displeasure, and despair."[59] Constituted as it is through the "fire" of attachment, the early Buddhist thinkers conclude that to exist, that is to be attached to phenomenal appearances, is necessarily to suffer. This suffering which they argue necessarily accompanies any form of attachment to existence is what gives rise to the primary value of existence as it is experienced by sentient beings.[60] Given the way our relation to reality necessitates our suffering, *being*, as it appears in conscious apperceptive clinging, the early Buddhist texts assert, can only be evaluated as a moral *evil*.[61] Hence the conclusion reached in the "Pāpavagga," or discourse on evil, as recorded in the *Dhammapada*, which suggests that "you will not find a spot in the world—not in the sky, not in the ocean, not inside a mountain cave—where you will be free from . . . evil."[62] Evil, for early Buddhism, is therefore the fundamental and inescapable *value* of existence for any and all who are aware of it.[63] And since, as we have seen, existence emerges, according to them, in and through our participation in it through our awareness of it, there can be no other value than this one. This necessary evil and useless suffering, they might say, is "the all," the sum total of existence. It follows from this then that for the early Buddhists everything which is, is necessarily and intractably evil and the primal cause of the existential suffering and moral harm of the world.

The reign of this primal evil is so pervasive, in fact, that every other apparent value which might be conceived of as good by a sentient being, such as pleasure or delight, is decidedly rejected by the early Buddhist philosophers as nothing other than evil in disguise. For, the argument goes, such apparent goods, by concealing the necessary moral harm of existence, lead us to desire (*taṇhā*) existence more and cling (*upādāna*) or remain attached to it longer and with even greater ardor in the desperate hope that we might somehow alleviate our suffering through its sensual comforts. As such, the teachings of the early Buddhists insist, every such apparent good is ultimately nothing more than a pathway to more suffering and the continuation of the evil of existence.[64] Thus, the early Buddhists argue, every apparent good is simply an illusion—one which does not oppose the evil of existence, but which merely deepens its moral predicament.

If any "good" is to be achieved from existence, the teachings of the early Buddhists conclude, it can only come from a negation of existence itself: a *renunciation* of being in the attempt to achieve *liberation* from it. In this regard, goodness for early Buddhism is not a separate or distinct ontological category which exists in and for itself. Instead, goodness appears, they reckon, exclusively in the *absence* of the evil of existence. Goodness is achieved, in other words, they think, when the innate evil of existence is evacuated and extinguished through the cessation of our clinging and attachment to phenomenal appearances. Such a relative good is achieved, therefore, entirely *negatively*, they maintain. Goodness is thus, within the Theravada tradition, a possibility which appears only in the absence of evil, understood to be the primary moral quality of existence itself. This relative sense of the good is something, it teaches, which can only be realized, then, through the actualization of pure nothingness.

Following this logic, the whole thrust of the early teachings of the Buddha as they are documented in the Pali Canon is to show how the evil of existence might be overcome and brought to an end (*nirodha*) through the concentrated renunciation, negation, and eventual obliteration of our attachment to perceptual reality as the source of being. The path (*magga*) to this obliteration, known as "the Noble Eightfold Path," promises to guide its adherents out of the moral predicament of existence—suffering and evil—by showing them how to slowly disentangle themselves from their natural attachment to perceptual reality and thereby from being itself and all of the moral harm it necessitates.[65]

In order to achieve this final liberation, the Eightfold Path teaches, we must first become aware of and attend mindfully to what is ultimately the ontological emptiness of existence (*suññatā*), the fact that existence has no independent or absolute reality or value in its own right. In other words, the first step in the negation of being is the rational recognition that existence is not only not good but is in fact evil; and the concomitant fact that existence is impermanent and does not exist independently from us, but is interdependent on and arises from our attachment to it. Thus, by ending perception and attachment, the early Buddhist texts teach, we may end our suffering and negate the evil of existence by ending existence itself through the cessation of our attachment to our own perceptions. It is only through recognition of this fact, the early Buddhists teach, that we can move beyond *being*, that is, beyond the commingled entanglement of self and existence, and thereby beyond evil, and achieve the purity of nothingness. And it is only in this way, they conclude, that we may realize the moral perfection of that which lies beyond good and evil, the liberation of non-being (*nibbana*)—that which remains when the fire of perception is snuffed out, the burning of existence ceases, and the evil of being is finally quenched.

By actively negating the will of existence in this way, the early Buddhists conclude, we might achieve a final peace where all "sorrow and lamentation, . . . pain and grief" fall away.[66] This release from the illusion of the self into the truth of "no-self" (*anattā*) by relinquishing our attachment to existence is the heart of early Buddhist ethics in the Theravada tradition.[67] It is our duty, the tradition therefore maintains, to negate the will of existence, both within ourselves and throughout the world, in order to "destroy the fetters of being," end the evil of existence, and achieve the purity of non-being.[68] This argument, which Schopenhauer understood to be the heart of early Buddhist ethics, significantly inspired his own pessimistic moral system.

While there is room to debate whether early Buddhism is really as pessimistic as Schopenhauer portrays it, it is clear that there are a number of overlapping points between his own metaphysical and moral pessimism and the teachings of early Buddhist philosophy in the Theravada tradition, at least as he understood it. For example, both argue that that the totality of existence lies in the interplay between materiality and perception—that there is nothing outside of, transcendent to, or beyond this interplay. Moreover, both maintain that a proper assessment of the nature of existence proves that it is not good to be—that, precisely the opposite is the case; namely, that, existence as we experience it is utterly and entirely evil, in large part because of the way it necessitate suffering by virtue of its very metaphysical structure, order, and operation. As such, both agree that any semblance of the "good" which might be achieved from the nightmare of being can only be secured negatively: through the active and conscientious negation and renunciation of existence.[69] Finally, both agree that the first step to such a renunciation is a mindful attentiveness to the truth of being, and a concomitant attempt to renounce existence in and through the practice of acts of compassion and asceticism.

It is due to these similarities that Nietzsche criticizes Buddhism with the same vehemence that he denounces Schopenhauer's pessimism. The problem with both, he maintains, is that in their development of an ethics of renunciation, both misinterpret the nature and value of existence and therefore fail to provide a practical guide to life. Instead, he suggests, both rely on a quietistic moral system from which no active or positive instructions can be gleaned.[70] For, Nietzsche rightly notes, both conclude that ultimately, to act ethically one must retreat from the horror of being by relinquishing their attachment to and engagement with reality. Indeed, both Schopenhauer and early Theravada Buddhism advocate for our withdrawal from the moral predicament of existence rather than for the active and practical confrontation of it. For both, the only right action we can achieve while bound within the moral nightmare of existence is to give up on being and to completely renounce its order and operation within us in the hope of diminishing its hold over us until some final and ultimate liberation comes for us in death. In this way, Nietzsche rightly notes, the best course for an ethical life, according to Schopenhauer and this interpretation of Buddhist ethics, is to retreat from existence entirely and to patiently await and prepare for our eventual extinction.

As we have already seen, however, the problem with this form of moral quietism is that it all too easily collapses back into a practical form of nihilism. Indeed, it was precisely for this reason, as we saw in the last chapter, that Nietzsche criticized Schopenhauer and early Buddhism so passionately.[71] In his opinion, although we may hope to escape the moral predicament we find ourselves in after Kant through some version of the pessimism that Schopenhauer and early Buddhist philosophy teach, their quietism ultimately entrenches us deeper in the mire of post-Kantian nihilism. And so, as we concluded with Nietzsche, while we must follow the pessimistic metaphysical and moral conclusions reached by Schopenhauer and early Buddhist philosophy, we must nevertheless find a way to push beyond their respective quietisms to define a more active, positive, and practical account of moral responsibility if we are to actually achieve any good in the world. Fortunately, we are not alone in this task. In fact, this was the specific aim of Philipp Mainländer, a neglected nineteenth-century German philosopher who drew equally from Schopenhauer's metaphysical and moral pessimism, early Buddhist philosophy, and the newly emergent science of thermodynamics in an effort to construct a new account of pessimistic ethics and politics.[72]

Mainländer's aim was to use the metaphysical and moral conclusions of Schopenhauerian pessimism and early Buddhist ethics to craft an active ethical and political agenda which, he argues, is capable of overcoming what he thinks (in anticipation of Nietzsche) are the dangers of moral quietism essential to their moral systems. By analyzing Mainländer's attempts to transform Schopenhauer's pessimistic rendering of early Buddhist philosophy into a practical ethics and an engaged social and political activism, we might therefore finally discover a scientifically justifiable path out of the morass of post-Kantian philosophy—a way, in other words, in which contemporary philosophy might offer an account of absolute truth, universal moral value, and ultimate meaning capable of responding actively to the social and political problems of the contemporary world.

Mainländer's Scientific Pessimism

Philipp Mainländer was not the first nineteenth-century thinker to try to expand or develop Schopenhauer's pessimism. Quite the contrary, there is a long history of pessimistic thinkers after Schopenhauer who explored and applied his work to a number of different fields.[73] None of them, however, is as original or, I would argue, as successful at developing a positive practical ethics from Schopenhauer's pessimism as Mainländer was. If we are to discover a way we might move beyond Schopenhauer's pessimistic version of Buddhist ethics to see how his recognition and renunciation of being as an absolute evil might give rise to a robust and practical system of ethical responsibility and political action, it is essential therefore that we study Mainländer's work. The problem with this is that no thorough account of Mainländer's thought has yet appeared in the English language, nor has any translation of his work into English been completed yet. The closest we have to either of these appears in Frederick Beiser's book *Weltschmerz: Pessimism in German Philosophy, 1860–1900*.[74] To enable our study of Mainländer's thought and see how it might contribute to the final conclusion of our aims then, I will provide in what follows my own introduction to, summation of, and analysis of Mainländer's principal work, his two-volume *Die Philosophie der Erlösung* (1876–86; *The Philosophy of Redemption*), by providing my own translation of its most illuminating and essential passages.

Mainländer's pessimism begins with the metaphysical assertion that, in anticipation of Nietzsche, "God has died"; that, in other words, there is no transcendent reality outside of or beyond the immanent reality of concrete material existence.[75] For Mainländer, as for Schopenhauer and the teachings of early Buddhism, the problem with so many of the philosophies of the past is that they appeal to some unifying or guiding nonphysical or spiritual reality which can only be approached through a dogmatic leap of faith. Against such dogmatic spiritualisms, Mainländer argues, with Schopenhauer and early Buddhism, that philosophy must limit itself exclusively to what is empirically verifiable if it is going to have any claim to legitimacy or practical import in the contemporary world.[76] "A true philosophy," Mainländer writes, "must be purely immanent, i.e., its substance must be both the world and its limit. It must explain the world on the basis of a principle which can be recognized by every human being in it, and must not seek help from . . . otherworldly powers of which absolutely nothing can be known."[77] For these reasons, Mainländer argues that a "true philosophy" must be consistent with and founded upon a fully scientific account of the world.

Thus, he admits, although "the natural sciences still have a wide field of work ahead of them," Mainländer argues that "they [nevertheless] must and will" eventually "come to a conclusion."[78] For this reason, he suggests that the sciences provide the best foundation for philosophers to understand the nature of the world and to rationally develop from their conclusions a speculative account of the meaning, ultimate nature, and universal moral value of existence. And, he claims, what the sciences show us is that "nothing at all transcendent, whatever its name, intervenes, coexists with, or exists in [nature]."[79] As such, he thinks, if any sense of the absolute truth, universal moral value, or ultimate meaning of being is to be developed by philosophers from the account of nature provided by the contemporary sciences, they must first recognize this fact. A fully and truly "immanent philosophy," Mainländer argues, must admit, other words, that it "knows of no miracles nor has anything to say of the operations of some unrecognizable 'other' world which could be of consequence to this world."[80] For these reasons, Mainländer suggests that if any normative system is to be developed by philosophers from a properly scientific account of the nature of reality, then it must first and foremost abandon the pretense that the basis for such a system could come from some otherworldly power or transcendental value, like the ones asserted in faith or dogmatically affirmed in pre-Kantian philosophy. Only once we take seriously an account of reality which flows entirely from scientific observation, Mainländer concludes, can we develop a more realistic account of existence, extract from it an actual sense of moral value, and develop from both a more practical and effective guide for ethical activity.[81]

In this regard, Mainländer's aspirations are in perfect accord with Schopenhauer's metaphysics and Buddhist ontology. Where he differs with both, however, is in his assessment of what such an exclusively scientific account of reality shows about the underlying nature of existence.

For Mainländer asserts against Schopenhauer, that a fully scientific account of reality does not reveal the presence, order, or operation of any one existent and unifying will with in nature. On the contrary, he argues, "a clear view of nature shows us [only] a diversity of individual wills."[82] Nevertheless, Mainländer agrees with Schopenhauer that the aim of each of the individual wills that make up the world is to live; each strives, in other words, he thinks, to maintain and perpetuate itself in every way possible and by any means necessary. As such, while there is no one unifying will at work in reality, Mainländer maintains with Schopenhauer that there is still only "one principle in the world: the individual will to live, and there is nothing other besides it."[83]

"Immanent philosophy," Mainländer concludes, "which acknowledges no source other than nature, [therefore] rejects the assumption of a hidden simple unity in, above, or behind the world."[84] The totality of existence, Mainländer claims, is nothing more than the "collective unit" of these diverse individual wills, inasmuch as each one strives to live and perpetuate itself over, and at times against, every other will. Mainländer thus figures the metaphysical totality of existence as a complex machinery comprised of divergent beings each striving in its own individual way, often against every other existent being, to maintain itself by consuming other beings or fighting against them for resources, all in the hope of sustaining itself from moment to moment and propagating itself into the future.[85] Thus, he argues, while there is no one existent and unifying will that is scientifically discoverable in nature, the diversity of living things nevertheless obeys one absolute principle or law which, he thinks, ensures that they are always and forever at war with one another. In this way, though not a strict monist like Schopenhauer, Mainländer nevertheless recognizes that there is only *one* reality (i.e., immanent material existence) and *one* absolute law at work within that reality (i.e., the will to live) which makes of reality, following Hobbes, a war of all against all.

In Mainländer's account, then, the *will to be*, which constitutes for him the inner life of each and every individual living thing as it is empirically accounted for, hides a deeper drive which can be speculatively extracted from the order and operation of the totality of existent reality. According to Mainländer, when we attend carefully through scientific observation to the operation of each existing material object, we note that behind every nominal existent's *will to be* there appears a hidden drive to destroy: to deteriorate, disintegrate, and collapse into nothingness everything which is—first the being of others and, ultimately, through them, its own being as well. This drive is, of course, precisely what is described by the second law of thermodynamics as defined by Boltzmann and others. Mainländer concludes that even more that the *will to be*, the hidden, true, or ultimate motivating power in every existent entity is this *will to destroy*.[86] Indeed, Mainländer contends, the ultimate power which fuels even the appearance of the *will to be* and *to live* in the existence of every individual being is this more primal *will toward annihilation*. For this reason, Mainländer argues, in its pursuit of life, every individual being is ultimately governed by a *drive toward death*. As such, he concludes, "the whole world, the universe, has a goal: non-being; and it achieves [this goal] by continually weakening the sum of its power."[87] In other words, Mainländer suggests that when we attend carefully to the order and operation of existence as documented in the sciences, we discover that "everything happens and is done, to speak figuratively, with a single objective: for the purpose and aim of non-being."[88] "The whole universe," he writes in summation, "moves from being to non-being, continually weakening its power, [and therefore] has an end: it is not endless, but leads to a pure absolute nothingness—to a *nihil negativum*."[89] The only reason why Mainländer resists the temptation to name this the ultimate unifying will or principle of reality is the fact that, as is implied by its aim, this drive toward nonbeing does not appear in what actually *is*, but only in what is not—since the aim of everything is directed toward nothingness. In fact, Mainländer maintains, this principle can only be speculatively deduced from the nature of existence as it is empirically described by the sciences. Nevertheless, he maintains, this speculatively achieved principle is the only logical explanation for the observable order and operation of each existent thing as a *will to be*. Moreover, as the ultimate aim or telos of everything that exists, Mainländer sees this speculatively derived drive to annihilate existence as the hidden essence of being. Being, for Mainländer, is this movement towards and agent of unbecoming.

Given the aim of this ultimate or absolute principle in reality, Mainländer suggests that the material world is not only ultimately and essentially finite, but that it is also actively working, through each existent thing's *will to live*—to consume, to grow, and to propagate—toward its own eventual dissolution and final obliteration.[90] It concretely achieves this, he thinks, by necessitating that the *will to live* is accomplished through the consumption and destruction of others. And so, Mainländer concludes that while the *will to live* is the only empirically accountable truth of actual reality, we can derive from it the speculative absolute truth that what is at work in the being of each existent thing and governing it in essence is an absolute *will to death*.[91]

According to Mainländer then, "the world, as the totality of individuals, which [ultimately] is what every individual is, is the will to die."[92] Mainländer asserts that this *will to die* is the true nature and inner essence of the actuality of being observed as the *will to live*. He writes: "the movement of all beings is not [ultimately] the will to live [therefore], but the will to death."[93] Hence his conclusion that while the observed facts of reality testify that every existent thing strives to live, the ultimate and absolute truth which can be speculatively deduced from this fact is that being as a whole pursues its own annihilation.[94] Indeed, he writes, "life, [when] understood in the inorganic realm, is always only . . . the gradual movement toward death."[95]

Mainländer thus defines life as little more than the complex means through which this will toward annihilation and nonexistence is accomplished.[96] He suggests that a properly scientific understanding of life is therefore of a sort of recursive loop within the absolute drive toward annihilation; one which momentarily arises as an indirect expression of the pursuit of this aim and ultimate end, the will to death, and which further accelerates the accomplishment of this aim in others. Mainländer suggests that given this fact, the best understanding we can gain of the nature of life is as a drive toward annihilation which has been "slowed down" through organic processes—life is something, in other words, that appears as a purely transitory phase in the accomplishment of absolute oblivion.[97] Mainländer concludes that while life may appear at first glance to work against and try to counter the *will to death* that lies immanent in all material objects—and thus, in the words of Václav Havel, "swim upstream against entropy"—in actual reality, life is merely the complex and abstruse means by which the annihilative trajectory of existence is more efficiently accomplished.[98]

Indeed, Mainländer suggests that it is precisely this pursuit of annihilation throughout the entirety of existence which grounds, conditions, and occasions the appearance of life itself; for, he argues, it is through the activity of the *will to life* that the annihilation of existence as a whole is ultimately accomplished. In this regard, he argues that the *will to life* is really nothing more than the efficient means through which the *will to death* is achieved. For these reasons, Mainländer concludes that while all living things must necessarily strive to maintain themselves and propagate their being while alive, "the movement of [life] is [nevertheless] from being to non-being."[99] Indeed, he argues, the movement of life *is* nothing more than this movement toward nihilation. Life, he thinks in other words, is how this movement appears and how this end is concretely achieved. "To sum up," Mainländer writes, "everything in the world is the will to death, which appears more or less veiled in the organic kingdom, as the will to live."[100]

Mainländer argues that the fact that beings inherently work against themselves, serving this *will to death* in and through their *will to live*, creates an inherent and inescapable tension within existence. Beings, he thinks, in other words, are fundamentally conflicted: they strive to maintain themselves, but cannot help but destroy themselves and others in the process. What's more, he concludes, this dynamic tension is inextricable from being itself; for, he argues, it is a consequent of very essence of being itself, driven as it is toward annihilation.

Given the fundamental contradiction that is immanent in and intrinsic to every living being, Mainlander argues that to exist is to be haunted by an impossible predicament; namely, to strive to live in in such a way that guarantees only death. To live, Mainländer argues, is therefore not merely to face the absolute fact that being ultimately ends in death; it is to face the fact that by living, by striving to be and to perpetuate themselves, beings are inextricably complicit in the accomplishment of their own annihilation, the destruction and death of others, and the ultimate obliteration of the totality of existence itself. Indeed, Mainländer argues, inasmuch as living beings strive to persist, to flourish, and to grow, they must necessarily consume and destroy, and thereby further advance their own death as well as the death of their surrounding world. After all, he reasons, what is survival for a living thing if not the active consumption of other beings through the metabolic process? And so, Mainländer concludes, existence is fundamentally absurd and irreconcilably at odds with itself. This is the foundation of his pessimistic evaluation of existence as it is accounted for by the modern sciences: the recognition that when it is understood properly and considered objectively, "life is the greatest nonsense."[101]

Given the fundamental trajectory of life toward death, Mainländer asserts that "nothing in the whole richness of life gifted to men . . . can be considered the purpose of life. Neither the creative joy, nor the delicious moments of brilliant understanding: nothing!"[102] And yet, he thinks, all living things nevertheless strive to maintain themselves: to enjoy, to flourish, and to grow. But, he reasons, insofar as they successfully accomplish these tasks, they necessarily deepen the fundamental conflict, tension, and predicament of their own existence. As a result, insofar as each being strives to maintain itself and even enjoy itself, he reasons, it is also bound to suffer.[103] Suffering is therefore, he reasons, a necessary consequence of being, especially for those who are endowed with the capacity to be aware of the essential and inescapable contradiction and inherent tension of their existence. Suffering, Mainlander concludes, is a necessary consequence of being itself. This suffering is, he agrees with Schopenhauer, especially apparent to every conscious entity that is capable of becoming aware of and understanding the inescapable contradictions of existence in general and life in particular.

Mainländer argues that the more conscious any being is, not to mention the more such a being strives to live and enjoy its life, the more its "suffering [necessarily] grows, and the sensitivity to it grows."[104] Consequently, Mainländer thinks, the only evaluative conclusion we can legitimately reach about the nature of existence is that "life in general is a 'wretchedly miserable thing': it has always been wretchedly miserable and will always be wretchedly miserable, and non-being is better than being."[105] Indeed, he concludes succinctly, "life is hell."[106] For Mainländer then, the only scientifically justifiable moral value we might ascribe to the nature of existence is that it is not good to be. This does not mean, however, he cautions his reader, that existence is potentially value-neutral. On the contrary, Mainländer insists, the only value we can legitimately ascribe to being from a scientifically informed understanding of existence is that it is fundamentally and inescapably *evil* to be.[107]

For Mainländer, following Schopenhauer, the fundamental question for moral philosophy arises from the intractable moral predicament of being itself, understood as a *will to death*. What, he asks in echo of Schopenhauer, is to be done practically about the great evil of our existence? How are we to deal with or actively confront the predicament of our reality, that is, the suffering and moral evil that our existence necessitates within ourselves and others? How are we to act if all we can hope to achieve from life and existence is to perpetuate conflict, suffering, misery, and evil in ourselves and the world? Given this predicament, Mainländer's ethics begin with an inquiry into the potential validity of Schopenhauer's rendition of Buddhist ethics which teaches that the only good which we can achieve is to resign ourselves to the problem of existence and attempt, as much as possible, to renounce the potency of being within us. But, in anticipation of Nietzsche's criticism of this ethics, Mainländer worries about the moral quietism this renunciation seemingly requires. It is in his attempt to craft a more active and practical ethics and social and political agenda from such a renunciation of the will of nature that Mainländer's contribution of pessimistic ethics appears.

It might seem at first glance that if Mainländer is to follow Schopenhauer's assessment of the moral horror of being, then he is left with only one option: to conclude that the sole path to lasting peace and relative goodness must be through the negation of existence and the renunciation of being—in a word, moral quietism. And, while Mainländer does not disagree with this conclusion in principle—indeed, he suggests that the only hope for any conception of goodness must come from an active negation of the innate tension and horror of existence—he nevertheless suggests that this renunciation of being might also found and justify a more robust account of practical ethics and political action. It is from an understanding of Mainländer's ethics and politics that we finally discover then a way out of the moral quietism of Schopenhauer's rendition of Buddhist ethics without resurrecting or relying on any form of dogmatic fideism.

Pessimism and the Ethical Duty of Social and Political Activism

Mainländer's ethics begins, like Schopenhauer's, with the claim that "the recognition that non-being is better than being is . . . the ultimate principle of all morality."[108] Given this fact, he argues, in further accord with Schopenhauer, that all conscious beings have a moral duty to pursue nonbeing over being, to resist the will to life within them, and to help other sentient beings renounce their own will to life. Mainländer thus concludes, in further affirmation of Schopenhauer's Buddhist-inspired ethics, that ethical activity must actively strive to accomplish rationally motivated works of compassion, works which he maintains alleviate the suffering of the world. What's more, he argues we can only commit ourselves to acts of this sort if we have first surrendered ourselves to the primal will of annihilation and achieved something approximating ego death.[109] Only in this way, he thinks, can we prepare ourselves and others for the death to come wherein we hope to achieve some final and eternal peace. All of this flows from his assessment that "life is hell," and that "the sweet silent night of absolute death is the destruction of hell."[110] It makes sense, then, that on this point Mainländer affirms Schopenhauer's claim that it must be the aim of every ethical activity to reconcile existence to this eventual "absolute death," first within the self, through acts of ascetic self-renunciation, and subsequently in the lives of others, through charitable acts of rationally inspired compassion and care. And thus, like Schopenhauer and the teaching of the first Buddhists, Mainländer identifies the highest expression of ethical action and moral duty with the attempt to oppose, resist, or renounce the will to life in ourselves and the world beyond us.

In further affirmation of these traditions, Mainländer identifies the best means of achieving this resistance as *contemplation*, through which he thinks individuals can learn to separate themselves from their own will; and *chastity*, the refusal to procreate and spread the suffering of existence, as the highest ethical duties which can be achieved. Through contemplation, he argues, we can learn to "look . . . into the absolute nothingness, the absolute emptiness, into the *nihil negativum*," and find satisfaction in the promise of its eventual extinction of reality.[111] And through chastity, he argues, we can learn to "love [death], for chastity is love for death."[112] Thus, he argues, through a commitment to contemplation and chastity a conscious subject can become increasingly comfortable with the absolute reality of the annihilative drive which lies forever at the heart of their existence and learn to lessen its effects both within themselves and, through them, in the lives of others. In this way, he thinks, the conscious subject can become an ethical agent and actively work to bend the *will to live* such that it aligns with and affirms the absolute *will to death*, neutralizing the inherent tension of existence. Thusly, he argues a conscious subject can achieve some semblance of peace and harmony within themselves and lessen their participation in the suffering of the world

Mainländer thus sees in contemplation and chastity a kind of "slow suicide."[113] It follows that more virtuous than both of these moral duties is suicide itself, by which, he argues, an individual can fully and "quickly" resolve the dilemma of their existence and, in so doing, end the problem of suffering and decrease the overall misery of the world.[114] For this reason, Mainländer argues, against Schopenhauer and early Buddhism, that suicide is one of the highest acts of personal virtue any individual can accomplish. Suicide, as the ultimate annihilation of the will, is an ethical act for Mainländer only inasmuch as it follows from what the novelist Graham Greene called "the courageous act [of] the clear-headed . . . mathematician" who "has judged by the laws of chance . . . that to live will be more miserable than to die" because "his sense of mathematics is greater than his sense of survival."[115] Only as the expression of a fully rational understanding of the mathematical laws of nature, Mainländer thinks, can we pursue suicide as an act of ethical virtue.

Inasmuch as he identifies virtuous action with acts of secularly motivated and scientifically inspired acts of ascetic renunciation, like contemplation, compassion, chastity, and ultimately, suicide, Mainländer's ethics initially seems to affirm the moral quietism of Schopenhauer and early Buddhist philosophy, albeit even more radically than both, given its approbation of suicide. And, Mainländer indeed praises Schopenhauer and early Buddhism alike as two of the most developed and scientifically justifiable moral philosophies in the history of philosophy.[116] But, where Mainländer breaks with Schopenhauer and early Buddhist philosophy, beyond his approval of suicide as an ethical act, is in his claim that despite the ethical legitimacy of these systems, both are ultimately insufficient to develop a truly practical and active ethics capable of informing us how we might enthusiastically work to help others achieve some relative goodness from and within their own existence. The best both achieve, he reasons, is to show us how we might lessen our contribution to that suffering, but not how to actively work to liberate them from the existential torment of being. As such, he concludes, neither system is sufficient to respond to the ethical demands of the world nor provides the kind of ethical activity which he thinks can be speculatively extracted from a recognition of the absolute evil of existence. According to Mainländer then, while Schopenhauer and early Buddhism each articulate methods for freeing the self from the suffering necessitated by the nature of reality, both ethical systems ignore the possibility of actively working to liberate others from the predicament of existence; and so, he concludes, in their quietism they are necessarily complicit in perpetuating the suffering of others and the overall evil of existence. Mainländer concludes therefore, that unless the moral quietism of both systems is overcome and a more practical ethics and sociopolitical activism is forwarded, both are bound to become accomplices in the moral harm which is necessitated by existence. Their moral systems are guilty, in other words, he thinks, more by moral omission than by moral commission. Against them, therefore, Mainländer argues for a more active and practical account of ethical responsibility and social and political activism. Only through such a moral activism, he thinks, can pessimism respond appropriately to the problem of existence.

To put a finer point on it, the problem with the kind of moral quietism advocated by Schopenhauer and early Buddhism according to Mainländer is that while it both help the individual who has already "awakened" to the fundamental conflict of existence to achieve some relative "goodness" from their lives, neither help those who lack access to the kind of education and social status which Mainländer thinks are necessary to develop this awareness in the first place to achieve this relative goodness. As such, he argues, the ethical activities of such quietisms when devoid of any definite social and political agenda, must be seen as fundamentally *unjust*. Unless some definite transformation of the existing social and political order is attempted whereby everyone is empowered to learn about the reality of existence, awaken to its moral value, and commit themselves to its alleviation, then, Mainländer reasons, moral quietism, in its pursuit of a personal good, is ultimately ethically unjustifiable. For Mainländer, such pursuits of personal moral perfection are, in other words, fundamentally *inequitable* if they are not made accessible to all; and this requires, he reasons, a robust social and political activism which aims to transform the way in which we live such that all are equally empowered to pursue these same ends. For this reason, Mainländer suggests that an active social and political project must be developed from the metaphysical and morally pessimistic evaluation of reality as an absolute evil if any semblance of a truly *just* account of even relative goodness is to be advanced by it. Put another way, in order to clear the way for one's own renunciation of being through asceticism, chastity, and eventually suicide, Mainländer thinks that one must actively work to create the conditions necessary in the social and political order which would empower everyone equally to pursue these ethical duties.

For this reason, Mainländer suggests that anyone who is truly committed to metaphysical and moral pessimism must actively work to develop and implement the kinds of social and political structures which would ensure that every individual has equal access to the education and lifestyle necessary to allow them to know the truth of being and to pursue the peace of contemplation and the ascetic practices essential to the full renunciation of that being. According to Mainländer, then, the full expression of pessimistic ethics is not merely the renunciation of being but the active pursuit of a more just social and political order which would assure the conditions necessary for each and every individual to pursue such a renunciation themselves. Put another way, for Mainländer, no one can be free from the ethical predicament of being unless they actively work to ensure that everyone can be free from it. And so, Mainländer concludes, for any pessimistic ethics to be worthy of its name, not only must it define those activities which each individual ought to pursue to be free of the moral and ontological horror of existence through the renunciation of the self, it must also define and actively work to construct whatever social and political structures are necessary to ensure that every individual, regardless of their social and political status, has access to the knowledge and socioeconomic freedom necessary to understand the predicament of existence and to commit themselves to the path of peace outlined within a pessimistic understanding of reality. Unless every social and political barrier which prevents this from happening is destroyed and a new social and political order is actively erected and maintained, he concludes, no semblance of the good can ever be achieved from a scientifically informed pessimistic metaphysics and ethics. For this reason, Mainländer argues that to truly combat the evil of existence we must actively commit ourselves to acts of social and political revolution.

Mainländer's commitment to ethical and political revolution grows directly from his commitment to counter the evil of existence by creating a world in which every individual has the opportunity to learn the truth of being and the freedom to try to alleviate the suffering which comes from the activity of the will to live within themselves and the lives of others.[117] Political revolution and social reform are thus essential to the cultivation and development of a rationally consistent pessimistic ethics according to Mainländer. Indeed, he maintains, this commitment to political activism is merely the logical extension of the kind of compassion that both Schopenhauer and early Buddhist philosophers argue that the recognition of existence as absolutely evil demands. For this reason, Mainländer defines his social and political agenda as a "subordinate principle" which is deducible from the fundamental claim of a properly pessimistic account of the value of being and the "recognition that non-being is better than being."[118] Hence his claim that the pursuit of social and political equality, as an outgrowth of pessimistic compassion, is "the last and highest consecration" of a rationally consistent pessimistic ethics.[119]

In order to create a world in which each individual is free from every structural limitation which might prevent them from pursuing this relative good—which is to say, the recognition and renunciation of the will to live—Mainländer thinks that we must actively work to overthrow every system which maintains any social injustice, imbalance, or inequity. Moreover, he argues, we must work to erect those political systems which assure everyone equal access to education, liberty, and the social and political status.[120] Mainländer therefore concludes that no truly pessimistic ethics is complete unless it actively champions "two great ideals: communism and free love [*freie Liebe*]."[121]

Through *communism*, Mainländer argues, we can achieve a political reality in which each individual has equal access to whatever is necessary to commit themselves to the liberation of being. Indeed, given its fundamental commitment to social and economic equality, Mainländer sees communism as a social and political extension of what he argues is our personal duty to resist and renounce the individual will to live through contemplation, compassion, and asceticism. Hence his claim that "where communism is fully realized, the individual existence is placed in the hands of the whole," which is precisely what he thinks is achieved through individual acts of compassionate service.[122] Like such acts, Mainländer reasons, communism achieves on a social and political level "the complete repeal of the self."[123] It does this, he thinks, by establishing the structural conditions necessary for every sentient being to equally participate in, benefit from, and commit themselves to the compassionate service of others, as opposed to the service of the self; service, that is, to the individual will to live. Communism accomplishes this end, he argues, first by discouraging and repressing what he sees as the inherent selfishness of the individual will to pursue one's own survival. Secondly, he argues, communism structurally institutes compassionate justice by actively eliminating social classes which bar and exclude certain individuals from accessing the kind of education and contemplative freedom which is necessary to overcome the impulse of the individual will to live. In this way, Mainländer argues, "pure communism would open up to all human beings all the paradise in which some have always lived since the beginning of civilization and would give humanity the best possible life."[124] Indeed, he thinks, within a perfect realized communist polis "[we] would be a hapless, if not a happy, humanity."[125] And so, Mainländer concludes, if we are truly committed to realizing the kind of negatively defined "good" which he thinks is deducible from a scientifically informed, pessimistic evaluation of existence as an absolute evil, then we must actively pursue the kind of social and political justice he believes is promoted by social and political communism.

Mainländer's commitment to social and political equality as an essential condition for the empowerment of every individual in the liberation of their own existence further motivates his advocacy of the *freie Liebe* or *free love* movement.[126] The free love movement was a popular sociopolitical movement in Europe and America in the late eighteenth and early nineteenth centuries which influenced a number of thinkers, including Nietzsche.[127] Inspired by the work of Henri de Saint-Simon, Charles Fourier, Robert Owen, and Victoria Woodhull, the free love movement sought to redefine the nature of sexual and marital relations outside the bounds of their traditional setting as a sacrament of faith, a state-sanctioned institution, or an economic necessity. In this regard, the free love movement grew out of and worked alongside the newly emergent women's rights movement and drew extensively from the work of Mary Wollstonecraft, Mary Grove, and Minerva Putnam to define and articulate its founding principles. Indeed, the very word "feminist" is often credited to Charles Fourier, one of the movement's principal architects, and was identified by him as a label that each of its adherents should actively embrace.[128] This movement is perhaps best understood then not by rendering it directly into English as the "free love" movement, since it might be confused thereby with the social libertinism which was also growing in popularity in Europe at the time. Instead, it is better understood as a movement aimed at the liberation of the sexes. The guiding principle and ultimate aim of the free love movement was indeed to liberate men and women from the bondage of the traditional sexual, gender, and family roles which enslaved them to one another in the service of procreation and or the maintenance of the state. By pursuing the liberation of men and women from what he sees as the repressive function of these roles, Mainländer argues that the free love movement accomplishes socioculturally what communism pursues sociopolitically: the equality and empowerment of all—which, as we have seen, he suggests is a necessary condition for the liberation of all from the evil of existence.

According to Mainländer, the free love movement works to achieve this aim by committing itself to the "complete annihilation of marriage."[129] Through the abolishment of marriage, Mainländer argues, sexual roles, identities, and relations will be liberated from the repressive strictures of contractual obligation and biological function; and can, in turn, be elevated into a free exchange between mutually empowered equals in co-pursuit of their own freedom from the evil of existence. Through the free love movement, Mainländer suggests then that women and men will be equally empowered to take ownership of their own bodies and sexual reproductivity, and ultimately, even, existence. In doing so, he argues, they will gain the autonomy they need to free themselves from the tyrannical biological drive to procreate, as well as the repressive sociocultural expectation that this should happen within the framework of marriage, as mandated by the church and/or sanctioned by the state. In this way, he thinks, they will be empowered to autonomously direct their own bodies against nature toward the good—that is, away from the impulse to survive and propagate and toward the virtue of chastity and eventually suicide.

In order to empower men and women mutually with this freedom, Mainländer argues that we must actively work to abolish traditional marriage roles, which perpetuate gender inequality and sexual puritanism and keep men and women alike enslaved to their bodies' biological functions, a fact which, he thinks, only serves to perpetuate the great evil of being. Only once everyone is granted the liberty which has traditionally been reserved for men alone, Mainländer thinks, can a truly just society be achieved; a situation, he suggests, which can only be achieved once everyone, regardless of their gender or sexuality, is free to pursue through education a proper understanding of the predicament of being and is empowered by social, political, and economic equality to actively renounce, in contemplative practice and compassionate service, the absurdity of their existence. Only through the kind of social equity and "unity" that is sought by the free love movement, Mainländer therefore reasons, can we accomplish "everything else: freedom, equality, and fraternity."[130] For as long as we are trapped in social and political roles which restrict our freedom to some biological/procreative function and thereby justify our bondage to one another, he makes clear, we will be doomed to perpetuate the absolute evil that is the will to live. In order to fully negate this will, Mainländer thus concludes that it is absolutely necessary that we actively strive to create a society in which gender and sexual liberation is fully realized. Hence his claim that a fully pessimistic metaphysics and ethics requires that we actively work towards those social and political orders which ensure equal freedom to any and every gender and sexual orientation.

According to Mainländer, it is only by actively pursuing revolutionary social and political goals like these that a negatively defined account of the good, established upon a scientifically informed pessimistic ethics, can be finally and fully achieved. Hence Frederick Beiser's conclusion that "while [Mainländer's] pessimism preaches resignation and quietism, his radical politics teaches the value of resistance and activism."[131] Indeed, for Mainländer, radical political commitments of these sorts are not only the natural expression of a truly pessimistic accounting of the absolute value of existence as a moral evil; they are for him the only way in which some semblance of the good can be achieved within and from existence. Given the abject evil of being, Mainländer reasons, it is our moral duty not only to overcome the will of nature at work in our individual lives; it is our responsibility to actively resist the negative effects of our individual existence within the social and political order as well by actively working to found and maintain social and political structures which empower everyone to work collectively against the will of existence: communism and free love. Only in this way, he argues, can a truly just and equitable society can be realized and the great moral horror of being be countered collectively. Only by abolishing whatever structures marginalize certain social and political classes, gender identities, and sexual orientations—and prevent them from understanding the problem of being and actively pursuing the lifestyle necessary to escape it—can some modicum of a "happy state of peace" be rationally hoped for and practically worked for.[132]

For Mainländer, the ethical power of the kind of ascetic renunciation of the *individual* will which is promoted by Schopenhauer and early Buddhist philosophy is fully developed only when we discover within it the possibility of actively pursuing *collective* actions against the vicissitudes of being by way of a politics of radical equality. Ultimately, for Mainländer, the true aim of every scientifically informed and speculative derived pessimistic evaluation of the absolute evil of being must be this: not merely to renounce the world, but to transform it! Only by committing ourselves to a revolutionary political transformation of this sort, he argues, can we hope to empower every individual to take up arms against the moral fact of existence and renounce and resist the evil it necessitates, both within themselves as individuals and within the social and political institutions to which they belong.

In this way, Mainländer's work shows us how a metaphysical and moral pessimism demands more than ethical quietism alone, but further requires a profound commitment to radical social and political activism. His work thus shows us concretely how we might ground a negatively defined normative system which actively works toward some practical social and political good. In other words, Mainländer's pessimism charts a way in which we might finally resolve the dilemma of post-Kantian philosophy, escape the miasma of contemporary moral, social, and political philosophy, and more effectively respond to the various moral, social, and political problems which confront us in the world today. The only question which remains for us is how we might apply this insight to the problems of the contemporary world. It is to this question that we will turn in the final chapter of this work.

10

New Directions in Pessimism

Cosmic Pessimism, Afropessimism, and Extinctual Nihilism

The Cosmic Pessimism of Thacker, Bataille, and Cioran

Philipp Mainländer was, of course, not the last pessimist in the history of Western thought. Nor was he the only thinker to suggest that a profound social and political potency could be extracted from pessimism's moral evaluation of existence as an absolute evil. To the contrary, there is a long line of thinkers, stretching from Schopenhauer through Mainländer and into the contemporary world, who have all been inspired by the ethical, social, and political potencies of metaphysical and moral pessimism. Indeed, philosophical pessimism has undergone something of a renaissance of late, with scholars from various disciplinary backgrounds using its evaluation of the horrors of existence to explore, explain, and respond to the vicissitudes of the contemporary world. Through a survey and evaluation of their work in light of what we've concluded concerning the metaphysics of decay in dialogue with Mainländer's pessimistically driven social and political activism—we can discover how we might develop more detailed marching orders from our ethical pessimism to respond to the problems of the contemporary world.

The most well-known of these "new pessimists" is undoubtedly Eugene Thacker, whose work highlights the continuing thread and power of philosophical pessimism in Western thought from Schopenhauer, through Mainländer, and beyond. According to Thacker, the real strength of the pessimistic tradition is that its account of the nature and value of reality moves beyond "an individual, personal attitude" to present "a cosmic one, an impersonal attitude" that is grounded in a proper understanding of the inhuman immensity of material reality itself.[1] In this regard, Thacker sees the philosophical pessimism of Schopenhauer and Mainländer as not merely a repudiation of any individual's particular experience of reality, but as a rendition of the ontological structure, material nature, and universal laws of existence itself. As such, he argues, pessimism escapes the inherent subjectivism of much of post-Kantian philosophy and recuperates an *absolute* account of reality without invoking any form of dogmatic logic. For this reason, he argues, metaphysical pessimism is not only more representative of the nature of the universe as we currently understand it in and through the material sciences; it is also the only legitimate basis we have for developing a practical approach to contemporary life.

For Thacker, what makes such a pessimism "cosmic" in scope and not merely a personal viewpoint is that it emerges from "a drastic scaling-up or scaling-down of the human point of view, the disorientation of deep space and deep time, all of this shadowed by an impasse, a primordial insignificance, the impossibility of ever adequately accounting for one's happenstance existence."[2] The "cosmic" perspective of pessimism is assured, in other words, Thacker thinks, through its commitment to understanding "the world as absolutely unhuman, and indifferent to the hopes, desires, and struggles of human individuals and groups"—an understanding of reality that is achieved through the lens of the mathematical sciences.[3] Indeed, for Thacker, pessimism is the natural speculative consequence of a properly scientific understanding of the world. For he thinks that what the contemporary mathematical sciences show us is the world as it actually is, outside and beyond the human perspective. Insofar as it does this, he argues, the mathematical sciences present humans with a sort of "limit-thought," a "thought that undermines itself, . . . that stumbles over itself, at the edge of an abyss."[4] By tarrying and wrestling with "limit-thoughts" of this sort, Thacker argues, human beings are forced to confront the fragility, insubstantiality, and ultimate irrationality of their own reason, not to mention the emptiness of their traditional objects of faith and devotion. In this regard, he suggests, the kinds of "limit-thoughts" which are presented by the mathematical sciences force us to abandon entirely our folk wisdoms and dogmatic convictions and to confront the universe on its own terms. And it is this confrontation, he concludes, that leads directly to philosophical pessimism. This is why Thacker sees philosophical pessimism as fundamentally "cosmic" in scope; and he maintains that it is the only proper and appropriate response to the "limit-thoughts" provoked by the account of nature which is achieved in the contemporary sciences.

Inasmuch as it embraces the profound challenge that the mathematical sciences present to our traditional understanding of our place in the universe, Thacker thinks that while pessimism is grounded in rational thought, it ultimately moves beyond the structures of rationality which constrict other schools of post-Kantian philosophy and presents a new and entirely inhuman and nonrational absolute. Given its aim to think alongside and in light of this radically inhuman account of reality, Thacker thinks that pessimism develops an entirely new ways of philosophizing. Examples of such new modes of philosophizing include, he notes, a mode of secularized "mysticism," or atheistic "hermeticism," and what he calls "a noumenal occultism."[5] Thacker highlights the work of Georges Bataille and Emil Cioran as exemplars of these modes of pessimistic post-Kantian philosophy.[6]

Bataille's Base Materialism

"Extending Bataille's ideas," Thacker writes, "one of the guiding questions for me here is whether it is possible to have, today, a mysticism without God, a negative mysticism, or really, a mysticism of the unhuman."[7] To develop a "mysticism of the unhuman" is indeed one of the principal aims of Bataille's work.[8] Or, as he puts it, his goal is to establish and define a new way of approaching the absolute truth of reality without invoking any form of "idealism" or rational "ethics"; a way that, in other words, is entirely "external and foreign to ideal human aspirations, and ... refuses to allow itself to be reduced to the great ontological machines resulting from these aspirations."[9] Bataille names this approach to thinking alongside the absolute nature of reality outside the bounds of human rationality "base materialism."[10]

Inasmuch as it attempts to confront the fundamentally irrational nature of the universe, Bataille argues that his base materialism "designate[s] the direct interpretation, excluding idealism, of raw phenomena."[11] In this regard, he claims, it provides a model for "affirming that the universe resembles nothing and is only formless."[12] This account of the universe as ultimately formless, Bataille claims, is the absolute truth of nature as it is presented by the contemporary sciences: as emerging from and steadily slouching toward annihilation. For this reason, he argues that his "base materialism" charts the path for a mode of philosophical thinking which is more representative of what he thinks the fundamental and absolute truth of being is than the metaphysics maintained by the philosophical dogmatisms and idealisms of the past: the truth that existence is ultimately nothing more than "an agitated void."[13]

In order to engage with this account of reality as an "empty infinity," Bataille argues, his new mode of thinking starts with the assertion that the "nothingness" of the universe is not that of a pure vacuum.[14] Instead, he claims, it manifests as the material presence of a cosmos which is entirely *devoid* of meaning, and is little more than a mute "cadaver."[15] The absolute fact that the materiality of the cosmos manifests as a form of mute "nothingness," Bataille claims, presents a "monstrous" challenge to the traditional account of the human that is maintained in the history of philosophy.[16] For, he argues, it forces every conscious or meaning-seeking mode of being like our own to confront the fact that ours is a "lacerated existence," a "catastrophe" that cannot be satisfied by nature and will never find any reflection of its hope and desires in what actually is the case.[17] Indeed, he thinks, it is this fundamental rejection of our hopes and dreams by nature which is the motivation for the classical philosophical turn to dogmatism and idealism. In Bataille's account, both these tendencies express a vainglorious attempt by humans to force the material muteness of the universe to speak and to give an account for the nature of its conscious creations, including their hopes, dreams, and desire for meaning.

"For academic men to be happy," Bataille writes, "the universe would have to take shape. All of philosophy has no other goal: it is a matter of giving a frock coat to what is, a mathematical frock coat."[18] The problem with this "frock coat," he argues, is that it is not only ill-fitting, it hides the monstrosity of the actual truth of reality in its absolute form. In order to overcome this intellectual version of the emperor's new clothes and not only see, but embrace the universe as he thinks it actually is—devoid of any transcendental meaning or form and terrible in its mute indifference to its products—Bataille posits his "base materialism" as the best way to renounce every form of dogmatic or idealistic dressing-up maintained in post-Kantian thought and to construct instead a mode of thinking that is more representative of the absolute truth of the universe. In this regard, he sees the aim of base materialism as the production of modes of thinking and being which are as devoid of form and structure as the universe itself—modes of thinking and being that are utterly empty, unfeeling, and horrifying from the traditional human perspective. In this way, he thinks, base materialism provides a way in which philosophy might become as brutal as the reality it attempts to describe and draw conclusions from.

To accomplish this aim, Bataille argues, philosophy must first give up the idea that reality can be objectively "known" as this or that determinate thing. Such idealized attempts to aggregate the chaos of existence into a coherent object of rational comprehension or description fundamentally betray what he sees as the true nature of being as it is accounted for in the contemporary sciences. What his base materialism strives to accomplish instead is to engage with and express the absolute meaninglessness of reality through what he calls a form of "nonknowledge," "inner experience," or "pure experience."[19]

"I give myself to nonknowledge," Bataille writes, and "this is communication, and as there is communication with the darkened world, rendered abyssal by nonknowledge, I dare say God: and it is in this way that there is new knowledge," a knowledge he designates as "mystical" in nature.[20] Indeed, Bataille argues, the ultimate product of such a "communication" with reality is an encounter with absolute materiality approached as a divine or mystical power. "Nonknowledge attained," he writes, "absolute knowledge is no more than one knowledge among others."[21] This "absolute knowledge," he thinks, is only achievable from a direct encounter or mystical union with matter in its primordial form; and he claims that this union can be attained only if the classical theoretical structures of rational knowledge are abandoned entirely in favor of the nonrational structures of reality as they are presented in the contemporary sciences.

For Bataille then, it would seem that while we might ascend to this "nonknowledge" of the material universe through the operation of reason and through the knowledge we gain from the mathematical sciences, once this truth has been encountered, if we hope to engage with it properly, on its own terms, as it were, we must "abandon the world of the civilized and its light" by ceasing to be "reasonable and educated," and we must instead endeavor to "become completely different."[22] Base materialism is for Bataille the way in which we become "completely different," in this way and, through the "pure experience" of reality in its absolute form, come into direct relationship with the ultimate truth of that reality. Hence his claim that his base materialism is not ultimately a mode of philosophical reflection, but rather a form of radical "mysticism" or "ecstasy" in the classical sense of the word (i.e., to stand outside of).[23]

Indeed, to illustrate the new way of experiencing the absolute material truth of being which Bataille thinks is possible through this process, he draws extensively from the classical Gnostics, seeing in their mystical practices a model for how we might encounter the absolute truth of reality as it is presented in the mathematical sciences in a new, transformative, and ultimately even practical way.[24] In the kind of religious experiences and poetic rhapsody which he sees as essential to the Gnostic traditions, Bataille outlines what he argues is the best path into the "extremity of the possible," the extremity of what he sees as the absolute nature of reality in all of its monstrous and horrible power.[25]

However such an encounter is achieved, whether through mystical transcendence or poetic reverie, Bataille argues that the only way we can confront the world as it actually is, as it is accounted for in the contemporary sciences, is to discover our "continuity with," our "perfect immanence" in, and our "intimacy" with the mute formlessness and meaninglessness of material reality in all its plenitude.[26] And to achieve this end, he thinks, we must reject and overturn traditional philosophical concepts of the "idealized subject" and the "objective world" and embrace instead the perfect "fusion of the object and the subject" which is given to us in a proper understanding of the universe as a base material object.[27] According to Bataille, only once we achieve this end, and collapse the distinction between ourselves and the absolute form of reality so that "there is no longer subject = object, but a 'gaping breach' between one and the other and, in the breach, subject and object are dissolved," can we discover that "there is a passage, communication, but not from one to the other: one and the other have lost their distinct existence."[28] Bataille concludes that what we learn from such a direct, inner, and pure communion with the brute reality of matter is the "nonknowledge" that being in its absolute form is not only indifferent to us, to itself, and to everything in between, it is also, ultimately, evil.[29] It is this attempt to forge a new way of relating human beings to *this* terrible truth about the cosmos, namely that, from the perspective of human understanding, being is utterly and completely evil, and to derive from this realization a kind of mystical union between humans and the horror of the universe, that Thacker counts as the practical value of Bataille's pessimism.

Cioran and the Ethics of Indifference

To this same end, Thacker praises the life and work of Emil Cioran as an alternative model for the kind of mystical thinking which he sees as constitutive of the new way of being in the world that a properly "cosmic" post-Schopenhauerian pessimism might provide for people today. According to Thacker, Cioran's greatness comes not only from his capacity to articulate the same basic truths of the cosmos described by Bataille, but to demonstrate in his very life the kind of mystical atheism which he counts as the natural expression of a fully pessimistic understanding of reality. Thacker thus designates Cioran as not only a great thinker, but a sort of "patron saint of pessimism."[30] Indeed, according to Thacker, Cioran's greatest accomplishment was to develop a lifestyle that reveled in an "ecstasy of the worst"; a lifestyle which demonstrated, in its daily ethical practices, the absolute truth of reality as a moral evil.[31] Cioran's capacity to practically engage with the abject horror of existence in this practical way grew, according to Thacker, from his constant "refus[al] to place his faith in human beings, let alone God or science."[32] Indeed, according to Cioran himself, if we are to directly encounter and reconcile ourselves to the true nature of the universe, such "absolute" or "unconditional" structures must be categorically rejected from the outset as not only false "idols," but as the source of human fanaticism and evil acts alike.[33]

Cioran expresses the danger of such transcendent structures thusly: "a man who loves a god unduly forces other men to love his god, [and is] eager to exterminate them if they refuse."[34] For Cioran, the real problem with such transcendental ideas is that they are all too easily used to justify murder, genocide, and other modes of cruelty.[35] For these reasons, Cioran concludes, transcendental idealities must be rejected entirely, not only because they are false, but because of what they can be used to justify. Instead, he argues, it is only by understanding and fully embracing the truth that the universe is devoid of any such transcendental idealities, that we can come to live in a more ethically honest and superior way.

According to Cioran, this process begins by recognizing that every transcendental idea, as well as every hope humans have in the ultimate meaningfulness or significance of their existence, is nothing more than the "fruit of the anxiety of our guts and the gurgle of our ideas."[36] The source of this primal anxiety and "gurgle of ideas" is a truth which Cioran thinks is buried within us; namely, that the universe, in its actual and absolute form, has no meaning, telos, or aim. "No one has found a valid goal for history," he writes.[37] This is the repressed truth of the universe which he thinks is papered over by our transcendental ideals: the terrifying fact that we all, if only secretly, know; namely, that when we "gaze . . . upon the heavens," we find "nothing there."[38] Hence Cioran's conclusion that "by all the evidence we are in the world to do nothing"; that, in other words, the totality of the evidence we can gain from the observation of nature is that nature has no plans for us and we are merely an accident of cosmic history.[39] Worse still than this buried truth of existence, Cioran reasons, is the fact that when we estimate the potential value of existence, devoid of meaning as it is, we can only conclude that the cosmos is aimed entirely at "injustice."[40] Unless contemporary philosophers are capable of reconciling themselves to this horrible truth without invoking the existence of some false god or transcendental idea to rescue them, he concludes, they will be destined to reproduce the kinds of idolatry and fanaticism that have hampered philosophy's efforts in the past.

Against what he sees as Western philosophy's complicity in maintaining the kinds of fanaticism which grow from our false idealities, Cioran frames his own philosophical project as an attempt to create a mode of thinking and being which acknowledges and accepts what he sees as the only rational claim that can be deduced from what is observable in the universe: the fact that injustice reigns supreme in existence and is the ultimate truth and absolute law of being. This is, he claims, an undeniable moral conclusion when one understands properly the reign of the second law of thermodynamics over and within existence.

"Decomposition presides over the laws of life," Cioran writes.[41] As a result, he argues, existence necessarily maintains itself by "each being feed[ing] on the agony of some other."[42] In perfect accord with Mainländer then, Cioran concludes that "everything [in existence] conspires, elements and actions alike, to harm you."[43] As such, he reasons, "every individual discomfort [which we experience in existence] leads back ultimately to a cosmogonic discomfort, each of our sensations expiating that crime of the primordial sensation, by which Being crept out of somewhere."[44] For this reason, Cioran thinks, the ultimate truth of being is the irrefutable ethical conclusion that existence is a "murderer"; and human existence, as that mode of being which is aware of the nature of being, is the worst of all murderers, a mode of being he likens to "leprosy" and a "fit of lunacy throttling matter."[45] Indeed, Cioran claims, "existence = torment," and human existence is its greatest tormentor.[46] Unless contemporary philosophy establishes itself upon this fundamental moral fact—one which he argues grows out of a proper understanding of the role of thermodynamic entropy in existence—it is bound to perpetuate the history of idolatrous pontification, dogmatic fideism, and idealistically justified fanaticism which has haunted its past and made it complicit in so much human suffering.

In order to respond authentically to the horror of existence, free contemporary philosophy from its past, and empower it to produce new and alternative ways of thinking and being, Cioran argues that we must renounce our hope that some robust sense of meaning might be wrenched from the horror inducing void that is existence and accept that "only aspiration to the Void saves us from that exercise of corruption which is the act of belief."[47] For Cioran, such an "aspiration" is not only *epistemologically* necessary for philosophical thinking to have any validity, assuring as it does that its products conform to what is actually observable of the universe, but even more importantly, it is *ethically* necessary, since it provides the only way we might attempt to counter the torment and horror of existence.

According to Cioran, at least one ethical injunction can be speculatively extracted from the absolute truth of being; namely, that it is our absolute duty to recognize the fundamental injustice of existence and to endeavor to reconcile ourselves to it fully. And, he thinks, this is a task which we can only accomplish by "suppressing our 'certitudes'" and cultivating in their place what he calls "a faculty of indifference"—that is, an indifference to ourselves, our hopes, our desires, and ultimately to our expectations that any final good or salvific meaning can be achieved from reality.[48] Only through such an attitude of "indifference," he thinks, can we hope to mirror in ourselves the fundamental and absolute truth of existence itself and, in this way, achieve some semblance of peace within the atrocity of being—or, at the very least, not contribute to it any more than we must. This is, for Cioran, the ultimate ethical aim of philosophical reflection upon the truth of being: to discover a way to become just as indifferent to the monstrosity of being as the monstrosity of being is indifferent to us; and in this way, to discover a mode of being in the world in which we are not accomplices to its murderousness through fanatical devotion to false ideals.

To exemplify this ethics of indifference, Cioran identifies three modes of being: the frivolity of the aesthete, the boredom of the idler, and the skepticism of the philosopher. In the frivolity of the aesthete, Cioran identifies a way of being which, "having discerned the impossibility of any certitude, ha[s] conceived a disgust for such things" and has cultivated in art, literature, and poetry a way to enjoy the "abyss" of existence "which, being by nature bottomless, can lead nowhere."[49] The glory of frivolity, he thinks, is that it shows us how to while away and even enjoy the meaninglessness of our own existence. For this reason, Cioran suggests that "frivolity is the most effective antidote to the disease of being what one is: by frivolity we abuse the world and dissimulate the impropriety of our depths."[50]

For those to whom such luxurious pursuits are not available due to social status, economic limitations, or political history, Cioran recommends instead the path of the "idle, empty mind—which joins the world only by grace of sleep."[51] In this cultivated boredom and indolence, Cioran outlines what he sees as an equally moral way in which we might cultivate within ourselves an interior reflection of the absolute meaninglessness and emptiness of the universe. In such shiftless inaction Cioran thinks we find another way in which we can reconcile ourselves to the law of inertia immanent in material reality itself and thus imitate more perfectly the absolute truth of existence. And so, Cioran suggests, "the idle apprehend[s] more things" and become even "deeper than the industrious."[52] More importantly still, he suggests, the idler finds a way, through their indolence, to neutralize the tendency of "the industrious" to murder in the name of their ideals, hopes, and dreams. In this regard, he reasons, those who are idle are in fact, ironically, always hard at work in the task of lessening the overall horror of human existence. Hence his conclusion that "the idle [are] the only ones not [inclined] to be murderers."[53] For, he reasons, "only the dilettante has no taste for blood, [and so] he alone is no scoundrel."[54] For this reason, Cioran identifies "ennui [as] the martyrdom of those who live and die for no belief" and one of the more ethical modes of being available to the human.[55]

Finally, for those who can neither give themselves over to the frivolity of artistic contemplation nor find themselves free to idle away their time in bored apathy, Cioran suggests "the art of thinking against oneself," which he sees as the heart of philosophical skepticism.[56] By learning to think "against oneself" in this way, Cioran argues, those who practice skepticism can learn to unravel the all too human tendency to prop up some false idol or transcendental ideal in the hope that they might resolve the inescapable problem of existence and become comfortable with the fundamental unresolvedness of reality.[57] To explain further this mode of ethical skepticism, Cioran identifies the first cynic, Diogenes of Sinope, as an exemplar.

"Only Diogenes proposes nothing," Cioran writes, and "the basis of his attitude—and of cynicism in its essence—is determined by a testicular horror of the absurdity of being man."[58] Like Diogenes, Cioran argues, someone "who rules and believes in nothing—behold[s] the model of a paradise of forfeiture, a sovereign solution to history."[59] And so Cioran thinks that in and through skepticism we might extract some modicum of goodness out of the horror of existence. This, he concludes, is the ethical aim of a life lived in pursuit of "nothing," a life consisting of a cultivated skepticism and philosophical cynicism.

Whatever form it takes, Cioran thinks that the only ethical response we can derive from the fundamental problem of existence is to reject the idolatry of philosophical and religious concepts by embracing the mode of being he sees exemplified in "the skeptics (or idlers or aesthetes)"; for "they propose nothing, because they, humanity's true benefactors—undermine fanaticism's purposes, [and] analyze the frenzy."[60] Cioran concludes that it is only through one of these modes of being that we can hope to authentically and responsibly embrace "life, which is the Great Unknown," and find some peace in the "pleasures of anguish" which arise from an "initiation . . . to nothingness—and to the mockery of being alive."[61] This, he thinks, is the best we can ever hope to achieve given the fundamental injustice of existence. For Cioran, the one ethical duty which can be deduced from the nature of existence as it is understood in and through the contemporary sciences is an injunction to resist the temptation to think that the universe might be made good or be forced to divulge some ultimate meaning. This is a resistance, he continues, which we actively pursue by means of frivolity, boredom, or skepticism.[62] Unless we learn to accept and reconcile ourselves to the evil and murderous indifference of the cosmos in one of these practical and ethical modes of being in the world, Cioran claims, we are not only bound to suffer the effects of reality within us, but to become complicit in its annihilative aims in the lives of others. If we are to lessen either of these fates, Cioran concludes, then we ought to reflect upon the fundamental reality of the universe and become utterly indifferent to its meaninglessness.

The Moral Impotence and Vicissitudes of Cosmic Pessimism

Thacker's aim in highlighting Bataille's mystical "base materialism" and Cioran's pessimistic "ethics of indifference" is to show how we might come to terms with and live practically within the kinds of "limit-thoughts" which he thinks are presented to us by the mathematical sciences: an account of the world as utterly indifferent, if not antagonistically opposed, to our mode of being.[63] For Thacker, "cosmic pessimism," whether or not it engages directly with the work of the contemporary sciences, fundamentally reflects the picture of reality granted to us by the sciences and therefore provides the only means by which contemporary philosophy can reinvent itself and provide an account for how we might practically live in the world today. Inasmuch as it accomplishes this task, Thacker thinks, "cosmic pessimism" is commendable and should be used to guide contemporary philosophy in the development of a new and practical ethics and politics.

Despite its originality and insightful engagement with the history of Western thought, however, there are fundamental problems and limitations with Thacker's account of "cosmic pessimism" as exemplified in Bataille and Cioran's work. First and foremost is the fact that neither one of those thinkers actually engages with the scientific accounts of the universe to which they claim to adhere in their work. In this regard, while not necessarily betraying or contradicting the conclusions of the mathematical sciences, their "cosmic pessimism" lacks a solid epistemological basis that is necessary to justify their metaphysical and ethical conclusions. On this front, as outdated as Mainländer's engagement with the sciences may seem, they are still more firmly grounded epistemologically than Thacker's account of "cosmic pessimism."

The practical consequence of this insufficiency in cosmic pessimism is that inasmuch as its variants strive to articulate new ethical activities that accurately reflect the universal and absolute truth of being, each one tends toward a personal or private account of truth as a kind of mystical encounter. Each mode of cosmic pessimism thus risks losing precisely the kind of universal validity that the sciences provide for philosophy and grant to Mainländer's pessimism. And as we saw in chapter 1, the danger of such an individualized approach to the absolute is that it risks resurrecting some new form of dogmatic fideism (only in this case of the individual's "pure experience") or collapsing into some form of nihilism, something that is irrefutably present in each of these modes of pessimism. As a result, while each variety of cosmic pessimism identified by Thacker aspires to derive some moral meaning and account of ethical responsibility from its reckoning with the meaninglessness of the material universe, the ethical injunctions they develop from their confrontation with the inhuman facts of reality are ultimately only a novel form of the same kind of moral quietism championed by Schopenhauer and early Buddhist philosophy. And, ultimately, this is the final and most damning weakness of the kind of cosmic pessimism which Thacker endorses as the path forward for contemporary philosophy.

Cioran, for his part, explicitly praises moral quietism as the only path by which the evils of human history might eventually come to an end.[64] In fact, it is Cioran's conviction that quietism is the only appropriate response to existence that inspires his praise for indifference as a sort of "apprenticeship to passivity."[65] For him, as for Schopenhauer and the historical Buddha before him, the only ethics which can be extracted from the fundamental injustice of existence is one that renounces existence entirely and pursues a life of what he calls "counterfeit living," which he defines as "a state of non-suicide."[66] The aim of ethical responsibility is fulfilled, according to him then, when we learn to live as if we were already dead. And what is this vision of ethical action if not a renewed form of exactly the kind of ascetic quietism promoted by Schopenhauer and decried by Nietzsche—and quite rightly so, since it is nothing more than a covert form of nihilism? It will come as no surprise then that Thacker, Bataille, and Cioran all equally draw from Schopenhauer and early Buddhist philosophy to model the kind of mystical indifference they see as the proper ethical response to the problem of existence.[67]

Bataille, for his part, decries the possibility of deriving any practically effective ethics from a truly pessimistic materialism. Indeed, he goes so far as to argue that the only appropriate response to the primal power of matter is to pursue "a crude liberation of human life from the imprisonment and masked pathology of ethics" by "appeal[ing] to all that is offensive, indestructible, and even despicable, [and] to all that overthrows, perverts and ridicules spirit."[68] If any ethical *ought* can be gleaned from Bataille's dark mysticism, then it is this alone: the injunction to reject every moral *ought* and to pursue the ecstasy of the inner experience of that which *is*—a position that is not only entirely nihilistic, but which lends itself all too easily to a new form of fanaticism. Indeed, Bataille even admits as much, suggesting that the nature of existence "forces one to dance with fanaticism."[69]

From this it should be clear that despite its merits, Thacker's "cosmic pessimism" leaves us with little hope to develop a robust normative system from which we might draw in our attempts to respond to the classical question: "How ought I live?" In this regard, Thacker's cosmic pessimism fails to achieve the kind of radical social and political potency that is articulated in Mainländer's pessimism. On the contrary, it risks collapsing back into a kind of practical moral nihilism or resurrecting some new form of mystical fideism which, as we have shown, post-Kantian philosophy must reject if it is to reclaim its relevance in the contemporary world. Fortunately, not every pessimism which has appeared in the last few years is as ethically and politically impotent as "cosmic pessimism." On the contrary, some use this same pessimistic evaluation of the horror of existence to justify a new absolute ethical imperative to engage in radical political activity. One particularly powerful example of such a socially and politically active model of ethical pessimism is what Frank B. Wilderson III, Saidiya Hartman, Steve Martinot, Jared Sexton, Hortense J. Spillers, Calvin Warren, and many others have called *Afropessimism*.[70]

Afropessimism and the Ontology of Social Death

Inspired by and drawing from Orlando Patterson's analysis of the structure, function, and effects of slavery on social life in his seminal work *Slavery and Social Death* (1982), Afropessimism starts with the premise that slavery is more than merely a tragic sociopolitical artifact or terrible accident of history.[71] Functioning as it did to reduce Black bodies to purely material objects, Afropessimists argue that slavery is first and foremost a metaphysical event—something which is structurally constitutive of and therefore inextricable from our contemporary conception and mode of being in the world. These metaphysical consequences of slavery are demonstrated, they document, in the way in which the institution of slavery transformed Black bodies from sites of subjective life to objects of pure and abject material potentiality, little more than brute *things* to be dominated, controlled, and used by some other subject who elevates itself beyond it and defines itself through this domination: the white slave owner and their peers. The "social death" effected by the institution of slavery thus operates, they argue, as a kind of ontological alchemy which transmutes some*one* (the Black individual) into some*thing* (the slave) and in this way transforms another *thing* (the white body) into some*one* (the conscious subject or rational agent). According to Patterson, this is the metaphysical power of the social and political institution of slavery and its contemporary heir, institutionalized racism.[72]

To understand Patterson's arguments properly, it is essential that we see that the ontological transformation which is effected through the "social death" constituted in slavery and anti-Black racism is not unidirectional—that is to say, its effect is not only to create passive objects from Black bodies. On the contrary, according to Patterson, the concomitant result of this "social death" is the creation of the active subjects or rational agent, as it is aspired to and fantasized by whites. Thus, Afropessimists argue, though the flow of power and the application of violence in slavery and racism are directed "downward" in the production of a purely material and passive object (the slave) from the Black body, the ontological effects of this "social death" is bidirectional—it creates through this downward flow of power an updraft of agency by which the non-black body elevates itself to the status of subjectivity: someone who freely wills and posits itself as existing and is, therefore, somehow outside of, beyond, and perhaps even in control of the purely material world which it identifies with the Black body. In this regard, as Saidiya Hartman argues, the fundamental dialectics of the history of Western thought are created: the subject/object split, the presumed ontological passivity of objects, the ideal of the subjective liberty or free-will of the conscious agent, if not the history of dualism itself. All of this, she shows, are products of the historical enslavement and contemporary suppression of Black bodies—products, in other words, of the metaphysical system it creates and upon which our contemporary world is founded.

Given "the longstanding and intimate affiliation of liberty and bondage," Hartman writes, it is "impossible to envision freedom independent of constraint or personhood and autonomy separate from the sanctity of property and proprietorial notions of the self."[73] For this reason, Frank B. Wilderson has argued that the very concept of the "Human," conceived of as it is in the history of Western thought, as a supposedly free subject and active agent who is somehow transcendent to the world of pure materiality, is inextricable from and ultimately "parasitic" upon the enslavement and suppression of Black bodies.[74] Hence he and his colleagues insistence on the ontological importance of slavery and racism in Western metaphysics as well as our entire understanding and experience of the world today.

"The Human is not an organic entity," Wilderson writes, "but a construct; a construct that requires its Other in order to be legible; [and]

the Human Other is Black."[75] In this regard, he argues, the very concept of the "Human" as a free, politically engaged, and morally valuable animal whose meaning is established not through its engagement with material reality, but in something transcendent to that reality is dependent on and inextricably complicit in the institution of slavery and all of its contemporary analogs.[76] "Violence against Black people is a mechanism for the usurpation of subjectivity, of life, of being," Wilderson writes.[77] As such, he concludes, "anti-Black violence [is] not a form of racist hatred but the genome of Human renewal; [it is] a therapeutic balm that the Human race needs to know and heal itself."[78] Wilderson concludes with Hartman that it is therefore impossible to work toward or hope to achieve some semblance of freedom, equality, and peace for people of African heritage within the current framework of our ontologies, which is to say the totality of the contemporary world, because the framing concepts of those ontologies and that world are absolutely interwoven with the subjugation of Black bodies. Every social and political agenda which grows out of such a metaphysics, they both conclude, no matter how committed it may be to the ideal of universal liberty, is necessarily doomed to reinforce the suppression and repression of Black bodies. Indeed, the very concept of liberty itself, they argue, conceived of as something which can be distributed to everyone, as if from a position of privilege, is integrally bound to and inextricable from the subjugation of Black bodies. The concept of "universal" liberation is in fact, they think, something of an oxymoron—a concept which is fundamentally self-defeating. For, they argue, liberation as it is conceived in the West can only be maintained through the enslavement and domination of the Black body. It is from this analysis of the metaphysical significance of the history of slavery and the institutionalized racism, which is its contemporary inheritor, that Afropessimism's skepticism toward every ethical and political agenda in the West grows, especially those which blithely aspire to the concept "liberty and justice for all."

Since, as Wilderson argues, the subjugation of Black bodies is the very condition for the possibility of existence as we know it today, especially the existence of the allegedly "free" and "rational" agent, every social and political agenda committed to maintaining or ameliorating that existence must, in one way or another, necessarily continue to do harm to Black bodies.[79] As such, he reasons, the enslavement and suppression of Black bodies is no mere accident of history; it is rather the very condition for the possibility of our current mode of being in the world and something which, therefore, is inextricable from every ethical and political project we might envision for that world. For this reason, Wilderson argues, "there is no antagonism like the antagonism between Black people and the world," for while "there is no world with Blacks, . . . there are not Blacks who are in the world."[80] To be in the world (i.e., to exist as a free agent), Wilderson concludes, is to benefit from the exclusion and subjugation of Black bodies. In this sense, Saidiya Hartman argues, the Black body can be seen as the absolute ground and material condition for the very possibility of every form of being in the world—from the ideas of humanity, subjectivity, individuality, and freedom which define the nature of that being, to the very concepts of moral value, ethical responsibility, and political activity which establish the hopes and aspirations of that being.[81]

As such, Wilderson identifies the Black body as the site of the "absolute dereliction" upon which the world at every level (metaphysical, ethical, and political) grows—in other words, as the nothing from which the being of the world emerges and against which it defines itself.[82] In this regard, Wilderson and his colleagues see in the Black body something of the raw materiality identified by Bataille as the base root of existence; nothing less than that which is seen as evil in itself. Indeed, Calvin Warren argues convincingly that for this reason blackness should be seen as the ultimate site in which the appearance of Bataille's concept of base material or Heidegger's account of *das nichts* is realized—that primordial "nothing" from which all other existent realities emerge, in contrast to which they must define themselves, and against which they must strive to maintain their existence and establish their idea of what is true, right, and ultimately good.[83] The reduction of the Black body to the status of *nothing* in this way, Warren argues, is the grounding condition for the possibility of every other mode of being in the world or ethical aspiration of and political hope for that being which is conceivable in the contemporary world.[84] In this regard, Warren argues, to be Black is to be constitutionally, ontologically, and ethically a *void* in-the-world.[85] As such, he concludes, this world emerges and is inextricable from a kind of "black nihilism."[86]

Given the ontological power of the enslavement and continued suppression of Black bodies in the world, Afropessimists argue that the position of the Black body in relation to the world is unique and incomparable to any other form of social or political marginalization. Indeed, Afropessimists argue that "to be" Black is not merely to be *marginalized* from the political discourse, it is to be fundamentally and absolutely *excluded* from the polis—and is therefore, ontologically, *not to be* at all. To "be" Black, in other words, Afropessimism argues, is to be absolutely, categorically, and irrevocably barred, denied, and excised from the realm of true being—it is "to be" effectively nothing; or, put another way, it is to be wholly and exclusively some*thing*, some passive or inert material object

CHAPTER 10

and not a living existential activity which constructs itself and constitutes itself through political engagement. For these reasons, they conclude, there can be no hope for Black bodies in this world or in any of its ethical ideals, social projects, or political aspirations. And, it is meaningless to think, they maintain, that there could be any ethical or political mode of being in the world, defined as it is through the subjugation of Black bodies, which could achieve or establish justice for all; and the more we attempt to extract ourselves from this fact through concepts like goodness and liberty, which are only available to us as a result of that subjugation, the more we must inevitably mire ourselves within the evil of this world and bind ourselves to the moral horror of history. By their account, the ontological order of our world and every concept of truth, moral value, and political hope within it is fundamentally inseparable then from the reduction of the Black body to that which these ideals define themselves against: passive, brute, and meaningless bits of matter with no intrinsic or absolute value, and no place, therefore, within the social and political discourses which allege to aspire to goodness and justice.

For these reasons, Wilderson concludes, we cannot reasonably hope that the injustices of our world might be overcome without a radical rejection of and revolution within our world, not merely at the level of social and political discourse, or even within the realm of our ethical imaginations, but at the level of metaphysical reality itself. Indeed, he argues, the true aim of a political revolution must be this: to overturn the very ontological structures of existence itself. For, Wilderson reasons, within the currently existing ontological order it is impossible to truly enfranchise or empower, which is to say to "liberate," Blackness in any real or meaningful sense. According to Wilderson, in the world as it currently exits "Blackness cannot become one of civil society's many junior partners: Black citizenship, or Black civic obligation, are oxymorons."[87] The so-called "liberation" of Black bodies from the historical condition of slavery within this world is necessarily an illusion then, the Afropessimists argue, for the very concept of liberty arises from the ontological order and social death which was instituted in slavery. For this reason, they conclude, any and every conception of "liberation" is ultimately just a rearrangement of the pieces which constitute the current ontological order which is established in and through the nihilation of the possibility of Black subjectivity. Indeed, Wilderson argues, in "emancipation the technology of enslavement simply morphs and shape shifts—it doesn't end."[88] Thus, they argue that the violence wrought upon the Black body in the constitution of our current metaphysical order cannot be overcome by merely rearranging the social and political deck chairs which exist within the subject's conception of its world; for the Black body is the dark sea which buoys that very subjectivity upon its back. Unless the very dynamics of this existence of this world is utterly rejected, they therefore conclude, and a new ontological order is created in its place, every social and political response to the consequences of slavery will simply re-institutionalize its foundational violence, only in a new and potentially even more violent way. For true justice to become even possible, to continue the metaphor, they argue, the boat must be capsized, and the world must be remade entirely.

Hence Wilderson and his allies claim that while a more inclusive politics might eventually function to accommodate those who have been historically disenfranchised by white men—for example, women, indigenous peoples, Latinx communities, and so on—no political order can ever exist within any of the current metaphysical frameworks which would be capable of fully incorporating a Black way of being. The constitutional violence against Black bodies is too foundational for that, he argues, for the Black body is the ontological other which must be excluded for our ethical hopes and political ideals of enfranchisement to even exist. Thus, in contrast to those who might aspire to be included in progressive political projects as "junior partners" in democracy, Wilderson argues that the Afropessimist recognizes that to be Black is to be fundamentally denied the possibility of personhood necessary to be included in any allegedly democratic project. This is the case, he concludes, because the founding metaphysical basis of each and every one of democracy's projects is the reduction of Blackness to exclusively and entirely a mode of *thinghood*. As such, he thinks, to "be" Black in this world is to be fundamentally denied the political hope which might be extended to members of other marginalized communities. For, he argues, where the marginalization of others is solely *political*, the exclusion of Blacks from civil society is, as we have seen, *ontological*.

This is the root of the ethical, social, and political "pessimism" at work in Afropessimism. Wilderson writes: "Afropessimism is premised on an iconoclastic claim: that Blackness is coterminous with Slaveness. Blackness *is* social death."[89] To be Black, he therefore argues, is to be metaphysically bound by the ontological effects of slavery. As such, it is to be essentially and structurally excluded from every form of *being* in the world: ethical, social, and political. And so, he concludes, there is no hope for liberation *in* the world; there is only perhaps a liberation "*from* the world" in death, or perhaps in radically overthrowing this world and remaking it anew, ontologically up.[90]

CHAPTER 10

The Revolutionary Political Ethics of Afropessimism

The fundamental question of Afropessimism, then, is this: What is to be done with this world? What, in other words, are we to do with the metaphysical structures established on the back of the ontological reduction of Blackness to thinghood? What ethical *ought* can we reasonably hope to develop in or from what *is* true of this world—or rather, from the "*is not*" achieved through the social death of the Black body upon which the world is established? "The question," as Saidiya Hartman puts it, in other words, "is whether it is possible to unleash freedom from the history of property that secured it, for the security of property that undergirded the abstract equality of rights bearers was achieved, in large measure, through black bondage."[91] To answer this question, Wilderson suggests, we must first recognize the ontological fact that "Blackness and Slaveness are inextricably bound in such a way that whereas Slaveness can be separated from Blackness, Blackness cannot exist as other than Slaveness."[92] Any ethical or political agenda which does not recognize the fact of this ontological reality, he argues, must necessarily fail. Indeed, it is for this reason, Wilderson argues, drawing upon the work of Frantz Fanon, that the traditional approach to liberation held out to Black communities is to feign whiteness—to take up what Fanon calls a "white mask."[93] But, Wilderson argues, since such a political masquerade ultimately fails to address the ontological conditions of Blackness or to unmake the world which emerges from this ontological condition, it cannot hope to transform the Black experience or the structures which constitute our world. Given its unique ontological status, Wilderson concludes, Blackness will never be successfully assimilated or enfranchised within any of the civil societies of this world through such a pantomime. At best, he thinks, such a project might function to earn certain individuals a limited tolerance from those who are empowered as subjects by the metaphysical history of the West. Ultimately, however, Wilderson assures us, the absolute truth of reality will reassert itself, and violently so, and the Black body will at some point be stripped of its mask and forced to face the base material reality to which it is metaphysically restricted by the constructs of our current version of reality.

For these reasons, Wilderson and his colleagues assert: "against this we choose, following Afro-pessimism, to understand Black liberation as a negative dialectic, a politics of refusal, and a refusal to affirm; as an embrace of disorder and incoherence; and as an act of political apostasy."[94] The only *ought* which can be derived from the *is* that is constituted by the ontological death forced upon the Black body, they therefore argue, is to radically *refuse, reject,* and *resist* the political and metaphysical structures of this world; for, they conclude, there is no good which can be hoped for in this world. Indeed, they argue, to be at all in this world, no matter how "good" one may appear to be, is to be an accomplice to and complicit in the violent suppression of Black bodies which founds it. Ethical responsibility and political liberation in the current status quo, they conclude, are fundamentally impossible and should not even be striven for. To the contrary, Afropessimism suggests, such ideals should be rejected entirely as instruments in the continued suppression of Black bodies. If any real or actual hope is to be established, they therefore think, all existing moral and political structures must be radically rejected and overthrown in an attempt to overturn, eventually, the ontological structures that found and justify them. Indeed, they argue, the only hope we might have for some semblance of "goodness," "liberty," or "justice" in this world is to be found in the active attempt to resist, reject, and overthrow every existing metaphysical, ethical, and social and political structure on offer in that world. What the Afropessimist argues that we must aim to accomplish if we are to work towards anything resembling the good, in other words, is the negation and nihilation of every element of being itself, as it currently exists within the ontological order of the day. Only in this way, they argue, can the structural evil of our current mode of existence be eliminated and some hope for the possibility of a truly just world emerge in its absence.

In the words of Frank Wilderson: "I do believe that there is a way out. But I believe that the way out is a kind of violence so magnificent and so comprehensive that it scares the hell out of even radical revolutionaries . . . The trajectory of violence that Black slave revolts suggest, whether it be in the 21st century or the 19th century, is a violence against the generic categories of life, agency being one of them."[95] In this regard, the only *ought* which Afropessimism thinks might be deducible from the ontological reality of the world as it currently *is* mirrors in many ways the kind of ethical commitment to revolutionary politics promoted by Philipp Mainländer, but even more radical still for its suspicion of every political aspiration would extend to include even his political ideals of equality. For both, the abject horror of existence demands a radical and revolutionary politics which works negatively against the very structure of the world itself, the world that defines the very nature of our being. For both, the only viable "ethics" which can be extracted from the lived conditions of our being is the moral demand to radically reject and resist the nature of existence as it appears today and, through such a radical and revolutionary sociopolitical and ontological transformation, to remake being itself. For both, then, the real aim of these pessimistic ethical

CHAPTER 10

and political projects is to negate the very structure of being itself at an ontological level. Only the Afropessimist sees, however, that the depravity of existence is so complete that even those ethical and political systems which are put in place to negate that being in the hopes of achieving some semblance of justice and equality will necessarily contribute to even greater injustice and inequality and eventually suppress in new and inventive ways the Black body.

In this regard, Afropessimism simultaneously fleshes out and calls into question Mainländer's ethical and political pessimism. By showing us in a specific and historically informed way how our active pursuit of the good might inadvertently reinforce actual injustices and moral harms, Afropessimism forces us to reconsider and radicalize Mainländer's ethical and political projects. Following their pessimistic assessment of our mode of being as absolutely evil, it is our moral duty, Afropessimists conclude, to actively reject and resist even Mainländer's hope in the possibility of liberty, justice, and equality, and along with it every form of white supremacy which might covertly be at work in any and every ethical and political aspiration. Instead, they assert, we must endeavor instead in and through our ethics and politics to overthrow reality itself, inclusive of our hope for the possibility of even a dialectically negative sense of political goodness.

"Want to be good?" we can imagine the Afropessimist asking, "then start by rejecting your commitment to your own sense of goodness. Reject moreover your very being, for you are structurally and constitutionally evil." The only hope for "goodness," they then maintain, is to consistently reject and to actively fight to overthrow the evil that is our very being in the world through the most radical form of political revolution imaginable: metaphysical obliteration. And how exactly are we to accomplish this, one might ask? Well, in the words of Wilderson, "as a professor I'm uniquely unqualified to actually make that answer. I rely on providing analysis and then getting those marching orders from people in the streets."[96] However such a metaphysical revolution might be envisioned or accomplished, Afropessimism provides invaluable insight for the kind of pessimistically driven practical ethics and politics we're pursuing— for it informs and provokes a suspicion in the efficacy of Mainländer's ethical and political activism by drawing attention to the actual historical facts of our mode of being in the world. In this regard, it provides a way of radicalizing his conclusions and directing us on how best we might develop "marching orders" in our attempt to actively negate the absolute evil of existence.

There is, however, one critical shortcoming to the ethical and political project of Afropessimism. In its historicity, it can at times lose the power that a fully scientifically informed metaphysics can offer this revolutionary project. This is demonstrated, for example, in Calvin Warren's appeal to what he calls "post-metaphysics," which he identifies with the "deconstruction" of traditional metaphysics as a universal "science" and the re-situating of such a metaphysical project within the actual lived social and political realities of history.[97] Such a "deconstruction," he argues, requires not only a rejection of traditional metaphysics, but of traditional science as well, since both appear in his work, and indeed in the history of the West, as co-conspirators in the subjugation of Black bodies.[98]

On this point, of course, Warren is irrefutably right. The history of metaphysics and science in the West is demonstrably complicit in and undeniably guilty of the racist subjugation of Black bodies. For this reason, Warren's suspicion of the role of science in metaphysics is justified, as is his suspicion of the value of any metaphysics, but particularly a scientifically grounded one. But this suspicion might be answered and quelled by the kind of scientifically informed naturalized metaphysics which is promoted by speculative realism—that is, the kind of radically inhuman, nonhuman, and irrational account of the universe which it claims is achieved and accomplished in the contemporary mathematical sciences. Indeed, as we have seen, what the naturalized metaphysics of speculative realism aspires to is what it sees as precisely the disruptive power of mathematics when applied to every human conception of itself, its order, meaning, and significance. In and through the radically inhuman perspective granted to us by the contemporary sciences, constituted as they are in and through the abstractive power of mathematics, Afropessimism might therefore discover a power which, in its inhuman hostility to the historical manifestation of the human as an active agent and rational subject, constitutes an ally in the fight against the history of white supremacy and the reality upon which that history is established: that is, the social death it subjected the Black body to in order to extract itself from the mire of matter and to construct the idea of the subjective human agent.

In the contemporary mathematical sciences, I would argue, Afropessimism could arm itself with what Badiou rightly identifies as a weapon of war against every form of fanatical social and political ideal, even and especially those ideals by which the human defines itself: free-will, agency, and immateriality. Without recognizing or utilizing this power to upend the history of suppression essential to the Western conception of the human, Warren's "post-metaphysics," and any ethical or political marching orders it might develop therein, will inevitably be bound within what Meillassoux calls some version of the "correlationist perspective."[99] Thus, while it is essential that we draw upon the ethical and political insights of Afropessimism to develop a potent account of the kind of practical pessimism accomplished by Mainländer, and to be wary even of how it might be complicit in the injustices of the world it aspires to negate, resist, and eventually annihilate, in order to make these insights all the more practically effective in their call to overturn the ontological order of the day, we mustn't lose sight of the radical power of mathematics to serve as a weapon in this battle. For within the primal antagonism of the entropic thrust of material reality as it is described by the mathematical sciences, we may, as Mainländer frames it, find a partner in the revolutionary project which is demanded by Warren, Wilderson, Hartman, and others.

What the contemporary mathematical sciences show us, after all, is that the absolute aim of the universe is to destroy existence as we know it, and with it, every form of humanity which has been established within in. In the absolute inhumanity of the cosmos as described by the mathematical sciences, we therefore discover a power to which we can turn to empower Warren, Wilderson, and Hartman's ethical call to reject and overturn the existing ontological order itself. Instead of reducing metaphysics to politics, as I think Warren does, I would argue that we must work to reestablish the kind of political revolution which is called for by Warren and his colleagues on the basis of the kind of absolute metaphysical reality which can be speculatively abstracted from the sciences. By embracing its account of the primal malicious inhumanity of the universe, and establishing itself upon the new metaphysics of decay this account justifies, Afropessimism might forge an ethical weapon and political lance by which it can practically challenge and eventually defeat the reality of this world. To this end, I think that Afropessimism might find a potential ally in our metaphysics of decay and even, perhaps, in the last of the "new" pessimisms which have appeared in recent years, a position which similarly sets itself against the prevailing humanisms of Western thinking, only in this case through the mobilization of what they see as the fundamentally *inhuman* fact of extinction, as guaranteed by the contemporary mathematical sciences.

The Absolute Reality of Extinction and the Nihilism of the Inhuman

First appearing in Jean-François Lyotard's *The Inhuman* (1988), this form of post-Schopenhauerian pessimism is founded upon what it sees as one of the most assured material facts uncovered by the contemporary mathematical sciences; namely, the absolutely inevitable extinction of all life on earth within a determinable time frame, and, eventually, the absolute extinction of existence itself at the far end of time.[100] This fact, which Lyotard sees as promised, at the very least, by the imminent explosion of the sun in roughly 4.5 billion years, should function, he argues, to radically challenge our intuitions concerning the importance and value of every human project. Indeed, he reasons, given what it promises for human beings and all that they have ever accomplished, thought, or hoped to achieve, the absolute annihilation which is guaranteed by this radically inhuman and cataclysmic event is "the sole serious question to face humanity today." It is, in other words, he argues, the one question by which every other philosophical pursuit and question should be measured.[101]

According to Lyotard, unless the products of our philosophical reasoning can justify and maintain their relevance in light of this scientifically assured fact, then they should be abandoned in favor of more pertinent and practical concerns. The problem is, he suggests, that when they are examined through the lens of this promised extinction, a number of the classical questions which have plagued Western thinkers for millennia suddenly "seem insignificant."[102] If philosophy is to achieve any use, validity, meaning, or importance for the contemporary world—which is to say, tarry no longer with questions of little to no material or practical significance—then, Lyotard reasons, it must begin to measure and ground its projects anew upon the absolute power, certainty, and perspective which is granted by the inevitability of our coming extinction—this singular and universal *inhuman* fact.

The fundamental problem with contemporary philosophy, Lyotard claims, is that it consistently refuses to do this. As a result, he argues, not only does it consign itself to irrelevance within and beyond the academy, but it further restricts itself to the imaginary and the ideal alone and, as such, remains firmly entrenched in the legacy of the "dogmatic slumber" from which critical philosophy endeavors to awaken. In this regard, contemporary philosophy's refusal to engage authentically with and take seriously the meaning and significance of our coming extinction, Lyotard argues, is yet another example of the lingering legacy of the dogmatic tendency to "X . . . out of writings—matter;" or, in other words, the tendency within the history of Western philosophy of treating material reality as if it were merely "an arrangement of energy created, destroyed, and re-created over and over again, endlessly," and thus unworthy of any real analysis—little more, in the final analysis, than a mute background against which the drama of human history is played out.[103] In as much as we maintain this tradition, Lyotard claims, philosophy will fail to realize the fact that this brute matter is the real grounding condition and ultimate essence of our being. What's more, he suggests, we will perpetually

CHAPTER 10

overlook something which is demonstratively true of matter; namely, that it is *not* eternal or infinitely re-creating, but is in fact determinately finite. Without accepting these facts which are irrefutably proven by the modern scientific account of reality and reckoning with that reality, Lyotard concludes, philosophy is doomed to remain stuck in its dogmatic past and, as such, remain utterly irrelevant to the contemporary world.

If philosophy is to finally escape its dogmatic past and secure its relevance to the contemporary world, Lyotard thus reasons, it must reject this tendency toward idealism and start to engage seriously with the scientifically verified fact that everything which exists is ultimately reducible to its material base and bound, therefore, by the same truths which define the nature of that material base: the truth that matter is not only finite, but working through its very being toward its ultimate extinction and the annihilation of everything else which exists. It is Lyotard's aim to force contemporary philosophy to acknowledge, reckon with, and measure itself against this fundamental and irrefutable *inhuman* truth, as he calls it, in the hopes that it might reground and reorganize itself anew.

To this end and in light of this fact, Lyotard surveys the state of contemporary philosophical projects (i.e., metaphysics, ethics, and politics) and notes that while we fritter away our time and energy debating various seemingly "deep" questions, we blithely ignore the scientifically demonstrable fact that "the sun is getting older" and will eventually explode.[104] And, he reminds us, that "with the sun's death your insoluble questions will be done with too."[105] When we measure our debates against this absolute fact, Lyotard thinks, we cannot help but discover the meaninglessness and insignificance of what we consider to be even the most pressing philosophical problems. Indeed, he argues, the fundamental power of this fact is to expose those problems to be empty, naked, meaningless, and fragile—little more than a kind of intellectual emperor's new clothes. In light of this fact, he concludes, our commitments to even the most apparently "hard" philosophical questions appear to be "futile," and meaningless.[106]

No matter how brilliant our philosophizing is, or how intricate and detailed our exposition of supposedly metaphysical truths, ethical values, and political imperatives may be, Lyotard argues that, in the end, we must all accept and reconcile ourselves to the inescapable fact that "in 4.5 billion years there will arrive the demise of your phenomenology and your utopian politics; and there'll be no one there to toll the death knell or hear it."[107] If our metaphysical speculations, ethical projects, and emancipatory politics are to have any value or use at all, he reasons, they must start by acknowledging this fact and proceed to account for themselves and for the validity of their projects in light of this fact. Unless it can reground these clearly *human* projects upon this absolutely *inhuman* fact, Lyotard thinks, philosophy must resign itself to being little more than an elaborate display of linguistic poetry and play—a sound and fury signifying nothing.[108] If, by contrast, philosophy is to have any practical import or claim to validity in the contemporary world, Lyotard concludes, then it must reorganize itself and reground these projects on a properly pessimistic evaluation of the meaning and value of existence in light of the absolute material fact that "after the solar explosion, there won't be any humanness, there won't be living creatures, [and] there won't be intelligent, sensitive, sentient earthlings to bear witness to it, since they and their earthly horizon will have been consumed," there will only be the vast emptiness of matter drifting steadily toward its own eventual annihilation.[109]

Inspired by this challenge to contemporary philosophy to reconceive itself and its products in light of the inevitability of what he calls the "solar catastrophe," Ray Brassier has endeavored to reframe the nature and aim of philosophical inquiry in the contemporary world. Brassier attends to this task by employing the epistemological methods of speculative realism, as defined by Meillassoux and Badiou, and the naturalized metaphysical claims of eliminative materialists like Paul and Patricia Churchland, in order to rethink the consequences of the eventual heat death of the universe, as predicted by the application of Boltzmann's law of entropic decay, upon philosophy's classical pursuits and projects.[110] According to Brassier, what we discover through such an epistemological vetting is not only the final death knell for the kind of correlationism critiqued by Meillassoux and challenged by naturalized metaphysics, but the radical reconfiguration of the limits and uses of philosophical reasoning itself.

As Brassier puts it, what ultimately "defies correlation is the thought that 'after the sun's death, there will be no thought left to know its death took place.'"[111] Since "extinction portends a physical annihilation which negates the difference between mind and world," Brassier argues that it effectively "turns thinking inside out, objectifying it as a perishable thing in the world like any other (and no longer the imperishable condition of perishing)."[112] As such, he continues, "extinction indexes the thought of the absence of thought."[113] Brassier concludes that while the fact of our ultimate extinction is "not empirical, since it is not of the order of experience," and it is not "ideal, since it coincides with the external objectification of thought unfolding at a specific historical juncture," it is nevertheless "real" and "transcendental."[114]

As the demonstrable transcendental reality of existence, Brassier argues that the eventual and ultimate extinction event which assured by the nature of matter itself should function as the proper ground upon which philosophy reestablishes itself and redefines its projects anew if it wants to justify its claims and assert its value to the contemporary world. In this way, he argues, "extinction has a transcendental efficacy [for philosophy] precisely insofar as it tokens an annihilation which is neither a possibility towards which actual existence could orient itself, nor a given datum from which future existence could proceed."[115] If philosophical reasoning, ethical evaluation, and moral and political normativity are to have any legitimate claim in the contemporary world, he concludes, then they must grow from a full recognition and understanding of the meaning and significance of the ultimate and transcendental reality of extinction which is assured by the inner essence of matter itself, or what we have called a "metaphysics of decay."

According to Brassier, however, what a proper reflection on the nature of this transcendental reality reveals is precisely the emptiness and meaninglessness of the vast majority of philosophical projects. Indeed, he argues, in light of the absolute fact of matter's eventual extinction, the bulk of the traditional metaphysical claims, moral values, ethical systems, and political agendas which have been outlined by philosophers are rendered *null and void*. Unless these projects are capable of crafting some new concept of the good, the right, and the true from the absolute fact of matter's eventual extinction, Brassier therefore argues, then they should be consigned to the dustbin of history, along with the dogmatisms of the past. Indeed, Brassier asserts, unless philosophy can learn to speak meaningfully of such things in light of the absolute fact of annihilation, then it should, in the words of Wittgenstein, learn to be silent. This, for Brassier, is the challenge which is put to philosophy by the absolute fact of the coming extinction of matter itself which is "unbound" by the contemporary scientific rendering of the world: to reconsider itself and its projects in light of the absolute fact of the ultimate nihilation of everything.

Despite its obviously destructive power, Brassier maintains that the nihilation of the classical aims and projects of philosophical reasoning which is loosed by this reckoning with the scientific accounting of matter is ultimately efficacious for contemporary philosophy; for, he thinks, while it eliminates much of what philosophers have traditionally hoped to accomplish through their reasoning, it supplies them at the same time with a new absolute ground for and clear parameters defining that which they can legitimacy hope to accomplish. For, he argues, insofar as contemporary philosophers can found and justify their metaphysical, ethical, and political claims anew upon the transcendental fact of extinction, they can be assured of the validity of their reasoning and its potential use to and value in the world. For this reason, Brassier argues that the absolute fact of extinction provides "a speculative opportunity" to philosophy: a chance to abandon its "human narcissism" and to reassess the scope and nature of its projects in light of an understanding of nature that is "indifferent to our existence and oblivious to the 'values' and 'meanings' which we would drape over it in order to make it more hospitable."[116] Thus, Brassier claims that the nihilistic "disenchantment of the world" which he thinks is "unbound" by the contemporary mathematical sciences should be "celebrated as an achievement of intellectual maturity, not bewailed as a debilitating impoverishment," even if it renders meaningless the bulk of what philosophy has aspired to accomplish in its long history.[117] For, he suggests, despite its destructive power, what the material fact of extinction provides to contemporary philosophers is not only a way to escape their solipsistic and humanistic past, but a way to rediscover a modicum of absolute reality upon which they might mount a new and scientifically justifiable synthetic account of existence.

Only insofar as contemporary philosophers redefine their aims and arguments in light of this new sense of what is absolutely and verifiably true of material reality itself, Brassier argues, can they hope to assert some justifiable claim concerning what *should* or *ought* to be done within that reality. To this end, Brassier proposes a number of possible paths forward for philosophical metaphysics, ethics, and politics by drawing extensively upon the work of Badiou and François Laruelle, both of whom he praises for their redefinition of philosophy negatively as a sort of "anti"-project.[118] But Brassier insists that if such a reframing of the ethical and political projects of philosophy is to proceed in the future, then it must grow from a full understanding and acceptance of the transcendental fact of the eventual extinction of life which, he rightly notes, is testified to in the contemporary sciences as a consequence of the nature of matter itself, understood to be the product of and efficient agent in entropic collapse. Unless these projects can be founded on and derived from this fact, Brassier concludes, philosophical ethics must relinquish its claim to be capable of contributing anything of practical value to the world and instead accept instead that it is ultimately no different in kind than of the other dogmatic dreams or fanciful idealisms of the past.

Reevaluating the Ethical and Political
Potency of the Inhuman

While Lyotard and Brassier's extinctual nihilism present a profound challenge to the history and projects of Western philosophy, one which must be responded to if philosophy is to maintain its claim to rationally achieve some account of what is absolutely right, ultimately true, and universally good, we should not be convinced entirely by their conclusion that philosophical metaphysics, ethics, and politics must necessarily perish in light of the absolute fact of annihilation. Their conclusion is based, after all, upon an assumption which we have already challenged; namely, the false belief that moral value is a purely human phenomenon—nothing more than a product of human thought, estimation, or sociopolitical history.[119] When Lyotard and Brassier call for the end of ethics and politics on the basis of this assumption, they unjustifiably dismiss the possibility that some absolutely inhuman moral value might be found within an entirely scientific account of matter. If, however, as we have already shown, some sense of absolute moral value can be discovered in and extracted from the inhuman structures of reality itself, then new ethical systems and political projects can be legitimately developed. Lyotard and Brassier's call to re-ground philosophy upon the absolutely inhuman annihilative principle inherent to material reality does not necessarily require us, in other words, to abandon the philosophical pursuit of an absolutely justified and scientifically informed account of moral value, ethical responsibility, and political activity. On the contrary, it may found and justify such pursuits anew; only, as we have seen, in an entirely negative and novel way—a way provided for us by metaphysical and moral pessimism.

The problem with Lyotard and Brassier's call for the end of metaphysics, ethics, and politics is ultimately that it confuses that which *will be* (i.e., the eventual nothingness toward which all of reality flows) with that which currently *is* (i.e., the proliferation of beings as agents of this coming nihilation). As a result, these thinkers conflate what we might call a *metaphysics of nihilation* with the *nihilation of metaphysics*, and through it, the nihilation of philosophical ethics and emancipatory politics. Against such a conflation, I think a proper speculative reckoning of the nihilating power of matter demands not the end of metaphysics, ethics, and politics, but their reinvention precisely as a nihilating power. This is what is implied by the metaphysics of decay we discovered in the first half of this book, and the pessimistic ethics which we have argued for in the second half. Hence, my claim that what we've seen concerning the absolute nature of material reality calls for the development of a new speculative account of being as a dissipative force, and my argument that a number of traditional concepts, like universal value and ultimate meaning, can be justified anew on the basis of this account of being and productively developed to yield new models of practical ethical duty and active political projects.

For this reason, despite what both see as the fundamentally nihilistic power of the *inhuman*, there is a way in which Lyotard and Brassier's account of the destructive potential of matter can be used to re-ground precisely the kind of radical metaphysical and revolutionary ethical and political projects we discovered in and through the work of Mainländer and contemporary Afropessimism. By identifying an absolutely *inhuman* potency within the annihilative trajectory of matter, one which is both fundamentally disruptive of and antagonistic to every *human* project, Lyotard and Brassier's work can be employed as an unexpected accomplice to the emancipatory ethics and politics called for by Mainländer and practically defined by Wilderson and others. This aid is supplied, however, against the intuitions of Lyotard and Brassier alike, who, for their part, remain dubious of the possibility of philosophy's capacity to derive a meaningful metaphysics and practically normative project from the annihilative fact of matter. Nevertheless, as we have shown, there is a negative power to the annihilative trajectory of matter as they describe it, one which can be used to ground and justify an account of reality as an absolute evil. This speculatively established ethical fact constitutes a strategic target against which every practical ethical practice and active emancipatory political project can define itself new, as an attempt to reject and resist the moral horror of being.

In this way, it becomes clear how Mainländer's metaphysical account of the foundations of ethical normativity and political action, when informed by Afropessimism's account of the moral duty to abolish and eradicate the ontological foundations of that reality through a radically emancipatory political revolution, points to a new way in which the extinctual promise of matter itself, as described by Lyotard and Brassier as "unbound" by the contemporary sciences, can be mobilized together in order to define a new, practical account of ethical duty and to justify in this way radical and revolutionary sociopolitical actions. The strength of these projects rests, however, upon a properly pessimistic evaluation of the annihilative trajectory of reality evaluated as absolutely evil. From such an evaluation, as we have seen, a new concept of the good becomes achievable as a relative aim, one which appears through a dialectical negation of the trajectory of nature, as Afropessimism rightly notes.

Understood in this way, the normative aims of this speculatively grounded pessimism become definable through a *disjunctive* deduction from the absolute *fact* of existence itself, evaluated as an absolute evil. In this way, not only is an absolute moral value rationally deducible from a speculative extension of what the contemporary mathematical sciences show us concerning the true nature being itself, but an absolutely justifiable account of ethical injunctions can be developed from that nature from which new and radically active sociopolitical projects can be devised. Given the absolute fact of material reality, the argument goes, it is our absolute ethical duty to work, however futilely, *against* the trajectory of reality by resisting our tendency to become accomplices in the destructive force of nature; and, to this end, we must actively work to erect social and political structures which aid us in this fight against the metaphysical facts of reality. These are the ethical, social, and political *oughts* which can be rationally deduced from that which actually *is* in nature itself—these, in other words, are the pessimistically driven ethical and political demands which we can absolutely justify from our metaphysics of decay.

When we inform Mainländer's commitment to emancipatory politics as a negative project through the analysis provided by Afropessimism of the historical injustices which have founded our current social and political order, we discover a strategic target for such a normative project; namely, to reject, resist, and attempt to overthrow entirely the history of white supremacy, patriarchy, and the capitalist class structures which are complicit in and work to maintain the absolute will of nature to harm, injure, destroy, and annihilate us, and through us itself. What we gain from our analysis of those pessimisms which have emerged since Schopenhauer and Mainländer is thus not only a more up-to-date account of the ground and nature of the absolute extinctual power of existence, but a more historically informed set of "marching orders" for the kinds of normative and political projects we should establish given our understanding of it.

By informing the ethical and political project of Philipp Mainländer with the Afropessimists' evaluation and critique of human history, and showing how this in turn might be re-grounded upon a more scientifically informed account of the annihilative power of reality as explored by Lyotard and Brassier, these new post-Schopenhauerian pessimisms reveal to us not only how we might finally escape the ethical miasma of post-Kantian philosophy, but how we might concretely pursue some semblance of the good in the contemporary world. In this way, they define the best path by which contemporary philosophy might reclaim its relevance to a suffering world.

Conclusion

Speculative Absolutes and Pessimistic Activism:

The Evangel of Entropy and the Ethics of Resistance

The Evangel of Entropy

We began this project with a seemingly simple question: Is it possible to absolutely ground and rationally justify universal ethical claims and normative sociopolitical activities after Kant's critique of dogmatic metaphysics? As we saw in the first chapter, the power of Kant's survey of the nature of rational thought was to reveal that every absolute appealed to in the history of Western thought was ultimately established upon and emergent from some structure of human consciousness and not, as had previously been believed, some independently existing reality in-itself. After Kant, as a result, it seemingly became impossible to appeal to any concept of absolute truth, universal moral value, or ultimate meaning without indulging in some kind of dogmatic fideism. If philosophy was remain within the limits of rationality alone, Kant therefore argued, then it must renounce such dogmatic tendencies and find new ways of grounding and justifying its claims. The history of Western philosophy after Kant is the history of the varied attempt to reckon with the effects of this critique.

As we saw, these attempts have traditionally been accomplished in one of three ways: (1) by abandoning the pursuit of some absolutely justifiable concept of the good, the right, and the true altogether in favor of some form of nihilism; (2) by erecting from the structures of reason itself some new foundation for the universal validity of truth, moral value, and meaning, albeit in a way that risks resurrecting either some form of nihilism or a new form of cultural imperialism; or (3) by rejecting Kant's restriction of philosophy to the realm of the rational and embracing the *exstasis* of singular experiences or exclusively local cultural practices wherein some new account of absolute truth, moral value, and meaning might be encountered, but again in a way that risks some form of relativistic nihilism or fanatical cultural and dogmatic imperialism. Each of these three approaches, lacking as they do any truly universal and actual absolute foundation upon which to ground and justify their claims, must inevitably fail, and with catastrophic consequences, as we detailed. As a result, the value, import, and practical use of philosophical reasoning has slowly withered in the West, to the detriment of both the discipline and social and political discourse at large.

But as we saw in chapters 2 and 3, a new hope has emerged in recent years for discovering an alternative path to absolute reality, one which, moreover, does not require betraying the basic insight of Kant's critique. This hope appears, as we detailed, in the epistemological claims of the so-called speculative realists, who argue that through a fully scientific naturalized metaphysics it might be possible to make meaningful claims about the nature of absolute reality once again without appealing to any form of dogmatic hope or singular personal experience. This work is accomplished, they argue, when we let the inhuman power of the mathematical and empirical sciences guide philosophical reasoning. Thus, they conclude, through the power of the contemporary mathematical sciences, we might move through reason to that which exists outside of and beyond reason alone: absolute reality in its own right. On this basis, they claim, philosophy can ground itself anew and reinitiate its attempt to make claims concerning absolute truth, universal moral value, and ultimate meaning; and, in this way, reclaim its relevance to the world.

To explore what possible absolutes might be available from such a speculatively justified survey of the scientific account of reality, we examined in chapter 4 the consensus of the contemporary mathematical sciences concerning the ordering principles and nature of reality as it is understood for today. There we discovered that nearly every contemporary scientist agrees that there is at least one absolutely grounding principle which conditions, organizes, regulates, and determines the nature of existence at every level: the law of entropic decay as articulated in the second law of thermodynamics. On the basis of this law, contemporary scientists agree, the universe can be understood from beginning to end as entirely *unbecoming*: as perpetually dissipating, dissolving, and decaying in pursuit of the absolute and eventual purity of thermal equilibrium. Indeed, as we saw there, material existence is nothing more than this steady dissipation of existence, whether in the form of matter, motion, or heat, toward the ultimate end of its complete annihilation. As a result, we concluded, it is possible to say with complete assurance that everything which exists must not only eventually disintegrate and disappear, leaving only a faint trace of background radiation more or less evenly distributed throughout an eternally expanding and utterly empty universe; but, moreover, that everything which exists is always already working toward this end—through its own development and its consumption of free energy from the surrounding environment for the maintenance and perpetuation of its own existence. From this fact, we know with certainty that the universe as a whole, as well as every existing thing which composes it, is radically and irrevocably *finite*; as well as the concomitant fact that everything which exists functions to hasten this end as expediently as possible—that existence, in other words, is an agent of oblivion. Indeed, as we saw, every being exists, no matter how complex, solely to accomplish this annihilative end more effectively and efficiently. Thus, we concluded that the entropic nature of matter not only defines the totality of material existence itself, but serves moreover as its formal organizing principle, its efficient driving force, and its final teleological end; and, in the sense, might be seen as the Aristotelian essence of existence. For this reason, we further concluded that not only might every existent object be defined as an agent of oblivion, but that being itself might be understood as little more than an annihilative machine. And so, we discovered that a new metaphysics might be established from the absolute facts of reality as described by the contemporary sciences—a metaphysics of decay. If the classical pursuit of an absolutely justifiable account of absolute truth, universal moral value, and ultimate meaning is to be established anew, we concluded, it must be founded upon and defined within this metaphysics of decay—this metaphysics which recognizes that *to be* is *to unbecome*.

This metaphysics, as we saw, necessarily lends itself to a pessimistic evaluation of being. Nevertheless, I argued, there is some unquestionably good news hidden behind the prima-facie nihilism of this pessimism. For what this pessimistic metaphysics provides is precisely the opposite: namely, a new and firm foundation for the reinauguration of philosophy's normative projects in a universal and practically meaningful way. In this way, far from contributing to nihilism, this pessimistic metaphysics effectively halts the slide of post-Kantian philosophy into either some form of nihilism, quietism, or fanatical neo-dogmatism; for it proves definitively that existence has a specific purpose and aim! Unfortunately, this good news does not come without its own accompanying bad news. Indeed, what the evangel of the absolute fact of entropy entails for philosophy is that reality faces an even more horrible fate than if it had no purpose at all. For, as it turns out, the purpose and aim of existence is solely to desolate, destroy, and ultimately obliterate itself; and, in doing so, to necessarily cause harm and provoke the suffering of every sentient being.

Everything eats and is eaten—everything destroys and will be destroyed. If any meaning for existence can be deduced from the second law of thermodynamics then it is this: that we, and indeed everything else, exist solely to consume, exterminate, and eventually annihilate reality. From this perspective, it becomes clear that humans are little more than cogs in a cataclysmic machine, and our existence is just one of the many pistons organized by the entropic principle of material reality to achieve its ultimate aim: to cease to be—to achieve absolute nothingness. From this we can conclude, as we have seen, not only the irrefutable fact that existence is fundamentally and irrevocably finite, structured as it is solely to end itself; but that existence is fundamentally antagonistic to itself, requiring as it does that each being maintain itself through the destruction of other existent beings. What this means concretely is not only that all things exist merely to decay, dissolve, and disappear but also to dismantle, damage, and destroy every other being, and indeed being itself, in the process. Moreover, it means that every conscious being which exists is necessarily bound by the structure and nature of existence itself to suffer and to contribute to the suffering and misery of everyone else capable of experiencing and anticipating their own decay, dissolution, and annihilation. This, as we've seen, is the consequence of the absolute fact that existence is an expression of an entropic drive to destroy.

If we can deduce any moral value from these facts, it is certainly not the classical claim that reality exists as a moral good, nor is it the much more palatable modern claim that existence is fundamentally value-neutral. Given the entropic antagonism inherent to reality as it is accounted for in the contemporary mathematical sciences, coupled with the fact the universe is not only indifferent to what it creates, but that it actively strives to destroy what it creates and necessitates, in the process, the suffering of all sentient beings within it, we can only conclude that if reality has any absolutely inherent moral value, it is less than zero. Indeed, if any absolute moral value can be speculatively extracted and rationally deduced from the absolute nature of reality as it is accounted for by contemporary science, it is this: that existence is a terrifying and monstrous *evil*.

From this it becomes clear that it is decidedly *not* good to be; in fact, it is better not to be at all, and best of all would be if nothing had ever come into being in the first place and we had never been born. From what we've seen concerning the nature of reality as an inescapable entropic power, existence appears to be a horrible curse and a miserable burden for all those condemned to consciousness by it. If any ethical claims can be extracted from this absolute truth, they must be grounded upon and deducible from this fact.

To show how we might justify this moral evaluation of nature, we explored in chapter 5 the classical distinction established between *facts* and *values* upon which the prohibition against so-called *naturalistic fallacy* was founded. Against those who argue for such a division, we showed how it might be possible to extract a moral value from that which *is* by understanding the classical definition of moral values. As we showed, the problem with much of modern philosophy is that it assumes that the apparent absence of any immediately obvious *ought* or *good* within the natural world is evidence for its moral neutrality. In point of fact, however, as we showed, when considered in terms of the classical definitions of evil, this apparent absence may in fact evince precisely the opposite; namely, the presence of another value altogether. Indeed, as we saw, the apparent *absence* of any *ought* or *good* in observable reality may in fact justify its evaluation as a moral *evil*. On this basis, we concluded that it is logically possible to speculatively derive a moral value from the account of material nature provided by the contemporary mathematical sciences. In this way, we saw how we might attribute a moral power to the entropic trajectory of the material universe and found new ethical and political projects upon this evaluation.

Following these conclusions, we proceeded in chapters 6, 7, and 8 to see how we might derive a viable and useful concept of ethical responsibility from this moral evaluation of existence. To this end, we explored the metaphysical and ethical materialistic monisms of Spinoza and Schopenhauer before turning to Nietzsche's critique and application of these materialisms to the question of ethical potency. Through Spinoza's thought, we discovered how we might maintain an account of ethical responsibility even when the concept of subjective agency and freedom is denied. From this, we saw how good and evil might be reconceived in such a system as either the acquiescence to or the resistance against the thrust of reality. The problem with Spinoza, however, as we detailed, was that he assumed the infinite potency of reality and, therefore, its goodness as well, all without cause. Realizing, as we do now, that the universe is fundamentally finite, we turned to Schopenhauer, who inverted Spinoza's moral categories to account for this primal finitude of existence. In this way we saw how we might extract an account of ethical responsibility from Schopenhauer's evaluation of nature as inescapably evil. Through his revision of Spinoza, we discovered a more useful model for ethical responsibility as the attempt to reject and resist the malicious thrust of reality. Unfortunately, however, as we eventually concluded, the problem with Schopenhauer's ethics is that they ultimately revert into a form of moral quietism that does not help us to define an active and engaged moral normativity or political project. In order to see how we might overcome this quietism, we turned to Nietzsche's revitalization of

CONCLUSION

Spinoza's monism to see how a more active ethics might be developed from Schopenhauer's metaphysics. Unfortunately, however, as we saw there, while Nietzsche's work affirms the possibility of deriving a more positive ethical *ought* from a scientific account of what *is*, it too rests on a faulty account of the infinitude of reality.

This problem inspired us to return again to Schopenhauer's more pessimistic account of nature and ethics to see whether a more active model of ethical responsibility might still be extracted from it. To this end, we explored the early Buddhist philosophies which inspired Schopenhauer's ethics, and we examined the scientifically driven pessimism of Philipp Mainländer which drew from an both. As we saw, in the work of Mainländer we finally discover a means of employing a pessimistic evaluation of reality to ground and justify a practical account of ethical normativity and sociopolitical action. In this way, we saw how we might finally achieve an absolutely justifiable account not only of absolute reality and truth, but of universal moral value, ethical duty, and active social and political projects as well all from a speculative extension of the testimony of the natural sciences.

As we saw there, given the nature and value of existence, Mainländer concludes that goodness exists exclusively as a dialectical possibility, one which appears only insofar as we attempt to negate, resist, and overturn the primal power and trajectory of reality itself. From this, Mainländer argues that it is our moral responsibility to work against the direction of nature as it appears within ourselves and the social and political order of the world by striving to overcome the inherently destructive will of nature in every form: first personally, through the cultivation of compassion, ascetic principles, and philosophical contemplation; and then sociopolitically, through the cultivation of equality and justice for all. It is through some version of Mainländer's pessimism, we concluded, that we might hope to develop a new post-Kantian sense of absolute moral value and deduce disjunctively from it a universally applicable account of ethical duty and emancipatory social and political action through which philosophy might reclaim its relevance to the world.

To inform what this account of an absolutely justified political action might look like today, we turned in the last chapter to more recent expressions of philosophical pessimism. Specifically, we examined the claims of the so-called cosmic pessimists, the work of Afropessimists, and the arguments of extinctual nihilists, respectively. What we gained from this investigation was what Frank B. Wilderson referred to as a new set of "marching orders" for contemporary ethics and politics; namely, to resist in every way the order and operation of reality and to work actively to counter the manifestation of the annihilative will of nature in history as it expresses itself in patriarchy, white supremacy, and class inequality. This, we concluded, is the absolute duty of everyone who strives to achieve some determinate good from a scientifically established evaluation of existence as an absolute evil. It is only in pursuit of such revolutionary emancipatory aims, we finally suggested, that some semblance of good might be achieved within our world. This pursuit of a more just and equitable world through the abolition of every structure which colludes with the will of nature as an absolute evil is absolutely justified from our speculative evaluation of nature as an absolute evil, an evaluation that follows from our metaphysics of decay. With this our project is therefore complete.

The Ethics of Perpetual Resistance

It is clear from all that we have seen that it is demonstrably not good to be. On the contrary, being is an absolute evil. Being is born of decay, sustains itself through the consumption and destruction of its products, and ultimately exhausts itself in service to this dissipation in pursuit of the final purity of nothingness. To exist within the regime of such a metaphysics of absolute decay is to be forever at war with existence itself and with every other existing thing in our surrounding environment. And to be condemned to sentience within the regime of this metaphysics of decay is to be consigned to a fate even worse than the death which inevitably awaits us as a result of it. For to be conscious within this metaphysical hegemony is necessarily to suffer its effects and to contribute to the suffering of others. This is an unavoidable and absolute moral fact of being, governed as it is entirely by the fact of entropic decay: to be is to be an accomplice to and victim of the torment and murder of being itself. To be is to be evil.

There is nothing supernatural to the absolute malevolence of our fate. On the contrary, it is the most natural thing there is. In fact, it is the only thing which is and the only thing which could ever potentially be. It is, in other words, nature itself. But the totality of this fact does not preclude the logical possibility of goodness. On the contrary, it allows us to postulate a new absolute good disjunctively as whatever works to oppose the tyranny of destruction, decay, suffering, and harm. The moral monism of material reality does not require then that we lay down our fight for justice or confine our ethical hopes to moral quietism. Nor does it require that we entrust our hopes for justice or political peace to the intervention of some supernatural power for which we have no evidence, or any justifiable reason to believe exists. On the contrary, it demands that we pursue the good by committing ourselves to constructing and fighting to realize normative aims and political goals which use the annihilative power of reality against itself, if only fleetingly, to win some respite from the otherwise ongoing and monotonous horror of reality.[1]

By striving to bend the entropic thrust of existence back upon itself in such a way that it momentarily neutralizes the destruction and suffering it necessitates, we can strive to prise some practical, if negatively achieved goodness from reality. When we envision and pursue goodness as a negative possibility in this way, as something which is accomplished from the dialectical negation of reality through itself, we can justify anew our hope not only for some semblance of an ethical good, but for the legitimacy of our emancipatory politics as well. And so, we discover the apex of this kind of ethical pessimism in the persistent attempt to use the annihilative flow of being to carve out a backwards-turning eddy of compassion, equality, and justice in our lives and in the social and political structures of our world. This aim can only be accomplished, however, entirely negatively: by endeavoring to oppose those constructs in our lives and social and political world which are built upon, justified by, and maintained through the destructive will of nature to harm, maim, repress, and ultimately destroy.

To aspire to some semblance of the good within a wholly evil reality requires actively fighting to dismantle, resist, and rearrange every structure which exists within ourselves and the sociopolitical order of our day that is complicit in the dissipative, destructive, and violent will of nature—structures like patriarchy, white supremacy, and socioeconomic class privilege. Only by pursuing the possibility of goodness negatively in this way, as the duty to perpetually resist that which works alongside and with the trajectory of existence itself, can we reanimate one of the central projects of philosophical inquiry lost as a result of Kant's critique: the construction of universal normative claims and the pursuit of an absolutely founded conception of political justice. What the pessimistic evaluation of the absolute nature of reality as an entropic machine empowers us to see, in other words, is how we might absolutely ground and justify the pursuit of new universal moral aims and emancipatory social and political projects without betraying the limits of Kant's critique. In this way we might finally overcome and escape the morass of post-Kantian moral and political philosophy and reclaim philosophy's relevance to the contemporary world.

Ultimately, of course, our pursuit of such goods is destined to fail, and all our efforts will eventually prove useless. In a universe entirely governed and determined by the principle of entropy, every project which strives to maintain human life and dignity against the destructive will of nature and the suffering of every sentient being it necessitates is fated to futility. No matter how fully we may commit ourselves to the act of perpetual resistance, individually or politically, we must acknowledge the irrefutable fact that we will never transcend or escape the conditions of our own material existence. No supernatural power can aid us in this project, nor can any rational hope be maintained for some final or transcendental salvation from the brutal facts of nature. So it is that we must admit that evil will ultimately win. We should not work for the good then under any false illusion that we might somehow extricate ourselves from the evil of existence or expiate ourselves from the suffering and destruction existence itself necessitates. This moral purity, perfection, and blamelessness cannot be the aim of a pessimistically driven ethics and politics. Its aim must be rather to ground and justify the active pursuit of some approximation of goodness and peace and to construct some temporary respite from the horrors of existence by directing our efforts not in favor of anything, but rather in opposition to, in resistance of, and against everything which contributes to the annihilative death march of being in our individual, social, and political lives. The aim of a truly pessimistic ethics and politics, in other words, is to use the power of nature to dismantle, disassemble, and dissolve its own structures, however fleetingly, so that we can achieve, however momentarily, a passing sense of calmness, peace, and goodness negatively from the absence of the otherwise relentless thrust of reality as it moves perpetually towards its own destruction. This is the work of a lifetime: to fight futilely to extract ourselves, as much as possible, from our affirmation of and complicity in the evil regime of existence and its social and political accomplices.

The moral value of our individual or collective actions should not be measured, then, according to their effectiveness in winning some final or complete victory over reality. Our actions cannot win and can never hope to be effective by this measure. The moral value of an ethical, social, or political action lies instead solely in its capacity to empower those who strive to be good to continue to tilt against the ill effects of nature, however fruitlessly, in their own lives, in the lives of those around them, and in the political systems to which they belong. It is with this aim that we must commit ourselves to resist in every form the injustice of reality in the hopes that through such useless activities we can remember that while evil may have the final word, it need not have every word—that, in other words, while evil will eventually win, it need not win right here, or right now.

Thus, while no final end to the useless suffering of existence can be rationally hoped for, we can nevertheless rest assured that the pursuit of some semblance of the good is absolutely justified and that, therefore, it is our duty to actively work to tear down those structures which exacerbate the useless suffering of sentient beings, and work to erect social and political systems which are more effective at negating the aim of reality by pitting us against one another solely to feed ourselves and survive day to day. On this basis, our pessimistic evaluation of nature allows us to justify our opposition to inequality and injustice in every form as well as our commitment to a radically emancipatory politics as the most effective ways to resist and oppose the absolute evil of existence at the sociopolitical level.

While such an ethics and politics of perpetual resistance will never achieve some final moral end or perfect political system, we can nevertheless defend our commitment to them absolutely through our metaphysical and moral pessimism. To do so, however, requires a clear-eyed rejection of every utopian hope as little more than a supernatural fantasy, a holdout from the history of dogmatic philosophy which has contributed to the melancholy record of horrors that is our history. For, as we have seen, within nature, destruction, war, suffering, and ultimately annihilation are guaranteed. This is undeniable, and there is no other nature to which we can turn to justify some fantastic hope in another way of being. We can be assured, then, that whatever new ethical structures we strive to establish in ourselves or in society through our dialectical account of the good will ultimately, in one form or another, become complicit again in the great evil of existence. This fact is inevitable. But, it does not necessitate our resignation to inaction or moral quietude. On the contrary, it can invigorate anew our commitment to never rest in our pursuit of the good, for we are assured that no matter what we have achieved through this pursuit, we have not yet achieved some final right way of being, some correct social order, or some truly just political system. The absolute fact of the evil of each and every form of reality should animate, in other words, our commitment to perpetually resist every existent order and system, even the ones we achieve in our pursuit of the right and good, as the only way to stay true to the good as a dialectically negative power. Given the absolute depravity of being, we must resist then the belief that we can ever finally achieve some final good through our political efforts and ethical actions. To the contrary, concomitant with our recognition that the only natural absolute value is evil, we must commit ourselves to perpetually and tirelessly oppose whatever current political order exists, even if it is one which we ourselves previously affirmed as a way of approximating the good. For goodness, as we have seen, can only ever be pursued within a pessimistic metaphysics and ethics negatively, in resistance to whatever is currently the case.

If we want to maintain any hope for the good, in other words, we must accept the fact that it will never exist in what we have already accomplished (in what is), but only in what might still come to be and only in as much as we are committed to resisting the structures of reality as they currently are. So it is that ethical pessimism requires that we must continuously take up arms in opposition to the inevitable, commit ourselves to the perpetual struggle against reality, and ceaselessly strive to overturn the order of existence. And, this commitment to resistance must come despite the fact that we can know with absolute certainty that our efforts will always ultimately be in vain, and that we must eventually collapse from exhaustion and give way before the march of time without having moved the scales of history one fraction of a degree toward justice. Nevertheless, we must fight on—forever onwards, in the words of Samuel Beckett, absolutely justified in our battle against the universe's slide "worstward."[2] "On. Somehow on" we must go, both against and into the "dim void" of annihilation, "ever try[ing]. Ever fail[ing]. No matter. Try[ing] again. Fail[ing] again. Fail[ing] better."[3] In this way, although we may grow "weak by time and fate," as Tennyson puts it, we must still "strive, to seek, to find, and not to yield" to the absolute evil of existence, but instead to resist all that is, all that has been, and all that still might be in the name of an absolutely justified sense of the good which can never be, but which can be justified nevertheless as a negative possibility which is logically deducible from the abject horror of existence itself.[4]

Notes

Chapter 1

1. Friedrich Nietzsche, *The Gay Science*, ed. Bernard Williams, trans. Josefine Nauckhoff and Adrian Del Caro (Cambridge: Cambridge University Press, 2001), 120; Martin Heidegger, "Nietzsche's Word: 'God Is Dead,'" in *Off the Beaten Track*, ed. and trans. Julian Young and Kenneth Haynes (Cambridge: Cambridge University Press, 2002), 162.

2. Albert Camus, *The Myth of Sisyphus and Other Essays*, trans. Justin O'Brien (New York: Vintage International, 1991); Jean-Paul Sartre, *Existentialism Is a Humanism*, trans. Carol Macomber (New Haven, CT: Yale University Press, 2007).

3. For more on the various approaches in contemporary Western philosophy after Kant, see Drew M. Dalton, *The Ethics of Resistance: Tyranny of the Absolute* (London: Bloomsbury, 2018), especially 11–13.

4. This position was infamously voiced by Florida Senator Marco Rubio, who quipped in a campaign speech that the problem with higher education is that it focused on seemingly abstruse subjects when what "we [really] need [is] more welders and less philosophers."

5. A. N. Whitehead, *Religion in the Making: Lowell Lectures, 1926* (Cambridge: Cambridge University Press, 1996), 26.

6. Immanuel Kant, "An Answer to the Question: 'What Is Enlightenment?'" in *Kant: Political Writings* (Cambridge: Cambridge University Press, 1970), 54.

7. See, for example, Immanuel Kant, *Critique of Pure Reason*, trans. and ed. Paul Guyer and Allen W. Wood (Cambridge: Cambridge University Press, 1998), 430–31. See also 646–47.

8. Kant, "What Is Enlightenment?" 54–55.

9. Kant, "What Is Enlightenment?" 54–55.

10. Kant, *Critique of Pure Reason*, 102. See also 119.

11. Kant, *Critique of Pure Reason*, 139.

12. Kant, *Critique of Pure Reason*, 133.

13. Kant, *Critique of Pure Reason*, 133.

14. Kant, *Critique of Pure Reason*, 340.

15. Kant, *Critique of Pure Reason*, 149.

16. Immanuel Kant, *Prolegomena to Any Future Metaphysics*, trans. and ed. Gary Hatfield (Cambridge: Cambridge University Press, 1997), 116.

17. Kant, *Prolegomena to Any Future Metaphysics*, 117.

NOTES TO PAGES 23–31

18. Kant, *Prolegomena to Any Future Metaphysics*, 117.
19. Kant, *Prolegomena to Any Future Metaphysics*, 114.
20. Kant, *Critique of Pure Reason*, 452. See also 704.
21. Kant, *Critique of Pure Reason*, 114.
22. Kant, *Critique of Pure Reason*, 119, 114, respectively.
23. Kant, *Critique of Pure Reason*, 119.
24. Kant, *Critique of Pure Reason*, 104.
25. Kant, *Critique of Pure Reason*, 101.
26. Kant, *Prolegomena to Any Future Metaphysics*, 134.
27. Kant, *Critique of Pure Reason*, 130ff. See also Kant, *Prolegomena to Any Future Metaphysics*, 16ff.
28. Kant, *Prolegomena to Any Future Metaphysics*, 17.
29. Kant, *Prolegomena to Any Future Metaphysics*, 54–55
30. For more on Kant's analytic of reason, any number of excellent secondary sources exist. See, for example, Henry E. Allison, *Kant's Transcendental Idealism: An Interpretation and Defense* (New Haven, CT: Yale University Press, 1983); Ralph C. S. Walker, ed., *Kant on Pure Reason* (Oxford: Oxford University Press, 1982); Sebastian Gardner, *Routledge Guidebook to Kant and the Critique of Pure Reason* (New York: Routledge, 1999); and more recently, Graham Bird, *The Revolutionary Kant: A Commentary on the Critique of Pure Reason* (Peru, IL: Open Court, 2006).
31. Kant, *Critique of Pure Reason*, 188–89.
32. Kant, *Critique of Pure Reason*, 186.
33. Kant, *Critique of Pure Reason*, 186.
34. Kant, *Critique of Pure Reason*, 230.
35. See, for example, Kant, *Critique of Pure Reason*, 326–28.
36. Kant, *Critique of Pure Reason*, 348.
37. Kant, *Critique of Pure Reason*, 190.
38. Kant, *Critique of Pure Reason*, 155.
39. Kant, *Critique of Pure Reason*, 155.
40. Kant, *Critique of Pure Reason*, 224.
41. Kant, *Critique of Pure Reason*, 348.
42. Kant, *Prolegomena to Any Future Metaphysics*, 84 (see also 67); Kant, *Critique of Pure Reason*, 190.
43. Kant, *Critique of Pure Reason*, 231. See also 360ff.
44. Kant, *Critique of Pure Reason*, 348.
45. Kant, *Critique of Pure Reason*, 414 and 231–32, respectively.
46. See Kant, *Critique of Pure Reason*, 417. For more on Kant's conception of the transcendental subject, see Siyaves Azeri, "Transcendental Subject vs. Empirical Self: On Kant's Account of Subjectivity," *Filozofia* 65, no. 3 (2010): 269–83; and Eduardo Molina, "Kant's Conception of the Subject," *CR: The New Centennial Review* 17, no. 2 (2017): 77–94.
47. Immanuel Kant, *Critique of Practical Reason*, trans. Mary Gregor (Cambridge: Cambridge University Press, 2015), 129.
48. Immanuel Kant, *Groundwork of the Metaphysics of Morals*, trans. and ed. Mary Gregor and Jens Timmermann (Cambridge: Cambridge University Press, 2012), 5, 25.

49. Kant, *Critique of Practical Reason*, 129.
50. Kant, *Groundwork of the Metaphysics of Morals*, 23.
51. Kant, *Groundwork of the Metaphysics of Morals*, 6.
52. Kant, *Critique of Practical Reason*, 18.
53. Kant, *Groundwork of the Metaphysics of Morals*, 34.
54. Kant, *Groundwork of the Metaphysics of Morals*, 33.
55. Kant, *Groundwork of the Metaphysics of Morals*, 52.
56. Kant, *Groundwork of the Metaphysics of Morals*, 41–42.
57. Kant, *Critique of Practical Reason*, 89–91.
58. Kant, *Critique of Practical Reason*, 52.
59. Kant, *Groundwork of the Metaphysics of Morals*, 10.
60. Kant, *Groundwork of the Metaphysics of Morals*, 12, 16, respectively.
61. Kant, *Prolegomena to Any Future Metaphysics*, 108. See also Kant, *Critique of Pure Reason*, 606–7.
62. Kant, *Critique of Practical Reason*, 129.
63. Kant, *Critique of Pure Reason*, 401.
64. Kant, *Critique of Pure Reason*, 350–51. See also 380.
65. Kant, *Critique of Pure Reason*, 402.
66. Kant, *Critique of Pure Reason*, 405–6.
67. Kant, *Critique of Pure Reason*, 611.
68. See, for example, Ludwig Feuerbach, *The Essence of Christianity*, trans. George Eliot (New York: Cosimo Classics, 2008).
69. Kant, *Critique of Pure Reason*, 375.
70. Kant, *Critique of Pure Reason*, 299.
71. Kant, *Critique of Pure Reason*, 299.
72. Kant, *Critique of Pure Reason*, 674.
73. Kant, *Critique of Pure Reason*, 677.
74. See, for example, Kant, *Critique of Pure Reason*, 678.
75. Kant, *Critique of Pure Reason*, 242.
76. Kant, *Critique of Pure Reason*, 236.
77. Kant, *Critique of Pure Reason*, 558.
78. Kant, *Critique of Pure Reason*, 608.
79. Kant, *Critique of Pure Reason*, 610.
80. Kant, *Critique of Pure Reason*, 611.
81. Kant, *Critique of Pure Reason*, 613.
82. Kant, *Groundwork of the Metaphysics of Morals*, 12.
83. Kant, *Critique of Practical Reason*, 92.
84. Kant, *Groundwork of the Metaphysics of Morals*, 39.
85. Immanuel Kant, "Toward Perpetual Peace," in *Practical Philosophy*, trans. and ed. Mary J. Gregor (Cambridge: Cambridge University Press, 1996), 328.
86. Inder S. Marwah, *Liberalism, Diversity, and Domination: Kant, Mill, and the Government of Difference* (Cambridge: Cambridge University Press, 2019), 119. See also 109.
87. See, for example, Lucy Allais, "Kant's Racism," *Philosophical Papers* 45 (2016): 1–36; Robert Bernasconi, "Who Invented the Concept of Race? Kant's Role in the Enlightenment Construction of Race," in *Race*, ed. Robert Bernasconi

(Oxford: Blackwell, 2001), 11–36; Pauline Kleingeld, "Kant's Second Thoughts on Race," *Philosophical Quarterly* 57, no. 229 (2007): 573–92; Charles Mills, "Kant's Untermenschen," in *Race and Racism in Modern Philosophy*, ed. Andrew Valls (Ithaca, NY: Cornell University Press, 2005), 169–93; and Helga Varden, "Kant and Women," *Pacific Philosophical Quarterly* 98 (2017): 653–94.

88. For more on Kant's relation to colonialism, see Katrin Flikschuh and Lea Ypi, eds., *Kant and Colonialism: Historical and Critical Perspectives* (Oxford: Oxford University Press, 2014).

89. David Harvey, *Cosmopolitanism and the Geographies of Freedom* (New York: Columbia University Press, 2009).

90. Pauline Kleingeld, "Kant's Second Thoughts on Colonialism," in *Kant and Colonialism: Historical and Critical Perspectives*, ed. Katrin Flikschuh and Lea Ypi (Oxford: Oxford University Press, 2014), 43–67.

91. Nina Glick Schiller and Andrew Irving, eds., *Whose Cosmopolitanism? Critical Perspectives, Relationalities, and Discontents* (Oxford: Berghahn Books, 2017).

92. For more on the nature of this transition from universalism to quietism, see Dalton, *The Ethics of Resistance*, 11–16. See also Matthew Altman, "The Limits of Kant's Cosmopolitanism: Theory, Practice, and the Crisis in Syria," *Kantian Review* 22, no. 2 (2017): 179–204.

Chapter 2

1. Levi Bryant, Nick Srnicek, and Graham Harman, "Towards a Speculative Philosophy," in *The Speculative Turn: Continental Materialism and Realism*, ed. Levi Bryant, Nick Srnicek, and Graham Harman (Melbourne: re.press, 2011), 3.

2. Bryant et al., "Towards a Speculative Philosophy," 4.

3. Bryant et al., "Towards a Speculative Philosophy," 4.

4. Quentin Meillassoux, *After Finitude: An Essay on the Necessity of Contingency*, trans. Ray Brassier (London: Bloomsbury, 2008), 4.

5. G. Anthony Bruno has argued convincingly that Meillassoux's criticism of Kant on this point was preceded, and perhaps even influenced by the work of Friedrich Heinrich Jacobi. For more on this link, see G. Anthony Bruno, "Jacobi's Dare: McDowell, Meillassoux, and Consistent Idealism," in *Idealism, Relativism, and Realism: New Essays on Objectivity beyond the Analytic-Continental Divide*, ed. Dominik Finkelde and Paul M. Livingston (Boston: De Gruyter, 2020), 35–66.

6. Bryant et al., "Towards a Speculative Philosophy," 4.

7. Bryant et al., "Towards a Speculative Philosophy," 3.

8. Meillassoux, *After Finitude*, 5.

9. Meillassoux, *After Finitude*, 5.

10. Meillassoux, *After Finitude*, 5.

11. Meillassoux, *After Finitude*, 5.

12. Meillassoux, *After Finitude*, 7.

13. Meillassoux, *After Finitude*, 7, italics mine.

14. Quentin Meillassoux, *Time without Becoming*, ed. Anna Longo (Italy: Mimesis International, 2014), 11.
15. Meillassoux, *Time without Becoming*, 9.
16. Meillassoux, *After Finitude*, 9–10.
17. See Meillassoux, *After Finitude*, 123.
18. Meillassoux, *After Finitude*, 44ff.
19. Meillassoux, *After Finitude*, 45.
20. Meillassoux, *After Finitude*, 44–45.
21. Meillassoux, *After Finitude*, 46.
22. Meillassoux, *After Finitude*, 47.
23. Meillassoux, *After Finitude*, 49.
24. Meillassoux, *After Finitude*, 51.
25. Meillassoux, *After Finitude*, 49.
26. Meillassoux, *Time without Becoming*, 12.
27. Meillassoux, *Time without Becoming*, 12, italics mine.
28. Meillassoux, *After Finitude*, 34.
29. Meillassoux, *After Finitude*, 36.
30. Meillassoux, *After Finitude*, 36.
31. Meillassoux, *After Finitude*, 34.
32. Meillassoux, *After Finitude*, 34.
33. Alain Badiou, preface to *After Finitude: An Essay on the Necessity of Contingency* by Quentin Meillassoux, trans. Ray Brassier (London: Bloomsbury, 2008), viii.
34. Meillassoux, *After Finitude*, 123.
35. Meillassoux, *After Finitude*, 22.
36. Meillassoux, *After Finitude*, 22.
37. Meillassoux, *After Finitude*, 8–10.
38. Meillassoux, *After Finitude*, 10.
39. Meillassoux, *After Finitude*, 9–10.
40. Meillassoux, *Time without Becoming*, 13.
41. Meillassoux, *After Finitude*, 10.
42. See, Meillassoux, *After Finitude*, 20.
43. Meillassoux, *After Finitude*, 17.
44. Meillassoux, *After Finitude*, 28.
45. Meillassoux, *After Finitude*, 51, italics mine.
46. Meillassoux, *After Finitude*, 50.
47. Meillassoux, *After Finitude*, 28.
48. Meillassoux, *After Finitude*, 28.
49. Meillassoux, *After Finitude*, 28.
50. Meillassoux, *After Finitude*, 53.
51. Meillassoux, *After Finitude*, 53.
52. Meillassoux, *After Finitude*, 53.
53. Meillassoux, *After Finitude*, 56.
54. Meillassoux, *After Finitude*, 52.
55. Mcillassoux, *After Finitude*, 73.

56. Meillassoux, *After Finitude*, 74, italics mine.
57. Meillassoux, *After Finitude*, 32.
58. Meillassoux, *After Finitude*, 33.
59. Meillassoux, *After Finitude*, 60, 32, respectively.
60. Meillassoux, *After Finitude*, 29.
61. Meillassoux, *After Finitude*, 29.
62. Meillassoux, *After Finitude*, 60.
63. Meillassoux, *After Finitude*, 62.
64. Meillassoux, *After Finitude*, 60. See also 53.
65. Meillassoux, *After Finitude*, 67, 76, respectively.
66. Meillassoux, *After Finitude*, 33–34.
67. Meillassoux, *After Finitude*, 33.
68. Quentin Meillassoux, "Appendix: Excerpts from *L'Inexistence divine*," in *Quentin Meillassoux: Philosophy in the Making*, trans. Graham Harman (Edinburgh: Edinburgh University Press, 2011), 195.
69. Meillassoux, "Appendix," 196.
70. Meillassoux, "Appendix," 194.
71. Meillassoux, "Appendix," 235.
72. Meillassoux, "Appendix," 207.
73. Meillassoux, "Appendix," 210.
74. Meillassoux, "Appendix," 206.
75. Meillassoux, "Appendix," 192.
76. Meillassoux, "Appendix," 193.
77. Meillassoux, "Appendix," 192.
78. Meillassoux, "Appendix," 206.
79. Meillassoux, "Appendix," 205.
80. James Ladyman and Don Ross, with David Spurrett and John Collier, *Every Thing Must Go: Metaphysics Naturalized* (Oxford: Oxford University Press, 2007).
81. Ladyman and Ross, *Every Thing Must Go*, vii.
82. Ladyman and Ross, *Every Thing Must Go*, vii.
83. Ladyman and Ross, *Every Thing Must Go*, 30.
84. Ladyman and Ross, *Every Thing Must Go*, vii.
85. Ladyman and Ross, *Every Thing Must Go*, 2.
86. Ladyman and Ross, *Every Thing Must Go*, 7, 25, respectively.
87. Ladyman and Ross, *Every Thing Must Go*, 130–31.
88. Ladyman and Ross, *Every Thing Must Go*, 67.
89. See Ladyman and Ross, *Every Thing Must Go*, 34, 248–49, 298ff.
90. Ladyman and Ross, *Every Thing Must Go*, 68, 53, respectively.
91. Ladyman and Ross, *Every Thing Must Go*, 4. See also 269–74.
92. Ladyman and Ross, *Every Thing Must Go*, 7, 17ff., respectively.
93. Ladyman and Ross, *Every Thing Must Go*, 288.

Chapter 3

1. Meillassoux, *Time without Becoming*, 12.
2. Meillassoux, *After Finitude*, 34.
3. Meillassoux, *After Finitude*, 114.
4. Meillassoux, *After Finitude*, 21.
5. Meillassoux, *After Finitude*, 22.
6. Meillassoux, *After Finitude*, 115.
7. Meillassoux, *After Finitude*, 7.
8. Meillassoux, *After Finitude*, 114–15; second set of italics mine.
9. Meillassoux, *After Finitude*, 113.
10. See Meillassoux, *After Finitude*, 28.
11. Quentin Meillassoux, "Interview with Quentin Meillassoux (August 2010)," trans. Graham Harman, in *Quentin Meillassoux: Philosophy in the Making*, by Graham Harman (Edinburgh: Edinburgh University Press, 2011), 167.
12. Meillassoux, *After Finitude*, 117.
13. Meillassoux, *After Finitude*, 116.
14. Meillassoux, *After Finitude*, 26.
15. Meillassoux, *After Finitude*, 117.
16. Meillassoux, *After Finitude*, 108.
17. Meillassoux, "Interview," 169.
18. Meillassoux, *After Finitude*, 126.
19. Ladyman and Ross, *Every Thing Must Go*, 2, italics mine.
20. Ladyman and Ross, *Every Thing Must Go*, 2.
21. Ladyman and Ross, *Every Thing Must Go*, 158.
22. Ladyman and Ross, *Every Thing Must Go*, 117–19. See also 159–61.
23. Ladyman and Ross, *Every Thing Must Go*, 16.
24. Ladyman and Ross, *Every Thing Must Go*, 93.
25. Meillassoux, "Interview," 161.
26. Meillassoux, *After Finitude*, 103.
27. Alain Badiou, *Being and Event*, trans. Oliver Feltham (London: Bloomsbury, 2013), 4.
28. Badiou, *Being and Event*, 4.
29. Badiou, *Being and Event*, 9, italics mine.
30. Alain Badiou with Gilles Haéri, *In Praise of Mathematics*, trans. Susan Spitzer (Cambridge: Polity, 2016), 65.
31. Alain Badiou, "Politics and Philosophy: An Interview with Alain Badiou," in *Ethics: An Essay on the Understanding of Evil*, trans. Peter Hallward (London: Verso, 2001), 127.
32. Badiou, *Being and Event*, 15–16.
33. Badiou, *Being and Event*, 8–9.
34. Alain Badiou, "Mathematics and Philosophy: The Grand Style and the Little Style," in *Theoretical Writings*, ed. and trans. Ray Brassier and Alberto Toscano (London: Continuum, 2004), 14.
35. Badiou, "Mathematics and Philosophy," 13–14.

36. Badiou, *Being and Event*, 6.
37. Badiou, *In Praise of Mathematics*, 7.
38. Badiou, *In Praise of Mathematics*, 74.
39. Badiou, *In Praise of Mathematics*, 64.
40. Badiou, *In Praise of Mathematics*, 49.
41. Badiou, *In Praise of Mathematics*, 73.
42. Badiou, *In Praise of Mathematics*, 21–22.
43. Badiou, "Mathematics and Philosophy," 16. See also Badiou, *In Praise of Mathematics*, 102ff.
44. Galileo Galilei, "The Assayer," in *The Essential Galileo*, ed. and trans. Maurice F. Finocchiaro (Indianapolis: Hackett, 2008), 183.
45. See Badiou, *In Praise of Mathematics*, 33ff.
46. This is why the famed "Golden Record," launched by NASA in 1977 as part of the interstellar Voyager 1 probe, contains both a simplified set of basic mathematical functions and samples of the music of Earth in the hope that if some form of intelligent alien life should ever find it, some form of basic communication might be achieved through one of these two universal languages.
47. Badiou, *In Praise of Mathematics*, 34.
48. Badiou, *In Praise of Mathematics*, 34.
49. Badiou, "Mathematics and Philosophy," 13.
50. Meillassoux, *After Finitude*, 62.
51. Meillassoux, *After Finitude*, 126.
52. Meillassoux, *Time without Becoming*, 25–26.
53. Meillassoux, *After Finitude*, 64.
54. Meillassoux, *After Finitude*, 101.
55. Meillassoux, *After Finitude*, 80.
56. See, Meillassoux, *After Finitude*, 82.
57. Meillassoux, *After Finitude*, 84.
58. Quentin Meillassoux, *Science Fiction and Extro-Science Fiction*, trans. Alyosha Edlebi (Minneapolis: Univocal Publishing, 2015), 10.
59. Meillassoux, *Science Fiction*, 41.
60. Meillassoux, *After Finitude*, 64.
61. Meillassoux, *Time without Becoming*, 25.
62. Meillassoux, *After Finitude*, 63.
63. Meillassoux, *L'Inexistence divine*, 189–90.
64. Meillassoux, *L'Inexistence divine*, 188.
65. Meillassoux, *L'Inexistence divine*, 190.
66. Meillassoux, *L'Inexistence divine*, 195; and Meillassoux, *Time without Becoming*, 27.
67. Alain Badiou, "Interview (with Ben Woodward)," in *The Speculative Turn: Continental Materialism and Realism*, ed. Levi Bryant, Nick Srnicek, and Graham Harman (Melbourne: re.press, 2011), 20.
68. Meillassoux, *L'Inexistence divine*, 189
69. Meillassoux, *L'Inexistence divine*, 189.
70. Meillassoux, *L'Inexistence divine*, 192.

NOTES TO PAGES 79-88

71. See, for example, Alain Badiou, *Number and Numbers*, trans Robin Mackay (Cambridge: Polity, 2008), 211–14.
72. Badiou, *Being and Event*, 5–6.
73. Badiou, *Being and Event*, 134. See also Alain Badiou, "Being-There: Mathematics of the Transcendental," in *Mathematics of the Transcendental*, ed. and trans. A. J. Bartlett and Alex Ling (London: Bloomsbury, 2014), 165.
74. Badiou, "Being-There," 165; Badiou, *Being and Event*, 191.
75. Badiou, *Being and Event*, 46.
76. Alain Badiou, "Topos, or Logics of Onto-Logy: An Introduction for Philosophers," in *Mathematics of the Transcendental*, ed. and trans. A. J. Bartlett and Alex Ling (London: Bloomsbury, 2014), 16.
77. Badiou, *Being and Event*, 55.
78. Badiou, *Being and Event*, 6, italics mine.
79. Badiou, "Topos," 14. See also Badiou, *In Praise of Mathematics*, 74–76.
80. Badiou, *In Praise of Mathematics*, 78.
81. See Badiou, "Mathematics and Philosophy," 16.
82. Alain Badiou, *Ethics: An Essay on the Understanding of Evil*, trans. Peter Hallward (London: Verso, 2001), 25–28.
83. Badiou, *Ethics*, 25.
84. Badiou, *Ethics*, 25.
85. Badiou, *Ethics*, 25.
86. Badiou, *Ethics*, 25.
87. Badiou, *Ethics*, 28.
88. Badiou, *Ethics*, 28.
89. Badiou, *Ethics*, 42.
90. Badiou, *Ethics*, 25.
91. Badiou, *Ethics*, 47.
92. Badiou, *Ethics*, 67.
93. Badiou, *Ethics*, 67.
94. Badiou, *Ethics*, 30, 38, respectively.
95. Badiou, "Mathematics and Philosophy," 16.
96. Badiou, *Ethics*, 60.

Chapter 4

1. Badiou, *In Praise of Mathematics*, 34.
2. Badiou's conflation of poetical and mathematical discourse is demonstrated in, for example, his analysis of the birth of philosophy in Parmenides. See, for example, Badiou, *Being and Event*, 131.
3. Alain Badiou, *Theory of the Subject*, trans. Bruno Bosteels (London: Continuum, 2009), 209.
4. One might also suspect that inasmuch as Meillassoux and Badiou engage with the products of mathematics and science metaphorically, they might inad-

vertently be engaging in the kind of project famously critiqued by Alan Sokal and Jean Bricmont in their book *Fashionable Nonsense: Post-Modern Intellectuals' Abuse of Science* (New York: Picador, 1998). This is, I think a legitimate concern and one which will be addressed at the beginning of the following chapter.

5. Meillassoux, *After Finitude*, 108.
6. Badiou, *Being and Event*, 132.
7. Erwin Schrödinger, *What Is Life? The Physical Aspects of the Living Cell* (Cambridge: Cambridge University Press, 1967), 68.
8. For more on this apparent difference, see Addy Pross, *What Is Life? How Chemistry Becomes Biology* (Oxford: Oxford University Press, 2012), 9–10.
9. The nature, origin, and logical problems with this dualism will be addressed in greater detail at the start of chapter 6.
10. Sean Carroll, *The Big Picture: On the Origins of Life, Meaning, and the Universe Itself* (New York: Penguin, 2016), 12
11. Nick Lane, *The Vital Question: Energy, Evolution, and the Origins of Complex Life* (New York: W. W. Norton, 2016), 55.
12. Lynn Margulis and Dorion Sagan, *What Is Life?* (Berkeley: University of California Press, 1995).
13. For more on the processes involved in the evolution of organic life from inorganic matter, see Peter M. Hoffmann, *Life's Ratchet: How Molecular Machines Extract Order from Chaos* (New York: Basic Books, 2012).
14. Pross, *What Is Life?* ix.
15. Pross, *What Is Life?* ix.
16. Pross, *What Is Life?* xiii.
17. Lane, *The Vital Question*, 64.
18. Pross, *What Is Life?* 161.
19. Francis Crick, *Life Itself* (New York: Simon and Schuster, 1981), 47.
20. Crick, *Life Itself*, 39.
21. Richard P. Feynman, "The Relation of Physics to Other Sciences," in *Six Easy Pieces: Essentials of Physics Explained by Its Most Brilliant Teacher*, by Richard P. Feynman, Robert B. Leighton, and Matthew Sands (Philadelphia: Basic Books, 2011), 48.
22. Charles S. Cockell, "The Laws of Life," *Physics Today*, vol. 70 (March 2017): 48.
23. Feynman, "The Relation of Physics to Other Sciences," 59.
24. Johnjoe McFadden and Jim Al-Khalili, *Life on the Edge: The Coming Age of Quantum Biology* (New York: Crown, 2014), 318.
25. For more on the advances toward a grand unified field theory in recent years, see, for example, Brian Greene, *The Fabric of the Cosmos: Space, Time, and the Texture of Reality* (New York: Alfred A. Knopf, 2004).
26. Frank Wilczek, *Fundamentals: Ten Keys to Reality* (New York: Penguin, 2021), xiii.
27. For more on the potential philosophical import of the laws of thermodynamics, see Shannon Mussett, *Entropic Philosophy: Chaos, Breakdown, and Creation* (London: Rowan and Littlefield, 2022).
28. For more on the history of the development and application of thermo-

dynamics, see Robert Hanlon, *Block by Block: The Historical and Theoretical Foundations of Thermodynamics* (Oxford: Oxford University Press, 2020).

29. See, for example, Peter Atkins, *Four Laws That Drive the Universe* (Oxford: Oxford University Press, 2007), v–vii.

30. Carlo Rovelli, *Seven Brief Lessons on Physics*, trans. Simon Carnell and Erica Segre (New York: Riverhead Books, 2014), 57–58.

31. Rovelli, *Seven Brief Lessons on Physics*, 57–58.

32. Pross, *What Is Life?* 80.

33. Albert Einstein, *Autobiographical Notes*, trans. and ed. Paul Arthur Schilpp (Chicago: Open Court, 1991), 31.

34. Einstein, *Autobiographical Notes*, 19.

35. Schrödinger, *What Is Life?* 10.

36. Schrödinger, *What Is Life?* 10.

37. Max Tegmark, *Our Mathematical Universe: My Quest for the Ultimate Nature of Reality* (New York: Vintage Books, 2014), 254.

38. Tegmark, *Our Mathematical Universe*, 249.

39. Schrödinger, *What Is Life?* 30, italics mine.

40. Graham Farmelo, *The Universe Speaks in Numbers: How Modern Math Reveals Nature's Deepest Secrets* (New York: Hachette Book Group, 2019).

41. Peter Atkins, *Conjuring the Universe: The Origins of the Laws of Nature* (Oxford: Oxford University Press, 2018), 159.

42. Atkins, *Conjuring the Universe*, 159, italics mine.

43. Meillassoux, *After Finitude*, 53.

44. This motion is known as Brownian motion and is named for Robert Brown, who first described the nature of this motion in 1827.

45. Quoted in Rovelli, *Seven Brief Lessons on Physics*, 53.

46. See, for example, Eric Johnson, *Anxiety and the Equation: Understanding Boltzmann's Entropy* (Cambridge, MA: MIT Press, 2018).

47. Joe Rosen, *The Capricious Cosmos: Universe beyond Law* (New York: Macmillan, 1991), 57 and 95, respectively.

48. Rosen, *The Capricious Cosmos*, 81.

49. See Rosen, *The Capricious Cosmos*, 75.

50. Atkins, *Conjuring the Universe*, 168.

51. John Bigelow, *The Reality of Numbers: A Physicist's Philosophy of Mathematics* (Oxford: Clarendon, 1988).

52. Bigelow, *The Reality of Numbers*, 175.

53. William Butler Yeats, "The Second Coming," in *The Collected Poems of W. B. Yeats* (London: Wordsworth Editions, 1994), 158.

54. Stephen Hawking, *The Illustrated A Brief History of Time* (New York: Bantam Books, 1996), 191.

55. Hawking, *The Illustrated A Brief History of Time*, 39.

56. Schrödinger, *What Is Life?* 57.

57. John von Neumann, *Mathematical Foundations of Quantum Mechanics*, trans. Robert T. Beyer, ed. Nicholas A. Wheeler (Princeton, NJ: Princeton University Press, 2018).

58. See, for example, McFadden and Al-Khalili, *Life on the Edge*, 291.

59. J. Bevan Ott and Juliana Boerio-Goates, *Chemical Thermodynamics: Principles and Applications* (Amsterdam: Elsevier, 2000), 1–2.

60. Schrödinger, *What Is Life?* 68; and Jacques Monod, *Chance and Necessity: An Essay on the Natural Philosophy of Modern Biology*, trans. Austryn Wainhouse (New York: Vintage Books, 1971), 123.

61. Eric D. Schneider and Dorion Sagan, *Into the Cool: Energy Flow, Thermodynamics, and Life* (Chicago: University of Chicago Press, 2002).

62. Lane, *The Vital Question*, 94–95. See also Pross, *What Is Life?* 118.

63. Hoffmann, *Life's Ratchet*, 86.

64. Jeremy England, *Every Life Is on Fire: How Thermodynamics Explains the Origins of Living Things* (New York: Basic Books, 2020).

65. Jeremy England, "Dissipative Adaptation in Drive Self-Assembly," *Nature and Nanotechnology*, vol. 10 (November 2015): 920.

66. Jeremy England, "Statistical Physics of Self-Replication," *Journal of Chemical Physics*, vol. 139 (2013): 141.

67. Carroll, *The Big Picture*, 264.

68. Carroll, *The Big Picture*, 274.

69. Lane, *The Vital Question*, 64.

70. Vaclav Havel, "Letter to Dr. Gustav Husak," in *Vaclav Havel: Living in Truth* (London: Faber and Faber, 2000), 23.

71. Hoffmann, *Life's Ratchet*, 87.

72. Carroll, *The Big Picture*, 240.

73. Fred Adams and Greg Laughlin, *The Five Ages of the Universe: Inside the Physics of Eternity* (New York: Touchstone Books, 1999), xxviii.

74. Adams and Laughlin, *Five Ages of the Universe*, 155.

75. Adams and Laughlin, *Five Ages of the Universe*, 155.

76. Lawrence M. Krauss, *A Universe from Nothing: Why There Is Something Rather Than Nothing* (New York: Atria Books, 2012), 179.

77. See, for example, Katie Mack, *The End of Everything (Astrophysically Speaking)* (New York: Scribner, 2020).

78. Alan Lightman, *The Accidental Universe: The World You Thought You Knew* (New York: Pantheon Books, 2013), 26.

79. Philip Ball, "How Life (and Death) Spring from Disorder," *Quanta Magazine*, January 26, 2017.

80. Lawrence M. Krauss and Glenn D. Starkman, "The Fate of Life in the Universe," *Scientific American* (November 1999): 60–61; and Steven Frautschi, "Entropy in an Expanding Universe," *Science* 2017, no. 4560 (August 13, 1982): 597.

81. Richard Dawkins, "Afterword," in *A Universe from Nothing: Why There Is Something Rather Than Nothing*, by Lawrence M. Krauss (New York: Atria Books, 2012), 188.

82. Schneider and Sagan, *Into the Cool*, 299ff.

83. This concept of the absolute contingency of necessity is explored in more detail, albeit in a definitely nonscientific and much more theological direction, in Tyler Tritten, *The Contingency of Necessity: Reason and God as Matters of Fact* (Edinburgh: Edinburgh University Press, 2017).

84. Sokal and Bricmont, *Fashionable Nonsense*.

Chapter 5

1. Sokal and Bricmont, *Fashionable Nonsense*, 14.
2. Sokal and Bricmont, *Fashionable Nonsense*, 180–81.
3. Sokal and Bricmont, *Fashionable Nonsense*, x.
4. See, for example, their note on Noam Chomsky: Sokal and Bricmont, *Fashionable Nonsense*, 12n11.
5. Sokal and Bricmont, *Fashionable Nonsense*, x.
6. Sokal and Bricmont, *Fashionable Nonsense*, x, xi, respectively.
7. Sokal and Bricmont, *Fashionable Nonsense*, 5.
8. Sokal and Bricmont, *Fashionable Nonsense*, 5.
9. Sokal and Bricmont, *Fashionable Nonsense*, 12.
10. Sokal and Bricmont, *Fashionable Nonsense*, 4, italics mine.
11. Sokal and Bricmont, *Fashionable Nonsense*, 13.
12. Sokal and Bricmont, *Fashionable Nonsense*, 9
13. Sokal and Bricmont, *Fashionable Nonsense*, 9.
14. Sokal and Bricmont, *Fashionable Nonsense*, 4
15. Sokal and Bricmont, *Fashionable Nonsense*, 4.
16. Sokal and Bricmont, *Fashionable Nonsense*, 5.
17. Sokal and Bricmont, *Fashionable Nonsense*, 5.
18. Sokal and Bricmont, *Fashionable Nonsense*, 10, 11, respectively.
19. Sokal and Bricmont, *Fashionable Nonsense*, 180–81.
20. See, for example, Badiou, *In Praise of Mathematics*, 34; and Badiou, *Being and Event*, 131.
21. William Shakespeare, "The Tragedy of Hamlet, Prince of Denmark," in *The Oxford Shakespeare: The Complete Works*, ed. Stanley Wells and Gary Taylor (Oxford: Oxford University Press, 2008), 681–718; William Shakespeare, *The Oxford Shakespeare: Hamlet* (Oxford: Oxford University Press, 2008).
22. Michel de Montaigne, "That the taste of good and evil things depends in large part on the opinion we have of them," and "To philosophize is to learn how to die," in *Michel de Montaigne: The Complete Essays*, trans. and ed. M. A. Screech (London: Penguin Books, 1997). Most contemporary Shakespeare scholars agree that Gonzalo's speech in act 2, scene 1 of *The Tempest* was inspired in no small part by Montaigne's "Of Cannibals," in *Michel de Montaigne: The Complete Essays*. See, for example, Kenji Go, "Montaigne's 'Cannibals' and 'The Tempest' Revisited," *Studies in Philology* 109, no. 4 (2012): 455–73.
23. See, for example, Epictetus, *Discourses and Selected Writings*, trans. and ed. Robert Dobbin (London: Penguin Books, 2008), 112, 223.
24. See, for example, Seneca, *The Stoic Philosophy of Seneca*, trans. Moses Hadas (New York: W. W. Norton, 1958), 256.
25. See, for example, Augustine, *On Free Choice of the Will*, trans. Thomas Williams (Indianapolis: Hackett, 1993), 92–108; and Thomas Aquinas, *Aquinas's Shorter Summa*, trans. Cyril Vollert (Manchester, NH: Sophia Institute, 2002), 125–33.
26. See, for example, Voltaire, "The Lisbon Earthquake," in *The Portable Voltaire*, ed. Ben Ray Redman (New York: Penguin Books, 1977), 560–69; and Jean-Jacques Rousseau, "Letter from J. J. Rousseau to M. de Voltaire," in *Rousseau: The Discourses and Other Early Political Writings*, ed. and trans. Victor Gourevitch (Cambridge: Cambridge University Press, 1997), 232–46.

27. See, for example, Kant, *Groundwork of the Metaphysics of Morals*, 66.

28. Jeremy Bentham, *An Introduction to the Principles of Morals and Legislation* (Mineola, NY: Dover, 2007), 103, 209.

29. Friedrich Nietzsche, *Human, All Too Human (I)*, trans. Gary Handwerk (Stanford, CA: Stanford University Press, 1995), 110. See also Friedrich Nietzsche, *Dawn Thoughts on the Presumptions of Morality*, trans. Brittain Smith (Stanford, CA: Stanford University Press, 2011), 279: "Not things, but opinions about things that do not even exist have confused and upset people so." For a more expanded assessment of Nietzsche's exploration of the moral potencies of nature, see chapter 8.

30. Martin Heidegger, *Being and Time*, trans. John Macquarrie and Edward Robinson (New York: Harper and Row, 1962), 96–98.

31. David Hume, *A Treatise of Human Nature*, ed. Ernest C. Mossner (London: Penguin Books, 1969), 519.

32. Hume, *A Treatise of Human Nature*, 517.

33. Hume, *A Treatise of Human Nature*, 520–21, italics mine.

34. Hume, *A Treatise of Human Nature*, 520.

35. Hume, *A Treatise of Human Nature*, 521.

36. Hume, *A Treatise of Human Nature*, 526.

37. Hume, *A Treatise of Human Nature*, 527.

38. G. E. Moore, *Principia Ethica*, ed. Thomas Baldwin (Cambridge: Cambridge University Press, 1993).

39. Moore, *Principia Ethica*, 59, 163, 69, and 89, respectively.

40. Moore, *Principia Ethica*, 62.

41. Moore, *Principia Ethica*, 62.

42. Moore, *Principia Ethica*, 68.

43. Moore, *Principia Ethica*, 90.

44. Moore, *Principia Ethica*, 91.

45. Moore, *Principia Ethica*, 62, 108–9, respectively.

46. For more on the history and debates of the idea of the naturalistic fallacy, see Neil Sinclair, ed., *The Naturalistic Fallacy* (Cambridge: Cambridge University Press, 2019).

47. Augustine, *The City of God*, trans. Marcus Dods (New York: Modern Library, 2000), book XI, chap. 9, p. 354. See also Augustine, *Enchiridion on Faith, Hope, and Love*, trans. Albert C. Outler (Aeterna, 2014), chap. 3, §11, 7.

48. See, for example, Fran O' Rourke, "Evil as Privation: The Neo-Platonic Background of Aquinas' *De Malo*," in *Aquinas's Disputed Questions on Evil*, ed. M. V. Dougherty (Cambridge: Cambridge University Press, 2015), 192–221; Paul Kontos, ed., *Evil in Aristotle* (Cambridge: Cambridge University Press, 2018); C. M. Chilcott, "The Platonic Theory of Evil," *Classical Quarterly* 17, no. 1 (1923): 27–31; and R. Hackforth, "Moral Evil and Ignorance in Plato's Ethics," *Classical Quarterly* 40, no. 3-4 (July–October 1946), 118–20.

49. Aquinas, *Aquinas' Shorter Summa*, §114ff., 126.

50. For more on this, see Michael Latzer, "Leibniz's Conception of Metaphysical Evil," *Journal of the History of Ideas* 55, no. 1 (1994): 1–15.

51. Immanuel Kant, *Religion within the Boundaries of Mere Reason*, ed. Alan

NOTES TO PAGES 129-134

Wood and George di Giovanni (Cambridge: Cambridge University Press, 1998), 25ff.

52. Hannah Arendt, *Eichmann in Jerusalem: A Report on the Banality of Evil* (New York: Penguin Books, 1963), 287.

53. One notable exception to this rule is Friedrich Schelling's analysis of evil in *Philosophical Investigations into the Essence of Human Freedom*, trans. Jeff Love and Johannes Schmidt (Albany: State University of New York Press, 2006), which we will examine shortly.

54. Plotinus, *The Enneads*, ed. Lloyd P. Gerson, trans. George Boys-Stones et al. (Cambridge: Cambridge University Press, 2018), I.8.3, 111–12.

55. Emmanuel Levinas, *Existence and Existents*, trans. Alphonso Lingis (Pittsburgh: Duquesne University Press, 2001), 52.

56. Emmanuel Levinas, "Meaning and Sense," in *Basic Philosophical Writings*, ed. Adriaan T. Peperzak, Simon Critchley, and Robert Bernasconi (Bloomington: Indiana University Press, 1996), 59.

57. Levinas, "Meaning and Sense," 59.

58. Emmanuel Levinas, *Alterity and Transcendence*, trans. Michael B. Smith (New York: Columbia University Press, 1999), 59–76. See also Emmanuel Levinas, *Totality and Infinity: An Essay on Exteriority*, trans. Alphonso Lingis (Pittsburgh: Duquesne University Press, 1969), 281.

59. Emmanuel Levinas, "Transcendence and Evil," in *Collected Philosophical Papers*, trans. Alphonso Lingis (Pittsburgh: Duquesne University Press, 1998), 180. For more on Levinas's relation to Plotinus, see John Izzi, "Proximity in Distance: Levinas and Plotinus," in *Levinas and the Ancients*, ed. Brian Schroeder and Silvia Benso (Bloomington: Indiana University Press, 2008), 196–209. See also Brian Schroeder, "A Trace of the Eternal Return: Levinas and Neoplatonism," in *Levinas and the Ancients*, 210–29.

60. Emmanuel Levinas, *Time and the Other*, trans. Richard A. Cohen (Pittsburgh: Duquesne University Press, 1987), 51.

61. Martin Heidegger, *Schelling's Treatise on the Essence of Human Freedom*, trans. Joan Stambaugh (Athens: Ohio University Press, 1985), 101.

62. Heidegger, *Schelling's Treatise*, 101.

63. Heidegger, *Schelling's Treatise*, 101, italics mine.

64. Heidegger, *Schelling's Treatise*, 100.

65. Heidegger, *Schelling's Treatise*, 101, italics mine.

66. Heidegger, *Schelling's Treatise*, 111–12.

67. Schelling, *Philosophical Investigations into the Essence of Human Freedom*.

68. Schelling, *Philosophical Investigations*, 39.

69. Schelling, *Philosophical Investigations*, 37.

70. Schelling, *Philosophical Investigations*, 38.

71. Schelling, *Philosophical Investigations*, 38.

72. Schelling, *Philosophical Investigations*, 41.

73. Schelling, *Philosophical Investigations*, 41–42.

74. Schelling, *Philosophical Investigations*, 44.

75. Schelling, *Philosophical Investigations*, 47.

76. Schelling, *Philosophical Investigations*, 48.

77. Schelling, *Philosophical Investigations*, 48.

78. For more on how a concept of ethical duty and the good might be conceived negatively in this way, through an active attempt to resist the temptation of a more primal mode of absolute evil, see Dalton, *The Ethics of Resistance*, 56–57, 112–14.

Chapter 6

1. Baruch Spinoza, *Ethics—Proved in Geometrical Order*, ed. Matthew J. Kisner, trans. Michael Silverthorne and Matthew J. Kisner (Cambridge: Cambridge University Press, 2018), Part IV, preface, 158.
2. Spinoza, *Ethics*, Part I, prop. 14–16, 14–18.
3. Spinoza, *Ethics*, Part II, prop. 9–12, 50–54.
4. Spinoza, *Ethics*, Part II, prop. 11, corollary, 53.
5. Spinoza, *Ethics*, Part II, prop. 13, scholium, 55.
6. Spinoza, *Ethics*, Part I, appendix, 36.
7. Spinoza, *Ethics*, Part II, prop. 35, scholium, 73.
8. Spinoza, *Ethics*, Part II, prop. 35, scholium, 73.
9. Spinoza, *Ethics*, Part II, prop. 44, corollary I, 81.
10. Spinoza, *Ethics*, Part II, prop. 48, 85.
11. Spinoza, *Ethics*, Part I, prop. 29, 28.
12. Spinoza, *Ethics*, Part IV, preface, 159.
13. Spinoza, *Ethics*, Part IV, preface, 159.
14. Spinoza, *Ethics*, Part IV, preface, 159.
15. Spinoza, *Ethics*, Part IV, def. 1, 160.
16. Spinoza, *Ethics*, Part IV, def. 2, 160. Note that the word translated as "bad" by Kisner, *malum*, is traditionally rendered as "evil." In keeping with this, when not directly quoting from the Kisner translation, I will refer to Spinoza's use of *malum* as "evil" henceforth.
17. Friedrich Nietzsche, "Ecce Homo," in *The Anti-Christ, Ecce Homo, Twilight of the Idols, and Other Writings*, ed. Aaron Ridley and Judith Norman, trans. Judith Norman (Cambridge: Cambridge University Press, 2005), 99. For more on the relationship between Nietzsche's concept of *Amor Fati* and Spinoza's ethics, see Joan Stambaugh, "*Amor Dei* and *Amor Fati*: Spinoza and Nietzsche," in *Studies in Nietzsche and the Judaeo-Christian Tradition*, ed. James O'Flaherty, Timothy F. Sellner, and Robert M. Helm (Chapel Hill: University of North Carolina Press, 1985), 130–42.
18. See, for example, Charles Jarrett, "Spinoza on the Relativity of Good and Evil," in *Spinoza: Metaphysical Themes*, ed. Olli Koistinen and John Biro (Oxford: Oxford University Press, 2002), 159–81. Nietzsche is also generally considered a relativist, but I will argue in chapter 8 that this is not so. After all, Nietzsche identifies a "highest virtue" which leads to joy and pleasure; namely, the "affirmation of life" as the "will to power," which, as we will see shortly, resembles Spinoza's identification of acquiescence as the highest virtue. See, for example,

Friedrich Nietzsche, *The Will to Power*, trans. Walter Kaufmann and R. J. Hollingdale (New York: Random House, 1967), 533.

19. Spinoza, *Ethics*, Part III, prop. 9, scholium, 103.
20. Spinoza, *Ethics*, Part IV, preface, 159.
21. For more on this, see Steven Nadler, *A Book Forged in Hell: Spinoza's Scandalous Treatise and the Birth of the Secular Age* (Princeton, NJ: Princeton University Press, 2011).
22. Spinoza, *Ethics*, Part V, prop. 15, 234.
23. Spinoza, *Ethics*, Part V, prop. 27, proof, 239. See also Part III, prop. 30, scholium, 118.
24. Spinoza, *Ethics*, Part V, prop. 30, 241.
25. Spinoza, *Ethics*, Part V, prop. 27, proof, 259.
26. Spinoza, *Ethics*, Part V, prop. 32, 242.
27. Spinoza, *Ethics*, Part V, prop. 33, proof and scholium, 242–43.
28. Spinoza, *Ethics*, Part V. prop. 33, scholium, 243.
29. Spinoza, *Ethics*, Part V, prop. 31, scholium, 241.
30. Spinoza, *Ethics*, Part V, prop. 42, proof, 250.
31. For more on the translation and concept of *acquiescentia* in Spinoza, see Claire Carlile, "Spinoza's *Acquiescentia*," *Journal of the History of Philosophy* 55, no. 2 (2017): 209–36.
32. Spinoza, *Ethics*, Part IV, prop. 52, 187–88.
33. For more on the nature of obedience in acquiescence, see Baruch Spinoza, *Theological-Political Treatise*, ed. Jonathan Israel, trans. Michael Silverthorne and Jonathan Israel (Cambridge: Cambridge University Press, 2007), 179–83.
34. Spinoza, *Ethics*, Part III, prop. 30, scholium, 118.
35. Spinoza, *Ethics*, Part III, "Definition of the Emotions," 25, 149.
36. Spinoza, *Ethics*, Part V, prop. 42, scholium, 249–50.
37. Spinoza, *Ethics*, Part IV, prop. 52, scholium, 198.
38. Spinoza, *Ethics*, Part V, prop. 42, scholium, 250
39. Indeed, Spinoza interacted significantly with Maimonides throughout his work, particularly in his letters. And despite disagreeing with him significantly on a number of points, Spinoza ultimately affirms what he sees as Maimonides's vision of the cosmos as the being of God. See, for example, Baruch Spinoza, "Letter 43," in *Spinoza: Complete Works*, trans. Samuel Shirley, ed. Michael L Morgan (Indianapolis: Hackett, 2002), 871. For more on Spinoza's relation to Maimonides, see Joshua Parens, *Maimonides and Spinoza: Their Conflicting Views on Human Nature* (Chicago: University of Chicago Press, 2012).
40. Spinoza, *Ethics*, Part IV, preface, 157–59.
41. Romans 8:28 (English Standard Version).
42. Arthur Schopenhauer, *Parerga and Paralipomena: Short Philosophical Essays*, vol. 2, trans. and ed. Adrian Del Caro and Christopher Janaway (Cambridge: Cambridge University Press, 2015), 94. See also Arthur Schopenhauer, "On Will in Nature," in *On the Fourfold Root of the Principle of Sufficient Reason and Other Writings*, trans. and ed. David E. Cartwrights, Edward E. Erdmann, and Christopher Janaway (Cambridge: Cambridge University Press, 2012), 443.

Chapter 7

1. For more on the relationship between Schopenhauer and Spinoza, see Henry Walter Brann, "Schopenhauer and Spinoza," *Journal of the History of Philosophy* 10, no. 2 (April 1972): 181–96.
2. Schopenhauer, "On Will in Nature," 323.
3. Schopenhauer, "On Will in Nature," 323.
4. Schopenhauer, "On Will in Nature," 315.
5. Schopenhauer, "On Will in Nature," 340.
6. Arthur Schopenhauer, *The World as Will and Representation*, vol. 1, trans. and ed. Judith Norman, Alistair Welchman, and Christopher Janaway (Cambridge: Cambridge University Press, 2010), 124.
7. See, for example, Schopenhauer, *Parerga and Paralipomena*, 2:96–100.
8. Schopenhauer, "On Will in Nature," 325.
9. See, for example, Arthur Schopenhauer, "The Critique of Kantian Philosophy," in *The World as Will and Representation*, vol. 1, trans. and ed. Judith Norman, Alistair Welchman, and Christopher Janaway (Cambridge: Cambridge University Press, 2010), 461–63.
10. Schopenhauer, "On Will in Nature," 323.
11. Cf. Kant, *The Critique of Pure Reason*, B246/A201, 311. Compare Schopenhauer, *Parerga and Paralipomena*, 2:97.
12. Schopenhauer, *The World as Will and Representation*, 1:421.
13. Schopenhauer, "On Will in Nature," 324.
14. Schopenhauer, "On Will in Nature," 324.
15. Schopenhauer, *Parerga and Paralipomena*, 2:95.
16. Schopenhauer, "On Will in Nature," 369.
17. Schopenhauer, "On Will in Nature," 392.
18. Schopenhauer, "On Will in Nature," 305.
19. Schopenhauer, *Parerga and Paralipomena*, 2:99.
20. Schopenhauer, *Parerga and Paralipomena*, 2:96.
21. Schopenhauer, *Parerga and Paralipomena*, 2:98.
22. Schopenhauer, "On Will in Nature," 340.
23. Schopenhauer, *Parerga and Paralipomena*, 2:86, 89.
24. Schopenhauer, *Parerga and Paralipomena*, 2:97. See also 100.
25. Arthur Schopenhauer, "Prize Essay on the Freedom of the Will," in *The Two Fundamental Problems of Ethics*, trans. and ed. Christopher Janaway (Cambridge: Cambridge University Press, 2009), 50.
26. Schopenhauer, "Prize Essay on the Freedom of the Will," 79.
27. Schopenhauer, "Prize Essay on the Freedom of the Will," 52.
28. Schopenhauer, *Parerga and Paralipomena*, 2:206.
29. Schopenhauer, "Prize Essay on the Freedom of the Will," 65.
30. Schopenhauer, "Prize Essay on the Freedom of the Will," 65.
31. Schopenhauer, *Parerga and Paralipomena*, 2:209.
32. Schopenhauer, "On Will in Nature," 341.
33. Schopenhauer, "Prize Essay on the Freedom of the Will," 47.
34. Schopenhauer, "Prize Essay on the Freedom of the Will," 79.

35. Schopenhauer, "Prize Essay on the Freedom of the Will," 48. See also Schopenhauer, "On Will in Nature," 386.
36. Schopenhauer, "Prize Essay on the Freedom of the Will," 66.
37. Schopenhauer, *Parerga and Paralipomena*, 2:216.
38. Schopenhauer, *Parerga and Paralipomena*, 2:213.
39. Schopenhauer, *Parerga and Paralipomena*, 2:183.
40. Schopenhauer, *Parerga and Paralipomena*, 2:183.
41. Schopenhauer, "On Will in Nature," 307, 305, respectively.
42. Schopenhauer, "On Will in Nature," 441.
43. Schopenhauer, "On Will in Nature," 442.
44. Schopenhauer, *Parerga and Paralipomena*, 2:262.
45. Schopenhauer, *Parerga and Paralipomena*, 2:94.
46. Schopenhauer, *Parerga and Paralipomena*, 2:274.
47. Schopenhauer, *Parerga and Paralipomena*, 2:196.
48. Schopenhauer, "On Will in Nature," 444.
49. Schopenhauer, *Parerga and Paralipomena*, 2:270.
50. Schopenhauer, *Parerga and Paralipomena*, 2:192.
51. Schopenhauer, *Parerga and Paralipomena*, 2:195.
52. Schopenhauer, *Parerga and Paralipomena*, 2:263.
53. Schopenhauer, *Parerga and Paralipomena*, 2:269, 270, respectively.
54. Schopenhauer, *Parerga and Paralipomena*, 2:262.
55. Schopenhauer, *Parerga and Paralipomena*, 2:269.
56. Schopenhauer, "Prize Essay on the Freedom of the Will," 107.
57. Schopenhauer, "Prize Essay on the Freedom of the Will," 105.
58. Schopenhauer, *Parerga and Paralipomena*, 2:273, 274.
59. Schopenhauer, "Prize Essay on the Freedom of the Will," 57.
60. Schopenhauer, "Prize Essay on the Freedom of the Will," 109.
61. Arthur Schopenhauer, "Prize Essay on the Basis of Morals," in *The Two Fundamental Problems of Ethics*, trans. and ed. Christopher Janaway (Cambridge: Cambridge University Press, 2009), 134.
62. Schopenhauer, "Prize Essay on the Basis of Morals," 150.
63. Schopenhauer, "Prize Essay on the Basis of Morals," 151.
64. Schopenhauer, "Prize Essay on the Basis of Morals," 200.
65. Schopenhauer, "Prize Essay on the Basis of Morals," 201.
66. Schopenhauer, "Prize Essay on the Basis of Morals," 200.
67. Schopenhauer, "Prize Essay on the Basis of Morals," 205.
68. Schopenhauer, "Prize Essay on the Basis of Morals," 140.
69. Schopenhauer, "Prize Essay on the Basis of Morals," 215.
70. Schopenhauer, "Prize Essay on the Basis of Morals," 219.
71. Schopenhauer, "Prize Essay on the Basis of Morals," 204.
72. Schopenhauer, "Prize Essay on the Basis of Morals," 204, italics mine.
73. Schopenhauer, "Prize Essay on the Basis of Morals," 204.
74. Schopenhauer, "Prize Essay on the Basis of Morals," 207.
75. See Schopenhauer, "Prize Essay on the Basis of Morals," 204.
76. Schopenhauer, *Parerga and Paralipomena*, 2:289.
77. Schopenhauer, *Parerga and Paralipomena*, 2:290.

78. Schopenhauer, *Parerga and Paralipomena*, 2:290.
79. William Shakespeare, *Hamlet*, act III, scene 1.
80. Schopenhauer, "Prize Essay on the Basis of Morals," 221ff.
81. Schopenhauer, "Prize Essay on the Basis of Morals," 226, See also 231.
82. Schopenhauer, "Prize Essay on the Basis of Morals," 227.
83. Schopenhauer, *The World as Will and Representation*, 393. See also Schopenhauer, *Parerga and Paralipomena*, 2:280.
84. Frederick C. Beiser, *Weltschmerz: Pessimism in German Philosophy, 1860–1900* (Oxford: Oxford University Press, 2016), 43.
85. Beiser, *Weltschmerz*, 43.

Chapter 8

1. Nietzsche, *The Gay Science*, 120.
2. Nietzsche, *The Will to Power*, 13.
3. Nietzsche, *Will to Power*, 9, 13, respectively.
4. Nietzsche, *Will to Power*, 13.
5. Nietzsche, *Will to Power*, 13.
6. Nietzsche, *Will to Power*, 14–15.
7. Nietzsche, *Human, All Too Human (I)*, 6. See also Nietzsche, *The Gay Science*, 244.
8. Friedrich Nietzsche, "Twilight of the Idols," in *The Anti-Christ, Ecce Homo, Twilight of the Idols, and Other Writings*, ed. Aaron Ridley and Judith Norman, trans. Judith Norman (Cambridge: Cambridge University Press, 2005), 155.
9. Nietzsche, *Human, All Too Human (I)*, 37.
10. Nietzsche, *Human, All Too Human (I)*, 37.
11. Nietzsche, *Human, All Too Human (I)*, 37.
12. See Nietzsche, *Human, All Too Human (I)*, 296.
13. Nietzsche, *Human, All Too Human (I)*, 21, 27–28. See also Friedrich Nietzsche, "Beyond Good and Evil," in *Beyond Good and Evil / On the Genealogy of Morality*, trans. Adrian Del Caro (Stanford, CA: Stanford University Press, 2014), 18.
14. Nietzsche, *Dawn Thoughts*, 69.
15. Nietzsche, *Dawn Thoughts*, 159.
16. Nietzsche, *Human, All Too Human (I)*, 41.
17. Nietzsche, "Twilight of the Idols," 155.
18. Friedrich Nietzsche, "On the Genealogy of Morals," in *Beyond Good and Evil / On the Genealogy of Morality*, trans. Adrian Del Caro (Stanford, CA: Stanford University Press, 2014), 244.
19. Friedrich Nietzsche, *Thus Spoke Zarathustra*, ed. Adrian Del Caro and Robert B. Pippin, trans. Adrian Del Caro (Cambridge: Cambridge University Press, 2006), 17. See also Nietzsche, "Beyond Good and Evil," 115.
20. Nietzsche, *The Gay Science*, 144. See also Nietzsche, *Will to Power*, 319.
21. Nietzsche, *Thus Spoke Zarathustra*, 5.

22. Nietzsche, *Thus Spoke Zarathustra*, 59.
23. Nietzsche, "Twilight of the Idols," 175.
24. Brian Leiter, *Nietzsche on Morality* (London: Routledge, 2002), 6.
25. See, for example, Friedrich Nietzsche, "Schopenhauer as Educator," in *Untimely Meditations*, ed. Daniel Breazeale, trans. R. J. Hollingdale (Cambridge: Cambridge University Press, 1997), 142.
26. Cosima Wagner, *Cosima Wagner's Diaries: 1869–1877*, vol. 1, ed. Martin Gregor-Dellin and Deitrich Mack, trans. Geoffrey Skelton (San Diego, CA: Harcourt Brace Jovanovich, 1978), 938.
27. Nietzsche, *Human, All Too Human (I)*, 10. See also Nietzsche, "Twilight of the Idols," 202–3, 210–11.
28. Nietzsche, *Human, All Too Human (I)*, 258.
29. Nietzsche, *Human, All Too Human (I)*, 258. While some have read this line as referring to the Bible, the couplet structure of the sentence makes the referent of this praise more likely Spinoza, especially given his critiques of Christian morality and the Bible through the rest of the text. For more of Nietzsche's praise of Spinoza, see Nietzsche, *Will to Power*, 36.
30. See Friedrich Nietzsche, "89—To Franz Overbeck (postmarked Sils Engd., July 30, 1881)," in *Selected Letters of Friedrich Nietzsche*, ed. and trans. Christopher Middleton (Chicago: University of Chicago Press, 1969), 177.
31. Nietzsche, *Human, All Too Human (I)*, 47.
32. See, for example, Nietzsche, *Dawn Thoughts*, 219.
33. Nietzsche, *Dawn Thoughts*, 9.
34. Nietzsche, *Will to Power*, 378.
35. Nietzsche, *The Gay Science*, 148.
36. Nietzsche, *The Gay Science*, 148.
37. Nietzsche, *Human, All Too Human (I)*, 20.
38. Nietzsche, *Dawn Thoughts*, 13.
39. Nietzsche, *Dawn Thoughts*, 71.
40. Nietzsche, *Dawn Thoughts*, 139–40.
41. Nietzsche, *Human, All Too Human (I)*, 21.
42. Nietzsche, *Human, All Too Human (I)*, 32.
43. Nietzsche, *Human, All Too Human (I)*, 33. See also 171–72.
44. Nietzsche, *Dawn Thoughts*, 219.
45. Nietzsche, *Dawn Thoughts*, 279.
46. Nietzsche, *The Gay Science*, 157. See also 109. For more on Nietzsche's account of nature as chaos, see Babette E. Babich, "Nietzsche's Chaos Sive Natura: Evening Gold and the Dancing Star," *Revista Portuguesa de Filosofia* 57, no. 2 (2001): 225–45.
47. Nietzsche, *Dawn Thoughts*, 98. See also Nietzsche, *The Gay Science*, 27, 32. For more on Nietzsche's appreciation of Darwin, see John Richardson, *Nietzsche's New Darwinism* (Oxford: Oxford University Press, 2004).
48. Friedrich Nietzsche, *Nietzsche Werke: Kritische Studienausgabe*, vol. 9, *Nachgelassene Fragmente 1880–1882*, ed. Giorgio Colli and Mazzino Montinari (Berlin: Walter de Gruyter, 1980), 197.

49. Nietzsche, "Twilight of the Idols," 155.
50. Nietzsche, *Dawn Thoughts*, 75. See also 92; and Nietzsche, *Will to Power*, 351–52, 546–47.
51. Nietzsche, *The Gay Science*, 109.
52. Nietzsche, *Human, All Too Human (I)*, 58.
53. Nietzsche, *The Gay Science*, 171.
54. Nietzsche, *Human, All Too Human (I)*, 83.
55. Nietzsche, *The Gay Science*, 32.
56. Nietzsche, *Human, All Too Human (I)*, 110.
57. Nietzsche, *Dawn Thoughts*, 114.
58. Nietzsche, *Dawn Thoughts*, 220.
59. Nietzsche, *The Gay Science*, 110.
60. Nietzsche, "Beyond Good and Evil," 81. Perhaps surprisingly, Nietzsche often uses the word "essence" in reference to the will to power throughout his later work. But when understood in the context of his definition of science as a "harmless" "future metaphysics," we are able to see that his use of the term is not meant to invoke any sense of "pure form" or "other-worldliness," but, instead, it merely references his conception of the true nature or inner power of reality.
61. Nietzsche, "Beyond Good and Evil," 40.
62. Nietzsche, *Will to Power*, 550.
63. Nietzsche, *Will to Power*, 547.
64. Nietzsche, *Will to Power*, 548.
65. Nietzsche, *Will to Power*, 549.
66. Nietzsche, *Will to Power*, 549.
67. Nietzsche, *Will to Power*, 550.
68. Nietzsche, *Will to Power*, 549.
69. Nietzsche, *Thus Spoke Zarathustra*, 178.
70. Nietzsche, *Will to Power*, 547.
71. Nietzsche, *Will to Power*, 549.
72. Nietzsche, "Beyond Good and Evil," 39.
73. Nietzsche, "Beyond Good and Evil," 39.
74. Nietzsche, "On the Genealogy of Morality," 267.
75. Nietzsche, "Beyond Good and Evil," 169.
76. Nietzsche, *Thus Spoke Zarathustra*, 90.
77. Nietzsche, *The Gay Science*, 110.
78. Nietzsche, *Human, All Too Human (I)*, 82.
79. Nietzsche, *Human, All Too Human (I)*, 49.
80. Nietzsche, *Human, All Too Human (I)*, 82.
81. Nietzsche, *Will to Power*, 354.
82. Nietzsche, *Human, All Too Human (I)*, 48. See also Nietzsche, "Twilight of the Idols," 181.
83. Nietzsche, "Twilight of the Idols," 182.
84. Nietzsche, *Will to Power*, 323.
85. Nietzsche, "Twilight of the Idols," 182.
86. Nietzsche, *Dawn Thoughts*, 220, italics mine.
87. Nietzsche, *Thus Spoke Zarathustra*, 17.

88. Nietzsche, *Thus Spoke Zarathustra*, 20.
89. Nietzsche, "On the Genealogy of Morality," 324.
90. Nietzsche, *Will to Power*, 43.
91. Nietzsche, *Thus Spoke Zarathustra*, 21.
92. Nietzsche, *Thus Spoke Zarathustra*, 6.
93. Nietzsche, *The Gay Science*, 110.
94. Nietzsche, *Will to Power*, 73; and Nietzsche, *Thus Spoke Zarathustra*, 229, respectively.
95. Nietzsche, *Will to Power*, 76.
96. Nietzsche, "Twilight of the Idols," 228.
97. Nietzsche, *The Gay Science*, 157.
98. Nietzsche, *The Gay Science*, 157. Note that this formulation of the "highest commandment," of his natural morality is a clear critique and reformation of the Christian account of the "highest commandment," "To love the Lord" (see Matthew 22:36–40).
99. Nietzsche, "Ecce Homo," 99.
100. Nietzsche, *Thus Spoke Zarathustra*, 185–87.
101. Nietzsche, *The Gay Science*, 169.
102. Nietzsche, *Thus Spoke Zarathustra*, 6.
103. See, for example, Nietzsche, "The Anti-Christ," 4.
104. Nietzsche, "The Anti-Christ," 4.
105. Nietzsche, "On the Genealogy of Morality," 228–29.
106. Nietzsche, "Ecce Homo," 81; and Nietzsche, *Thus Spoke Zarathustra*, 6.
107. Nietzsche, *Human, All Too Human (I)*, 76.
108. Nietzsche, "Twilight of the Idols," 202; and Nietzsche, *The Gay Science*, 167.
109. Nietzsche, *Will to Power*, 11.
110. Nietzsche, "Twilight of the Idols," 210.
111. Nietzsche, "On the Genealogy of Morality," 324. For more on Nietzsche's ethics as life-affirmation, see Bernard Reginster, *The Affirmation of Life: Nietzsche on Overcoming Nihilism* (Cambridge, MA: Harvard University Press, 2009).
112. Nietzsche, "Ecce Homo," 81.
113. Nietzsche, *Thus Spoke Zarathustra*, 263.
114. Nietzsche, *Thus Spoke Zarathustra*, 112.
115. Nietzsche, *The Gay Science*, 38.
116. Nietzsche, "Twilight of the Idols," 228.
117. Nietzsche, *Will to Power*, 36.
118. For more on Nietzsche's Spinozism, see Andreas Urs Sommer, "Nietzsche's Readings on Spinoza: A Contextualist Study, Particularly on the Reception of Kuno Fischer," *Journal of Nietzsche Studies* 43, no. 2 (2012): 156–84; and Yirmiyahu Yovel, "Nietzsche and Spinoza: *Amor Fati* and *Amor Dei*," in *Nietzsche as Affirmative Thinker*, ed. Yirmiyahu Yovel (Dordrecht: Springer, 1986), 183–203.

Chapter 9

1. Beiser, *Weltschmerz*, 26.
2. See, for example, Ludwig Boltzmann, "On a Thesis of Schopenhauer's," in *Theoretical Physics and Philosophical Problems*, ed. Brian McGuinness, trans. Paul Foulkes (Dordrecht: D. Reidell, 1974), 193–95.
3. See, for example, Johnson, *Anxiety and the Equation*, 52–53.
4. Boltzmann, "On a Thesis of Schopenhauer's," 195.
5. John Blackmore, ed., *Ludwig Boltzmann: His Later Life and Philosophy, 1900–1906, Book I: A Documentary History* (Dordrecht: Kluwer/Springer, 1995), 165.
6. Schopenhauer, "On Will in Nature," 442.
7. Schopenhauer, *The World as Will and Representation*, 378.
8. Schopenhauer, *The World as Will and Representation*, 439.
9. Schopenhauer, *The World as Will and Representation*, 378.
10. Schopenhauer, *The World as Will and Representation*, 343–44, 359–60.
11. Schopenhauer, *The World as Will and Representation*, 378.
12. Schopenhauer, *Parerga and Paralipomena*, 2:270.
13. Schopenhauer, *The World as Will and Representation*, 378.
14. Schopenhauer, *The World as Will and Representation*, 376.
15. Schopenhauer, *The World as Will and Representation*, 389.
16. Schopenhauer, *The World as Will and Representation*, 389.
17. Schopenhauer, *The World as Will and Representation*, 394.
18. Schopenhauer, *The World as Will and Representation*, 398.
19. Schopenhauer, *The World as Will and Representation*, 389.
20. Schopenhauer, *The World as Will and Representation*, 389.
21. Schopenhauer, *The World as Will and Representation*, 389.
22. Schopenhauer, *The World as Will and Representation*, 427.
23. Schopenhauer, *The World as Will and Representation*, 314.
24. Schopenhauer, *The World as Will and Representation*, 314.
25. Schopenhauer, *The World as Will and Representation*, 314.
26. Schopenhauer, *The World as Will and Representation*, 311; see also 334.
27. Schopenhauer, *The World as Will and Representation*, 389.
28. Schopenhauer, *The World as Will and Representation*, 389.
29. Schopenhauer, "Prize Essay on the Basis of Morals," 215.
30. See, for example, Schopenhauer, *The World as Will and Representation*, 402.
31. Schopenhauer, *The World as Will and Representation*, 405.
32. Schopenhauer, *The World as Will and Representation*, 439.
33. Schopenhauer, *The World as Will and Representation*, 408–9. Remember that for Schopenhauer, suicide is not an option for those who strive to act justly because it fails to use the power of the will to alleviate the suffering of others, opting as it does exclusively to alleviate one's own suffering. See, for example, 425–28.
34. Schopenhauer, *The World as Will and Representation*, 419.
35. Schopenhauer, *The World as Will and Representation*, 410.
36. Schopenhauer, *The World as Will and Representation*, 394.

37. Schopenhauer, *The World as Will and Representation*, 416; see also 357.
38. Schopenhauer, *The World as Will and Representation*, 334 and 360.
39. Schopenhauer, *The World as Will and Representation*, 439.
40. Schopenhauer, *The World as Will and Representation*, 439.
41. For more on the influence of Buddhism on Schopenhauer's thought, see Peter Abelsen, "Schopenhauer and Buddhism," *Philosophy East and West* 43, no. 2 (1993): 255–78.
42. Schopenhauer, *The World as Will and Representation*, 383.
43. Schopenhauer, "On Will in Nature," 435.
44. For examples of the various positions on this debate, see, for example, Oliver Lacombe, "Buddhist Pessimism," in *Buddhist Studies in Honor of W. Rahula*, ed. Somaratna Balasooriya (London: Roundwound, 1980), 113–17; and David E. Cooper, "Buddhism as Pessimism," *Journal of World Philosophies*, vol. 6 (Winter 2021): 1–16.
45. Schopenhauer, "On Will in Nature," 435.
46. Though there are many different Buddhist traditions and interpretations, for the purposes of simplicity here I will focus on the core teachings of early Buddhism as they are documented in the Theravada Pali Canon. While the teachings preserved there were expanded upon and modified in later systems and schools of thought, they are nevertheless accepted within all strains of Buddhist thought and thus serve as a broad basis to make the kind of general claims I will pursue here without inspiring too much controversy or debate.
47. Bhikkhu Bodhi, trans., *The Connected Discourses of the Buddha: A Translation of the Saṃyutta Nikāya* (Boston: Wisdom Publications, 2000), 1140.
48. Bodhi, *The Connected Discourses*, 1140.
49. Bodhi, *The Connected Discourses*, 1140.
50. Bodhi, *The Connected Discourses*, 1140.
51. Maurice Walshe, trans., *The Long Discourses of the Buddha: A Translation of the Dīgha Nikāya* (Boston: Wisdom Publications, 1995), 190.
52. Walshe, *The Long Discourses*, 190.
53. Bhikkhu Ñāṇamoli and Bhikkhu Bodhi, trans., *The Middle Length Discourses of the Buddha: A Translation of the Majjhihima Nikāya* (Boston: Wisdom Publications, 1995), 83–90.
54. Bodhi, *The Connected Discourses*, 1270.
55. Bodhi, *The Connected Discourses*, 1269.
56. Bodhi, *The Connected Discourses*, 535–36.
57. Bodhi, *The Connected Discourses*, 1838.
58. Bodhi, *The Connected Discourses*, 1839.
59. Bodhi, *The Connected Discourses*, 1143.
60. For more on the negative value of the natural world in early Buddhism, see Damien Keown, "Buddhism and Ecology: A Virtue Ethics Approach," *Contemporary Buddhism* 8, no. 2 (2007): 97–112.
61. See, for example, H. Saddhatissa, trans., *The Sutta-Nipāta* (London: Routledge, 1985), 25.
62. Gil Fronsdal, trans., *The Dhammapada: A New Translation of the Buddhist Classic with Annotations* (Boston: Shambhala, 2006), 33.
63. For more on the early Buddhist conception of evil, see Trevor Oswald

Ling, *Buddhism and the Mythology of Evil: A Study in Theravada Buddhism* (London: Allen and Unwin, 1962).

64. See, for example, Bodhi, *The Connected Discourses*, 1844ff.
65. See, for example, Bodhi, *The Connected Discourses*, 1528–30.
66. Ñāṇamoli and Bodhi, *The Middle Length Discourses of the Buddha*, 145.
67. Bodhi, *The Connected Discourses*, 951.
68. Ñāṇamoli and Bodhi, *The Middle Length Discourses of the Buddha*, 87.
69. Schopenhauer, *The World as Will and Representation*, 424.
70. This, of course, is not necessarily the case with later schools of Buddhist philosophy, most notably Mahayana Buddhism, where the six perfections are touted as a positive ethical code. But we are restricting ourselves exclusively to the study of early Theravada Buddhism here since it was the only form of Buddhism with which Schopenhauer seems to have been familiar.
71. See, for example, Nietzsche, "The Anti-Christ," 16–20.
72. Mainländer's work has yet to be translated into English, and there is little or no scholarly interaction with his thought in the English-speaking world. The one major exception to this rule is Frederick Beiser's excellent *Weltschmerz: Pessimism in German Philosophy, 1860–1900*. To remedy this, in what follows I will be providing my own translations of the relevant passages of Mainländer's two major works: *Die Philosophie der Erlösung* (Berlin: Grieben, 1876); and *Die Philosophie der Erlösung*, vol. 2: *Zwölf philosophischer Essays* (Frankfurt: C. Koenitzer, 1886, second edition, 1984).
73. For more on these figures, see Beiser, *Weltschmerz*.
74. Beiser, *Weltschmerz*.
75. Mainländer, *Die Philosophie der Erlösung*, 1:108. It should be noted that this phrase first appears in Mainländer and *not* in Nietzsche who, if anything, seems to have taken it from Mainländer who, incidentally, he decries as a "sickeningly sentimental apostle of virginity" (Nietzsche, *The Gay Science*, 220).
76. Mainländer, *Die Philosophie der Erlösung*, 1:3 and 199.
77. Mainländer, *Die Philosophie der Erlösung*, 1:3.
78. Mainländer, *Die Philosophie der Erlösung*, 1:310.
79. Mainländer, *Die Philosophie der Erlösung*, 1:310.
80. Mainländer, *Die Philosophie der Erlösung*, 1:219.
81. Mainländer, *Die Philosophie der Erlösung*, 1:223.
82. Mainländer, *Die Philosophie der Erlösung*, 1:50.
83. Mainländer, *Die Philosophie der Erlösung*, 1:50.
84. Mainländer, *Die Philosophie der Erlösung*, 1:199.
85. Mainländer, *Die Philosophie der Erlösung*, 1:199.
86. Mainländer, *Die Philosophie der Erlösung*, 1:328, 331, respectively.
87. Mainländer, *Die Philosophie der Erlösung*, 1:327
88. Mainländer, *Die Philosophie der Erlösung*, 1:342.
89. Mainländer, *Die Philosophie der Erlösung*, 1:341–42. See also Mainländer, *Die Philosophie der Erlösung*, 2:510.
90. Mainländer, *Die Philosophie der Erlösung*, 1:36. See also Mainländer, *Die Philosophie der Erlösung*, 2:626.
91. Mainländer, *Die Philosophie der Erlösung*, 1:216. It is almost definitely

from Mainländer that Freud derived his claim in *Beyond the Pleasure Principle* that "the aim of all life is death." Sigmund Freud, *Beyond the Pleasure Principle*, trans. James Strachey (New York: W. W. Norton, 1961), 46.

92. Mainländer, *Die Philosophie der Erlösung*, 2:650.
93. Mainländer, *Die Philosophie der Erlösung*, 1:241.
94. Mainländer, *Die Philosophie der Erlösung*, 1:250.
95. Mainländer, *Die Philosophie der Erlösung*, 1:330.
96. Mainländer, *Die Philosophie der Erlösung*, 1:331.
97. Mainländer, *Die Philosophie der Erlösung*, 1:334–35.
98. See, for example, Mainländer, *Die Philosophie der Erlösung*, 1:330.
99. Mainländer, *Die Philosophie der Erlösung*, 1:215.
100. Mainländer, *Die Philosophie der Erlösung*, 1:334.
101. Mainländer, *Die Philosophie der Erlösung*, 1:210.
102. Mainländer, *Die Philosophie der Erlösung*, 1:210.
103. Mainländer, *Die Philosophie der Erlösung*, 1:242.
104. Mainländer, *Die Philosophie der Erlösung*, 1:593
105. Mainländer, *Die Philosophie der Erlösung*, 1:208.
106. Mainländer, *Die Philosophie der Erlösung*, 1: 216. See also 1:575.
107. See, for example, Mainländer, *Die Philosophie der Erlösung*, 2:211–12.
108. Mainländer, *Die Philosophie der Erlösung*, 1:575.
109. See, for example, Philipp Mainländer, "Aus meinem Leben," in *Schriften*, ed. Winfried H. Müller-Seyfarth (Hildesheim: Olms Verlag, 1996), 4:368; as cited in Beiser, *Weltschmerz*, 211.
110. Mainländer, *Die Philosophie der Erlösung*, 1:216.
111. Mainländer, *Die Philosophie der Erlösung*, 1:345.
112. Mainländer, *Die Philosophie der Erlösung*, 1:216.
113. Mainländer, *Die Philosophie der Erlösung*, 1:262.
114. Mainländer, *Die Philosophie der Erlösung*, 1:349.
115. Graham Greene, *The Comedians* (New York: Open Road Media, 2018), 122.
116. Mainländer, *Die Philosophie der Erlösung*, 1:245–46.
117. Mainländer, *Die Philosophie der Erlösung*, 1:593 and 349, respectively.
118. Mainländer, *Die Philosophie der Erlösung*, 1:575.
119. Mainländer, *Die Philosophie der Erlösung*, 1:357
120. See, for example, Mainländer, *Die Philosophie der Erlösung*, 1:57–58, 169.
121. Mainländer, *Die Philosophie der Erlösung*, 2:333.
122. Mainländer, *Die Philosophie der Erlösung*, 1:280.
123. Mainländer, *Die Philosophie der Erlösung*, 1:279, 281.
124. Mainländer, *Die Philosophie der Erlösung*, 2:305.
125. Mainländer, *Die Philosophie der Erlösung*, 2:305.
126. Mainländer, *Die Philosophie der Erlösung*, 2:306.
127. For more on the free love movement, see Lisa Cochran Higgins, "Adulterous Individualism, Socialism, and Free Love in Nineteenth-Century Anti-Suffrage Writing," *Legacy* 21, no. 2 (2004): 193–209; and Iain McCalman,

"Females, Feminism, and Free Love in an Early Nineteenth Century Radical Movement," *Labour History*, no. 38 (May 1980): 1–25.

128. Karen Offen, "Sur l'origine des mots 'féminisme' et 'féministe,'" *Revue d'Histoire Moderne et Contemporaine* 34, no. 3 (1987): 492–96.

129. Mainländer, *Die Philosophie der Erlösung*, 2:279.

130. Mainländer, *Die Philosophie der Erlösung*, 2:347.

131. Beiser, *Weltschmerz*, 203.

132. Mainländer, *Die Philosophie der Erlösung*, 1:218.

Chapter 10

1. Eugene Thacker, *Starry Speculative Corpse: Horror of Philosophy*, vol. 2 (Washington, DC: Zero Books, 2015), 127.

2. Eugene Thacker, *Infinite Resignation* (London: Repeater Books, 2018), 11.

3. Eugene Thacker, *In the Dust of This Planet: Horror of Philosophy*, vol. 1 (Washington, DC: Zero Books, 2011), 17.

4. Thacker, *In the Dust of This Planet*, 17; and Thacker, *Starry Speculative Corpse*, 14.

5. Thacker, *In the Dust of This Planet*, 17. Whether these modes of philosophizing avoid resurrecting the kinds of fanaticism which we decried as a necessary product of mystical thought in chapter 1 will be addressed later in this chapter.

6. See, for example, Thacker, *Starry Speculative Corpse*, 21, 36–38; and Thacker, *Infinite Resignation*, 260–72.

7. Thacker, *Starry Speculative Corpse*, 21.

8. Georges Bataille, *Visions of Excess: Selected Writings, 1927–1939*, ed. Allan Stoekl, trans. Allan Stoekl with Carl R. Lovitt and Donald M. Leslie, Jr. (Minneapolis: University of Minnesota Press, 1985), 16.

9. Bataille, *Visions of Excess*, 45, 32, and 51, respectively.

10. See, for example, Bataille, *Visions of Excess*, 15–16, 32.

11. Bataille, *Visions of Excess*, 16.

12. Bataille, *Visions of Excess*, 31. See also 43, 79.

13. Bataille, *Visions of Excess*, 179.

14. Bataille, *Visions of Excess*, 133.

15. Bataille, *Visions of Excess*, 133.

16. Bataille, *Visions of Excess*, 55, 101, respectively.

17. Bataille, *Visions of Excess*, 134.

18. Bataille, *Visions of Excess*, 31.

19. Georges Bataille, *Inner Experience*, trans. Stuart Kendall (Albany: State University of New York Press, 2014), 16, 57, 15, and 58–59, respectively.

20. Bataille, *Inner Experience*, 56.

21. Bataille, *Inner Experience*, 60.

22. Bataille, *Visions of Excess*, 179.

23. Bataille, *Inner Experience*, 63.

NOTES TO PAGES 248-253

24. Bataille, *Visions of Excess*, 49.
25. Bataille, *Inner Experience*, 45. See also Georges Bataille, *Literature and Evil*, trans. Alastair Hamilton (New York: Penguin Books, 2012), especially 18; and Georges Bataille, *The Impossible*, trans. Robert Hurley (San Francisco: City Lights Books, 2001), especially 10.
26. Georges Bataille, *Theory of Religion*, trans. Robert Hurley (New York: Zone Books, 1992), 32, 19, and 44, respectively.
27. Bataille, *Inner Experience*, 16.
28. Bataille, *Inner Experience*, 64. See also 50.
29. Bataille, *Visions of Excess*, 13.
30. Thacker, *Infinite Resignation*, 260–72.
31. Thacker, *Infinite Resignation*, 271.
32. Thacker, *Infinite Resignation*, 265.
33. E. M. Cioran, *A Short History of Decay*, trans. Richard Howard (New York: Arcade, 2012), 3.
34. Cioran, *A Short History of Decay*, 3.
35. Cioran, *A Short History of Decay*, 3.
36. Cioran, *A Short History of Decay*, 138.
37. Cioran, *A Short History of Decay*, 26.
38. Cioran, *A Short History of Decay*, 141.
39. Cioran, *A Short History of Decay*, 44.
40. Cioran, *A Short History of Decay*, 38. See also E. M. Cioran, *The Trouble with Being Born*, trans. Richard Howard (New York: Arcade, 2012), 190.
41. Cioran, *A Short History of Decay*, 40.
42. Cioran, *A Short History of Decay*, 38.
43. Cioran, *A Short History of Decay*, 29.
44. Cioran, *The Trouble with Being Born*, 16.
45. Cioran, *The Trouble with Being Born*, 176, 179, respectively.
46. Cioran, *The Trouble with Being Born*, 116.
47. Cioran, *A Short History of Decay*, 138.
48. Cioran, *A Short History of Decay*, 4, 3, respectively.
49. Cioran, *A Short History of Decay*, 8.
50. Cioran, *A Short History of Decay*, 9.
51. Cioran, *A Short History of Decay*, 7.
52. Cioran, *A Short History of Decay*, 23.
53. Cioran, *A Short History of Decay*, 23.
54. Cioran, *A Short History of Decay*, 72.
55. Cioran, *A Short History of Decay*, 162.
56. E. M. Cioran, *The Temptation to Exist*, trans. Richard Howard (New York: Arcade, 2012), 35.
57. See, for example, E. M. Cioran, *Tears and Saints*, trans. Ilinca Zarifopol-Johnston (Chicago: University of Chicago Press, 1998); Cioran, *A Short History of Decay*, 49; and Cioran, *The Temptation to Exist*, 151–64.
58. Cioran, *A Short History of Decay*, 64.
59. Cioran, *A Short History of Decay*, 89.
60. Cioran, *A Short History of Decay*, 4.

61. Cioran, *A Short History of Decay*, 10, 12, respectively.
62. See, for example, Cioran, *A Short History of Decay*, 27.
63. Thacker, *In the Dust of this Planet*, 8.
64. See, for example, Cioran, *A Short History of Decay*, 4.
65. Cioran, *The Temptation to Exist*, 35.
66. Cioran, *A Short History of Decay*, 104, 19, respectively.
67. On Buddhism, see, for example, Thacker, *Infinite Resignation*, 18–19; Georges Bataille, *The Accursed Share*, vol. 1, trans. Robert Hurley (New York: Zone Books, 1991), 93–110; and Cioran, *The Trouble with Being Born*, 4, 14.
68. Bataille, *Visions of Excess*, 32.
69. Bataille, *Visions of Excess*, 179.
70. See, for example, *Afropessimism: An Introduction*, ed. Frank B. Wilderson III, Saidiya Hartman, Steve Martinot, Jared Sexton, and Hortense J. Spillers (Minneapolis: Racked and Dispatched, 2017).
71. Frank B. Wilderson III, "Blacks and the Master/Slave Relation," in *Afropessimism: An Introduction*, ed. Frank B. Wilderson III, Saidiya Hartman, Steve Martinot, Jared Sexton, and Hortense J. Spillers (Minneapolis: Racked and Dispatched, 2017), 17–18.
72. See, for example, Orlando Patterson, *Slavery and Social Death: A Comparative Study* (Cambridge, MA: Harvard University Press, 2018), 38–45.
73. Saidiya Hartman, "The Burdened Individuality of Freedom," in *Afropessimism: An Introduction*, ed. Frank B. Wilderson III, Saidiya Hartman, Steve Martinot, Jared Sexton, and Hortense J. Spillers (Minneapolis: Racked and Dispatched, 2017), 32.
74. Frank B. Wilderson III, *Afropessimism* (New York: W. W. Norton, 2020), ix, 16; see also 164.
75. Wilderson III, *Afropessimism*, ix.
76. Wilderson III, *Afropessimism*, 41–42; see also 218–29.
77. Wilderson III, "Blacks and the Master/Slave Relation," 25.
78. Wilderson III, *Afropessimism*, 17.
79. Frank B. Wilderson III, "The Prison Slave as Hegemony's (Silent) Scandal," in *Afropessimism: An Introduction*, ed. Frank B. Wilderson III, Saidiya Hartman, Steve Martinot, Jared Sexton, and Hortense J. Spillers (Minneapolis: Racked and Dispatched, 2017), 67.
80. Wilderson III, *Afropessimism*, 40, 42, respectively.
81. See, for example, Hartman, "The Burdened Individuality of Freedom," 44, 46–67.
82. Wilderson III, "The Prison Slave as Hegemony's (Silent) Scandal," 77.
83. Calvin Warren, *Ontological Terror: Blackness, Nihilism, and Emancipation* (Durham, NC: Duke University Press, 2018), 5–6.
84. Warren, *Ontological Terror*, 47.
85. Warren, *Ontological Terror*, 32.
86. Warren, *Ontological Terror*, 6, 9–15, respectively.
87. Wilderson III, "The Prison Slave as Hegemony's (Silent) Scandal," 67; see also Wilderson III, *Afropessimism*, 102.
88. Wilderson III, "Blacks and the Master/Slave Relation," 18.

89. Wilderson III, *Afropessimism*, 226.
90. Frank B. Wilderson III, "The Vengeance of Vertigo: Aphasia and Abjection in the Political Trials of Black Insurgents," in *Afropessimism: An Introduction*, ed. Frank B. Wilderson III, Saidiya Hartman, Steve Martinot, Jared Sexton, and Hortense J. Spillers (Minneapolis: Racked and Dispatched, 2017), 145
91. Hartman, "The Burdened Individuality of Freedom," 39.
92. Wilderson III, *Afropessimism*, 42; see also 19, 217, 228–29.
93. Frantz Fanon, *Black Skin, White Masks*, trans. Richard Philcox (New York: Grove, 2008).
94. Frank B. Wilderson et al., "Editor's Introduction," in *Afropessimism: An Introduction*, ed. Frank B. Wilderson III, Saidiya Hartman, Steve Martinot, Jared Sexton, and Hortense J. Spillers (Minneapolis: Racked and Dispatched, 2017), 11.
95. Wilderson III, "Blacks and the Master/Slave Relation," 30.
96. Wilderson III, "Blacks and the Master/Slave Relation," 30.
97. Warren, *Ontological Terror*, 4–5, 7, 10.
98. Warren, *Ontological Terror*, 99, 108–13, respectively.
99. Meillassoux, *After Finitude*, 37.
100. Jean-François Lyotard, *The Inhuman: Reflections on Time*, trans. Geoffrey Bennington and Rachel Bowlby (Stanford, CA: Stanford University Press, 1991), 2. The fact of extinction is also a feature of Thacker's "cosmic pessimism." See, for example, Thacker, *In the Dust of This Planet*, 17, 120–26.
101. Lyotard, *The Inhuman*, 9.
102. Lyotard, *The Inhuman*, 9.
103. Lyotard, *The Inhuman*, 9.
104. Lyotard, *The Inhuman*, 8.
105. Lyotard, *The Inhuman*, 8.
106. Lyotard, *The Inhuman*, 9.
107. Lyotard, *The Inhuman*, 9.
108. Lyotard, *The Inhuman*, 9.
109. Lyotard, *The Inhuman*, 10.
110. Ray Brassier, *Nihil Unbound: Enlightenment and Extinction* (Basingstoke, UK: Palgrave Macmillan, 2007), 223, 228.
111. Brassier, *Nihil Unbound*, 229.
112. Brassier, *Nihil Unbound*, 229.
113. Brassier, *Nihil Unbound*, 229–30.
114. Brassier, *Nihil Unbound*, 238.
115. Brassier, *Nihil Unbound*, 230.
116. Brassier, *Nihil Unbound*, xi.
117. Brassier, *Nihil Unbound*, xi.
118. See, for example, Brassier, *Nihil Unbound*, chapters 4 and 5, respectively.
119. See, for example, Brassier's footnote on Laurelle's attempts at erecting a new ethics and politics: Brassier, *Nihil Unbound*, 132, 152n19.

Conclusion

1. For more on how a reading of the fundamental power of entropy might be productive of a new ethical and political order, see Mussett, *Entropic Philosophy*.
2. Samuel Beckett, "Worstword Ho," in *Company / Ill Seen Ill Said / Worstword Ho / Stirrings Still*, ed. Dirk Van Hulle (London: Faber and Faber, 2009), 81–103.
3. Beckett, "Worstword Ho," 81.
4. Alfred Lord Tennyson, "Ulysses," in *Tennyson: Poems* (New York: Alfred A. Knopf, 2004), 90.

Bibliography

Abelsen, Peter. "Schopenhauer and Buddhism." *Philosophy East and West* 43, no. 2 (1993): 255–78.
Adams, Fred, and Greg Laughlin. *The Five Ages of the Universe: Inside the Physics of Eternity*. New York: Touchstone Books, 1999.
Allais, Lucy. "Kant's Racism." *Philosophical Papers* 45 (2016): 1–36.
Allison, Henry E. *Kant's Transcendental Idealism: An Interpretation and Defense*. New Haven, CT: Yale University Press, 1983.
Altman, Matthew. "The Limits of Kant's Cosmopolitanism: Theory, Practice, and the Crisis in Syria." *Kantian Review* 22, no. 2 (2017): 179–204.
Aquinas, Thomas. *Aquinas's Shorter Summa*, trans. Cyril Vollert. Manchester, NH: Sophia Institute, 2002.
Arendt, Hannah. *Eichmann in Jerusalem: A Report on the Banality of Evil*. New York: Penguin Books, 1963.
Atkins, Peter. *Conjuring the Universe: The Origins of the Laws of Nature*. Oxford: Oxford University Press, 2018.
———. *Four Laws That Drive the Universe*. Oxford: Oxford University Press, 2007.
Augustine. *The City of God*, trans. Marcus Dods. New York: Modern Library, 2000.
———. *Enchiridion on Faith, Hope, and Love*, trans. Albert C. Outler. Aeterna, 2014.
———. *On Free Choice of the Will*, trans. Thomas Williams. Indianapolis: Hackett, 1993.
Azeri, Siyaves. "Transcendental Subject vs. Empirical Self: On Kant's Account of Subjectivity." *Filozofia* 65, no. 3 (2010): 269–83.
Babich, Babette E. "Nietzsche's Chaos Sive Natura: Evening Gold and the Dancing Star." *Revista Portuguesa de Filosofia* 57, no. 2 (2001): 225–45.
Badiou, Alain. *Being and Event*, trans. Oliver Feltham. London: Bloomsbury, 2013.
———. "Being-There: Mathematics of the Transcendental." In *Mathematics of the Transcendental*, ed. and trans. A. J. Bartlett and Alex Ling, 163–268. London: Bloomsbury, 2014.
———. *Ethics: An Essay on the Understanding of Evil*, trans. Peter Hallward. London: Verso, 2001.
———. *In Praise of Mathematics*, with Gilles Haéri, trans. Susan Spitzer. Cambridge: Polity, 2016.
———. "Interview (with Ben Woodward)." In *The Speculative Turn: Continental Materialism and Realism*, ed. Levi Bryant, Nick Srnicek, and Graham Harman, 19–20. Melbourne: re.press, 2011.
———. "Mathematics and Philosophy: The Grand Style and the Little Style." In

Theoretical Writings, ed. and trans. Ray Brassier and Alberto Toscano, 3–20. London: Continuum, 2004.

———. *Number and Numbers*, trans Robin Mackay. Cambridge: Polity, 2008.

———. "Politics and Philosophy: An Interview with Alain Badiou." In *Ethics: An Essay on the Understanding of Evil*, trans. Peter Hallward, 95–142. London: Verso, 2001.

———. Preface to *After Finitude: An Essay on the Necessity of Contingency*, by Quentin Meillassoux, trans. Ray Brassier. London: Bloomsbury, 2008.

———. *Theory of the Subject*, trans. Bruno Bosteels. London: Continuum, 2009.

———. "Topos, or Logics of Onto-Logy: An Introduction for Philosophers." In *Mathematics of the Transcendental*, ed. and trans. A. J. Bartlett and Alex Ling, 11–161. London: Bloomsbury, 2014.

Ball, Philip. "How Life (and Death) Spring from Disorder." *Quanta Magazine*, January 26, 2017.

Bataille, Georges. *The Accursed Share*, vol. 1, trans. Robert Hurley. New York: Zone Books, 1991.

———. *The Impossible*, trans. Robert Hurley. San Francisco: City Lights Books, 2001.

———. *Inner Experience*, trans. Stuart Kendall. Albany: State University of New York Press, 2014.

———. *Literature and Evil*, trans. Alastair Hamilton. New York: Penguin Books, 2012.

———. *Theory of Religion*, trans. Robert Hurley. New York: Zone Books, 1992.

———. *Visions of Excess: Selected Writings, 1927–1939*, ed. Allan Stoekl, trans. Allan Stoekl with Carl R. Lovitt and Donald M. Leslie, Jr. Minneapolis: University of Minnesota Press, 1985.

Beckett, Samuel. "Worstword Ho." In *Company / Ill Seen Ill Said / Worstword Ho / Stirings Still*, ed. Dirk Van Hulle, 81–103. London: Faber and Faber, 2009.

Beiser, Frederick C. *Weltschmerz: Pessimism in German Philosophy, 1860–1900*. Oxford: Oxford University Press, 2016.

Bentham, Jeremy. *An Introduction to the Principles of Morals and Legislation*. Mineola, NY: Dover, 2007.

Bernasconi, Robert. "Who Invented the Concept of Race? Kant's Role in the Enlightenment Construction of Race." In *Race*, ed. Robert Bernasconi, 11–36. Oxford: Blackwell, 2001.

Bigelow, John. *The Reality of Numbers: A Physicalist's Philosophy of Mathematics*. Oxford: Clarendon, 1988.

Bird, Graham. *The Revolutionary Kant: A Commentary on the Critique of Pure Reason*. Peru, IL: Open Court, 2006.

Blackmore, John, ed. *Ludwig Boltzmann: His Later Life and Philosophy, 1900–1906, Book I: A Documentary History*. Dordrecht: Kluwer/Springer, 1995.

Bodhi, Bhikku, trans. *The Connected Discourses of the Buddha: A Translation of the Saṃyutta Nikāya*. Boston: Wisdom Publications, 2000.

Boltzmann, Ludwig. "On a Thesis of Schopenhauer's." In *Theoretical Physics and Philosophical Problems*, ed. Brian McGuinness, trans. Paul Foulkes, 193–95. Dordrecht: D. Reidell, 1974.

Brann, Henry Walter. "Schopenhauer and Spinoza." *Journal of the History of Philosophy* 10, no. 2 (April 1972): 181–96.
Brassier, Ray. *Nihil Unbound: Enlightenment and Extinction*. Basingstoke, UK: Palgrave Macmillan, 2007.
Bruno, G. Anthony. "Jacobi's Dare: McDowell, Meillassoux, and Consistent Idealism." In *Idealism, Relativism, and Realism: New Essays on Objectivity beyond the Analytic-Continental Divide*, ed. Dominik Finkelde and Paul M. Livingston, 35–66. Boston: De Gruyter, 2020.
Bryant, Levi, Nick Srnicek, and Graham Harmon. "Towards a Speculative Philosophy." In *The Speculative Turn: Continental Materialism and Realism*, ed. Levi Bryant, Nick Srnicek, and Graham Harman, 1–18. Melbourne: re.press, 2011.
Camus, Albert. *The Myth of Sisyphus and Other Essays*, trans. Justin O'Brien. New York: Vintage International, 1991.
Carlile, Clarie. "Spinoza's *Acquiescentia*." *Journal of the History of Philosophy* 55, no. 2 (2017): 209–36.
Carroll, Sean. *The Big Picture: On the Origins of Life, Meaning, and the Universe Itself*. New York: Penguin, 2016.
Chilcott, C. M. "The Platonic Theory of Evil." *Classical Quarterly* 17, no. 1 (1923): 27–31.
Cioran, E. M. *A Short History of Decay*, trans. Richard Howard. New York: Arcade, 2012.
———. *Tears and Saints*, trans. Ilinca Zarifopol-Johnston. Chicago: University of Chicago Press, 1998.
———. *The Temptation to Exist*, trans. Richard Howard. New York: Arcade, 2012.
———. *The Trouble with Being Born*, trans. Richard Howard. New York: Arcade, 2012.
Cockell, Charles S. "The Laws of Life." *Physics Today*, vol. 70 (March 2017): 43–48.
Cooper, David E. "Buddhism as Pessimism." *Journal of World Philosophies* 6 (Winter 2021): 1–16.
Crick, Francis. *Life Itself*. New York: Simon and Schuster, 1981.
Dalton, Drew M. *The Ethics of Resistance: Tyranny of the Absolute*. London: Bloomsbury, 2018.
Dawkins, Richard. Afterword to *A Universe from Nothing: Why There Is Something Rather Than Nothing*, by Lawrence M. Krauss. New York: Atria Books, 2012.
Einstein, Albert. *Autobiographical Notes*, trans. and ed. Paul Arthur Schilpp. Chicago: Open Court, 1991.
England, Jeremy. "Dissipative Adaptation in Drive Self-Assembly." *Nature and Nanotechnology*, vol. 10 (November 2015): 919–23.
———. *Every Life Is on Fire: How Thermodynamics Explains the Origins of Living Things*. New York: Basic Books, 2020.
———. "Statistical Physics of Self-Replication." *Journal of Chemical Physics*, vol. 139 (2013): 139–46.
Epictetus. *Discourses and Selected Writings*, trans. and ed. Robert Dobbin. London: Penguin Books, 2008.

BIBLIOGRAPHY

Fanon, Frantz. *Black Skin, White Masks*, trans. Richard Philcox. New York: Grove, 2008.

Farmelo, Graham. *The Universe Speaks in Numbers: How Modern Math Reveals Nature's Deepest Secrets.* New York: Hachette Book Group, 2019.

Feuerbach, Ludwig. *The Essence of Christianity*, trans. George Eliot. New York: Cosimo Classics, 2008.

Feynman, Richard P. "The Relation of Physics to Other Sciences." In *Six Easy Pieces: Essentials of Physics Explained by Its Most Brilliant Teacher*, by Richard P. Feynman, Robert B. Leighton, and Matthew Sands. Philadelphia: Basic Books, 2011.

Flikschuh, Katrin, and Lea Ypi, eds. *Kant and Colonialism: Historical and Critical Perspectives.* Oxford: Oxford University Press, 2014.

Frautschi, Steven. "Entropy in an Expanding Universe." *Science* 2017, no. 4560 (August 13, 1982): 593–99.

Freud, Sigmund. *Beyond the Pleasure Principle*, trans. James Strachey. New York: W. W. Norton, 1961.

Fronsdal, Gil, trans. *The Dhammapada: A New Translation of the Buddhist Classic with Annotations.* Boston: Shambhala, 2006.

Galilei, Galileo. "The Assayer." In *The Essential Galileo*, ed. and trans. Maurice F. Finocchiaro. Indianapolis: Hackett, 2008.

Gardner, Sebastian. *Routledge Guidebook to Kant and the Critique of Pure Reason.* New York: Routledge, 1999.

Glick Schiller, Nina, and Andrew Irving, eds. *Whose Cosmopolitanism? Critical Perspectives, Relationalities, and Discontents.* Oxford: Berghahn Books, 2017.

Go, Kenji. "Montaigne's 'Cannibals' and 'The Tempest' Revisited." *Studies in Philology* 109, no. 4 (2012): 455–73.

Greene, Brian. *The Fabric of the Cosmos: Space, Time, and the Texture of Reality.* New York: Alfred A. Knopf, 2004.

Greene, Graham. *The Comedians.* New York: Open Road Media, 2018.

Hackforth, R. "Moral Evil and Ignorance in Plato's Ethics." *Classical Quarterly* 40, no. 3–4 (July–October 1946): 118–20.

Hanlon, Robert. *Block by Block: The Historical and Theoretical Foundations of Thermodynamics.* Oxford: Oxford University Press, 2020.

Hartman, Saidiya. "The Burdened Individuality of Freedom." In *Afropessimism: An Introduction*, ed. Frank B. Wilderson III, Saidiya Hartman, Steve Martinot, Jared Sexton, and Hortense J. Spillers, 31–48. Minneapolis: Racked and Dispatched, 2017.

Harvey, David. *Cosmopolitanism and the Geographies of Freedom.* New York: Columbia University Press, 2009.

Havel, Vaclav. "Letter to Dr. Gustav Husak." In *Vaclav Havel: Living in Truth*, 23. London: Faber and Faber, 2000.

Hawking, Stephen. *The Illustrated A Brief History of Time.* New York: Bantam Books, 1996.

Heidegger, Martin. *Being and Time*, trans. John Macquarrie and Edward Robinson. New York: Harper and Row, 1962.

———. "Nietzsche's Word: 'God Is Dead.'" In *Off the Beaten Track*, ed. and trans.

BIBLIOGRAPHY

Julian Young and Kenneth Haynes, 157–99. Cambridge: Cambridge University Press, 2002.

———. *Schelling's Treatise on the Essence of Human Freedom*, trans. Joan Stambaugh. Athens: Ohio University Press, 1985.

Higgins, Lisa Cochran. "Adulterous Individualism, Socialism, and Free Love in Nineteenth-Century Anti-Suffrage Writing." *Legacy* 21, no. 2 (2004): 193–209.

Hoffmann, Peter M. *Life's Ratchet: How Molecular Machines Extract Order from Chaos.* New York: Basic Books, 2012.

Hume, David. *A Treatise of Human Nature*, ed. Ernest C. Mossner. London: Penguin Books, 1969.

Izzi, John. "Proximity in Distance: Levinas and Plotinus." In *Levinas and the Ancients*, ed. Brian Schroeder and Silvia Benso, 196–209. Bloomington: Indiana University Press, 2008.

Jarrett, Charles. "Spinoza on the Relativity of Good and Evil." In *Spinoza: Metaphysical Themes*, ed. Olli Koistinen and John Biro, 159–81. Oxford: Oxford University Press, 2002.

Johnson, Eric. *Anxiety and the Equation: Understanding Boltzmann's Entropy.* Cambridge, MA: MIT Press, 2018.

Kant, Immanuel. "An Answer to the Question: 'What Is Enlightenment?'" In *Kant: Political Writings*, 54–60. Cambridge: Cambridge University Press, 1970.

———. *Critique of Practical Reason*, trans. Mary Gregor. Cambridge: Cambridge University Press, 2015.

———. *Critique of Pure Reason*, trans. and ed. Paul Guyer and Allen W. Wood. Cambridge: Cambridge University Press, 1998.

———. *Groundwork of the Metaphysics of Morals*, trans. and ed. Mary Gregor and Jens Timmermann. Cambridge: Cambridge University Press, 2012.

———. *Practical Philosophy*, trans. and ed. Mary J. Gregor. Cambridge: Cambridge University Press, 1996.

———. *Prolegomena to Any Future Metaphysics*, trans. and ed. Gary Hatfield. Cambridge: Cambridge University Press, 1997.

———. *Religion within the Boundaries of Mere Reason*, ed. Alan Wood and George di Giovanni. Cambridge: Cambridge University Press, 1998.

Keown, Damien. "Buddhism and Ecology: A Virtue Ethics Approach." *Contemporary Buddhism* 8, no. 2 (2007): 97–112.

Kleingeld, Pauline. "Kant's Second Thoughts on Colonialism." In *Kant and Colonialism: Historical and Critical Perspectives*, ed. Katrin Flikschuh and Lea Ypi, 43–67. Oxford: Oxford University Press, 2014.

———. "Kant's Second Thoughts on Race." *Philosophical Quarterly* 57, no. 229 (2007): 573–99.

Kontos, Paul, ed. *Evil in Aristotle.* Cambridge: Cambridge University Press, 2018.

Krauss, Lawrence M. *A Universe from Nothing: Why There Is Something Rather Than Nothing.* New York: Atria Books, 2012.

Krauss, Lawrence M., and Glenn D. Starkman. "The Fate of Life in the Universe." *Scientific American* (November 1999): 58–65.

Lacombe, Oliver. "Buddhist Pessimism." In *Buddhist Studies in Honor of W. Rahula*, ed. Somaratna Balasooriya, 113–17. London: Roundwound, 1980.
Ladyman, James, and Don Ross. *Every Thing Must Go: Metaphysics Naturalized*, with David Spurrett and John Collier. Oxford: Oxford University Press, 2007.
Lane, Nick. *The Vital Question: Energy, Evolution, and the Origins of Complex Life*. New York: W. W. Norton, 2016.
Latzer, Michael. "Leibniz's Conception of Metaphysical Evil." *Journal of the History of Ideas* 55, no. 1 (1994): 1–15.
Leiter, Brian. *Nietzsche on Morality*. London: Routledge, 2002.
Levinas, Emmanuel. *Alterity and Transcendence*, trans. Michael B. Smith. New York: Columbia University Press, 1999.
———. *Existence and Existents*, trans. Alphonso Lingis. Pittsburgh: Duquesne University Press, 2001.
———. "Meaning and Sense." In *Basic Philosophical Writings*, ed. Adriaan T. Peperzak, Simon Critchley, and Robert Bernasconi, 33–64. Bloomington: Indiana University Press, 1996.
———. *Time and the Other*, trans. Richard A Cohen. Pittsburgh: Duquesne University Press, 1987.
———. *Totality and Infinity: An Essay on Exteriority*, trans. Alphonso Lingis. Pittsburgh: Duquesne University Press, 1969.
———. "Transcendence and Evil." In *Collected Philosophical Papers*, trans. Alphonso Lingis, 175–86. Pittsburgh: Duquesne University Press, 1998.
Lightman, Alan. *The Accidental Universe: The World You Thought You Knew*. New York: Pantheon Books, 2013.
Ling, Trevor Oswald. *Buddhism and the Mythology of Evil: A Study in Theravada Buddhism*. London: Allen and Unwin, 1962.
Lyotard, Jean-François. *The Inhuman: Reflections on Time*, trans. Geoffrey Bennington and Rachel Bowlby. Stanford, CA: Stanford University Press, 1991.
Mack, Katie. *The End of Everything (Astrophysically Speaking)*. New York: Scribner, 2020.
Mainländer, Philipp. "Aus meinem Leben." In *Schriften*, vol. 4., ed. Winfried H. Müller-Seyfarth. Hildesheim: Olms Verlag, 1996.
———. *Die Philosophie der Erlösung*. Berlin: Grieben, 1876.
———. *Die Philosophie der Erlösung, II: Zwölf philosophischer Essays*. Frankfurt: C. Koenitzer, 1886, 2nd edition, 1984.
Margulis, Lynn, and Dorion Sagan. *What Is Life?* Berkeley: University of California Press, 1995.
Marwah, Inder S. *Liberalism, Diversity, and Domination: Kant, Mill, and the Government of Difference*. Cambridge: Cambridge University Press, 2019.
McCalman, Iain. "Females, Feminism, and Free Love in an Early Nineteenth-Century Radical Movement." *Labour History*, no. 38 (May 1980): 1–25.
McFadden, Johnjoe, and Jim Al-Khalili. *Life on the Edge: The Coming Age of Quantum Biology*. New York: Crown, 2014.
Meillassoux, Quentin. *After Finitude: An Essay on the Necessity of Contingency*, trans. Ray Brassier. London: Bloomsbury, 2008.
———. "Appendix: Excerpts from *L'Inexistence divine*." In *Quentin Meillassoux: Phi-*

BIBLIOGRAPHY

losophy in the Making, by Graham Harman, 175–238. Edinburgh: Edinburgh University Press, 2011.

———. "Interview with Quentin Meillassoux (August 2010)," trans. Graham Harman. In *Quentin Meillassoux: Philosophy in the Making*, by Graham Harman, 159–74. Edinburgh: Edinburgh University Press, 2011.

———. *Science Fiction and Extro-Science Fiction*, trans. Alyosha Edlebi. Minneapolis: Univocal Publishing, 2015.

———. *Time without Becoming*, ed. Anna Longo. Italy: Mimesis International, 2014.

Mills, Charles. "Kant's Untermenschen." In *Race and Racism in Modern Philosophy*, ed. Andrew Valls, 169–93. Ithaca, NY: Cornell University Press, 2005.

Molina, Eduardo. "Kant's Conception of the Subject." *CR: The New Centennial Review* 17, no. 2 (2017): 77–94.

Monod, Jacques. *Chance and Necessity: An Essay on the Natural Philosophy of Modern Biology*, trans. Austryn Wainhouse. New York: Vintage Books, 1971.

Montaigne, Michel de. *Michel de Montaigne: The Complete Essays*, trans. and ed. M. A. Screech. London: Penguin Books, 1997.

Moore, G. E. *Ethica*, ed. Thomas Baldwin. Cambridge: Cambridge University Press, 1993.

Mussett, Shannon. *Entropic Philosophy: Chaos, Breakdown, and Creation*. London: Rowan and Littlefield, 2022.

Nadler, Steven. *A Book Forged in Hell: Spinoza's Scandalous Treatise and the Birth of the Secular Age*. Princeton, NJ: Princeton University Press, 2011.

Ñāṇamoli, Bhikkhu, and Bhikkhu Bodhi, trans. *The Middle Length Discourses of the Buddha: A Translation of the Majjhihima Nikāya*. Boston: Wisdom Publications, 1995.

Nietzsche, Friedrich. "Beyond Good and Evil." In *Beyond Good and Evil / On the Genealogy of Morality*, trans. Adrian Del Caro, 1–205. Stanford, CA: Stanford University Press, 2014.

———. *Dawn: Thoughts on the Presumptions of Morality*, trans. Brittain Smith. Stanford, CA: Stanford University Press, 2011.

———. "Ecce Homo." In *The Anti-Christ, Ecce Homo, Twilight of the Idols, and Other Writings*, ed. Aaron Ridley and Judith Norman, trans. Judith Norman, 69–152. Cambridge: Cambridge University Press, 2005.

———. *The Gay Science*, ed. Bernard Williams, trans. Josefine Nauckhoff and Adrian Del Caro. Cambridge: Cambridge University Press, 2001.

———. *Human, All Too Human (I)*, trans. Gary Handwerk. Stanford, CA: Stanford University Press, 1995.

———. *Nietzsche Werke: Kritische Studienausgabe*, vol. 9, *Nachgelassene Fragmente 1880–1882*, ed. Giorgio Colli and Mazzino Montinari. Berlin: Walter de Gruyter, 1980.

———. "On the Genealogy of Morals." In *Beyond Good and Evil / On the Genealogy of Morality*, trans. Adrian Del Caro, 206–351. Stanford, CA: Stanford University Press, 2014.

———. *Selected Letters of Friedrich Nietzsche*, ed. and trans. Christopher Middleton. Chicago: University of Chicago Press, 1969.

———. "Schopenhauer as Educator." In *Untimely Meditations*, ed. Daniel

Breazeale, trans. R. J. Hollingdale, 125–94. Cambridge: Cambridge University Press, 1997.

———. *Thus Spoke Zarathustra*, ed. Adrian Del Caro and Robert B. Pippin, trans. Adrian Del Caro. Cambridge: Cambridge University Press, 2006.

———. "Twilight of the Idols." In *The Anti-Christ, Ecce Homo, Twilight of the Idols, and Other Writings*, ed. Aaron Ridley and Judith Norman, trans. Judith Norman, 153–230. Cambridge: Cambridge University Press, 2005.

———. *The Will to Power*, trans. Walter Kaufmann and R. J. Hollingdale. New York: Random House, 1967.

Offen, Karen. "Sur l'origine des mots 'féminisme' et 'féministe.'" *Revue d'Histoire Moderne et Contemporaine* 34, no. 3 (1987): 492–96.

O'Rourke, Fran. "Evil as Privation: The Neo-Platonic Background of Aquinas' *De Malo*." In *Aquinas's Disputed Questions on Evil*, ed. M. V. Dougherty, 192–221. Cambridge: Cambridge University Press, 2015.

Ott, J. Bevan, and Juliana Boerio-Goates. *Chemical Thermodynamics: Principles and Applications*. Amsterdam: Elsevier, 2000.

Parens, Joshua. *Maimonides and Spinoza: Their Conflicting Views on Human Nature*. Chicago: University of Chicago Press, 2012.

Patterson, Orlando. *Slavery and Social Death: A Comparative Study*. Cambridge, MA: Harvard University Press, 2018.

Plotinus, *The Enneads*, ed. Lloyd P. Gerson, trans. George Boys-Stones, John M. Dillon, Lloyd P. Gerson, R. A. H. King, Andrew Smith, and James Wilberding. Cambridge: Cambridge University Press, 2018.

Pross, Addy. *What Is Life? How Chemistry Becomes Biology*. Oxford: Oxford University Press, 2012.

Reginster, Bernard. *The Affirmation of Life: Nietzsche on Overcoming Nihilism*. Cambridge, MA: Harvard University Press, 2009.

Richardson, John. *Nietzsche's New Darwinism*. Oxford: Oxford University Press, 2004.

Rosen, Joe. *The Capricious Cosmos: Universe beyond Law*. New York: Macmillan, 1991.

Rousseau, Jean-Jacques. "Letter from J. J. Rousseau to M. de Voltaire." In *Rousseau: The Discourses and Other Early Political Writings*, ed. and trans. Victor Gourevitch, 232–46. Cambridge: Cambridge University Press, 1997.

Rovelli, Carlo. *Seven Brief Lessons on Physics*, trans. Simon Carnell and Erica Segre. New York: Riverhead Books, 2014.

Saddhatissa, H., trans. *The Sutta-Nipāta*. London: Routledge, 1985.

Sartre, Jean-Paul. *Existentialism Is a Humanism*, trans. Carol Macomber. New Haven, CT: Yale University Press, 2007.

Schelling, F. W. J. *Philosophical Investigations into the Essence of Human Freedom*, trans. Jeff Love and Johannes Schmidt. Albany: State University of New York Press, 2006.

Schneider, Eric D., and Dorion Sagan. *Into the Cool: Energy Flow, Thermodynamics, and Life*. Chicago: University of Chicago Press, 2002.

Schopenhauer, Arthur. "The Critique of Kantian Philosophy." In *The World as Will and Representation*, vol. 1, trans. and ed. Judith Norman, Alistair Welch-

BIBLIOGRAPHY

man, and Christopher Janaway, 441–556. Cambridge: Cambridge University Press, 2010.

———. "On Will in Nature." In *On the Fourfold Root of the Principle of Sufficient Reason and Other Writings*, trans. and ed. David E. Cartwright, Edward E. Erdmann, and Christopher Janaway, 303–448. Cambridge: Cambridge University Press, 2012.

———. *Parerga and Paralipomena: Short Philosophical Essays*, vol. 2, trans. and ed. Adrian Del Caro and Christopher Janaway. Cambridge: Cambridge University Press, 2015.

———. "Prize Essay on the Basis of Morals." In *The Two Fundamental Problems of Ethics*, trans. and ed. Christopher Janaway, 113–258. Cambridge: Cambridge University Press, 2009.

———. "Prize Essay on the Freedom of the Will." In *The Two Fundamental Problems of Ethics*, trans. and ed. Christopher Janaway, 31–112. Cambridge: Cambridge University Press, 2009.

———. *The World as Will and Representation*, vol. I, trans. and ed. Judith Norman, Alistair Welchman, and Christopher Janaway. Cambridge: Cambridge University Press, 2010.

Schrödinger, Erwin. *What Is Life? The Physical Aspects of the Living Cell*. Cambridge: Cambridge University Press, 1967.

Schroeder, Brian. "A Trace of the Eternal Return: Levinas and Neoplatonism." In *Levinas and the Ancients*, ed. Brian Schroeder and Silvia Benso, 210–29. Bloomington: Indiana University Press, 2008.

Seneca. *The Stoic Philosophy of Seneca*, trans. Moses Hadas. New York: W. W. Norton, 1958.

Shakespeare, William. "The Tragedy of Hamlet, Prince of Denmark." In *The Oxford Shakespeare: The Complete Works*, ed. Stanley Wells and Gary Taylor, 681–718. Oxford: Oxford University Press, 2008.

Sinclair, Neil, ed. *The Naturalistic Fallacy*. Cambridge: Cambridge University Press, 2019.

Sokal, Alan, and Jean Bricmont. *Fashionable Nonsense: Post-Modern Intellectuals' Abuse of Science*. New York: Picador, 1998.

Sommer, Andreas Urs. "Nietzsche's Readings on Spinoza: A Contextualist Study, Particularly on the Reception of Kuno Fischer." *Journal of Nietzsche Studies* 43, no. 2 (2012): 156–84.

Spinoza, Baruch. *Ethics—Proved in Geometrical Order*, ed. Matthew J. Kisner, trans. Michael Silverthorne and Matthew J. Kisner. Cambridge: Cambridge University Press, 2018.

———. "Letter 43." In *Spinoza: Complete Works*, trans. Samuel Shirley, ed. Michael L Morgan, 871. Indianapolis: Hackett, 2002.

———. *Theological-Political Treatise*, ed. Jonathan Israel, trans. Michael Silverthorne and Jonathan Israel. Cambridge: Cambridge University Press, 2007.

Stambaugh, Joan. "*Amor Dei* and *Amor Fati*: Spinoza and Nietzsche." In *Studies in Nietzsche and the Judaeo-Christian Tradition*, ed. James O'Flaherty,

Timothy F. Sellner, and Robert M. Helm, 130–42. Chapel Hill: University of North Carolina Press, 1985.

Tegmark, Max. *Our Mathematical Universe: My Quest for the Ultimate Nature of Reality*. New York: Vintage Books, 2014.

Tennyson, Alfred Lord. "Ulysses." In *Tennyson: Poems*, 88–90. New York: Alfred A. Knopf, 2004.

Thacker, Eugene. *Infinite Resignation*. London: Repeater Books, 2018.

———. *In the Dust of This Planet: Horror of Philosophy*, vol. 1. Washington, DC: Zero Books, 2011.

———. *Starry Speculative Corpse: Horror of Philosophy*, vol. 2. Washington, DC: Zero Books, 2015.

Tritten, Tyler. *The Contingency of Necessity: Reason and God as Matters of Fact*. Edinburgh: Edinburgh University Press, 2017.

Varden, Helga. "Kant and Women." *Pacific Philosophical Quarterly*, vol. 98 (2017): 653–94.

Voltaire. "The Lisbon Earthquake." In *The Portable Voltaire*, ed. Ben Ray Redman, 560–69. New York: Penguin Books, 1977.

von Neumann, John. *Mathematical Foundations of Quantum Mechanics*, trans. Robert T. Beyer, ed. Nicholas A. Wheeler. Princeton, NJ: Princeton University Press, 2018.

Wagner, Cosima. *Cosima Wagner's Diaries: 1869–1877*, vol. 1, ed. Martin Gregor-Dellin and Deitrich Mack, trans. Geoffrey Skelton. San Diego, CA: Harcourt Brace Jovanovich, 1978.

Walker, Ralph C. S., ed. *Kant on Pure Reason*. Oxford: Oxford University Press, 1982.

Walshe, Maurice, trans. *The Long Discourses of the Buddha: A Translation of the Dīgha Nikāya*. Boston: Wisdom Publications, 1995.

Warren, Calvin. *Ontological Terror: Blackness, Nihilism, and Emancipation*. Durham, NC: Duke University Press, 2018.

Whitehead, A. N. *Religion in the Making: Lowell Lectures, 1926*. Cambridge: Cambridge University Press, 1996.

Wilczek, Frank. *Fundamentals: Ten Keys to Reality*. New York: Penguin, 2021.

Wilderson III, Frank B. *Afropessimism*. New York: W. W. Norton, 2020.

———. "Blacks and the Master/Slave Relation." In *Afropessimism: An Introduction*, ed. Frank B. Wilderson III, Saidiya Hartman, Steve Martinot, Jared Sexton, and Hortense J. Spillers, 15–30. Minneapolis: Racked and Dispatched, 2017.

———. "The Prison Slave as Hegemony's (Silent) Scandal." In *Afropessimism: An Introduction*, ed. Frank B. Wilderson III, Saidiya Hartman, Steve Martinot, Jared Sexton, and Hortense J. Spillers, 67–79. Minneapolis: Racked and Dispatched, 2017.

———. "The Vengeance of Vertigo: Aphasia and Abjection in the Political Trials of Black Insurgents." In *Afropessimism: An Introduction*, ed. Frank B. Wilderson III, Saidiya hHartman, Steve Martinot, Jared Sexton, and Hortense J. Spillers, 123–47. Minneapolis: Racked and Dispatched, 2017.

Wilderson III, Frank B., et al. "Editor's Introduction." In *Afropessimism: An Intro-*

duction, ed. Frank B. Wilderson III, Saidiya Hartman, Steve Martinot, Jared Sexton, and Hortense J. Spillers, 7–14. Minneapolis: Racked and Dispatched, 2017.

Wilderson III, Frank B., Saidiya Hartman, Steve Martinot, Jared Sexton, and Hortense J. Spillers, eds. *Afropessimism: An Introduction*. Minneapolis: Racked and Dispatched, 2017.

Yeats, William Butler. "The Second Coming." In *The Collected Poems of W. B. Yeats*, 158. London: Wordsworth Editions, 1994.

Yovel, Yirmiyahu. "Nietzsche and Spinoza: *Amor Fati* and *Amor Dei*." In *Nietzsche as Affirmative Thinker*, ed. Yirmiyahu Yovel, 183–203. Dordrecht: Springer, 1986.

Index

absence, 54, 80, 112, 225; as presence, 10, 132–34; of thought, 269; of value, 126, 127–29, 131–32, 135, 211, 275, 279. *See also* annihilation; being: non-being/void; nothing; void
absolute, 13–16, 19, 21, 29–31, 33–38, 41–47, 50–55, 63–65; being/reality, 9, 13, 20, 29–30, 34–36, 45–50, 61, 65–66, 70–71, 74, 85, 118, 135, 150, 169–72, 187, 218, 236, 266, 271, 276; truth, 1–2, 28, 54–55, 60, 63–64, 73, 111, 188, 199, 231–32, 246–47, 251–52, 277–78; value, 54–56, 88, 114, 121, 151–56, 160, 170, 185, 189, 193–94, 202, 204, 208, 212, 217, 260, 284
acquiescence, 162–63, 279, 302n18, 303n33; as complicity, 161; as virtue, 151, 154, 157, 159, 207
aestheticism, 17, 185, 204, 252–53
Afropessimism, 256, 259, 261–66, 273, 274
ancestral, 49–55, 58, 64. *See also* fossil matter
animals, 89, 140, 170, 173, 183–84
annihilation, 106, 109–14, 136, 161, 178, 207, 212, 223, 231–33, 246, 267–78, 284–85. *See also* being: non-being/void; nothing; void
Aquinas, Thomas, 89, 128–29, 155
Arendt, Hannah, 129
Augustine, 121, 128, 155

Badiou, Alain, 48, 77–84, 111, 115, 189, 265, 269, 271; on mathematics; 68–71, 73–74, 85–88, 95–97, 100, 118, 120
Bataille, Georges, 16, 246–49, 254–56, 259
Beckett, Samuel, 285
being, 14, 29, 49, 52, 57, 60, 69–71, 73, 80, 171, 263–64, 277; as becoming, 56, 64, 76–77, 110, 112–14, 197–99, 206, 208; essence of, 79–80, 107, 111, 114, 130–31, 134–35, 144–45, 161, 171, 178, 197–99, 231–33, 270, 277, 308n60; as event, 78–82; as evil, 130–33, 135–39, 161–63, 176, 180–82, 209, 211–18, 221–22, 224–26, 234–37, 241–42, 249, 251, 264, 278, 281; as good, 154–57; as material, 52, 134, 145, 169, 173, 257, 267, 272; as non-being/void, 226, 231–33, 246, 259; as static, 8, 56, 110, 158, 195, 198, 203; as unbecoming, 109–10, 113, 120; 137, 161, 164, 208, 210–13, 231–33, 268, 277–78; unity of, 37, 90, 112, 142–47, 153–54, 156, 164–66, 174, 187, 199, 230. *See also* absolute: being/reality; metaphysics; void
Bentham, Jeremy, 122
biology, 89–92, 104–5, 106, 117, 210, 241
blessedness, 152–55, 157, 159–62
Boltzmann, Ludwig, 94, 98, 103, 106, 213–14, 230
Brassier, Ray, 269–74. *See also* nihilism: extinctual
Bricmont, Jean, 113, 115–21. *See also* Sokal, Alan
Buddhism, 221–27, 228–29, 234, 235, 236–37, 255, 311n46, 312n70

Camus, Albert, 14
chaos, 98, 247; in Meillassoux, 74–76, 84; in Nietzsche, 194–95, 197, 200, 202, 207, 209, 307n46. *See also* disorder
chemistry, 23, 90–92, 95, 103–4, 107, 109, 117, 170, 210
Cioran, E. M., 246, 249–54, 255
colonialism, 18–19, 38–39, 290n88; post-colonialism, 18, 38–39
communism, 239–40, 242

331

INDEX

compassion, 180–84, 206, 219–20, 227, 235–36, 239, 280, 282
contingency, 53, 53–61, 74–77, 79, 96, 98–100, 111–12, 298n83
correlationism, 43–47, 50, 54–56, 60, 63–65, 68, 75, 85, 111, 115, 265, 269
cosmic pessimism, 12, 244–46, 254–56
cynicism, 17, 82, 88, 253

death: biological, 106, 177, 210, 216, 220, 224, 227; cosmic, 76, 107–8, 231, 268–69; of God, 13–14, 33–37, 186, 189–90, 228; social, 256–57, 260–62, 265; will to, 231–36, 281. *See also* extinction
Deleuze, Gilles, 16
Diogenes, 253
disorder, 77, 95, 101, 108, 134, 200, 262. *See also* chaos
dissipation, 102–5, 107, 110, 161, 184, 272, 276, 281–82; dissipative driven adaptation; 104–5, 110. *See also* entropy; evolution
dogmatism, 16, 20–21, 40, 87, 93, 141–42, 211–12, 245, 275–77, 284; and contemporary pessimism, 246–47, 251, 267–68, 270–71; and Hume; 124–26; Kant, 21–25, 28, 31–36, 115, 118, 165–69, 275; and Nietzsche, 186–99, 202–8; and Schopenhauer, 165–75, 215, 221; and speculative realism, 41–49, 51–60, 63–65, 70–73, 76, 83, 85; and Spinoza, 155, 157, 161. *See also* fanaticism; fideism; metaphysics: classical/dogmatic
dualism, 91, 139–42, 144–48, 158, 164–68, 171–76, 215, 257

entropy, 101–12, 114–15, 120, 161–62, 208, 210, 251, 318n1; and contemporary pessimism, 232, 261, 266, 269, 271; as essence/being, 107, 109–13, 114, 276–78; and value, 126, 135–36, 137, 178–79, 212–14, 278–79, 281–82. *See also* dissipation
Epictetus, 121
equality, 17, 120–21, 239–43, 258, 262–64, 280, 282, 285
eternity, 151, 154–56, 158, 160–63, 203, 206. *See also* finitude
ethics, 3–4; 7–9, 120–21, 138–39; of affirmation, 191, 201–7; Buddhist, 221–27;

of acquiescence, 151–55, 159, 162–63, 279, 302n18, 303n33; and extinctual nihilism, 271–72; of fidelity, 77–84; of hope, 74–77; of indifference, 249–54; after Kant, 31–38, 42, 53, 57, 62, 67, 85, 88–89, 176, 186–87, 211–13; of resistance, 133–36, 163, 180, 184, 209, 212–20, 228, 234–43, 262–66, 273–74, 279, 281–85, 302n78; quietistic, 184–85, 191, 254–56; relativism, 14, 46–49, 51, 56, 59, 62, 71, 75, 82–83, 149–55, 189, 302n18. *See also* value: moral
evil, 4–7, 135–36, 141, 160–61, 183, 187–90, 196, 205–6, 281; of existence, 130–33, 135–39, 161–63, 176, 180–82, 209, 211–18, 221–22, 224–26, 234–37, 241–42, 249, 251, 264, 278, 281; from good, 82–83; natural, 121–22, 176–79, 211–12; positivity of, 127–29, 130–35, 211–18, 279; as privation, 6, 127–29, 132, 137–39, 148–53, 156–58, 211–12, 279;. *See also* being: as evil
evolution, 3, 90–91, 94, 102, 104–5, 114, 199, 296n13. *See also* dissipation: dissipative driven adaptation
extinction, 106–8, 110, 176, 212, 236, 266–67; extinctual nihilism, 266–71, 273–74, 317n100. *See also* death
extremism, 24–25, 38–40, 42–49, 56–57, 62–67, 76, 82–83, 138, 250–51, 256, 314n5. *See also* fanaticism

facts, 61–62, 84, 100, 105–7, 110–11, 113–14, 120–21, 138, 179; factial/facticity, 53–56, 58–59, 75–76, 79; moral, 131, 138, 215–16, 242, 251, 281; vs. values, 123–28, 130–31, 138, 154, 160
fallacy: appeal to ignorance, 98; appeal to inappropriate authority, 117; equivocation, 127–28; naturalistic fallacy, 113, 121, 123–27, 214–15, 278–79, 300n46; of presumption, 128
fanaticism, 24–25, 38–40, 42–46, 48–49, 56–57, 62–67, 76, 82–83, 138, 250–51, 256, 314n5. *See also* extremism
Fanon, Frantz, 262
fate, 94, 141, 157, 184, 200, 211, 213, 216, 277, 281, 285; love of (*amor fati*), 149, 152, 203–6. *See also* necessity
feminism, 240. *See also* equality; Free-Love (movement)

INDEX

Feuerbach, Ludwig, 35
Fichte, Johann Gottfried, 15
fideism, 15, 24–25, 46–53, 56, 62–65, 71, 83–87, 112, 115, 138, 165, 235, 251, 255–56, 275
finitude, 8, 161–62, 208, 214–15, 223, 231, 268, 277–78, 279. *See also* annihilation; death; and infinite
fossil matter, 49–50, 102. *See also* ancestral
Free-Love (movement), 239–42, 313n127. *See also* feminism
free will, 37, 123–24, 139–43, 146–48, 157–59, 163, 174–75, 200, 205, 257, 265. *See also* fate; necessity
Freud, Sigmund, 313n91

Galilei, Galileo, 72
Gnosticism, 129, 246, 248
God, 22, 31, 34–37, 55, 57, 80, 140, 168, 246–48, 250; death of, 13–14, 33–37, 186, 189–90, 228; as evil/monstrous, 162; or nature (*sive natura*), 142–47, 151–55, 161, 195, 303n39
good, 4–7, 17, 59, 127–29, 134–35, 136, 211, 275–76; derived disjunctively, 138, 183–85, 273, 280–81; as relative/privative, 180, 217–19, 225, 242, 273; of resistance, 133–36, 163, 180, 184, 209, 212–19, 228, 234–43, 262–66, 273–74, 279, 281–85, 302n78; reversibility of, 82–83, 127–29, 130–35

Hartman, Saidiya, 256–59, 262, 266
Havel, Vaclav, 105, 232
Hegel, G. F. W., 15, 18
Heidegger, Martin, 13, 122, 130, 132, 134, 135, 137, 259
humanism, 89, 204, 257–59, 265–66, 269, 271–72, 273–74. *See also* inhuman
Hume, David, 123–27, 129–31, 214
Husserl, Edmund, 15

infinite, 55, 113, 131, 144, 147, 151, 160, 198–99, 207, 279–80; transfinite, 77, 79, 81, 88
inhuman, 3, 52, 54–55, 73–74, 118, 192–95, 244–46, 255, 265–69, 271–73
irrational (unreason), 28, 39, 48, 58, 124, 125, 141, 169; nature as, 52–55, 199, 246, 265

joy, 152–55, 157, 159–62, 198, 206–8, 219–20, 233, 302n18
justice, 120–21, 209, 213, 239–40, 280–82; impossibility of, 258–64; after Kant, 17–19, 24, 41; in Schopenhauer, 181–84; and speculative realism, 46, 56–59, 77–79, 111
Kant, Immanuel: on absolutes, 28–31, 33–36; and colonialism, 18–19, 38–39, 290n88; critical philosophy, 21–31; effects on the history of thought, 13–21, 41–49, 54–59, 64–65, 85, 89, 115, 186–93, 203, 275–76, 282; on ethics and moral value; 31–33, 122, 124–25, 129; Schopenhauer's critique of, 165–70, 174–75
Kierkegaard, Søren, 15

Ladyman, James, 60–62, 68, 73, 74, 85. *See also* Ross, Don
laws (of nature), 89–94, 95–100, 140–41, 161, 207–8, 236; Kant on, 34–37; Meillassoux on, 54, 60, 75–76, 84; Nietzsche on, 200–1, Schopenhauer on, 172–74, 178–79; Spinoza on, 142–47, 153–54, 157; thermodynamic, 94–113, 119–20, 137, 210, 213, 251
Leibniz, Gottfried Wilhelm, 129
Levinas, Emmanuel, 130–32, 134–35
liberalism, 17–20, 38, 257–58
Lyotard, Francois, 266–69, 271–74

Mainländer, Philipp, 227–43, 244, 251, 254–56, 263–64, 266, 273–4, 280, 312n72
materialism: base, 246–48, 254; Kant's critique of, 22–24, 41; metaphysics, 111; Nietzsche's, 189; Schopenhauer's, 175; speculative, 48–49, 52–53, 55–57, 59, 61, 64, 85; Spinoza's, 139, 159, 163
mathematics, 1–4, 236; abuse of, 115–21, 247–48; as epistemological method, 51, 65–71, 192–94, 245, 254, 271, 276; as language of the universe (universal), 72–74, 86–88; 266; mathematization of nature, 65–68, 75–77, 78–80, 84, 85–87, 109–11, 121, 202; as ontology, 70, 72, 273; in the sciences, 94–100, 103; set-theory, 69, 79–80; statistical mechanics, 94–96, 100–3, 109, 120; and suppression/social death, 265

INDEX

Meillassoux, Quentin: on the absolute, 51–56, 67–68, 71, 74–77, 84, 111–12; ethics of, 55–59, 76–78, 85–86; on Kant and correlationism, 43–47, 265, 290n5; on mathematical sciences, 47–50, 63–68, 73, 78–79, 86–88, 96–98, 189. *See also* ancestral; correlationism; facts: factial/facticity; fossil matter

metaphysics, 13, 55, 118; classical/dogmatic, 13, 23; death of, 13–16; entropic/of decay, 109–13, 114, 161–63, 208, 210–12, 266, 270, 272, 277–78, 281; Kant and the possibility of, 23–25, 28, 31–36, 118, 165–69, 275; Mainländer's, 228–33; monistic, 138, 142, 163, 166–67, 217, 281; naturalized, 59–62 202, 211, 265, 269, 276; Nietzsche's, 194–95; 197–99; pessimistic, 238, 242, 277, 281, 284; Schopenhauer's, 169–71, speculative, 59–62, 70, 72, 74–77; Spinoza's, 142–46

Montaigne, Michel de, 121, 299n22

Moore, G. E., 124–27, 129–32, 214

mysticism, 169, 246–48, 255

nationalism, 19–20, 46

naturalism: ethical, 124, 211; metaphysical, 60–61, 190–95; scientific/reductionistic, 22–25, 36

necessity: of contingency, 48, 55, 58, 61, 68, 75–77, 111–12, 298n83; of decay, 161, 210; of nature, 92, 110, 112–13, 120, 138, 142–43, 159, 172–75, 200–7; of suffering, 176–85, 209–16, 222–26, 233–34, 277–78, 281–85; *See also* fate; free will; laws (of nature)

Nietzsche, Friedrich: on Buddhism, 227; on chaos, 194–95, 197, 200, 202, 207, 209, 307n46; on dogmatism, 186–99, 202–8; ethics of, 201–6; on free will, 200–201; on Kant, 13–14, 186–90; and Mainländer, 228, 234, 240, 312n75; materialism/naturalism, 189, 200–201; on mathematics and science, 192–95; metaphysics, 194–95; 197–99; and moral value, 122, 193–97; on Spinoza, 149, 190–91, 203, 302n17, 307n29; on Schopenhauer, 185, 205–7, 212–13; on thermodynamics, 199; will to power, 197–202, 204–6, 302n18, 308n60

nihilism, 3, 14, 21, 38–40, 42, 44, 115, 138, 227, 275–77; and Afropessimism, 259; Badiou on, 65, 71, 82, 88; and cosmic pessimism, 255–56; extinctual, 266–71; Meillassoux on, 48, 56, 75; Nietzsche on, 186–90, 192–94, 199–203, 206

nothing, 79–80, 132, 246–47, 250, 253, 278, 281; Afropessimism on, 259; Buddhism on, 225–26; Mainländer on, 230–32, 236; and nature, 108–9, 111–12, 177, 210–11, 272, 278; Schopenhauer on, 214, 220–21. *See also* absence; annihilation; being: non-being/void; void

noumena (*thing-in-itself*), 98, 114, 124; Schopenhauer on, 165, 169–71; and speculative realism, 40, 55, 55, 64, 70, 74, 85; Kant on, 28–31, 33–36

Patterson, Orlando, 256–57. *See also* death: social

peace, 129, 252–53, 258, 281, 283; Buddhism on, 226; Kant and perpetual peace, 17–18, 24, 38–39; Mainländer on, 238–38, 242–43; Schopenhauer on, 219–21; speculative realism on, 57, 59, 76; Spinoza on, 153–54, 157, 159–62. *See also* politics; equality

pessimism, 7, 163, 273, 278, 280; Afropessimism, 256–66; and Buddhism, 221–22, 226; cosmic, 244–46, 249, 254–56; entropic, 212–14; ethical/moral, 8–9, 12, 163, 212–14, 256, 272, 282, 285; metaphysical, 175–79, 212, 245; Nietzsche on, 191, 196, 201, 205–7, 227; Schopenhauer's, 175–79, 209, 213–14; Mainländer's, 227–29, 237–38, 242–43, 264–66. *See also* Afropessimism; cosmic pessimism

physics, 61, 68, 101, 103, 105, 210; abuse of, 115–21, 247–48; astrophysics, 108–9; laws of, 91–95, 98, 147; mathematics and, 96–100

Plotinus, 128, 129

politics: activism, 212, 228, 235–39, 242, 244, 264; emancipatory, 46, 239–42, 258, 260, 268, 272–74, 280–82, 284; justice, 120–21, 209, 213, 239–40, 258–64, 280–82; after Kant, 17–19, 41; peace, 242–43, 258, 281, 283; revolution, 115, 238–43, 242, 260,

262–66, 273, 281. *See also* equality; justice; peace

realism, 68, 265; anti-, 44, 46–47, 50, 56, 65, 75, 111, 115; ethical/moral, 69; scientific/structural, 59–91; speculative, 42–44, 46–47, 51, 54, 56, 63–65, 84, 88

resistance: ethics of, 110, 133–36, 163, 180, 184, 209, 212–20, 228, 234–38, 253, 279–85; 302n78; politics of, 238–43, 262–66, 273–74, 280–85. *See also* ethics: of resistance

Ross, Don, 60–62, 68, 73, 74, 85. *See also* Ladyman, James

Rousseau, Jean-Jacques, 122

Russell, Bertrand, 15

science, 1–3, 107, 110; biology, 89–92, 104–5, 106, 117, 210, 241; chemistry, 23, 90–92, 95, 103–4, 107, 109, 117, 170, 210; mathematical, 2–4, 49, 51, 66–72, 84, 94, 96–100; material, 45, 47–49, 52–55, 63–66, 68, 74, 77, 95–97; physics, 61, 68, 91–95, 98, 101, 103, 105, 108–9, 210

scientism, 22–25, 36

Schelling, F. W. J., 132–35

Schopenhauer, Arthur: on Buddhism, 221–23, 226–28, 255; dogmatism, 165–75, 215, 22; ethics, 179–85, 191, 214–21; on justice, 181–84; on Kant, 165–70, 174–75; on the laws of nature, 172–74, 178–79; metaphysics, 169–71, 175; on peace, 219–21; pessimism, 175–79, 209, 213–14; on reality-in-itself, 165, 169–71

Seneca, 121

Shakespeare, William, 121, 127, 183, 299n22

Sokal, Alan, 113, 115–21. *See also* Bricmont, Jean

speculative realism, 42–56, 61, 63, 84–85, 88, 111, 189, 192, 265, 269

Spinoza, Baruch: on dogmatism/classical metaphysics, 155, 157, 161; ethics, 151–55, 159, 162–63, 279, 302n18, 303n33; on God/nature (*sive natura*), 142–47, 151–55, 161, 195, 303n39; on infinitude, 144, 147, 151, 160; on the laws of nature, 142–47, 153–54, 157; on materialism, 139, 159, 163; metaphysics, 142–46; on peace, 153–54, 157, 159–62

suffering, 4, 39, 52, 78, 137, 160–63, 251, 274; necessity of, 176–85, 209–16, 222–26, 233–34, 277–78, 281–85

suicide, 184, 238, 241, 255, 310n33

Tennyson, Alfred Lord, 285

Thacker, Eugene, 244–46, 249, 254–56

thermodynamics (laws of), 94–113, 119–20, 137, 179, 210, 213, 230, 251, 276, 278; Nietzsche on, 198–200, 203, 207

thing-in-itself (*noumena*), 98, 114, 124; Kant on, 28–31, 33–36; Schopenhauer on, 165, 169–71; and speculative realism, 40, 50, 55, 64, 70, 74, 85. *See also* noumena

value: moral, 3–4; neutral, 7–8, 121–41, 176, 208, 211, 234, 278; origin of, 4–7

Vienna Circle, 15

void, 54, 58, 80, 82, 84, 111–12, 133, 208, 211, 246, 25, 259. *See also* absence; annihilation; nothing; being: non-being/void

Voltaire, 122

Warren, Calvin, 256, 259, 265–66

Whitehead, A. N., 21

Wilderson III, Frank B., 256–66, 273, 280

will: annihilative/entropic, 162, 184, 250–51, 274, 276–78, 280–83; free, 37, 123–24, 139–43, 146–48, 157–59, 163, 174–75, 200, 205, 257, 265; in nature/self (Schopenhauer), 169–85, 213, 215–21; of God/nature (Spinoza), 143–48, 156–59; to be/life and to destroy/death (Mainländer), 230–42, 313n91; to power (Nietzsche), 195, 197–202, 204–6 302n18, 308n60

Yeats, William Butler, 101